FAMILY LAW IN PRACTICE

FAMILY LAW IN PRACTICE

Inns of Court School of Law

Institute of Law, City University, London

OXFORD

UNIVERSITY PRESS

OXFORD

UNIVERSITY PRESS

Great Clarendon Street, Oxford OX2 6DP

Oxford University Press is a department of the University of Oxford.
It furthers the University's objective of excellence in research, scholarship,
and education by publishing worldwide in

Oxford NewYork

Athens Auckland Bangkok Bogotá Buenos Aires Cape Town
Chennai Dar es Salaam Delhi Florence Hong Kong Istanbul Karachi
Kolkata Kuala Lumpur Madrid Melbourne Mexico City Mumbai Nairobi
Paris São Paulo Shanghai Singapore Taipei Tokyo Toronto Warsaw

with associated companies in Berlin Ibadan

Oxford is a registered trade mark of Oxford University Press
in the UK and certain other countries

Published in the United States
by Oxford University Press Inc., New York

A Blackstone Press Book

British Library Cataloguing in Publication Data

Data available

Library of Congress Cataloging in Publication Data

Data available

ISBN 1-84174-312-7

1 3 5 7 9 10 8 6 4 2

Typeset by Montage Studios Limited, Tonbridge, Kent
Printed in Great Britain
on acid-free paper by
Ashford Colour Press, Gosport, Hampshire

FOREWORD

These manuals are designed primarily to support training on the Bar Vocational Course, though they are also intended to provide a useful resource for legal practitioners and for anyone undertaking training in legal skills.

The Bar Vocational Course was designed by staff at the Inns of Court School of Law, where it was introduced in 1989. This course is intended to equip students with the practical skills and the procedural and evidential knowledge that they will need to start their legal professional careers. These manuals are written by staff at the Inns of Court School of Law who have helped to develop the course, and by a range of legal practitioners and others involved in legal skills training. The authors of the manuals are very well aware of the practical and professional approach that is central to the Bar Vocational Course.

The range and coverage of the manuals have grown steadily. All the practice manuals are updated every two years, and regular reviews and revisions of the manuals are carried out to ensure that developments in legal skills training and the experience of our staff are fully reflected in them.

This updating and revision is a constant process, and we very much value the comments of practitioners, staff and students. Legal vocational training is advancing rapidly, and it is important that all those concerned work together to achieve and maintain high standards. Please address any comments to the Bar Vocational Course Director at the Inns of Court School of Law.

With the validation of other providers for the Bar Vocational Course it is very much our intention that these manuals will be of equal value to all students wherever they take the course, and we would value comments from tutors and students at other validated institutions.

The enthusiasm of the publishers and their efficiency in arranging the production and publication of these manuals is much appreciated.

The Hon. Mr Justice Elias
Chairman of the Advisory Board of the Institute of Law
City University, London
December 2001

CONTENTS

CONTENTS

LIST OF ABBREVIATIONS

ADR	Alternative dispute resolution
AE	Additional element
BE	Basic element
CA 1989	Children Act 1989
CAFCASS	Children and Family Court Advisory and Support Service
CALM	Comprehensive Accredited Lawyer Mediators
CAO	Child assessment order
CCR	County Court Rules
CGT	Capital gains tax
CSA	Child Support Agency
DPMCA 1978	Domestic Proceedings and Magistrates' Courts Act 1978
DVMPA 1976	Domestic Violence and Matrimonial Proceedings Act 1976
EPO	*Ex parte* order
FA 1988	Finance Act 1988
FAO	Family assistance order
FLA 1996	Family Law Act 1996
FMA	Family Mediators Association
FMS	Family Mediation Scotland
FP	Income support family premium
FPC(MP)R 1991	Family Proceedings Courts (Matrimonial Proceedings etc.) Rules 1991
FPCR 1991	Family Proceedings Courts (Children Act 1989) Rules 1991
FPR 1991	Family Proceedings Rules 1991
F(No. 2)A 1992	Finance (No. 2) Act 1992
GAL	Guardian *ad litem*
ICTA 1988	Income and Corporation Taxes Act 1988
ITA 1984	Inheritance Tax Act 1984
MCA 1973	Matrimonial Causes Act 1973
MHA 1983	Matrimonial Homes Act 1983
MR	Maintenance requirement
NFM	National Family Mediation
PA	Income support personal allowance
PET	Potentially exempt transfer
PSO	Prohibited steps order
RSC	Rules of the Supreme Court
SFLA	Solicitors Family Law Association
SIO	Specific issue order
TCGA 1992	Taxation of Chargeable Gains Act 1992

TABLE OF CASES

TABLE OF STATUTES

TABLE OF STATUTORY INSTRUMENTS

ONE

INTRODUCTION

Family law is an important area of specialisation at the Bar. It is also a common ingredient of general practice, and research has shown that about two thirds of barristers entering practice do some family work in their early years. There has been some decline in publicly-funded work but it is important for the majority of those entering practice to have at least some knowledge of how to approach a family law case.

This Manual takes a practical approach so as to prepare the newly qualified for the reality of practice. It includes relevant statute and case law, which inevitably form both a framework and a starting point for any research that may be required to tackle the wide range of cases that can arise in family work. The main emphasis of this Manual, however, is on the *practical* considerations involved in the analysis and conduct of family law disputes. These often spring from marital breakdown or other trauma and require a high degree of skill and understanding. As will become clear, family law involves the deployment of the entire range of practitioner skills. Effective social skills are of particular importance, as are confidence in drafting and arithmetic calculation.

This Manual concentrates on the areas that are most likely to arise early in practice, such as applications for financial orders (or to vary or enforce such orders), and applications relating to domestic violence and the occupation of the matrimonial home. It is less likely that someone in early practice will be asked to deal with any major dispute relating to a child, or with capital provision on divorce where there are substantial assets, but these matters are included to provide a reasonably coherent picture. Throughout, the focus is on how best to serve the practical needs of the client, and how to deal with facts and figures to find apt and feasible solutions.

To get a feel for how different family law in practice is from a purely academic study of family law, one only has to look at 'At a Glance', published annually by the Family Law Bar Association. This is an essential tool for any practitioner who does much family work. The booklet provides up-to-date information on many areas, from tax and social security benefit rates to house-price indices and international living costs. Although it summarises recent leading cases, most of the booklet is full of figures that the practitioner needs not only to understand but to be able to handle fluently.

Family law is undergoing major changes:

(a) The fault based procedure for seeking a divorce has attracted significant criticism. Legislation was in place (in the Family Law Act 1996) for moving to a system providing for no fault divorce which emphasised identifying and solving issues relating to children and finance and encouraged the use of discussion and mediation. However, pilot projects revealed practical difficulties, and in January 2001 the government announced that these proposals would not be implemented.

(b) Following a pilot project the procedure for seeking financial relief ancillary to divorce has been changed, with the Family Proceedings Regulations 1991 being significantly amended by the Family Proceedings (Amendment No. 2) Rules

1999. The new procedure is based on an exchange of standard forms providing detailed financial information and provides for much more court control of evidence and costs.

(c) In the case of *White* v *White* [2001] 1 All ER 1, the House of Lords has suggested a quite important shift towards equality in allocating financial assets on divorce.

(d) Pension rights are often one of the biggest financial assets owned by a couple and there has been significant change in statutory and regulatory provision over the last few years, particularly with the introduction of pension sharing where a divorce petition has been issued on or after 1 December 2000 (Welfare Reform and Pensions Act 1999).

(e) The working of the Child Support Agency has attracted criticism, and significant changes in procedure and the quantification of payments have been made by the Child Support, Pensions and Social Security Act 2000.

(f) The Human Rights Act 1998 is having a significant impact in family law cases relating to children.

In the light of these changes it is very important to ensure that legal advice is up-to-date, for example by using properly updated loose-leaf works rather than textbooks that do not have a recent new edition. The journal, *Family Law*, is a particularly good source of practical up-to-date comment, and it has a web site at www.familylaw.co.uk. The Lord Chancellors Department may also provide useful information at www.lcd.gov.uk/family.

TWO

DOMESTIC VIOLENCE AND OCCUPATION OF THE FAMILY HOME

2.1   Introduction

Modern living brings with it benefits, but at the price of increasing insecurity for many people. Sadly, but not surprisingly, this has an impact on family life and one result is that domestic violence, like divorce, is on the increase. Although procedurally, the law in this area is now predictable and rational, if not entirely straightforward, nevertheless it remains an aspect of practice requiring great care and skill. Whether domestic violence is a cause or a by-product of family breakdown, it remains a traumatic occurrence.

Before the implementation of the Family Law Act 1996, the law relating to remedies for victims of domestic violence was full of inconsistencies and anomalies. These were largely the result of piecemeal statutory development over the years, together with attempts to adapt existing legislation to meet a variety of needs. Increasingly it became clear that, to be both fair and effective, the law in this area needed to be completely overhauled — as epitomised by Lord Scarman's famous outburst of judicial exasperation in *Richards* v *Richards* [1984] AC 206 where he described the provisions then in force as:

> A hotch potch of enactments of limited scope passed into law to meet specific situations or to strengthen the powers of specific courts. The sooner the range, scope and the effect of these powers are rationalised into a coherent and comprehensive body of statute law the better.

The route to reform was slow and not without its difficulties. In 1995, legislation was proposed giving effect to the recommendations of the Law Commission in its excellent report, 'Family Law: Domestic Violence and Occupation of the Family Home' (Law Commission Report No. 207, May 1992). The Family Homes and Domestic Violence Bill was due to be enacted in November 1995 when it was summarily revoked at the eleventh hour by a politically weak government responding to the demands of a vociferous, and many would say uninformed, minority. This so-called 'family values' lobby insisted that the legislation undermined the sanctity of marriage by giving cohabitees the same protection from domestic violence as married couples.

As hastily as it was withdrawn, the legislation was redrafted so as to reinforce the special status of matrimony. It was then tacked on to the end of the Family Law Bill, which at the time was itself proceeding through parliament, resulting in a rather unhappy marriage of convenience between it (Part IV) and the rest of the legislation's attempt to reform the basis and mechanics of obtaining divorce (Parts I–III).

Somewhat ironically, the divorce reforms never got beyond the pilot testing of certain of its features, which revealed various problems. They have now been scrapped — leaving Part IV practically the sole operative survivor of this rather tortured journey onto the statute books.

Notwithstanding that the procedure in this area has been rationalised, it is important to remember that the complexity and stress surrounding domestic violence remains the same whatever labels are attached. Changing terminology and simplifying the system of remedies, albeit a major step forward, can never remove the distress suffered by the people involved. Try always to remember when you are advising and representing lay clients that, more often than not, they will be in a highly volatile and emotional state. Decisions on how to proceed in a way which best protects the interests of your client usually means giving careful consideration not only to that person's individual needs, but the overall family situation as well.

2.2 The Family Law Act 1996 (Part IV)

Part IV of the Family Law Act 1996 (FLA 1996) created a single set of remedies, available in all courts having jurisdiction in family matters, to give personal protection from domestic violence and to regulate the occupation of the family home. Relevant sections of the legislation are reproduced in **Appendix A**.

There are two kinds of remedy, a non-molestation order and an occupation order, each with its own criteria, but capable of combination with one another and other family remedies. Both types of order may be made in relation to 'associated persons' and 'relevant child(ren)'.

2.3 Associated Persons

This is the initial prerequisite for those seeking protection under the legislation.

Part IV of the FLA 1996 applies to all 'associated persons' which is defined in such a way as to encompass those living in almost any family or domestic living arrangement. The result has been to include many categories of people excluded by the previous legislation and so increase generally the availability of protection against domestic violence, especially non-molestation orders.

Associated persons, as defined by s. 62(3) include: spouses or former spouses; cohabitants or former cohabitants (i.e., persons living together 'as man and wife'); couples who have agreed to marry (so long as the agreement was not terminated more than three years previously); parties to the same family proceedings (other than under the FLA 1996 itself); and a variety of relatives. Significantly, it also includes people who live or have lived in the same household other than as a mere employee, tenant, lodger or boarder (i.e., a domestic rather than business relationship). Thus a cohabiting gay couple would be associated, although a girlfriend and boyfriend who did not live together (and never had), would not. In *Re H (A Minor) (Occupation Order: Power of Arrest)* [2001] FCR 370, a father obtained a non-molestation and occupation order against his 17-year-old son.

Also 'associated' are the parents of the same child, individuals (not, e.g., a local authority) who have or have had parental responsibility for the same child; and persons connected by virtue of the adoption process (s. 62(5)).

2.4 Relevant Child

Children are a common feature of family life. As you might expect, they also frequently figure in matters of family strife. The 'relevant child' is therefore a recurring concept in the legislation.

By s. 62(2), a 'relevant child' in relation to any proceedings under the FLA 1996 includes:

(a) any child living, or who might reasonably be expected to live, with either party to the proceedings;

(b) a child involved in existing children proceedings; and

(c) any other child whose interest the court considers relevant.

2.5 Non-Molestation Order

A non-molestation order is a form of injunction containing either or both of the following:

(a) a provision prohibiting the respondent from molesting another person who is associated with the respondent,

(b) a provision prohibiting the respondent from molesting a relevant child (FLA 1996, s. 42(1)).

The Law Commission considered in depth whether there should be a statutory definition of 'molestation' — a curiously archaic term used in previous legislation and which seemed incapable of simple, yet accurate up-dating. In the absence of any evidence of problems caused in the past by lack of such a definition, and given the possibility that any delineation might be over-restrictive, it was decided that the term should not be defined in the legislation. Thus the courts continue to be guided by the old case law which established that 'violence is a form of molestation but molestation may take place without the threat or use of violence and still be serious and inimical to mental or physical health' (per Viscount Dilhorne in *Davis* v *Johnson* [1979] AC 264). Lack of a statutory definition keeps the remedy flexible and able to adapt to novel circumstances.

In *Horner* v *Horner* [1982] 2 All ER 495, sending threatening letters and intercepting the applicant on the streets was regarded as molestation. In *Johnson* v *Walton* [1990] 1 FLR 350, it was suggested that sending partially nude photographs of the applicant to the press so as to cause her distress would amount to molestation. Thus, any serious form of pestering or harassment is included in the concept of molestation.

There are, however, limits and the need for direct contact between perpetrator and victim was stressed in *C* v *C* [1998] 1 FLR 554. In that case, a husband and wife were in the process of divorcing. Newspaper articles, critical of the husband's marital conduct, were published with the assistance of information provided by his wife. The husband claimed the articles were harmful to him and sought an order restraining his wife from speaking to the press so as to procure further such articles. The issue on appeal was whether the wife's behaviour amounted to molestation. Sir Stephen Brown, then President of the Family Division, confirmed that molestation 'implies some quite deliberate conduct which is aimed at a high degree of harassment of the other party, so as to justify the intervention of the court'. But he held that the wife's revelations of her marital past 'comes nowhere near molestation as envisaged by s. 42'. He found the lack of direct communication between the parties relevant and concluded that the (by then ex) husband was concerned with damage to his reputation rather than molestation as such. This case seems to confirm that molestation needs to be of a direct and personally harmful nature, which excludes invasions of privacy which may be said to damage one's reputation. The remedy for the latter lies in defamation.

The court may make a non-molestation order on application by a person who is:

(a) 'associated with the respondent' whether or not other family proceedings have been initiated (s. 42(2)(a)); or

(b) on its own initiative, in any family proceedings to which the respondent is a party if it considers that the order should be made for the benefit of any other party to the proceedings or to any relevant child (s. 42(2)(b)).

In deciding whether to grant the non-molestation order, the court by virtue of s. 42(5) shall have regard to *all of the circumstances* of the case, *including* the 'health, safety and well-being' of the applicant (or, in a case falling within s. 42(2)(b), the person for whose benefit the order is made) and any relevant child.

General molestation will be restrained by 'forbidding' the respondent from 'using violence against, threatening, harassing, intimidating or pestering' the applicant (note that the word 'molestation' does not appear in the actual order). In addition, specific kinds of behaviour can also be restrained by more precise wording — usually set out after the general prohibition.

Non-molestation orders may last for a specified period or until further order (s. 42(7)). This gives the court total flexibility. In general, non-molestation orders are intended as a temporary ameliorating measure to last only until a long-term solution is found (e.g., reconciliation or separation), but in extreme cases they can effectively be permanent. In *M v W (Non-Molestation: Duration)* [2000] FLR 107, for example, it was said that a non-molestation order is designed to 'give a breathing space to parties' and unless there are exceptional circumstances, it should be for a specified period. A non-molestation order made in the course of other family proceedings ceases if those proceedings are dismissed or withdrawn (s. 42(8)).

2.6 Occupation Orders: the General Scheme

Known colloquially as 'ouster orders', these regulate the occupation of the family home. Such orders come in various, if essentially standard, permutations and their availability depends on the rights and/or relationship of both parties to the application. The greatest protection is given to property owners and married couples.

The FLA 1996 distinguishes, in the first instance, between applicants who are entitled to occupy the family home ('entitled applicants') and those who are not. Occupation orders are draconian in their nature, and are easiest to justify in the case of an applicant who is independently entitled to occupy the property. They are most difficult to justify where the applicant has no such right but the respondent does. Therefore, an applicant who is 'associated' with the respondent and is entitled to occupy the family home can get access to the fullest protection that is available under the Act, *irrespective* of her relationship to the respondent (although often it is this relationship which is the source of entitlement (see **2.8.1**)).

Non-entitled applicants, on the other hand, may *only get orders against former spouses, cohabitants or former cohabitants* and are discriminated against in terms of the possible duration of such orders. A further distinction is made between those who have been married and those who have not — as demanded by the 'family values' lobby. Cohabitants are specifically deprived of the potential benefits of the so-called 'balance of harm' test (see **2.8.4**) which compels the court, when dealing with spouses or former spouses, to make an order in the applicant's favour in certain circumstances.

These various permutations are reflected in the five separate, but subtly unequal, sections under which applications are made. Given that the parties must be 'associated persons' (see **2.3**), which section is appropriate then depends on their further status as follows:

- If the applicant is *entitled* — apply under s. 33 (whatever the respondent's status).

- If the applicant is *not entitled*, but the respondent *is* — apply under s. 35 if the parties are former spouses or under s. 36 if the parties are existing or former cohabitants.

- If *neither* applicant nor respondent is *entitled* — apply under s. 37 if the parties are existing or former spouses, or under s. 38 if the parties are existing or former cohabitants.

2.7 Two Types of Order

There are two types of occupation order: declaratory and regulatory. The latter, as their name suggests, regulate the occupation of the family house. The former declare, extend or create rights and are a necessary prerequisite to a regulatory order where the respondent is entitled, but the applicant is not.

Declaratory orders are possible in respect of any dwelling that is, has been or was intended to be a family home. They are not, however, applicable where neither party is 'entitled' (see **2.10**).

2.8 Entitled Applicant: Section 33

Under FLA 1996, s. 33(1)(a)(i) and (ii), an applicant is an 'entitled applicant' if he or she is entitled to occupy the dwelling home by virtue of:

- a beneficial estate or interest (e.g., resulting trust);

- a contract (e.g., tenancy agreement);

- any enactment giving the applicant the right to remain in occupation; or

- matrimonial home rights in relation to the dwelling house (see **2.8.1**).

2.8.1 MATRIMONIAL HOME RIGHTS

Where one spouse has legal or other rights of occupation in the matrimonial home, and the other spouse does not, the latter is given 'matrimonial home rights under FLA 1996, s. 30(1) (called 'rights of occupation' under the previous legislation). These in effect give both parties to a marriage equal rights to occupy the family home.

Matrimonial home rights are defined in s. 30(2) as being:

(a) *If in occupation*: a right not to be evicted or excluded from the dwelling-house or any part of it by the other spouse except with the leave of the court given by an order under s. 33.

(b) *If not in occupation*: a right with the leave of the court to enter into and occupy the dwelling-house.

Matrimonial home rights (like the power to regulate the exercise of those rights) apply to any dwelling-house which is, has been or (to fill a gap in the old law) *was intended* to be the matrimonial home (s. 30(7)). In the normal course, such rights expire on divorce or the death of either spouse, but can be extended by the court (s. 33(5)).

Most applications under the Act fall within s. 33.

2.8.2 POSSIBLE SECTION 33 ORDERS

On application under s. 33, the court may make any one of the following 'regulatory' orders (s. 33(3)):

(a) enforcing the applicant's entitlement to remain in occupation as against the respondent;

(b) requiring the respondent to permit the applicant to enter and remain in the dwelling house or part of the dwelling house;

(c) regulating the occupation of the dwelling house by either or both parties;

(d) prohibiting, suspending or restricting the exercise by the respondent of his or her right to occupy the dwelling house;

(e) restricting or terminating the respondent's matrimonial home rights;

(f) requiring the respondent to leave the dwelling house or part of the dwelling house;

(g) excluding the respondent from a defined area in which the dwelling house is included.

There is usually no need for a declaratory order under s. 33 because the applicant, by definition, already has full entitlement to occupy the matrimonial home.

2.8.3 THE CRITERIA FOR SECTION 33 ORDERS

The test for regulatory orders is contained in s. 33(6) and (7). In deciding whether, and in what terms, to make a regulatory order, the court must have regard to *all the circumstances* of the case and, *in particular*, the:

- housing needs and resources of the parties and any relevant children;

- financial resources of the parties;

- likely effect of an order (or lack of one) on the health, safety and well-being of the parties or any relevant child;

- conduct of the parties in relation to each other and otherwise.

These factors, which are essentially a matter of common sense, might usefully be described as the '*core criteria*' to be considered by the court. They are common to *all* applications for occupation orders under the Act.

2.8.4 THE 'BALANCE OF HARM' TEST

In addition, the court must apply what is known as the 'balance of harm' test. This *requires* the court to make a regulatory order *if* it appears that the applicant (or relevant child) is likely to suffer *significant harm* (attributable to the respondent) if the order is not made *unless* it appears that the respondent (or relevant child) is likely to suffer equal or greater harm if the order is made (whether attributable to the applicant or not): s. 37(7).

Harm is defined in s. 63. In relation to an adult it means ill-treatment or the impairment of health, and in relation to a child it means the above and/or the impairment of development (apparently adults do not develop any further after a certain age!).

Although the *core criteria* are obviously relevant when weighing the balance of harm, ss. 33(6) and (7) are distinct stages of the decision-making process. In particular, the mandatory nature of subsection (7) *only* comes into play if the applicant or relevant child is likely to suffer 'significant harm'. The dictionary definition of 'significant' (i.e., 'considerable, noteworthy or important') accepted by Booth J in *Humberside County Council v Second Defendants* [1993] 1 FLR 257 (a Children Act case), is taken as applying equally in this context (see s. 63). In *Chalmers v Johns* [1999] 1 FLR 392, the Court of Appeal allowed a husband's appeal against the making of an occupation order because the judge had wrongly applied the balance of harm test in a case where the harm which the applicant and child might suffer if the order were not made was, given the history, too slight to be considered 'significant'. Confirming both the draconian nature of ouster orders generally and the fact that subsection (7) is 'designed to cater for (the) more extreme situations', Thorpe LJ went on to say at p. 396:

> The court has first to consider whether the evidence establishes that the applicant or any relevant child is likely to suffer significant harm attributable to the conduct of the respondent if the order is not made. If the court answers that question in the affirmative, then it must make the order unless balancing one harm against the other, the harm to the respondent or the child is likely to be as great. If, however, the court answers the question in the negative, then it enters the discretionary regime provided by subsection (6).

One might have said 'returns' rather than 'enters' the discretionary regime of subsection (6), since the *core criteria* set out there are obviously relevant to the question of risk of significant harm. The point remains, however, that where there is not a risk of significant harm, the court has the *power* to make an order taking into account the *core criteria* (i.e., housing needs, conduct etc.), but is under *no obligation* to do so.

In the sad case of *Banks* v *Banks* [1999] 1 FLR 726, a husband, aged 75, applied for non-molestation and occupation orders against the wife, aged 79, who suffered from senile dementia. The wife could be both verbally and physically aggressive, but had never physically injured the husband. After a spell in hospital, her doctors thought that it was in her best interests to be at home in familiar surroundings. Her husband, however, felt too frail, physically and emotionally, to cope and sought an order under the Act — in effect to force her return to hospital. Although sympathetic to the husband, the court dismissed his application on the basis that there was no risk to him of significant injury if the order were not made. The judge also seemed to say that even had there been a risk of significant harm to the husband, the balance of harm in any event would have favoured the wife. (It is also worth noting that a non-molestation order was also refused, principally because the wife would have been mentally incapable of understanding, much less abiding by it.)

In the all too prevalent cases, however, where the court does find that there is a likelihood of significant harm, the discretion becomes a duty and the court *must* make an order if, after weighing the harm likely to be suffered by both parties and by any relevant children, the 'balance of harm' favours the applicant (or relevant child). If both parties are able to establish significant harm, but the applicant is unable to show the risk of greater harm, then the court still has the power, but again is under no obligation, to make an appropriate order. See, for example, *B* v *B (Occupation Order)* [1999] 1 FLR 715. In that case, after suffering substantial violence at the hands of her husband, a wife moved out of the family home with the couple's two-year-old daughter. They were temporarily housed in bed and breakfast accommodation by the local authority while the husband remained in the family house with his six-year-old son by a previous relationship. Both children were 'relevant' children. The wife obtained an occupation order against the husband. The husband appealed.

The Court of Appeal allowed the appeal against the order because the judge had wrongly applied subsection (7), in part due to his mistaken belief that the local authority would be obliged to permanently re-house the husband and his son. However, a husband removed from his home on account of his violence, would be considered intentionally homeless, requiring the local authority only to give advice and temporary shelter. By contrast, if the mother and daughter were made homeless on account of the husband's violence, the local authority was obliged to provide them with suitable permanent accommodation. The Court of Appeal thus held that:

- the judge had been perfectly correct to decide that the wife and daughter would suffer significant harm were an order not made; but

- he had erred in balancing the risks of harm. In weighing the risk as regards the two children, the balance came down not in the favour of the applicant and daughter, as the judge had supposed, but in favour of the husband's child who would be very precariously housed were an occupation order made. Therefore, the judge had not been *required* by subsection (7) to make the order and in the circumstances, had he realised he had a choice, it was unlikely that he would have exercised his discretion to do so.

This case also confirms the fact that where there are significant risks to children, their interests are likely to become paramount in weighing up the balance of harm. Indeed, the Court of Appeal were at pains to ensure that the outcome of this case, which turned on a very particular set of facts, should not be viewed as condoning what had been very serious domestic violence.

2.8.5   DURATION

FLA 1996, s. 33(10) provides that orders under s. 33 may be for a specified period, until the occurrence of a specified event, or until further order. In other words, these orders can be of unlimited duration.

2.9   Unentitled Applicant and Entitled Respondent

The rest of the legislation follows the above pattern, with adaptations as appropriate to the circumstances and to produce the result that the further away one gets from property rights or matrimony, the more dilute is the protection given under the Act.

2.9.1   FORMER SPOUSES: SECTION 35

2.9.1.1   Possible orders

Possible regulatory orders under s. 35(5) are an adaptation of those available under FLA 1996, s. 33. Because the applicant is (as yet) 'unentitled', those regulatory orders included in the s. 33(3) list (see **2.8.2**), but excluded from the s. 35(5) list are orders (a), (b) and (e), which are dealt with by way of declaratory order. In effect, the court cannot make a regulatory order under s. 35 without first making the relevant declaratory order, which is intended to give the applicant rights of occupation to match those of the respondent before any regulation of those rights is then imposed.

Thus, where the court makes a regulatory order under s. 35, it *must* also include a declaratory order giving the applicant relevant occupation rights, i.e.:

- *If the applicant is already in occupation of the property*: there must be a provision giving the applicant the right not to be evicted or excluded from the dwelling-house or any part of it by the respondent for the period specified in the order, plus a provision prohibiting the respondent from evicting the applicant during this period (s. 35(3)).

- *If the applicant is not in occupation*: there must be a provision giving the applicant the right to enter into and occupy the dwelling-house for the period specified, plus a provision requiring the respondent to permit the exercise of that right (s. 35(4)).

It is, of course, possible (but uncommon) for a court to make a declaratory order without going on to make further regulatory orders.

2.9.1.2   Criteria for section 35 orders

In deciding whether, and in what terms, to make a s. 35 declaratory order the court is to have regard to the *core criteria* (see **2.8.3**), plus certain additional matters relating to the circumstances; namely the length of time that has elapsed since the parties ceased living together, the length of time since the marriage was terminated and the existence of any relevant pending family proceedings (regarding property or children).

As to whether to go on to make further regulatory orders (which the court may, usually will, but need not necessarily do), the court shall have regard to the *core criteria*, plus the length of time which has elapsed since the parties ceased living together. In addition, the court **must** make a regulatory order under s. 35(5) if the balance of harm test is satisfied (see **2.8.4**).

2.9.1.3 Duration

The duration of any order granted under FLA 1996, s. 35 must, on the first occasion, not exceed six months, but may be extended on subsequent occasions for no more than six months at any one time (s. 35(10)).

2.9.2 COHABITANTS AND FORMER COHABITANTS: SECTION 36

2.9.2.1 Possible orders

The same menu of order possibilities applies for FLA 1996, s. 36 as for s. 35. Thus, if the court is to make a regulatory order under s. 36, it must first make the relevant declaratory order (s. 36(3) and (4)). Declaratory orders can stand alone, but almost inevitably will be followed by a further regulatory order (s. 36(5)).

The differences, and in-built discrimination against cohabitants, arise in the following aspects of the legislation and are indicated in bold italics.

2.9.2.2 Criteria for section 36 orders

In deciding whether, and in what terms, to make a s. 36 declaratory order the court is to have regard to the *core criteria* (see **2.8.3**), plus certain additional matters relating to the circumstances; namely the length of time the parties lived together as man and wife, whether there are or were any children, the length of time which has elapsed since the parties ceased living together and the existence of any relevant pending family proceedings (regarding property or children). *In addition, the court must have regard to the nature of the relationship, i.e., the fact that the parties have not given each other 'the commitment involved in marriage'* (s. 36(6)(e) and s. 41).

2.9.2.3 Balance of harm: no duty

As to whether to go on to make further regulatory orders (which the court may, usually will, but again need not necessarily do), the court shall, in addition to the *core criteria*, have regard to:

- whether the applicant or any relevant child is likely to suffer significant harm attributable to the conduct of the respondent if a regulatory order is not included in the order; and

- whether the harm likely to be suffered by the respondent or child if the provision is included is as great or greater than the harm (attributable to the conduct of the respondent) which the applicant or child is likely to suffer if the provision is not made.

Note that in the s. 36 context, these are merely additional factors to be taken into account and impose no duty. *There is no obligation on the court to make an order, even where it is the case that the applicant will suffer significant and the greater harm if an order is not made*.

2.9.2.4 Duration

Like s. 35, orders under FLA 1996, s. 36 are limited in the first instance to a specified period, not exceeding six months. *However, s. 36 orders may only be extended on one occasion.*

2.10 Both Applicant and Respondent Unentitled

In most cases, at least one of the parties will be entitled to occupy the property in question, so applications under this head will be relatively rare. Situations where both parties are unentitled include squatters and bare licensees (e.g., a couple living with one of the parties' parents).

2.10.1 SPOUSES/FORMER SPOUSES: SECTION 37

2.10.1.1 Possible orders
Only regulatory orders are possible. These are the same possibilities as set out in FLA 1996, s. 33(3), but excluding those, namely (a), (d) and (e), which enforce or restrict what, in this context, are non-existent rights. As neither party has any rights of occupation, parity between the parties already exists in this regard — there is thus no scope for a declaratory order.

2.10.1.2 Criteria for section 37 orders
In deciding whether and in what terms to make a regulatory order under FLA 1996, s. 37, the court shall have regard to the *core criteria* (see **2.8.3**). In addition, the court **must** make a regulatory order if the balance of harm test (see **2.8.4** is satisfied): s. 37(4)).

2.10.1.3 Duration
As under FLA 1996, s. 35 — see **2.9.1.3**.

2.10.2 COHABITANTS/FORMER COHABITANTS: SECTION 38

2.10.2.1 Possible orders
The possibilities are the same here as under s. 37 (see **2.10.1**).

2.10.2.2 Criteria for section 38 orders
In deciding whether and in what terms to make an order under s. 38, the court shall have regard to the *core criteria* (see **2.8.3**). In addition, the court shall have regard to the risks of significant harm as set out above at **2.9.2.3**. As with s. 36, there is *no duty* to make an order even if the balance of harm were to favour the applicant or any relevant children.

2.10.2.3 Duration
As under s. 36 — see **2.9.2.4**.

2.11 Ancillary orders

When an occupation order has been made under either FLA 1996, s. 33, 35 or 36 (i.e., where at least one of the parties is entitled to occupy), the court has power to make relevant ancillary orders which impose obligations relating to repair and maintenance, discharge of rent, mortgage repayments and other outgoings, and the use of furniture and other household equipment. Such may be particularly useful where the occupation order is to last for any length of time or where an order for financial provision following divorce is awaited.

2.12 *Ex Parte* Orders

The FLA 1996 preserves the power of the court to grant both occupation and non-molestation orders *ex parte* (i.e., without notice to/hearing from the respondent). As regards occupation orders, the extreme caution that characterised the treatment of such applications under the old law continues so that such orders are not generally granted until both sides of the story have been heard. The courts are less cautious about granting non-molestation orders *ex parte* since it is somewhat less of a derogation from a person's rights that he or she be required to behave 'properly'.

Section 45(1) says that the court should only exercise its discretion to make an order *ex parte* where it is 'just and convenient to do so'. In determining whether to grant an order *ex parte* the court must have regard to *all the circumstances* (s. 45(2)), *including*:

(a) any risk of significant harm to the applicant or a relevant child, attributable to conduct of the respondent if the order is not made immediately;

(b) whether it is likely that the applicant will be deterred or prevented from pursuing the application if an order is not made immediately;

(c) whether there is reason to believe that the respondent is aware of the proceedings, but is deliberately evading service and that the applicant or a relevant child will be seriously prejudiced by the delay involved in effecting service of the proceedings (where the court is a magistrates' court) or (in any other case) in effecting substituted service (now known in the mainstream civil courts as service by an alternative method, or alternative service).

These provisions encompass both the notion of urgency and the need for secrecy. Section 45(2)(b) represents an especially welcome recognition of the fact that some applicants may be so genuinely terrified of the respondent that the secrecy afforded an *ex parte* application is needed to gain meaningful protection under the Act.

It is imperative that the application and supporting evidence explain *why* an application is being made *ex parte*.

Section 45(3) provides that where the court does make an *ex parte* order it must give the respondent an opportunity to make representations as soon as just and convenient at a full hearing of which notice has been given to all the parties in accordance with rules of court. This suggests, and is taken by many to mean, that an order made *ex parte* must state a return date (the date when both parties very soon return to put their cases).

2.13 Undertakings and Power of Arrest

2.13.1 APPLICATIONS ON NOTICE ('*INTER PARTES*')

Traditionally, the acceptance by the court of undertakings (in lieu of making an order) has been a useful, and often used, device in domestic violence cases. Undertakings can defuse fraught situations. They avoid a traumatic court hearing, thereby saving time, saving tempers and saving face (by allowing a party to avoid the stigma of the imposition of a court order).

Not surprisingly, therefore, FLA 1996, s. 46, enables the court to accept an undertaking from any party where it has the power to make an occupation order or a non-molestation order. This power, however, is subject to severe restrictions imposed by s. 46(3). To understand these constraints it is important to understand that a power of arrest *cannot* be attached to an undertaking, which is otherwise enforceable as if it were a court order (see below).

Section 46(3) prevents the court from accepting an undertaking in a case where, if an order were made, a power of arrest would have to be attached. Because there is a very strong statutory impetus to attach a power of arrest to orders (in the interest of giving greater and more effective protection), this makes it more difficult for judges to accept undertakings instead.

Thus, if (and to the extent that) the court takes the view that the grounds are made out for attaching a power of arrest to a non-molestation or occupation order, it is constrained in its ability to accept an undertaking. Section 47 imposes on the court an *obligation* to attach a power of arrest in all cases where it 'appears' to the court that the respondent has *used or threatened* violence against the applicant or a relevant child, *unless* it is satisfied that in all the circumstances of the case the applicant or the child in question will be adequately protected without one. It is worth noting that a power of arrest should be attached only to that part of the order to which it relates, i.e., the terms dealing with violence.

It would seem that the possible calming properties of undertakings cannot come into the equation when deciding whether an applicant would be adequately protected without a power of arrest because when making this decision the court must put itself in the position it would be in were it in fact making an order (and not being offered undertakings in lieu). But the enhanced powers of enforcement (see below) probably can. Those who favour undertakings tend to find adequate protection in better enforcement of court orders or take refuge in lack of time or opportunity to make proper findings about allegations of violence. Those not so disposed to undertakings, let the policy behind ss. 46 and 47 prevail. In this context, it is clearly important to 'know your tribunal'.

2.13.2 APPLICATIONS WITHOUT NOTICE ('*EX PARTE*')

A power of arrest may be attached to an order made *ex parte* where it is shown that the respondent has used or threatened violence against the applicant (or relevant child) *and* that there is a risk of significant harm to the applicant (or the child) from the respondent if the power of arrest is not attached immediately (s. 47(3)). This reflects the Law Commission's recommendation that attaching a power of arrest to an order when the respondent has not had the opportunity to be heard should, as previously, be treated with some caution. However, where there has been some actual or threatened violence and there is additionally a risk of significant harm to the applicant or child, a power of arrest will be attached to an *ex parte* order.

The acceptance of undertakings in lieu of a court order is not, of course, applicable to *ex parte* applications where only the applicant is present.

2.14 Enforcement

Where there is no power of arrest attached to any part of an order, and the respondent (having been properly served etc.) is in breach of the order (or an undertaking in lieu of an order), the applicant can apply for a warrant for the respondent's arrest. Such an application must be supported by evidence *on oath* to satisfy the court that there are reasonable grounds for believing that the respondent has failed to comply with the order/undertaking. This procedure is an improvement upon the traditional (and more time consuming) proceedings for contempt.

Where a power of arrest has been attached to an order, a police officer may arrest without warrant where he or she has reasonable cause for suspecting the respondent of being in breach of the provisions of the order (lodged with the local police station) to which the power of arrest attaches.

See **Appendix B** for a detailed step-by-step guide to the various enforcement procedures.

2.15 Variation of Occupation and Non-Molestation Orders

An application can be made by either the applicant or respondent to vary or discharge an order. If the court has made an order on its own initiative, then it can vary or discharge the order (FLA 1996, s. 49).

2.16 Applications by Children under the Age of Sixteen

A child under the age of sixteen may make an application for a non-molestation order or an occupation order but only with the leave of the court (FLA 1996, s. 43(1)). The test that the court must apply in deciding whether to give leave is whether the court is 'satisfied that the child has sufficient understanding to make the proposed application' (s. 43(2)). In the case of *Gillick v West Norfolk & Wisbech Area Health Authority* [1986] AC 112, Lord Scarman suggested that sufficiency of understanding came with 'the attainment by a child of an age of sufficient discretion to enable him or her to exercise a wise choice in his or her own interests'.

This provision, which has wide-ranging possibilities, has yet to generate much controversy.

2.17 Jurisdiction

Section 57 of the FLA 1996 provides for a unified jurisdiction between the High Court, county courts and the magistrates' courts (i.e. the Family Proceedings Court). In certain circumstances procedure varies slightly and/or proceedings must be commenced in a particular court. As a general rule, however, the ethos and effect of the FLA 1996 is to create a single jurisdiction between all of the family courts enabling choice as well as equality of access and speed for all parties seeking a remedy under the Act.

2.18 Rules of Procedure

Applications for a non-molestation or occupation order are to be made in Form FL 401 whether the application is free-standing or in other proceedings. In the High Court and county courts, the application should be supported by evidence in the form of a 'statement which is signed by the applicant and is sworn to be true' — an affidavit in all but name. In the Family Proceedings Court (i.e. the magistrates' court) only a declaration of truth is required. Whatever form the supporting evidence takes, it should convey, as economically as possible, a clear and complete picture of why and on what grounds the order is sought (see example **2.21**). The application will be heard in chambers (i.e. in private) unless the court otherwise directs.

The procedural rules governing applications under the FLA 1996 are to be found in the following:

- *In the High and county court*: the Family Proceedings (Amendment No. 3) Rules 1997 (SI 1997 No. 1893), which amend the Family Proceedings Rules 1991 (SI 1991 No. 1247).

- *In the Family Proceedings Court*: the Family Proceedings Courts (Matrimonial Proceedings etc.) (Amendment) Rules 1997 (SI 1997 No. 1894) which amend the Family Proceedings Courts (Matrimonial Proceedings etc.) Rules 1991 (SI 1991 No. 1991).

- The Family Law Act 1996 (Part IV) (Allocation of Proceedings) Order 1997 (SI 1997 No. 1896).

- The Family Proceedings Fees Order 1999 (SI 1999 No. 690) as amended by the Family Proceedings Fees (Amendment No. 2) Order 2000 (SI 2000 No. 938).

- The Family Proceedings (Allocation to Judiciary) Directions 1999.

2.19 Amendments to the Children Act 1989

2.19.1 OUSTER ORDER

The FLA 1996, s. 52 and sch. 6 amended the Children Act 1989 (CA 1989), creating ss. 38A, 38B, 39(3B), 44A, 44B, 45(8A) and 45(8B) and enabling the court to make an ouster order for the protection of children when making an interim care order (CA 1989, s. 38) or an emergency protection order (CA 1989, s. 44) (see generally **Chapter 7**). These changes were intended to introduce improvements in the *emergency* protection of children by permitting the removal, albeit as a temporary short-term measure, of a suspected abuser from the family home as an alternative to removing the child from the source of the suspected abuse. This power is intended to supplement the emergency protection order or interim care order, rather than provide a long-term alternative to a care order. To reinforce this auxillary purpose, the expression 'exclusion requirement' is used instead of 'ouster' or 'occupation order'.

2.19.2   THE CONDITIONS

The conditions for attaching an exclusion requirement, as set out in CA 1989, ss. 38A(2) and 44A, are:

(a)   that there is reasonable cause to believe that, if a person ('the relevant person') is excluded from a dwelling-house in which the child lives, the child will cease to suffer, or cease to be likely to suffer significant harm, and

(b)   that another person living in the dwelling-house (whether a parent of the child or some other person):

(i)   is able and willing to give to the child the care which it would be reasonable to expect a parent to give him; and

(ii)   consents to the inclusion of the exclusion requirement.

These provisions do not seem to be utilised very much — presumably because of the difficulty of obtaining the necessary cooperation and consent from the child's other parent or carer. It is an unhappy feature of domestic child abuse that very often the relationship of that person with the suspected abuser is such that the former assumes the role, if not of co-abuser, then of colluder. Even if the collusion is the result of incompetence, rather than malice, it can still be difficult to be assured of the required level of responsibility from the remaining adult to give the child the necessary protection.

2.19.3   THE NATURE OF THE EXCLUSION REQUIREMENT

The exclusion requirement provisions are set out in CA 1989, s. 38A(3)–(10). The requirement can be to leave a dwelling house in which the child lives, not to enter a dwelling-house in which the child lives, or to be excluded from a defined area in which the dwelling-house where the child lives is situated.

The court can attach a power of arrest to an exclusion requirement to last for the period of the main order or a shorter period. Enforcement procedure is the same as for any order with a power of arrest (see **2.13**).

An exclusion requirement ceases to have effect at the same time as the interim care order or emergency protection order. The 'package' is thus intended as a short-term solution.

The court may accept an undertaking from a relevant person in lieu of attaching an exclusion requirement (CA 1989, ss. 38B and 44B).

A person excluded can apply to vary or discharge the exclusion requirement whether or not he or she is entitled to make an application in relation to the main order itself (CA 1989, s. 39(3A)). If a power of arrest is attached, an application can be made for it to be discharged.

2.20   Protection from Harassment Act 1997

Part IV of the FLA 1996 was implemented after a long and public debate. In contrast, the protection from Harassment Act 1997 seemed to slip onto the statute books almost unnoticed. It is, however, an important piece of legislation with far-reaching implications. Drafted primarily to provide protection against 'stalkers', it appears that this Act may have more potential (and more pitfalls) than the legislators anticipated. Before the FLA 1996, there were many categories of people without a remedy against molestation or harassment under the domestic violence legislation as it then stood, who had to rely instead on the general civil or criminal law. The FLA 1996 has considerably widened the range of people who can apply for protection under the Act, but there will still be those who fall outside the class of 'associated person' who will need to look elsewhere for protection. There is no tort of harassment at common law (see *Burnett* v *George* [1992] 1 FLR 525) although some inroads into this principle have recently taken place (see, e.g., *Khorasandjian* v *Bush* [1993] QB 727 and *Burris* v *Azadani* [1995] 1 WLR 1372). As for the criminal law, proof is often fraught with predictable difficulties, not the least being the reluctance of witnesses to give evidence and the more onerous standard of proof required in criminal proceedings. Again, however, the courts have shown some willingness to stretch the concepts of assault and bodily harm as necessary (see, e.g., *R* v *Ireland*; *R* v *Burstow* [1998] 1 FLR 105).

The Protection from Harassment Act 1997 is unique in that in certain circumstances:

(a)   breach of a civil injunction is a crime, and

(b)   in effect, the criminal courts can grant injunctive relief.

This mixture of the criminal and civil law is novel, and may pose problems, especially as regards the different burden and standards of proof.

On the face of it, the FLA 1996 should and will be invoked to protect victims of family strife arising in the many domestic situations catered for in the legislation. Its improved methods of enforcement give the available remedies strength, without criminalising the violence involved, which may be particularly pertinent in the domestic context. However, there will be (still relatively rare) circumstances, most notably when the parties are not 'associated', but also as between 'associated persons' when criminal sanctions are more appropriate (e.g., to deter or punish stalking by a former spouse as envisaged in *R* v *Hills* [2001] Fam Law 185), when it may be necessary to make use of the provisions of the 1997 Act.

2.21 An Example of Domestic Violence Proceedings in the County Court

Instructions to counsel

IN THE CLERKENWELL COUNTY COURT   Case No. 02/162

IN THE MATTER OF THE FAMILY LAW ACT 1996

BETWEEN

EMMA JANE BROWN   Applicant

and

ARTHUR HAROLD BROWN   Respondent

INSTRUCTIONS TO COUNSEL

Counsel has herewith:

1. Copy application dated 4.1.2002

2. Copy sworn statement of the Applicant sworn on 4.1.2002

3. Statement of Mr Brown

Counsel acts for the Respondent Mr Brown. On 4 January 2002 his wife, Mrs Brown, obtained *ex parte* a non-molestation injunction supported by a power of arrest. The return day is 11 January 2002. Counsel is referred to the Application and sworn statement of Mrs Brown.

Counsel is instructed to settle the sworn statement of Mr Brown of 9 Holiday Road, London N1 in reply to the application of Mrs Brown to exclude him from the matrimonial home at the above address and to renew her application for a non-molestation injunction. Counsel will note from the statement of Mr Brown that he disputes the recent allegation of violence but makes some admissions to the older allegations of violence.

Mr Brown says that he cannot go and stay with his brother John Hanks because he now has a lodger and there would be no room for him to move in. Instructing Solicitors are of the view that there is a chance of Mr Brown being excluded from the property despite not having anywhere to live. Instructing solicitors spoke with Mr Brown this morning and the entrance to the flat is at the back of the building on a different street. Mr Brown says that yesterday his wife did return when he was there and things were fine although she did go back to sleep at her friend's flat.

OYEZ

Application for:
a Non-Molestation Order
an Occupation Order

Family Law Act 1996 (Part IV)
The Court

To be completed by the Court

Date issued

Case number

Clerkenwell County Court

Please read the accompanying notes as you complete this form.

1. About you (the Applicant).

State your title (Mr, Mrs etc), full name, address, telephone number and date of birth (if under 18):

Mrs Emma Jane Brown
9 Holiday Road
London N1

State your solicitor's name, address, reference, telephone, FAX and DX numbers:

Messrs Ling & Ton
2 Upper Street London N1
tel. 020 7226 4175
fax. 020 7226 4299

2. About the Respondent.

State the Respondent's name, address and date of birth (if known):

Arthur Harold Brown
9 Holiday Road
London N1

3. The Order(s) for which you are applying.

This application is for:

☑ a non-molestation order

☑ an occupation order.

☐ Tick this box if you wish the Court to hear your application without notice being given to the Respondent. The reasons relied upon for an application being heard without notice must be stated in the statement in support.

[P.T.O.

4. Your relationship to the Respondent (the person to be served with this application).

Your relationship to the Respondent is:

Please tick only one of the following

1 ☑ Married.

2 ☐ Were married.

3 ☐ Cohabiting.

4 ☐ Were cohabiting.

5 ☐ Both of you live or have lived in the same household.

6 ☐ Relative. State how related:

7 ☐ Agreed to marry. Give the date the agreement was made. If the agreement has ended, state when.

8 ☐ Both of you are parents of or have parental responsibility for a child.

9 ☐ One of you is a parent of a child and the other has parental responsibility for that child.

10 ☐ One of you is the natural parent or grandparent of a child adopted or freed for adoption, and the other is:

        (i)   the adoptive parent

   or (ii) a person who has applied for an adoption order for the child

   or (iii) a person with whom the child has been placed for adoption

   or (iv) the child who has been adopted or freed for adoption.

State whether (i), (ii), (iii) or (iv):

11 ☐ Both of you are parties to the same family proceedings (see also section 11 below).

5. Application for a non-molestation order.

If you wish to apply for a non-molestation order, state briefly in this section the order you want. Give full details in support of your application in your supporting evidence.

The Respondent be forbidden to use or threaten violence against the Applicant. The Respondent be forbidden to intimidate, harass or pester the Applicant.

6. Application for an occupation order.

If you do not wish to apply for an occupation order, please go to section 9 of this form.

(A) State the address of the dwelling-house to which your application relates:

9 Holiday Road
London
N1

(B) State whether it is occupied by you or the Respondent now or in the past, or whether it was intended to be occupied by you or the Respondent:

Both Applicant and Respondent

(C) State whether you are entitled to occupy the dwelling-house: ☑ Yes ☐ No

If yes, explain why:

Provided by employers

(D) State whether the Respondent is entitled to occupy the dwelling-house: ☑ Yes ☐ No

If yes, explain why: Matrimonial home rights

[P.T.O.

On the basis of your answer to (C) and (D) above, tick one of the boxes 1 to 5 below to show the category into which you fit:

1 [✓] a spouse who has matrimonial home rights in the dwelling-house, or a person who is entitled to occupy it by virtue of a beneficial estate or interest or contract or by virtue of any enactment giving him or her the right to remain in occupation.

If you tick box 1, state whether there is a dispute or pending proceedings between you and the Respondent about your right to occupy the dwelling-house.

2 [ ] a former spouse with no existing right to occupy, where the Respondent spouse is entitled.

3 [ ] a cohabitant or former cohabitant with no existing right to occupy, where the Respondent cohabitant or former cohabitant is so entitled.

4 [ ] a spouse or former spouse who is not entitled to occupy, where the Respondent spouse or former spouse is also not entitled.

5 [ ] a cohabitant or former cohabitant who is not entitled to occupy, where the Respondent cohabitant or former cohabitant is also not entitled.

Matrimonial Home Rights.
If you do have matrimonial home rights please:
State whether the title to the land is registered or unregistered (if known):

N/A

If registered, state the Land Registry title number (if known):

N/A

If you wish to apply for an occupation order, state briefly here the order you want. Give full details in support of your application in your supporting evidence.

An order excluding the Respondent from the property known as 9 Holiday Road London N1.

7. Application for additional order(s) about the dwelling-house.

If you want to apply for any of the orders listed in the notes to this section, state what order you would like the Court to make:

8. Mortgage and rent.

Is the dwelling-house subject to mortgage? ☐ Yes ☑ No

If yes, please provide the name and address of the mortgagee:

Is the dwelling-house rented? ☑ Yes ☐ No

If yes, please provide the name and address of the landlord:

9. At the Court.

Will you need an interpreter at Court ? ☐ Yes ☑ No

If yes, specify the language:

If you need an interpreter because you do not speak English, you are responsible for providing your own.

If you need an interpreter or other facilities because of a disability, please contact the Court to ask what help is available.

[P.T.O.

10. Other information.

State the name and date of birth of any child living with, or staying with, or likely to live with or stay with you or the Respondent:

N/A

State the name of any other person living in the same household as you and the Respondent, and say why they live there:

N/A

11. Other Proceedings and Orders.

If there are any other current family proceedings or orders in force involving you and the Respondent, state the type of proceedings or orders, the court and the case number. This includes any application for an occupation order or non-molestation order against you by the Respondent.

None

This application is to be served upon the Respondent.

Signed   Messrs Ling & Ton   Date   4.1.02

OYEZ The Solicitors' Law Stationery Society Ltd. Oyez House, 7 Spa Road, London SE16 3QQ

Family Law Act—FL401

Statement by Mrs Brown

Filed on behalf of Applicant
Deponent: E J Brown
Date of Swearing: 4.1.02
Date of Filing: 4.1.02

IN THE CLERKENWELL COUNTY COURT   Case No. 02/162

IN THE MATTER OF THE FAMILY LAW ACT 1996

BETWEEN   EMMA JANE BROWN   <u>Applicant</u>

and

ARTHUR HAROLD BROWN   <u>Respondent</u>

I, EMMA JANE BROWN, of 9 Holiday Road, London N1, canteen assistant, the above-named Applicant, MAKE OATH and say as follows:

1. I make this sworn statement in support of my application herein for an injunction, supported by a power of arrest, forbidding the Respondent from using violence against me or from threatening, intimidating, harassing or pestering me. I also seek an order requiring the Respondent to vacate the matrimonial home at 9 Holiday Road aforesaid forthwith.

2. I met the Respondent in March 2001 and we got married on 18 April 2001. He moved into my flat above the canteen where I work. It is a one bedroom flat.

3. I did not know of the Respondent's serious drink problem until after we were married. Very shortly after our honeymoon he began to drink to excess on a regular basis. When he gets drunk he becomes abusive and violent but particularly his drunkeness manifests itself in an uncontrollable paranoia that I am engaging in affairs with different men.

4. The Respondent began visiting the canteen where I work, usually without warning, and sometimes many times in the day, to see if I had any men hidden behind the serving area or in the store cupboard. He was also rude to the male customers telling them to 'keep their hands off his missus' and not to 'eye me up'. This was extremely distressing for me and embarrassing for both me and my customers.

5. One day last July the Respondent and I were walking down the street when we met a married couple who are friends of mine. After we chatted for a few minutes the Respondent shouted at the man to 'stop imagining that you are having sex with my wife'. I did not know what to do or say so I just kept quiet.

6. On 10 August 2001 the Respondent and I went to a party where we met one of his friends. The friend complimented me in front of the Respondent who immediately lost his temper. He punched his friend in the face, broke his nose and there was blood everywhere. I was very embarrassed and frightened and did not dare say anything to the Respondent about this outburst.

7. The next day the Respondent noticed that I was wearing some silver earrings. I bought these before we were married and have worn them many times. However, he was convinced that they were a present from one of my customers. He grabbed me by the wrists, pulled the earrings out of my ears and tore my lobes as he did so.

8. The Respondent has assaulted me on more occasions than I can remember. He began going to the pub more and more and would often come home and beat me or kick me or bend back my fingers. I felt too ashamed to go to the doctor for help. I wore trousers and long sleeved tops so that nobody noticed the bruises.

9.   Two nights ago the Respondent and I decided to hold a party with a Mexican theme for about twenty of the Respondent's friends and a couple of my girlfriends. I spent the whole day preparing the food whilst the Respondent provided the alcohol. Unfortunately he drank a glass of tequila with each guest as they arrived and got very drunk. He then got jealous of everyone complimenting me on the food, how pretty I looked in the spanish dress that I was wearing and the attention that I was receiving. He got hold of a bowl of dip and threw it at me causing the dip to run down my dress. He shouted at me to 'stop behaving like a tart' and said 'now you will want to strip off your dress you slapper'. He then grabbed me by the wrists and dragged me to the bedroom trying to rip off my dress. He slapped me around the face and told me to change clothes. I felt humiliated because everyone was watching so I stayed in the bedroom and waited for everyone to go.

10.   About an hour later the Respondent staggered into the bedroom and hurled an empty bottle at me narrowly missing me and hitting the wall behind. He jumped on top of me on the bed and twisted back my arms. I received a large bruise on my left upper arm. Then he pulled my hair right back, slapped my face and then started to hit my head against the headboard. He only stopped when I poked his eyes with my fingers. He then rolled over and fell off the bed. I quickly ran to the bathroom and locked the door and stayed there all night.

11.   Last night I slept on the sofa of Janice Ham, a work colleague who lives close to the Angel. She has a small flat and I cannot stay there for more than a few days. I have nowhere else to stay. My flat is provided by my employers, at a very reasonable rent. I only earn £80 per week net and I cannot afford to rent any other accommodation. The Respondent can go and stay with his brother in Finchley where he lived prior to the marriage. His brother has a two bedroom house and it is not far for him to commute to work in his car. He is a garage mechanic working at Highbury Corner.

12.   I am too frightened to return to my flat. The Respondent behaves irrationally and I believe that he will continue to assault me if he is allowed to remain in the flat. I am frightened by how the Respondent will react to my applying for this injunction and I therefore seek an order *ex parte* in the terms set out in paragraph 1 of this sworn statement.

Sworn this 4th day of January 2002
at 10 Highbury Crescent
London N1

Emma Jane Brown

Before me
Commissioner of Oaths

Statement of Mr Brown

STATEMENT OF MR BROWN

I can't believe what she is saying. Whilst it is true that I used to go and visit her at work a lot, that was only because we had just got married and I missed her when we came back from our honeymoon. It was out of affection and not out of jealousy. I did accuse Emma of receiving the earrings from a customer but it is very difficult because she gets lots of builders and the like coming into her canteen and they are always being sweet on her. I asked her to take them off because it upset me seeing her wearing them and she refused. She just smiled and said nothing. She refused to answer my questions so I did take them off her. Maybe I was a bit heavy handed but they are very tricky things to remove. Anyway, she never complained about it at the time.

I admit that I did accuse Dave Canker of imagining that he was having sex with my wife when we met them in the street but that is because he has a reputation of having affairs and started chatting up Emma in front of Amy, his wife and she was getting all upset and crying and Emma was laughing at her and I wanted to help Amy because Dave is so thoughtless and would not stop.

I admit that I got drunk on the 10 August last year and punched Frank, but Frank asked for it. He has always been going on at me about how pretty Emma is and how he fancied her and so when he met her for the first time at that party and started coming on strong I was furious. I don't trust him an inch. He is a slippery fish and if he could get his hands on Emma he would.

Emma is very aware of the effect she has on men. She can switch on the charm and sex appeal when she wants to and she does it to tease me. It is true that I have hit her a couple of times in the past but that is only because she was trying to get my attention by chatting up other men. She knows that I get jealous and she does it on purpose. I have never kicked her. I have bent back her fingers but that is to stop her poking out my eyes. It is true that I go to the pub most evenings and some lunchtimes but that is because most of my mates go down there. As I have said, I do not get drunk and beat up Emma; rather, she teases me to get me jealous.

How Emma has described the Mexican party is a pack of lies. I did not drink a glass of tequila with every guest on their arrival. How would she know because she was not standing by the door greeting guests as they came in. Rather she was doing provocative dances with some of my mates from work. That is why I threw the food at her. It was the only way I could stop her dancing those close up Latin American dances. She was trying to attract my attention and to get me jealous. She stormed into the bedroom. When I came in later to see if she was alright she attacked me. She was screaming and kicking and when I tried to defend myself she tried to poke my eyes out.

I cannot stay with my brother in Finchley. He has rented out his spare room to a lodger and my car is not reliable enough to travel the distance to work. I cannot afford to be late for work because I already have a warning at work over my time-keeping. There is nobody else who has the room to put me up and I can't afford to rent because I am trying to pay off my credit card. I owe about £4,300 and I make payments of £200 a month. This comes out of my take home pay of £255 a week.

2.22 Drafting the Sworn Statement in a Support

The sworn statement is the party's evidence before the court and is an absolutely crucial document. It takes a high degree of skill — and lots of practice — to draft such statements effectively.

When drafting a sworn (or other witness) statement you want to put forward the relevant facts as convincingly as possible. In effect your job is to put a persuasive presentational 'spin' on the evidence so that it has the best chance of achieving its purpose. Remember that judges often have to sit and read such statements all day long. If yours can be that much more compelling, clear and to the point than the rest, you will be doing yourself and your client a valuable service.

You should refer to **Chapter 21** of the ***Drafting Manual*** for the rules of presentation of affidavits and witness statements.

2.22.1   CONTENT

It is imperative that the story you tell is the *client's story* — not your story or a story you think you would rather be telling.

In the sworn statement your client should set out the relief or outcome sought and the eligibility for such relief, e.g., the category of associated person and rights of occupation in the property. If the application is *ex parte* then the statement *must* include an explanation of why the application is being made without notice.

The statement should contain the relevant facts available to show why the party needs the court's protection or on what basis he or she resists the injunction(s) sought. It should focus on the main incidents said to justify the making (or not) of the order(s). The statement does *not* recite the law, but it needs to be drafted with the law clearly in mind. What it must do is set out the facts to satisfy the criteria which the District Judge will apply under the relevant section of the FLA 1996. If it is a sworn statement in reply, it should show why the criteria are not satisfied and/or why the court's discretion should be exercised in favour of the respondent and not the applicant.

2.22.2   STRUCTURE

It is important to tell your client's story *well*. The facts should be presented logically (chronologically is usually best), setting out clearly the incidents of violence (or replying to each allegation of violence). Try to develop a 'theory of the case' and draft accordingly. Describing a steady escalation of violence will require a different presentation from the portrayal of an out-of-the-blue series of attacks. Always set the scene carefully and think in terms of a 'strong finish'. Tailor the statement's structure to meet the needs of your case; never use 'off-the-peg' statements.

Be as specific as you can. In Mrs Brown's statement she asserts that she has been assaulted on more occasions than she can remember. Unless she really has been attacked so many times it has affected her short-term memory, she will be challenged on this telling lack of detail.

A sworn statement in reply would normally adopt the order of the applicant's statement and should always respond to *every* allegation.

2.22.3   LANGUAGE

A sworn statement is the witness' evidence and it is important to set out the facts so that his or her 'voice' comes through. Having said this, it is also important to recast sentences in the proof so that they are grammatically correct and readily comprehensible. The aim is not to make the statement unnecessarily formal but to make it clear and compelling. If it is appropriate to include the actual words spoken by some person this should be done in the normal way using quotation marks.

2.22.4 '   PERSUASIVENESS

The sworn statement is the witnesses' evidence and the aim is to persuade the court to make the order applied for or to resist the making of the order. Your 'theory of the case' must be an effective one; you must set out the facts in such a way that the inference you wish the District Judge to draw is one which will achieve your goal. For example, in **2.21** Mrs Brown's theme is that her husband is of a jealous disposition which manifests itself when he is drunk. He misinterprets situations, is increasingly violent towards her and will continue to do this unless she obtains protection from the court. She gives examples of his behaviour: he pesters her at work; he accuses her of having affairs; he tore out her earrings; he has developed a habit of getting drunk and using violence towards her. When there is a history of violence an applicant is more likely to get the extra protection of a power of arrest or occupation order if she can show an escalation of violence.

Mr Brown's theme is that he does not misinterpret situations, but rather that his wife deliberately behaves in an alluring manner towards other men so as to make him jealous. Whilst he does admit to occasions when he has lost his temper in response to such behaviour, e.g., throwing the dip, he asserts that the allegations greatly exaggerate the situation and that his wife is herself capable of violence.

2.23   At the *Ex Parte* Hearing

This hearing, of which Mr Brown is not given notice, is held in chambers (i.e., in private). Mrs Brown's counsel will introduce himself or herself, explain that the application is for a non-molestation order and an order excluding Mr Brown from the matrimonial home situate at 9 Holiday Road, London, supported by a power of arrest. Counsel will then briefly give some background facts — the short courtship; the date of the marriage; the immediacy of his unfounded suspicions and pestering which escalated into violence first towards others and then to his wife.

The District Judge should then be given an opportunity to read the sworn statement if he or she has not done so already (always be prepared to read it out in full to the court but you will very rarely be called upon to do this).

Counsel will then get into the heart of the application. The essence of the case is that Mr Brown is of a jealous disposition which manifests itself when he is drunk and he uses violence towards his wife. Counsel will refer to the paragraphs in Mrs Brown's sworn statement to support this theory and the fact that Mr Brown's conduct towards his wife has got worse, e.g., at the Mexican party he threw a bowl at her; grabbed her by the wrists; returned later and threw a bottle at his wife; jumped on top of her and twisted her arms back; pulled her hair back; slapped her face and started to hit her against the headboard. Highlight relevant facts and repeat useful detail, but do not merely recite whole paragraphs which the court has already read.

Counsel will then seek to persuade the District Judge that Mrs Brown needs proper protection and importantly, draw attention to her reasons for applying *ex parte* (see **2.12**). Much will be made of the fact that Mrs Brown sought refuge in the bathroom and sanctuary at her friends and that she cannot stay for long at Janice Ham's on the sofa but her husband could stay with his brother in Finchley and drive to work. In the absence of Mr Brown, Mrs Brown's counsel must be mindful of the need for full and frank disclosure (which is sometimes difficult to achieve given the emotions involved in such family crises). In any case, you should always be aware of and prepared to deal with weakness in the case (e.g., lack of medical evidence).

The outcome will likely be based on Mrs Brown's sworn statement and one would not expect her to be called unless, for example, the District Judge wishes to hear evidence on her injuries because there is no medical evidence to support her case (if possible, you should get a medical report). Also, if there have been other incidents since the swearing of the statement then Mrs Brown can be called to give evidence of these.

The District Judge is unlikely to make an occupation order excluding Mr Brown because these are not exceptional circumstances (see **2.12**). He or she would, however, be likely to grant an injunction prohibiting Mr Brown from using violence or threatening violence (supported by a power of arrest) and prohibiting Mr Brown from intimidating, harassing or pestering Mrs Brown.

The District Judge would then fix a return day for the *inter partes* hearing which is usually about seven days later. Both parties will have the opportunity to put their case at this time. The *ex parte* order will last until the *inter partes* hearing.

Costs are usually reserved. If Mrs Brown is publicly funded (which would be indicated on the front page of the brief to her Counsel) then the District Judge might order an assessment of her costs. If not, then Counsel at the *inter partes* hearing must remember to ask for it to be granted retrospectively. Counsel will then ask for a certificate for counsel.

The *ex parte* hearing is likely to last only five to ten minutes. It is vital to present a focused and succinct application. Not only is this apt to be more persuasive but the courts are very busy and will have a number of matters listed for the day.

Mrs Brown should have been advised before the hearing that she was unlikely to get the occupation order at this stage, and so should not be unduly surprised if she has not. She may, however, still have concerns so after the hearing Counsel should explain the outcome, and especially the effect and added protection of the power of arrest, if this was granted.

The order will only take effect once it has been drawn up and served upon Mr Brown personally — if appropriate, by an enquiry agent. Mrs Brown should be advised when the order has been served and what to do if her husband is in breach of the terms.

2.24   At the *Inter Partes* Hearing

Again the hearing is in private. This time, however, both parties are able to put their case.

Counsel for Mrs Brown will introduce the case (including both parties' advocates) and remind the court that non-molestation injunctions were ordered at the *ex parte* hearing on 4 January 2002 with a power of arrest and that this is the return day for the applications.

Counsel will refer the Judge/District Judge to the two sworn statements in the matter and then call Mrs Brown as a witness. Having taken the oath she will be asked to identify herself and then to confirm that she did swear her statement on 4 January 2002 and that its contents contain her account of events to the date of it being sworn. If there are no other matters which need to come out in chief, then generally Mrs Brown should not be asked questions-in-chief but be tendered for cross-examination. As with the *ex parte* hearing, if you want to get a power of arrest attached to the order you need the court to make a finding that there has been the use of or threat of violence. You may feel better able to show this if Mrs Brown tells her side of the story by relating the serious incidences of violence prior to cross-examination. Some District Judges like to hear some evidence-in-chief in order to assess credibility. But some District Judges will stop you. You need to be flexible and learn to know your tribunal. If in conference before the hearing Mrs Brown tells Counsel of new matters since the statement was sworn, e.g., new incidents of violence, accommodation and financial matters, then she can be asked questions in chief to elicit this information.

Counsel for Mr Brown will cross-examine Mrs Brown. He or she will question her on all the disputes of fact, putting his or her client's case to her. Counsel will seek to advance Mr Brown's theory of the case and to discredit hers. For example, counsel will seek to obtain from Mrs Brown admissions that she has behaved in an alluring manner to other men knowing that her husband would be provoked by this. Counsel might point out omissions in her sworn statement. For example, she cannot recall details of the other incidents which might indicate that they are invented, or the fact that in her sworn statement she says her husband bends her fingers back but omits to say that this is to avoid her poking out his eyes. There may be a telling lack of medical evidence.

Counsel for Mrs Brown will re-examine if necessary. Assuming there are no other witnesses, that concludes the case for the applicant.

Counsel for the respondent then calls Mr Brown. The same points concerning examination-in-chief apply here and if Mr Brown undertakes not to use violence, threaten, intimidate, harass or pester his wife, the court is told of this if it is not already contained within his sworn statement. Then Counsel for Mrs Brown cross-examines him with any necessary re-examination to follow.

Finally, the closing speeches. The respondent goes first, giving the applicant the last word. The most effective submissions will take the District Judge through the s. 33 'core criteria' and balance of harm test (see **2.8.3** and **2.8.4**), applying them to the facts. You are more likely to be successful if you relate each part of the test to the relevant facts and articulate your arguments fully while at the same time being concise and focused on matters likely to influence the decision.

The District Judge is well familiar with the legislation, so concentrate on persuading him or her that, *on the facts of the case*, your client is entitled to the remedy/outcome he or she seeks. In a case like the Browns, be aware of how s. 33(6) and (7) relate to one another (see **2.8.4**). Apply the s. 33(6) criteria to each party, relying on your own version of the events (as adapted through any concessions made in cross-examination), and compare and contrast with the version of events put forward by the other side.

When dealing with the balance of harm test contained in s. 33(7) think both in terms of whether the test applies (i.e., whether there is a risk of 'significant harm') and of whether the balance favours your client. Set out the facts that support your submission on these points and contrast with any argument your opponent can/has made. Deal with the mandatory/discretionary parts of s. 33 in such a way that it advances your own case.

As with the *ex parte* hearing, any order made at the *inter partes* hearing will only take effect once it has been drawn up and served personally on Mr Brown. In addition, if an occupation order is made under ss. 33, 35 or 36, the applicant must serve a copy of the order on the mortgagee or landlord (as the case may be) of the property in question. Costs will be apt to follow the event, although if both parties are publicly funded, the court will make no order as to costs. Counsel should ask for certificate for Counsel.

Again, after the hearing, Counsel should spend a moment explaining the outcome of the case, and its practical implications to the lay client and deal with any questions or concerns which he or she might still have.

2.25   The Human Rights Act 1998

The Human Rights Act 1998 came into force on 2 October 2000. Its effect is to make rights under the European Convention for the Protection of Human Rights and Freedoms 'directly enforceable' against 'public authorities' (which is defined to include the courts) thus obviating the need for individuals to apply to the European Court of Human Rights. Under s. 3 of the Human Rights Act 1998, the courts must minimise interference with the Convention and interpret legislation so as to be compatible with it. In addition, domestic law must now be enacted, amended and interpreted so as to be compatible with the Convention. The higher courts can make declarations that legislation is 'incompatible' with a Convention right, although they cannot directly strike down primary legislation.

Because an occupation order usually has the effect of precluding an individual's right to occupy his or her home, it necessarily interferes with the right to 'private and family life' (Article 8). But the right is qualified and the State is entitled to infringe it in certain circumstances, including in order to 'protect health or morals' or to 'protect the rights and freedom of others'. The Family Law Act 1996 was drafted so as to comply with the Convention, and it seems that the balance which the Convention strikes between the rights of the individual and the rights of others has been adequately reflected in the legislation.

The ability to obtain non-molestation and/or occupation orders on applications which have been made without giving the other side notice (*ex parte*) raises a possible conflict with Article 6, the right to a fair trial. However, it seems that Article 6 is complied with so long as the need to apply *ex parte* is made out (e.g., urgency) and such orders last only for so long as it takes to hear the respondent's representations at an *inter partes* hearing.

The requirement for a public hearing under Article 6 accepts the need for privacy in several circumstances, including the protection of the private life of the parties and the interests of children. There may need to be some adjustment of procedural rules, but it would seem likely that the prevalence of private hearings in most family law cases, and especially cases of domestic violence, will continue.

THREE

APPLICATIONS FOR FINANCIAL PROVISION WHEN NO DIVORCE IS SOUGHT

There are many circumstances in which it may be necessary to seek, vary or enforce orders for financial provision although no divorce proceedings are pending or contemplated. Spouses may separate experimentally, or temporarily, and financial problems can arise very quickly if there are housing and food bills to be met and previous financial arrangements have broken down. This chapter outlines briefly the power of the courts to deal with financial matters when no divorce is pending. More practical detail on how to prepare and present a case is provided in **Chapter 6**. Financial provision for children is dealt with in more detail in **Chapter 7**.

3.1 The High Court and County Courts

The High Court and the county court have the following powers to make orders relating to financial provision and property rights when no divorce is sought.

3.1.1 POWERS TO AWARD MAINTENANCE

Either party to a marriage can seek an order that the other should provide maintenance on the basis that he or she:

- has failed to provide reasonable maintenance for the applicant; or

- has failed to provide or make a proper contribution towards reasonable maintenance for any child of the family.

The factors that are relevant to the level of provision made are similar to those on divorce and are dealt with in **3.2.3**. The relevant statutory provisions are in **Appendix C** (MCA 1973, s. 27). The orders that can be made include periodical payments, secured periodical payments or a lump sum for the applicant or for the benefit of a child.

3.1.2 POWERS TO DEAL WITH MAINTENANCE AGREEMENTS

It is possible for spouses to make enforceable agreements for the payment of maintenance by contract or deed without going to court. There are powers relating to maintenance agreements in MCA 1973, ss. 34 to 36, although these are not widely used.

3.1.3 POWERS TO DECIDE OWNERSHIP OF PROPERTY

Orders as to the ownership of property can be made under Married Women's Property Act 1882, s. 17:

> *In any question between husband and wife as to the title to or possession of property, either party may apply by summons or otherwise in a summary way to the High Court or such county court as may be prescribed and the court may, on such an application (which may be heard in private), make such order with respect to the property as it thinks fit.*
>
> ...

Note that this section does not provide any discretion, but simply a power to declare existing rights. One spouse may have an interest in property owned by the other under an implied, constructive or resulting trust, due to contributions made to the purchase price, etc.

3.1.4   PROCEDURE

Application is made by originating summons or application, supported by affidavit or evidence in standard form. The procedure and principles relevant to the assessment of maintenance are very similar to those on divorce. (See **Chapter 6**.)

3.2   Family Proceedings Courts

The family proceedings courts (i.e., specially constituted magistrates' courts) have no power to order provision ancillary to divorce (though note that they do have powers relating to the enforcement of an order made by a county court where that order is registered in a magistrates' court).

Although they have no jurisdiction in respect of divorce, family proceedings courts do have powers to order maintenance for spouses and children. The powers of the magistrates and the factors that they can take into account in making orders are closely aligned to the powers of the higher courts, but their jurisdiction is much more limited. The powers of the court are set out in the Domestic Proceedings and Magistrates' Courts Act 1978 (DPMCA 1978).

The possible advantages of going to a family proceedings court are that it may be cheaper, and possibly also quicker as the procedure is relatively straightforward. However, it also has disadvantages in that often less information is available before a hearing, and there are limits on the orders that can be made. For example, a lump sum cannot exceed £1,000.

3.2.1   POWERS TO AWARD MAINTENANCE AND LUMP SUMS

The powers (see DPMCA 1978, ss. 1 and 2 in **Appendix C**) of the family proceedings courts are broadly similar to those of the High Court and the County Courts already outlined.

The powers are wider in that, in addition to being able to make an order where there is a failure to provide reasonable maintenance for a spouse or child, an order can be made where the respondent has deserted the applicant, or has behaved in such a way that the applicant cannot reasonably be expected to live with the respondent.

An order may provide for periodical payments or a lump sum, but cannot include secured periodical payments, or a lump sum in excess of £1,000.

3.2.2   DURATION OF ORDERS

The duration of any order should be specified and is essentially at the discretion of the court. An order cannot be backdated before the making of the application for provision, though the order can cover liabilities and expenses already reasonably incurred. An order cannot last beyond the death or remarriage of an applicant. It is quite common for periodical payments to be specified to be payable for a set period of years, or 'until further order'.

Payments to or for the benefit of a child will normally stop when the child reaches school leaving age, and should in any event cease when a child is 18 unless the child is still undergoing education or training or there are other special circumstances justifying ongoing provision. The relevant statutory provisions are set out in **Appendix C** (DPMCA 1978, ss. 4 and 5):

3.2.3 RELEVANT FACTORS

The factors relevant to the making of provision under DPMCA 1978, s. 3, are similar to those on divorce, for which, see **5.3.1**.

3.2.4 AGREED PROVISION

Magistrates have powers under DPMCA 1978, ss. 6 to 7, to make an order where provision has been agreed. An order can be made where the court is satisfied that there is an agreement that provision be made and it would not be contrary to the interests of justice to make an order in those terms (s. 6). Alternatively, an order can be made where the parties have been living apart for at least three months and maintenance has in fact been paid, to ensure that such maintenance continues and becomes enforceable (s. 7).

Orders under these sections can include maintenance for a spouse or child. An order by agreement under s. 6 can also include a lump sum. These provisions are set out in full in **Appendix C**.

3.2.5 PROCEDURE

The proceedings for an order under DPMCA 1978, s. 2 or 6, are commenced by written application. Following this, a summons will be issued to the spouse from whom provision is sought. Affidavits do not have to be filed, but it is necessary for a statement of means to be completed, for which there is a standard form. The documents are lodged with the court for service on the respondent.

3.2.6 THE HEARING

The applicant will make his or her claim and the other side will reply. Evidence will be partly oral, with skills in examination-in-chief and cross-examination required in getting out the facts of the case. There is advance disclosure of argument and evidence, including a schedule of figures relating to the current and proposed financial position of the client. As you might expect, the practical arithmetic of the situation is at the heart of the case (see **6.3.6**).

The Maintenance Enforcement Act 1991, empowers the court to order payment by standing order or by attachment of earnings when making a maintenance order.

FOUR

THE DIVORCE PROCESS

This chapter provides a basic, practical outline of grounds upon which a divorce may be obtained, the procedure for getting a divorce and examples of relevant drafting. Irretrievable breakdown is the sole basis upon which a divorce may be sought, but this must be shown by alleging and proving one of five facts, three of which are entirely fault based. The current procedure has been subject to significant criticism for a variety of reasons:

- fault based divorce encourages recrimination rather than resolution;

- using the model of petitioner and respondent encourages litigation rather than mediation and settlement;

- current procedure permits a divorce to be granted relatively quickly, with important matters relating to children and money remaining unresolved for some considerable time;

- current procedure places little emphasis on seeking to retrieve a marriage that may be going through a difficult period.

A comprehensive attempt to address these problems was made in the Family Law Act 1996, which proposed the introduction of a wholly new procedure which was not based on fault, sought to support marriages that could be saved, encouraged mediation rather than litigation, and provided for the resolution of matters relating to children and money before a divorce was finalised. Because the changes being made were quite fundamental, various pilot projects were carried out before the legislation was brought into effect. Unfortunately, these projects highlighted difficulties with some of the proposed changes, and in January 2001 the government announced that it no longer intended to put the legislation into effect. While this decision is understandable, it is regrettable that the defects of the current system will therefore continue until alternative reform proposals are evolved.

4.1 Getting Married

It is prerequisite of a divorce that the couple be validly married. The law on the validity of marriage is not within the scope of this Manual and will need to be researched if necessary. The rules governing capacity to marry can be found in the Matrimonial Causes Act 1973 (MCA 1973), s. 11. In effect they allow persons who are not closely related, who are of the opposite sex to one another, not already married and who are aged over 18, or over 16 with parental consent, to marry. Special rules allow those who are not domiciled in England or Wales to marry polygamously outside of England or Wales.

Even where the parties have the capacity to marry, the validity of the marriage may be questioned if the formalities have not been complied with (MCA 1973, s. 11), or if the marriage has not been consummated or one of the parties either did not consent to it or had not the capacity to consent to it or married a person who was pregnant by another or suffering from venereal disease at the time of the marriage (MCA 1973, s. 12). Note that MCA 1973, s. 13 provides defences to some of these grounds.

When s. 12 applies, a decree annulling the marriage must be obtained; whereas when s. 11 applies a declaration from the court should be obtained.

Formalities for the marriage service are governed primarily by the Marriage Act 1949. The Marriage Act 1994 allows a marriage to take place in any approved building. Over 1,000 places have been approved, including several football stadia, London Zoo, and a James Bond theme pub! See also the Marriage Ceremony (Prescribed Words) Act 1996.

4.2 The Ground for Divorce

Where a problem relating to finance, the care of children or the occupation of a home arises during a marriage, a variety of applications may be made to court even if no divorce is sought. It is important to appreciate this, and the main powers that may be used where the marriage is continuing are referred to in this Manual. However, for many couples, problems concerning children and money arise when they decide that their marriage should end, and are therefore sorted out in the context of divorce, which is why the divorce process is central to this Manual. The basis on which a divorce can currently be sought is briefly outlined here for convenience.

If a client decides that their marriage is over, a divorce is available under the MCA 1973, s. 1, only on the ground that the marriage has broken down irretrievably. This irretrievable breakdown may be shown in one of five ways:

(a) That the respondent has committed adultery and the petitioner finds it intolerable to live with the respondent.

(b) That the respondent has behaved in such a way that the petitioner cannot reasonably be expected to live with the respondent.

(c) That the respondent has deserted the petitioner for a continuous period of at least two years immediately preceding the presentation of the petition.

(d) That the parties to the marriage have lived apart for a continuous period of at least two years immediately preceding the presentation of the petition and the respondent consents to the decree being granted.

(e) That the parties to the marriage have lived apart for a continuous period of at least five years immediately preceding the presentation of the petition.

Only the first two involve no interval of time and can be used immediately, and therefore tend to be the most popular. However, both are based on the fault of the other spouse and are therefore to some extent antagonistic. The fourth ground is the only one which is consensual and makes no allegation of fault, but this does require two years of separation before a divorce can be granted.

Sometimes the parties are not agreed on whether their case should be dealt with in this jurisdiction or in some other country. This complex topic of jurisdiction is beyond the scope of this Manual, but for a recent case on the subject, see *W v W (Financial Relief: Appropriate Forum)* [1997] 1 FLR 257.

4.3 The Procedure for Obtaining a Divorce

The great majority of divorce petitions are not defended, and in the case of an undefended divorce there is a special procedure allowing the divorce to be granted without a hearing. A divorce can be defended on the basis that the facts alleged are not true or do not justify the grant of a decree. In the case of five years' separation there is a statutory defence if it can be shown that a divorce would result in grave financial or other hardship for the respondent (MCA 1973, s. 5). This is rarely used, and may be avoided if it is possible to find some way of making financial provision.

Divorce is a two stage process, consisting of an interim decree ('decree nisi') and a final decree ('decree absolute'), and the parties are only free to remarry once the decree absolute has been obtained. Generally it is the petitioner who will apply for the decree absolute six weeks after the decree nisi has been granted by the court, but the respondent can apply once a further three months have elapsed if the petitioner has not applied. The hearing of ancillary matters relating to money and children is normally adjourned to be heard in private.

There may be a delay in the issue of the decree absolute if the judge feels it is necessary to use the court's powers with relation to the children (MCA 1973, s. 41). Arrangements need not be detailed and final, but the judge must feel confident that there are no major potential problems. Formerly there was a special hearing to consider this, but now a decision is taken on the basis of a written Statement of Arrangements. If the judge is satisfied, the divorce will proceed under the special procedure. If the judge is not satisfied, he or she can ask for further evidence and if necessary there can be a hearing relating to the child. The divorce can be delayed under s. 41 if there are exceptional circumstances and it is felt that delay would be in the interests of the child.

Under the current law there are a variety of tactical and practical considerations that may be relevant in bringing or defending a divorce. The facts given by the client may provide a choice as to the basis on which a divorce could be sought. Although it is possible to allege more than one basis in a petition, it is common, for costs reasons if no other, to plead only one basis, and a decision should be taken not only on the strength of the evidence but also on the likely reaction of the other side. The precise legal interpretation of each possible basis for divorce should be checked. For example, the test for behaviour is partly objective, but is also subjective, allowing a wife to divorce a dogmatic and chauvinistic husband (*Birch* v *Birch* [1992] Fam Law 290).

4.4   Drafting a Divorce Petition

A divorce must be originated by petition (Family Proceedings Rules 1991, r. 2.2). In recent years, with simplifications in procedure, it has become rarer for a barrister to be asked to draft a petition, but it is still important for the barrister to be aware of what should be in a petition and to check it if briefed to appear on applications in connection with the divorce. The proposals for reform would have replaced the petition with a simpler form.

4.4.1   RULES FOR A PETITION

Rules for the contents of a petition are laid down in FPR 1991, r. 2.3 and Appendix 2, and a standard form is commonly used.

Appendix 2 provides:

1.   Every petition other than a petition under rules 3.12, 3.13, 3.14 or 3.15 (seeking specific declarations) shall state:
    (a)   the names of the parties to the marriage and the date and place of the marriage;
    (b)   the last address at which the parties to the marriage have lived together as husband and wife;
    (c)   where it is alleged that the court has jurisdiction based on domicile—
        (i)   the country in which the petitioner is domiciled, and
        (ii)   if that country is not England and Wales the country in which the respondent is domiciled,
    (d)   where it is alleged that the court has jurisdiction based on habitual residence—

(i)   the country in which the petitioner has been habitually resident throughout the period of one year ending with the date of the presentation of the petition, or

(ii)   if the petitioner has not been habitually resident in England and Wales, the country in which the respondent has been habitually resident during that period, with details in either case, including the addresses of the places of residence and the length of residence at each place;

(e)   the occupation and residence of the petitioner and the respondent;

(f)   whether there are any living children of the family and, if so—

(i)   the number of such children and the full names (including surname) of each and his date of birth or (if it be the case) that he is over 18, and

(ii)   in the case of each minor child over the age of 16, whether he is receiving instruction at an educational establishment or undergoing training for a trade, profession or vocation;

(g)   whether (to the knowledge of the petitioner in the case of a husband's petition) any other child now living has been born to the wife during the marriage and, if so, the full names (including surname) of the child and his date of birth or, if it be the case, that he is over 18;

(h)   if it be the case, that there is a dispute whether a living child is a child of the family;—

(i)   whether or not there are or have been any other proceedings in any court in England and Wales or elsewhere with reference to the marriage or to any children of the family or between the petitioner and the respondent with reference to any property of either or both of them, and if so—

(i)   the nature of the proceedings,

(ii)   the date and effect of any decree or order, and

(iii)   in the case of proceedings with reference to the marriage, whether there has been any resumption of cohabitation since the making of the decree or order,

(j)   whether there are any proceedings continuing in any country outside England and Wales which relate to the marriage or are capable of affecting its validity or subsistence and, if so—

(i)   particulars of the proceedings, including the court in or tribunal or authority before which they were begun,

(ii)   the date when they were begun,

(iii)   the names of the parties,

(iv)   the date or expected date of any trial in the proceedings, and

(v)   such other facts as may be relevant to the question whether the proceedings on the petition should be stayed under Schedule 1 to the Domicile and Matrimonial Proceedings Act 1973;

and such proceedings shall include any which are not instituted in a court of law in that country, if they are instituted before a tribunal or other authority, having power under the law having effect there to determine questions of status, and shall be treated as continuing if they have been begun and have not been finally disposed of;

(k)   where the fact on which the petition is based is five years' separation, whether any, and if so what, agreement or arrangement has been made or is proposed to be made between the parties for the support of the respondent or, as the case may be, the petitioner or any child of the family;

(l)   in the case of a petition for divorce, that the marriage has broken down irretrievably;

(m)   the fact alleged by the petitioner for the purposes of section 1(2) of the Act of 1973 or, where the petition is not for divorce or judicial separation, the ground on which relief is sought, together in any case with brief particulars of the individual facts relied on but not the evidence by which they are to be proved,

(n)   any further or other information required by such of the following paragraphs and by rule 3.11 as may be applicable . . .

4.   Every petition shall conclude with:—

(a)   a prayer setting out particulars of the relief claimed, including any application for an order under any provision of Part I or Part II of the Children Act 1989 with respect to a child of the family, any claim for costs and any application for ancillary relief which it is intended to claim;

(b)   the names and addresses of the persons who are to be served with the petition, indicating if any of them is a person under disability,

(c) the petitioner's address for service, which, where the petitioner sues by a solicitor, shall be the solicitor's name or firm and address. Where the petitioner, although suing in person, is receiving legal advice from a solicitor; the solicitor's name or firm and address may be given as the address for service if he agrees. In any other case, the petitioner's address for service shall be the address of any place in England or Wales at or to which documents for the petitioner may be delivered or sent.

The petition to commence the divorce proceedings is filed in the local divorce county court or in the Divorce Registry in London, as appropriate. With it are filed:

(a) A statement of arrangements for children (if there are 'any children under 16 or over 16 but under 18 who are at school or college or are training for a trade, profession or vocation' (form M4)).

(b) The marriage certificate.

(c) A solicitors' certificate that reconciliation has been attempted (form M3).

(d) An affidavit in support of the petition (in short formal form).

Under FPR 1991, r. 2.4, a petitioner who seeks to rely on a conviction under the Civil Evidence Act 1968, ss. 11 or 12, must give appropriate details in the petition.

Under FPR 1991, r. 2.5, a petition should be signed by counsel if settled by counsel, or by the solicitor or petitioner as appropriate.

Under FPR 1991, r. 2.7, a person with whom it is alleged the respondent has committed adultery should be made a party to the proceedings unless that person is not named in the petition, or is dead, or the court otherwise directs. If some other improper association is alleged with a named person, the court may direct that that person be made a party.

In practical terms, a petition does not have to follow any set wording exactly, so long as it has the specified contents, but it is vital that it be complete and absolutely accurate. In practice, the general form set out below is commonly followed.

Form of petition

<table>
<tr><td></td><td>In the (County Court)
(Divorce Registry)</td><td>No. of
Matter</td></tr>
<tr><td></td><td colspan="2">THE PETITION OF   SHOWS THAT</td></tr>
</table>

(Insert and/or delete as appropriate)

(1) On 20
the Petitioner was lawfully
married to (hereinafter
called the Respondent)

at
(2)   The Petitioner and the Respondent last lived together at

(3)   The Petitioner is domiciled in England and Wales;

(or as the case may be)

the Petitioner is a and resides at
and the Respondent is a and resides at

(4)   There is/are children of the family
now living namely

Delete as

(5)   (In the case of a husband's petition) No other child now living has been born to
the Respondent during the marriage so far as is known to the Petitioner (or in the case of a wife's petition) No other child now living has been born to the Petitioner during the marriage (except

appropriate

(6)   The Petitioner alleges that
is (not) a child of the family.

(7)   There are, or have been no other proceedings in any court in England and Wales or elsewhere with reference to the marriage (or to any children of the family) or between the Petitioner and the Respondent with reference to any property of either or both of them (except

(8)   There are no proceedings continuing in any country outside England and Wales which relate to the marriage or are capable of affecting its validity or subsistence (except

(9)   No agreement or arrangement has been made or is proposed to be made between the parties for the support of the Respondent (or the Petitioner) (and any child of the family) except

(10)   (In the following paragraphs, state the ground or grounds and fact or facts relied upon in support thereof.)

The Petitioner therefore prays
(Signed)

The names and addresses of the persons who are to be served with this Petition are

The Petitioner's address for service is

Dated this day of 20

Generally, paras 1 to 8 are formal and simply recount practical matters such as the date of the marriage, the facts giving jurisdiction to the court, details about each spouse and about any children. Details must be checked and be correct, taking information about the marriage from the marriage certificate if necessary.

As regards addresses, the petitioner may get leave to withhold his or her address if there is a real threat of danger from the respondent.

Details of children must include all children of the family, and of any other child born to the wife, giving name and date of birth of each.

Details of any proceedings affecting the marriage or the parties to it must also be given, including domestic violence proceedings, existing maintenance orders etc.

Paragraphs 9 and 10 set out the ground of divorce, with the facts relied on and any appropriate particulars (MCA 1973, ss. 1 and 2). In many cases the facts can be alleged briefly and concisely, as is often the case for adultery or desertion, but all appropriate details must be given, for example, any periods of resumed cohabitation after separation.

More details are likely to be required where behaviour is relied on, and a full statement, linked if necessary with a conference with the client, is a vital basis for pleading. It is important to organise allegations to produce a clear and strong draft. In general terms when raising behaviour:

(a) Use an overall structure, whether it be chronological or putting the worst allegations first and then lesser allegations.

(b) Put each allegation in a separate numbered paragraph.

(c) Draft each allegation concisely and clearly.

(d) If there are many allegations, choose the strongest.

(e) Allege facts, not evidence.

(f) Try to include specific actions rather than generalisations and emotions.

(g) Choose appropriate vocabulary, to put the client's words into a suitable form for presentation to the court.

There may be important considerations in deciding which basis for divorce to allege if there is any choice on the information provided by the client. Of course the basis chosen must be soundly, legally based on available evidence, but if there is a choice it should be carefully made. Adultery and behaviour are most commonly used as they allow for immediate divorce, whereas the alternatives require a wait of at least two years. Two years' separation and consent has the advantage of a parting by agreement. If more than one basis for divorce may be alleged, choice may be based on the strength of available evidence, or on tactics. To give an example, an allegation of behaviour may be useful if it lays a foundation for claims to be made in financial or children hearings, but may be unwise if it upsets a spouse with whom it is hoped a good financial settlement will be negotiated.

It is technically possible to draft a petition relying on more than one basis in the alternative, but this should be avoided if possible as it is likely only to increase costs, and may suggest the case is weak.

The prayer is one of the most vital parts of the petition as it should list all forms of relief which the spouse seeks, including financial relief, residence order, costs, etc. Relief sought should be checked with the client, but it is generally thought wise to claim widely at this early stage, thus keeping all options open.

4.4.2   EXAMPLE PETITION

IN THE OXFORD COUNTY COURT   No. of matter

The petition of SANDRA ANNE CUTFORTH shows that:

1.   On 15 June 1992 the Petitioner was lawfully married to James Andrew Cutforth (the Respondent) at the Tottenham Register Office, High Street, Tottenham, London N1.

2.   The Petitioner and the Respondent last lived together at 13 Jasmine Road, Oxford, Oxfordshire.

3.   The Petitioner is domiciled in England and Wales. The Petitioner is a receptionist and resides at 13 Jasmine Road, Oxford. The Respondent is a computer engineer and resides at Flat 3 Alexandra Mansions, New Way, London NW22.

4.   There are two children of the family, namely Damian John Cutforth born on 16 December 1993 and Gemma Jane Cutforth born on 3 May 1995.

5.   No other child now living has been born to the Petitioner during the marriage.

6.   There are or have been no other proceedings in the court in England and Wales with reference to the marriage or the children of the family or between the Petitioner and the Respondent with reference to any property of either or both of them, save in that on 20 May 2001 the Oxford County Court made an order under the Family Law Act 1996 requiring the Respondent to leave the matrimonial home, and an order that the Respondent should not use or threaten to use violence against the person of the applicant.

7.   The marriage has broken down irretrievably.

8.   The Respondent has behaved in such a way that the Petitioner cannot reasonably be expected to live with the Respondent.

PARTICULARS

(i)   From about January 1998 the Respondent has become increasingly cold and neglectful towards the Petitioner, and unjustifiably critical of her abilities as a housewife.

(ii)   From March 1998 the Respondent began working late, often not returning home until the late evening. When the Petitioner asked about the reason for this the Respondent merely said that he liked work, and the Petitioner would not understand anything about his work.

(iii)   In May 1998 the Respondent refused to take the Petitioner to an important social function connected with his employment, saying that the function was only for those who supported their spouses in their work, and falsely claiming that she gave him no support at all.

(iv)   On several occasions over the summer of 1998 the Petitioner suggested that the Respondent should take her out for the evening, but he always refused, saying that he was too tired, and that in any event he found the Petitioner's company boring, and she should be spending more time keeping the house clean and learning to cook.

(v)   In December 1998 the Respondent invited several business associates to the matrimonial home, giving the Petitioner little notice of their arrival. When they left, the Respondent flew into a temper, throwing crockery at the Petitioner, and breaking several items from a dinner service that had been a wedding present from the Petitioner's parents.

(vi)   From March to September 1999 the Respondent insisted on attending a course which took him away from home most weekends, although the Petitioner requested him to spend more time with herself and the children of the family. When the Respondent was at home, he spent most of his time in his study, becoming angry with the children whenever he heard them playing. On one occasion in August 1999 he falsely accused the Petitioner of being an incompetent mother who could not control her own children. On completion of the course, the Respondent continued to spend many weekends away from the home, despite the entreaties of the Petitioner.

(vii)   From January 2000, the Respondent has consumed alcohol in excessive quantities. The petitioner has remonstrated with him on several occasions, but the Respondent refuses to accept that he drinks excessively, saying only that he needs a drink to help him to relax. The Petitioner has become most concerned for the welfare of the chidren of the family when the Respondent is drunk.

(viii) In November 2000 the Petitioner returned home early one evening to find the Respondent in a drunken stupor, although he had undertaken to look after the children of the family for the day, thereby putting the welfare of the children at risk.

(xi)   In May 2001 the Petitioner remonstrated with the Respondent on finding several empty whisky bottles secreted about the matrimonial home. The Respondent became extremely angry and struck the Petitioner, causing her injury which required hospital treatment and the insertion of five stitches on the side of her head. It was as a result of this incident that the Petitioner was granted the order referred to in paragraph 6 above. The Respondent left the matrimonial home as a result of this order and has not returned since.

The Petitioner therefore prays:

1.   That the marriage may be dissolved.

2.   That the children Damian John and Gemma Jane be ordered to reside with her.

3.   That the court may order such payments by way of maintenance pending suit and may make such orders for financial provision or adjustment of property for the benefit of the Petitioner and the children as may be just.

4.   That the Respondent may be ordered to pay the costs of this suit.

Anne O'Nimous

The name and address of the person to be served with this petition is:

James Cutforth
Flat 3
Alexandra Mansions
New Way
London NW22

The Petitioner's address for service is:
c/o Brown and Brown Solicitors
121 High Street
Oxford

4.4.3   ALTERNATIVE BASES FOR DIVORCE

These are examples of how the various alternatives for para. 8 of the petition might be drafted.

Adultery
The respondent has committed adultery and the petitioner finds it intolerable to live with the respondent.

(i)   The Respondent committed adultery with Mary Mopp (the Co-respondent) on 16 October 1999 at the Grand Hotel, Station Road, London SW40.
(ii)   The Respondent also committed adultery with another woman the Petitioner could identify if called upon to do so.
(iii)   The Respondent has since 1 July 2000 lived, cohabited and committed adultery with the Co-respondent at 26 Wild Street, Dorchester, Dorset.
(iv)   The Respondent on 30 April 2000 committed adultery at 11 Queen Street, Slough, Berkshire, with a person known to the Petitioner only as 'Jonnie'.
(v)   The Petitioner resumed cohabitation with the Respondent at 11 Queen Street, Slough, Berkshire from 1 May 1999 to 20 June 1999 a period amounting to less than six months.

Behaviour
The respondent has behaved in such a way that the petitioner cannot reasonably be expected to live with the respondent.

PARTICULARS

(See example in **4.4.2**.)

Desertion
The respondent has deserted the petitioner for a continuous period of at least two years immediately preceding the presentation of the petition.

PARTICULARS

The Respondent informed the Petitioner on 17th December 1997 while she was in hospital that he would not allow her to return to the matrimonial home, since which day the parties have lived separate and apart.

Two years' separation and consent
The parties have lived apart from a continuous period of at least two years immediately preceding the presentation of the petition and the respondent consents to a decree being granted.

PARTICULARS

The parties separated by agreement on 25th December 1996 since which day they have lived apart save that cohabitation was resumed for the following periods, namely:
From 1st April 1998 to 1st June 1998 at 6 High Street and from 28th June 1999 to 30th June 1999 at 6 High Street, which periods amount to less than six months in all.

Five years' separation
The parties have lived apart for a continuous period of at least five years immediately preceding the presentation of the petition.

PARTICULARS

On 28th February 1988 the Petitioner ejected the Respondent from the matrimonial home, since which day the parties have lived separate and apart.

4.5 Drafting an Answer

4.5.1 THE ROLE OF THE ANSWER

The petition is served on the respondent with a form for acknowledgment of service, and a notice of proceedings informing the respondent what courses he or she can take. If the respondent wishes to defend the case, he or she should give notice of intention to defend within eight days.

It is not essential that an answer be filed at all. An answer is only required, within 21 days of the date for filing the notice of intention to defend, under FPR 1991, r. 2.12, if a respondent or co-respondent:

(a) Wishes to defend the petition, or dispute any facts alleged in it.

(b) Wishes to cross-petition, that is, to seek a divorce on an alternative basis.

(c) Wishes to oppose the grant of divorce under MCA 1973, s. 5 (petition alleging five years' separation and there is a defence of grave financial or other hardship).

It is not necessary to file an answer simply to be heard on ancillary matters relating to finance or the children. The decision whether to file an answer may involve practical considerations, bearing in mind that the majority of divorces are undefended and that defending will normally have the effect of making the divorce procedure longer and more expensive. This may require some discussion with the client, whose emotions may not immediately suggest the wisest course. In practical terms, an answer will be required:

(a) If the respondent does not want a divorce at all, and has some basis for defending the allegation in the petition.

(b) If the respondent really cannot accept the basis on which a divorce is sought in the petition, and has good reason for alleging an alternative basis.

(c) If the petition makes allegations that may prejudice the respondent in the financial hearings or those concerned with children.

4.5.2 CONTENTS OF AN ANSWER

An answer effectively fulfils the role of a defence, and should thus generally deal with those allegations in the petition which are disputed and add any further relevant points, see FPR 1991, r. 2.15. There is no set format for an answer: it must be drafted to suit the case. An answer remains an important document although relatively few cases are defended (*Lawlor* v *Lawlor* [1995] 1 FLR 269).

The heading, as in the example given in **4.5.4**, should set out the names of the petitioner and the respondent as parties. If any allegation of adultery with a named person is made in the petition, that person will be added as co-respondent. If any allegation of adultery is made against a named person in the *answer*, that person should be added as a party, called the 'party cited'.

The answer should start by dealing with any matters arising from the formal paragraphs in the petition. Generally there will be no dispute on the basic facts of the marriage, occupation of spouses etc., and there will therefore be no need to deal with these paragraphs of the petition at all. The respondent should, however, say whether or not he or she agrees with what is alleged regarding the children of the family.

It is then necessary to state whether or not the marriage has broken down. It should of course be admitted that the marriage has broken down if the respondent wants a divorce, even if he or she wishes to rely on a different basis.

The respondent must then deal with the basis for divorce relied on in the petition, pleading both to the fact alleged, and to any details provided. A bare denial is permissible (*Haque* v *Haque* [1977] 1 WLR 888) but it is better policy to respond in more detail, especially as regards allegations of behaviour (*Andrews* v *Andrews* [1974] 3 All ER 643). Indeed there may be good reason for responding to behaviour allegations in some detail, especially to confess and avoid, to give further information to explain, or to put a different interpretation on facts alleged.

Note that there is the specific statutory defence of grave financial or other hardship where the petition alleges five years' separation, and this should be specifically included in the answer, if it has to be relied on (MCA 1973, s. 5).

4.5.3   CROSS-PETITION

A cross-petition may be added to an answer, just as a counter-claim can be added to a defence. A cross-petition seeks a divorce on a basis other than that alleged in the petition. No subheading is required. One simply continues the numbered paragraphs to raise the basis alleged as one would in a petition.

4.5.4   EXAMPLE ANSWER AND CROSS-PETITION

IN THE OXFORD COUNTY COURT   01 D   No. 288

BETWEEN   SANDRA ANNE CUTFORTH   Petitioner

and

JAMES ANDREW CUTFORTH   Respondent

and

JUSTIN REDMOND   Party Cited

The Respondent in ANSWER to the petition filed in this suit says that:

1.   No other child now living has been born to the Petitioner during the marriage, so far as is known to the Respondent.

2.   It is admitted that the marriage has broken down irretrievably.

3.   It is denied that the Respondent has behaved in such a way that the Petitioner cannot reasonably be expected to live with him, as alleged in the petition or at all.

4.   Save as is expressly admitted, the Respondent denies each and every allegation contained in paragraph 8 of the petition.

5.   The Respondent denies that he became cold or neglectful towards the Petitioner as alleged or at all. Insofar as he may appear to have done so, this was entirely justified by the Petitioner's lack of ability as a housewife and mother. The matrimonial home was rarely cleaned, the Petitioner failed to discipline the children of the family properly, and the Petitioner rarely presented proper meals, normally resorting to pre-packed dishes.

6.   The Respondent admits that he frequently worked late. This was necessary as the joint bank account held by the Petitioner and the Respondent was frequently overdrawn, largely due to the sums spent by the Petitioner. The Respondent did not try to discuss his work with the Petitioner as she frequently said that she did not understand how computers worked. The function in May 1998 was only open to employees of the Respondent's employer.

7.   The Petitioner herself asked the Respondent to invite some of his colleagues from work to the matrimonial home. Having stated that she would cook a meal, the Petitioner merely provided light snacks, thereby causing much embarrassment to the Respondent.

8.   The Respondent admits that he attended a course between March and September 1999. He did so in expectation of promotion at work. The Petitioner failed to support him in this enterprise.

9.   The Respondent denies that he has ever consumed alcohol in excessive quantities as alleged or at all. As to the incident referred to in November 2000, the Respondent in fact had a bad cold and had simply taken a cold remedy.

10.   The Respondent admits that he did strike the Petitioner in May 2001, but this was an isolated incident, the Respondent not being a violent man. The injury to the Petitioner was accidental in that she hit her head on a table as she fell.

11.   The Petitioner has committed adultery and the Respondent finds it intolerable to live with the Petitioner.

<u>PARTICULARS</u>

(a)   The Petitioner committed adultery with Justin Redmond (the Party Cited) on a day or days unknown to the Respondent in about July 1999, at a place or places unknown to the Respondent.

(b)   Since 8 April 2000 the Petitioner has committed adultery with Justin Redmond on a day or days unknown to the Respondent at a place or places unknown to the Respondent, but including 13 Jasmine Road, Oxford, Oxfordshire.

The Respondent therefore prays:

1.   That the prayer of the petition may be rejected.

2.   That the marriage may be dissolved.

3.   That the children Damian and Gemma be ordered to reside with him.

4.   That the Party Cited may be ordered to pay the costs of this suit.

Jonathan Brown

Name, addresses etc.

4.6   Reply

It is possible for the petitioner to respond with a reply to allegations made in the answer (FPR 1991, r. 2.13). However, a reply is rare.

4.7   Void and Voidable Marriages

It should be kept in mind that divorce is not the only option if a client wishes to end a marriage. It is possible that the marriage may be void (MCA 1973, s. 11) or voidable (MCA 1973, s. 12). If either spouse is not domiciled in England and Wales, or was not so domiciled at the time of the marriage, then conflict of law points should be considered.

The grounds on which a marriage may be void are:

(a)   That the parties are within a prohibited degree of relationship.

(b)   That either party is under the age of 16.

(c)   That vital formalities relating to the marriage were disregarded.

(d)   That at the time of the marriage either party was already lawfully married.

(e)   That the parties are not respectively male and female.

(f)   That in the case of a polygamous marriage entered into outside England and Wales, either party was at the time of the marriage domiciled in England and Wales.

The grounds on which a marriage may be voidable are:

(a)   That the marriage has not been consummated owing to the incapacity of either party.

(b)   That the marriage has not been consummated owing to the wilful refusal of the respondent.

(c)   That either party to the marriage did not validly consent to it, whether in consequence of duress, mistake, unsoundness of mind or otherwise.

(d)   That at the time of the marriage either party was suffering from mental disorder of such a kind or to such an extent as to be unfitted for marriage.

(e)   That at the time of the marriage the respondent was suffering from venereal disease in a communicable form, and the petitioner did not know this.

(f)   That at the time of the marriage the respondent was pregnant by some person other than the petitioner, and the petitioner did not know this.

The last four of these may only be used within three years of the marriage. In the case of either a void or a voidable marriage, it is possible for the court to order financial provision and to make orders for the care of children.

4.8   Judicial Separation

A final alternative is judicial separation (MCA 1973, s. 17). This does not end the marriage, but is appropriate where the client does not want the marriage to end finally for emotional or religious reasons. A decree of judicial separation may be granted where one of the bases for a divorce is made out, and it is possible for the court to make orders for financial provision, and orders regarding the care of children when making an order that the parties live apart.

FIVE

FINANCIAL PROVISION ON DIVORCE

5.1 Introduction

This chapter is intended to provide a broad framework on which to base the very practical work involved in financial provision applications. Fact management skills are essential when dealing with such applications, as is the ability to research and keep abreast of the evolving case law relating to the exercise of the courts' powers. The importance of numerical skills will become obvious!

5.1.1 THE LEGAL FRAMEWORK

Broad powers to order financial provision are provided by statute, primarily in the Matrimonial Causes Act 1973, as amended. Many of the relevant sections are set out in these materials, but you should (and will, if you practice in this area) become generally familiar not only with the statutory provisions, but also the supporting Rules of Court and Practice Directions. The most important of these is the Family Proceedings Rules 1991 (SI 1991 No. 1247), as amended by the Family Proceedings (Amendment No. 2) Rules 1999 (SI 1999 No. 3491) which is set out in **Appendix D**. The powers of the court with regard to maintenance for children have been limited by the Child Support Act 1991 (see **Chapter 6**).

Because every case will involve different assets and different problems, the powers provided by statute are very wide to allow orders to be tailored to fit each individual case. For this reason, the statutory provisions themselves include only general guidance as to how the powers should be exercised. This means that case law is very important as an *illustration* of how the powers were actually (or ought to have been) used in particular cases. Some of these are referred to here by way of example, but always remember that each case will turn on its *own facts* and not the facts of some other case (unless they are remarkably similar).

5.1.2 THE NEW PROCEDURE

On 5 June 2000 a new set of procedural rules for dealing with applications for financial provision ancillary to divorce came into being. Previously, two forms of procedure were running in tandem. Alongside the traditional procedure, a modern alternative had been evolving as a more efficient way of reaching decisions. The *powers* of the court to make financial orders are the same — it is the *procedure* which was changed.

The traditional procedure was based on sworn statements (affidavits) and was very adversarial. In practice it was found to be inefficient in terms of defining issues and collecting information, and proved to be time consuming and costly. This old procedure is now gone, but is mentioned in passing as you may still encounter it in a case that was commenced before the new rules took effect.

The new procedure was originally drawn up by a working party of barristers, solicitors and other relevant experts, chaired by Lord Justice Thorpe. It is based on the completion and use of standard forms and involves tight timetables, more court control and a greater emphasis on defining issues and reaching agreements.

That should all sound very familiar. The new rules were extensively 'piloted' in various courts around the country and resulted in much cross-fertilisation with the reforms then on-going in civil practice generally. The new procedure has a distinctly Woolf-like feel about it, from the overriding objective to active case management by the court. There is even a pre-action protocol!

As you might expect, therefore, the main aims of the new procedure are to:

- give the court more control over the issues raised and the evidence used in each case,

- provide better ways of controlling costs,

- direct parties towards settlement where possible,

- encourage full and frank disclosure, but discourage excessive and/or tactical requests for information.

The main elements of the new procedure are:

- That once there has been an application for ancillary relief there will be a first appointment within 12–16 weeks.

- Before that appointment there will be a simultaneous exchange of statements of the financial position of both spouses containing specified information in a common format.

- Just before the first appointment both parties will file questionnaires covering areas on which further information is sought, and a list of documents to be produced.

- At the first appointment the District Judge will review the case with a view to limiting the issues and saving costs. The judge will be able to set a date for an interim or final hearing, and more usually direct that the case should go to a Financial Dispute Resolution hearing (along the lines of a mediation).

- Both parties should file a precise statement of the orders sought before a final hearing.

- Both sides should have an estimate of current costs available at each hearing.

These are discussed in detail below at **5.5.3**. For additional information about how the new rules work in practice you should refer to one of the published guides to the new procedure, such as Nicholas Mostyn QC and John Nicholson, *Ancillary relief — A Guide to the New Rules*, Butterworths, 2000, or Roger Bird, *Ancillary Relief Handbook*, Family Law, 2000.

5.1.3 THE PRACTICAL APPROACH

Because statute provides general powers and case law merely examples, there is rarely a single, simple answer as to the correct financial provision in a particular case. There is no set formula, and indeed trying to apply the same formula in different circumstances could itself be unjust. Rather, there are a variety of factors from which a case can be built, and an overall basis for provision found.

It is important to appreciate this. This is not an area where legal principles can simply be learned and applied. Everything depends on a complete and thorough *factual* analysis of the individual case, and an intelligent development of arguments. This makes a really practical approach vital. Although the powers of the courts are wide, you cannot give a general or waffly answer. In each case the facts must be carefully gathered and analysed, the detailed arithmetic done, and the client's objectives clearly kept in view. The important points are:

(a) What sort of provision does the client want? In terms of capital? In terms of income?

(b) What assets does your client have?

(c) What assets does the other spouse have?

(d) What are the relevant factors which favour your client's claims?

(e) What are the relevant factors which weaken your client's claims?

(f) What is the appropriate overall basis for provision? Are there any options?

(g) Work out full details for all provision on the appropriate basis.

(h) Do full arithmetic to show the position which each spouse will be left in if that provision is ordered, taking into account tax, etc.

(i) Check that the detailed proposals are practical, realistic, and meet your client's objectives as far as possible.

(j) Remember that lawyers representing parties in a case have a duty to investigate figures fully and to advise their clients properly about their options (see *Kelly* v *Corston* [1998] 1 FLR 986 and *Frazer Harris* v *Scholfield, Roberts & Hill* [1998] Fam Law 500).

(k) Use your common sense! It is an indispensable tool.

5.2   Court Powers to Make Orders

5.2.1   MAKING THE CHOICE

(a) Identify the court to which application should be made. If the application is ancillary to divorce the application will be to the county court or the High Court, depending on the court in which the divorce case proceeds. If the application is not ancillary to divorce, the basic choice will be between the county court and the family proceedings court, depending on the orders sought and the costs (see **Chapter 3**).

(b) Identify the powers of the court with regard to income provision, if sought.

(c) Identify the powers of the court with regard to capital provision, if sought.

(d) In consultation with the client, identify precisely what orders should be sought. Although it may be clear what orders your client *wants*, it will usually be sensible to *apply* for the whole range of orders, to keep all options open. Include orders for children as well as for the spouse if appropriate.

Although maintenance may be paid under a deed or contract, or even under no binding legal agreement, it will usually be better to have a court order. The powers of the court to make orders with regard to maintenance for children has been severely limited by the Child Support Act 1991.

Note that jurisdiction will depend on the domicile and residence of the spouses. Problems of jurisdiction are not covered here, and will have to be researched if appropriate. If a case has an international element then courts in another country may also have jurisdiction, and points relating to the different potential entitlement in each jurisdiction, and where best to proceed may need to be considered (*Chebaro* v *Chebaro* [1987] 1 FLR 456).

5.2.2 APPLICATIONS ANCILLARY TO DIVORCE

5.2.2.1 Maintenance pending suit and other interim orders

Marital breakdown can cause immediate financial strains. Maintenance pending suit is intended to 'tide' a party over, where necessary, until a final determination of the application(s) for financial provision can be made and put into effect. Such orders, which take the form of requiring one spouse to make regular (e.g., monthly or weekly) payments to the other, are therefore very much a temporary measure.

Once a petition has been filed, maintenance pending suit may be ordered to be paid by one spouse to the other. Of necessity it will not be possible to have full information available at this stage of the case, so the court will only seek to determine what figure is reasonable for immediate needs rather than seeking to make complex calculations or to apply all the factors outlined later in this chapter. However, it is still important to present the figures you do have and the arguments for what is reasonable as clearly as possible. It may also be necessary to seek a separate maintenance order in favour of any children.

MCA 1973, s. 22:

> *On a petition for divorce, nullity of marriage or judicial separation, the court may make an order for maintenance pending suit, that is to say, an order requiring either party to the marriage to make to the other such periodical payments for his or her maintenance and for such term, being a term beginning not earlier than the date of the presentation of the petition and ending with the date of the determination of the suit, as the court thinks reasonable.*

Do not confuse maintenance pending suit (made before the court has power to make a final order for financial provision) with other interim financial provision orders. The latter are appropriate where the court has *power* to make a final order (i.e. after decree absolute), but is not yet in a *position* to do so — perhaps because some relevant information is still outstanding. Interim orders for financial provision mimic orders for maintenance pending suit in that they are usually confined to periodical payments orders (*Wicks* v *Wicks* [1998] 3 FLR 470).

The procedure for obtaining maintenance pending suit (and other interim orders) was modified by the Family Proceedings (Amendment No. 2) Rules 1999 and is set out in r. 2.69F of the Family Proceedings Rules 1991, as amended. An application can be made at any stage in the proceedings by issuing a notice of application, the date fixed for hearing being at least 14 days later. If the application is made before Form E (which provides details of financial resources and needs) has been filed, the applicant must file and serve on the respondent a draft of the order sought, together with a short sworn statement that provides relevant information about means and explains why the order sought is necessary. Similarly, if the respondent has not yet filed a copy of Form E, he or she must file a short sworn statement of means at least seven days before the date fixed for hearing. Applications for maintenance pending suit are commonly made at the 'first appointment' (see **5.5.4.2**).

When preparing for the hearing you should bear in mind that at this stage the court will focus on what the applicant really needs to cover reasonable outgoings, together with what the respondent can reasonably afford to pay. To present information on this clearly and concisely, it is best to draw up a schedule which summarises the income of each party from all sources and the reasonable outgoings of each. If relevant, also include other liabilities and assets that may have a bearing on the appropriate order. Ensure that all figures are given on the same basis, i.e. monthly or weekly, net or gross.

If you act for the applicant your first objective is to show the shortfall between your client's income and reasonable outgoings; your second, is to show how the respondent can reasonably afford to cover this gap. If you act for the respondent your main aims will be to show that the applicant could earn more, and/or is extravagant, and/or that in any event your client cannot afford to pay the order sought. To convince the judge of your case it is very important to use accurate and full figures.

At the interim stage the District Judge will be concerned to meet immediate needs, not to try to pre-judge in any detail what will be ordered when financial provision is finally decided. This is especially true of orders for maintenance pending suit. Therefore awards tend to be on the low side. It is also difficult to get orders with regard to capital at an interim stage (*Wicks v Wicks*). On possible costs problems, see *A v A (Maintenance Pending Suit: Provision for Legal Fees)* [2001] 1 FLR 377.

5.2.2.2   Financial provision on divorce: MCA 1973, ss. 23-25D
On divorce (nullity or judicial separation) the court has power to make any of the following:

- Order for periodical payments to a party to the marriage or to/for a child of the family (s. 23).

- Order for secured periodical payments to a party to the marriage or to/for a child of the family (s. 23).

- Order that a lump sum be paid to a party to the marriage or to/for a child of the family (s. 23). This includes 'earmarking' of pensions orders made under ss. 25B and 25C.

- Transfer of property order, i.e., an order that one party to the marriage transfer property to the other party or to/for the benefit of a child of the family (s. 24).

- Settlement of property order (s. 24).

- An order varying the effect of any ante or post-nuptial agreement (s. 24).

- Order for sale (s. 24A).

- Pension sharing orders (s. 24B).

The provisions are set out in **Appendix C**.

5.2.2.3   Limitations on and duration of orders: MCA 1973, ss. 28 and 29

Payments to a party to the marriage
Periodical payments orders (secured or not) may not be expressed to begin before the date of the application (i.e., the court can 'back-date' an order to that point, but no earlier), nor can they continue after the death of either the payee or the payer. Nor, significantly, may such orders continue after the remarriage of the person in whose favour the order was made (an important factor when advising on or negotiating in respect of an ancillary relief application). Otherwise the duration of such orders shall be that which the court thinks just in the circumstances. Applications for extensions (as opposed to repeat applications) are usually possible.

Payments to/for children
Save in appropriate circumstances (e.g., education beyond 16 or 18) or special need:

- no financial provision may be made in respect of a child who has reached 18 years of age;

- no orders for periodical payments to or for a child (which may begin from the date of application) shall extend, in the first instance, beyond school-leaving age and in any event beyond the date of the child's eighteenth birthday.

Periodical payments orders to or for a child shall cease upon the death of the payer (save for any arrears).

Lump sum payments
Note that although only one lump sum may be ordered, the payment may be intended to be used for more than one purpose. See, e.g., *Hobhouse* v *Hobhouse* [1999] 1 FLR 961.

See **Appendix C** where the detailed provisions of ss. 28 and 29 are set out in full.

5.3 Relevant Factors

5.3.1 THE FACTORS

On an application to court for financial provision, there is no standard method for calculating appropriate provision. Indeed if it were that simplistic, there would be little role for lawyers in arguing the case! Although there may be broad similarities between cases, the details of each are different in terms of available assets and the needs of both spouses. The system for determining provision has to be sufficiently flexible to allow for this, and therefore a list of relevant factors is provided by statute, rather than a single rule.

The relevant factors to take into account on divorce are listed in MCA 1973, s. 25. Similar factors are taken into account in applications that are not ancillary to divorce.

Section 25 provides:

(1)   It shall be the duty of the court in deciding whether to exercise its powers under sections 23 or 24 or 24A ... and, if so, in what manner, to have regard to all the circumstances of the case, first consideration being given to the welfare while a minor of any child of the family who has not attained the age of eighteen.
(2)   As regards the exercise of the powers of the court under section 23(1)(a), (b) or (c), 24 or 24A ... in relation to a party to the marriage, the court shall in particular have regard to the following matters—
(a)   the income, earning capacity, property and other financial resources which each of the parties to the marriage has or is likely to have in the foreseeable future, including in the case of earning capacity any increase in that capacity which it would in the opinion of the court be reasonable to expect a party to the marriage to take steps to acquire;
(b)   the financial needs, obligations and responsibilities which each of the parties to the marriage has or is likely to have in the foreseeable future;
(c)   the standard of living enjoyed by the family before the breakdown of the marriage;
(d)   the age of each party to the marriage and the duration of the marriage;
(e)   any physical or mental disability of either of the parties to the marriage;
(f)   the contributions which each of the parties has made or is likely in the foreseeable future to make to the welfare of the family, including any contribution by looking after the home or caring for the family;
(g)   the conduct of each of the parties, if that conduct is such that it would in the opinion of the court be inequitable to disregard it,
(h)   in the case of proceedings for divorce or nullity of marriage, the value to each of the parties to the marriage of any benefit (for example, a pension) which, by reason of the dissolution or annulment of the marriage, that party will lose the chance of acquiring.
(3)   As regards the exercise of the powers of the court under sections 23(1)(d), (e) or (f), (2) or (4), 24 or 24A ... in relation to a child of the family, the court shall in particular have regard to the following matters—

(a)   the financial needs of the child;

(b)   the income, earning capacity (if any), property and other financial resources of the child;

(c)   any physical or mental disability of the child;

(d)   the manner in which he was being and in which the parties to the marriage expected him to be educated or trained;

(e)   the considerations mentioned in relation to the parties to the marriage in paragraphs (a), (b), (c) and (e) of subsection (2) above.

(4)   As regards the exercise of the powers of the court under section 23(1)(d), (e) or (f), (2) or (4), 24 or 24A ... against a party to a marriage in favour of a child of the family who is not the child of that party, the court shall also have regard—

(a)   to whether that party assumed any responsibility for the child's maintenance, and, if so, to the extent to which, and the basis upon which, that party assumed such responsibility and to the length of time for which that party discharged such responsibility;

(b)   to whether in assuming and discharging such responsibility that party did so knowing that the child was not his or her own;

(c)   to the liability of any other person to maintain the child.

5.3.2   USING THE FACTORS

The factors listed by statute are effectively the building blocks from which the barrister constructs an argument in an individual case. They are not equally important, but will have to have their relative weights assessed in each case. Dealing with the relevant factors in a practical and professional way can only come with practice, but as a suggested starting-point in a case:

(a)   Identify which factors from the general list are relevant to the particular case (ignoring those which are not relevant).

(b)   Weigh up each relevant factor, deciding by reference to the facts which are central to the case and those which are less important.

(c)   Clearly identify the relevant factors which *favour* your client, which will therefore be central to your case.

(d)   Clearly identify the relevant factors which *undermine* your client's case or favour the other side, and which you will therefore have to try to counter.

If one factor overshadows all others in the case, it may suggest an overall basis for provision, see **5.4**. If no factor is substantially more important than others, all relevant factors will go into the balance.

5.3.3   WHAT THE FACTORS MEAN

The meaning of each of the statutory factors has been explored in a substantial body of case law, which may require thorough legal research in any particular instance. Only a few cases are included in these notes to give general guidance.

5.3.3.1   The welfare of the children of the family under 18

This means that the need to provide a home and maintenance for any children of the family will be given priority in dividing assets on divorce. For example, a spouse awarded a residence order in respect of minor children may well get the right to live in the former matrimonial home until the children come of age (though that spouse will not necessarily get ownership of the home — this will depend on other factors). If necessary, a parent may be expected to accept a cut in standard of living to provide for the children (*Roots* v *Roots* [1988] 1 FLR 89). Any special needs of a child, such as illness or disability, will also be considered to be of particular importance.

The welfare of the children of the family is a 'first', but not paramount consideration. This simply means that their needs come first. Certainly they take priority over the needs of any other children for whom a party may have become responsible. The intention is not that part of the capital assets of a parent should be directly made over to a child (*Kiely* v *Kiely* [1988] 1 FLR 248) though in exceptional circumstances this could happen, see *Tavoulareas* v *Tavoulareas* [1998] 2 FLR 418. The needs of the child should not, however, unduly prejudice the need of the non-carer spouse for a home (*M* v *B (Ancillary Proceedings: Lump Sum)* [1998] 1 FLR 53). If a child is nearly 18, its need will generally have less importance than these of a younger child (*Leadbeater* v *Leadbeater* [1985] FLR 789). The needs of a child can be relevant even if the child is not the child of the spouse ordered to make provision (*Fisher* v *Fisher* [1989] 1 FLR 423). Payments under the Child Support Act 1991 will have to take priority over other provision.

5.3.3.2   **Income, earning capacity and other financial resources**
This is clearly one of the most critical factors in many cases — it does not matter how strong claims for provision are if there are not sufficient resources to meet them. A party's resources can be highly relevant not only to the amount, but also to the *type* of provision ordered. Lump sum payments, for example, require sufficient capital and/or income to raise the funds. Equally, if there is not sufficient income available to the person wanting to remain in the matrimonial home to pay the mortgage and outgoings, there may be no realistic alternative to selling it. The importance of getting full details and figures for capital and income cannot be over-emphasised.

Note that 'any' financial resources are relevant, and this is widely interpreted to include, for example, free or cheap accommodation available with a job. Rights under a trust may also be included (*J* v *J (C Intervening) (Minors: Financial Provision)* [1989] Fam 29). There are, however, some limits; for example, proceeds of drug-trafficking that are liable to be forfeit may not be taken into account (*Re Peters* [1988] QB 871).

As regards earnings, it is important to appreciate that the court can take into account not only what a spouse is earning, but what he or she may be *capable* of earning. Clear evidence of relevant skills, marketability and opportunity will be required. However, the court will not make assumptions. Nor will it be likely to take the view that mothers of very young children should be made to go out to work. If it takes the view that an applicant may need some time to retrain and/or otherwise adjust to future financial independence, the court can make a fixed term periodical payments order (as an alternative to a normal open-ended order putting the onus on the other party to apply for a variation).

Only resources that are in practical, realistic terms available, can be taken into account, which may not include personal injury damages (*C* v *C (Financial Provision: Personal Damages)* [1995] 2 FLR 171). A court may draw inferences as to resources that are available provided there is sufficient reason to do so (*Thomas* v *Thomas* [1995] 2 FLR 668), especially if there is serious non-disclosure (*Baker* v *Baker* [1995] 2 FLR 829). A resource which is considered too remote (e.g., a possible future inheritance) will be disregarded.

Resources available from a third party such as a cohabitee may also be relevant, but the position of a cohabitee cannot be fully equated with that of a spouse, and the income of a party's cohabitee will not simply be added to that of the party (*Macey* v *Macey* [1981] 3 FLR 7). It will be assumed, however, that cohabitees with an income, use some of it to contribute to the household in which they live (*Atkinson* v *Atkinson (No. 2)* [1996] 1 FLR 51). If a claimant spouse remarries, his or her right to maintenance will of course cease, and a claimant spouse who is intending to remarry a wealthy person may get only limited capital provision (*H* v *H (Family Provision: Remarriage)* [1975] Fam 9).

The situation may be complicated where an asset was purchased or inherited by one spouse before the marriage. It is clear that such property may be taken into account (*O'D* v *O'D* [1976] Fam 83), but on the actual facts of the case it may be left out of account (see *Heseltine* v *Heseltine* [1971] 1 WLR 342).

5.3.3.3 Financial needs and obligations

As regards needs, it is obviously vital to get details of the mortgage, gas and electricity bills etc. The term 'needs' can be interpreted widely to include any reasonable expense of living, and this should be fully investigated — get the client to think of everything that has to be paid for. Remember that for the spouse seeking provision you would try to include all possible needs, whereas in representing a spouse from whom provision is sought you would try rather to argue that the needs of the claimant should be kept within reasonable bounds.

The term 'obligations' can include any legal or moral obligation to meet an expense, including obligations to third parties such as relatives, cohabitees or children who are being supported (see *Ette* v *Ette* [1964] 1 WLR 1433 and *Barnes* v *Barnes* [1972] 1 WLR 1381). In some cases this may mean that the resources of one man have to be divided between his former wife and his new wife or cohabitee, and any children. The claims of the applicant spouse will normally take precedence, as will the requirements of the divorcing couples' children, but the need to take new children and partners into account can lead both to overstretched resources and ill-feeling.

5.3.3.4 The standard of living of the family before the breakdown

Although the standard of living that the spouse enjoyed during the marriage is relevant, this is only in a general sense, as it will rarely be possible to maintain that standard. If the money that has financed a single household has to be split to finance two, there will almost certainly have to be some drop in the standard of living.

A standard of living can really only be maintained where the couple are wealthy — the so-called 'big money' cases. In the more typical scenario the court will keep the previous standard of living in mind, and try to ensure that neither party's individual standard of living slips more than is really necessary.

5.3.3.5 The age of each party

The age of a party will have a bearing on the case where it affects one of the other factors or gives rise to special needs. For example, if the age of a party means that it is unrealistic to expect that party to work, it is more likely that the court will order maintenance for that party. Age is also of particular relevance when a party is near to retirement, in which case the effect that retirement will have on needs and resources must be investigated and taken into account.

5.3.3.6 The duration of the marriage

In many cases the duration of the marriage will only be generally relevant, in that a marriage which has lasted several years or more will tend to lead to full entitlement for an applicant. The length of a marriage is only likely to have a substantial bearing on the outcome where the marriage is very short.

Only in the case of an extremely short marriage is the court likely to order no financial provision at all, for example where a marriage effectively lasted only two weeks (*Krystman* v *Krystman* [1973] 1 WLR 927). It is particularly likely that no provision will be ordered where neither spouse has suffered financially as a result of the marriage. For a marriage that has lasted more than a few weeks it is quite possible that some provision will be ordered, even if it is at a low level, such as the award of a small lump sum to allow the claimant to adjust (see *Brett* v *Brett* [1969] 1 WLR 487).

In the case of a short marriage, the court is likely to look at any loss that a claimant spouse has suffered because of the marriage. For example, if the claimant has moved out of his or her own home to marry, and now needs sufficient money to move back again, an award may be made to cover expenses for that (*S* v *S* [1977] Fam 127). Even after a short marriage, the needs of any children must be put first (*C* v *C (Financial Relief: Short Marriage)* [1997] 2 FLR 27).

Even if a marriage is not so short as to have a substantial effect on the overall level of provision, a relatively short marriage may have the effect of keeping provision at the lower end of what might otherwise be reasonable.

5.3.3.7 Any physical or mental disability

This point is fairly straightforward. If either spouse has a physical or mental disability which makes it difficult or impossible to be self-supporting, then that spouse will usually have a good claim for provision against the other spouse.

However, the fact of the disability must be put in context. If the spouse who has a disability can claim social security benefits, while the spouse against whom a claim is made has a limited income, it is possible that no order will be made (see *Ashley* v *Blackman* [1988] Fam 85).

5.3.3.8 Contributions to the welfare of the family

Contributions to the welfare of the family can take many forms. Often it is financial, but this provision also puts value on non-monetary contributions by making particular reference to looking after the household. Thus the contribution of a spouse in caring for a home and/or children will be relevant to the level of provision. There is no concept in law of a notional 'wage' for housework, nor any idea that one spouse should acquire a legal interest in family assets because of keeping house while the assets have been built up. Having said that, the tendency increasingly is to view monetary and non-monetary contributions to the family with a degree of equality of value, so that a spouse who has cared for a home and/or children for some years should not, at least in theory, be discriminated against because of the nature of those contributions (see **5.4.4** and **5.4.5**).

5.3.3.9 Conduct

Conduct is not an easy issue on divorce. One spouse may be very upset at the way that the other has behaved — indeed the conduct may to them personally be the most important issue in the case. However, the court is loath to go into a detailed examination of the causes and effects of marital breakdown, as this can be very expensive in terms of time and money, and is rarely productive. In any case, there is often fault on both sides. As a result, the court will only take the most serious misconduct into account.

The test initially adopted following MCA 1973 was that conduct would be taken into account if it was 'gross and obvious', but in 1984 this was modified into the current test, that conduct will be taken into account if it is such that 'in the opinion of the court it would be inequitable to disregard it'. The change was intended to make the test slightly less strict. It has not made previous case law irrelevant, but older case law should be read in the light of the change of wording.

In fact there have been relatively few reported cases where the court has held that conduct is sufficiently bad to have a substantial effect on the level of provision ordered. It is clear that adultery will not be sufficiently serious to be taken into account unless there is some aggravating factor, for example, if the adultery is with a father-in-law (*Bailey* v *Tolliday* (1982) 4 FLR 542), or is being committed when the husband puts property into the name of the wife (*Cuzner* v *Underdown* [1974] 1 WLR 641). A serious attack by a husband on a wife may have a substantial effect on provision (*A* v *A (Financial Provisions: Conduct)* [1995] 1 FLR 345 and *H* v *H (Financial Provisions: Conduct)* [1994] 2 FLR 801). In *Evans* v *Evans* [1989] 1 FLR 351 it was held that a wife's right to maintenance should end after she was convicted of inciting the murder of her husband, and in *Kyte* v *Kyte* [1987] 3 All ER 1041 a wife's conduct in condoning her husband's suicide attempts was held to be relevant to her level of entitlement. The conduct of a spouse who has knowingly married bigamously will deprive him or her of a claim (*Whiston* v *Whiston* [1995] 2 FLR 268). Serious financial misconduct may also be relevant (*Young* v *Young* [1998] 2 FLR 1132), particularly where it depletes the family assets.

Bad conduct, where relevant, is apt to keep provision at the low end of the range of what might otherwise be thought reasonable rather than to result in no provision or a drastically reduced level of provision being ordered (*Griffiths* v *Griffiths* [1974] 1 WLR 1454). But it depends on the conduct and its effects; for an astonishing recent case involving what Thorpe LJ described as the worst case of matrimonial conduct he had ever seen, see *Clark* v *Clark* [1999] 2 FLR 498.

5.3.3.10 Value of any benefit the claimant will lose the chance of acquiring

The point here is that if it is clearly foreseeable that, had the marriage continued, the claimant spouse would have benefited from some financial benefit accruing to the other spouse, then this can be taken into account in assessing financial provision on divorce. This might include future pension rights, early retirement or redundancy rights, or inheritance rights.

The resources that a party is likely to have in the future may also be taken into account, so it is important to look forward as well as simply looking at existing figures but not at figures that are too uncertain (*H v H (Financial Provisions: Capital Assets)* [1993] 2 FLR 335).

The possible loss of pension rights may be of particular importance, especially for older couples where accrued pension rights may be as valuable, or even more valuable than, the family home. Over the last few years there has been substantial discussion as to what powers the courts should have over pension rights on divorce. Historically the courts have had very limited powers, in that although accrued pension rights could be a relevant asset on divorce, a court could not make an order affecting third-party rights and the pension fund is not a party to the divorce proceedings. There were increasing calls for the courts to have powers to make orders relating to pensions, especially where a wife has limited pension rights of her own and may otherwise end up in a very disadvantageous financial position.

There was government resistance to radical legislation (not least because it is thought that a change is likely to be expensive for pension funds and for the government), so change has come in stages as follows:

(a) Through the courts. The case of *Brooks v Brooks* [1995] 2 FLR 13, the House of Lords decided that in certain circumstances a pension could be seen as an anti-nuptial settlement which the courts had power to alter. However, it must be said that the case involved a small private company, and it will not necessarily assist in all cases. Note however *W v W (Periodical payments: Pensions)* [1996] 2 FLR 480.

(b) Pension attachment. The Pensions Act 1995, ss. 166 and 167 have amended s. 25 of the Matrimonial Causes Act 1973 to oblige the courts to have regard to the value of a pension on divorce, and enabling the court to give directions to the trustees or managers of a pension fund to pay a lump sum or maintenance to the former spouse from the benefits due to a pension member spouse (sometimes called 'ear-marking'). However, money can only be 'attached' by court order, and can only be paid once the money is due to be paid to the spouse with the pension rights. These provisions came into force for petitions filed after 1 July 1996 where an order is made after April 1997. From 1 December 2000, these provisions are amended by sch. 4 to the Welfare Reform and Pensions Act 1999.

(c) Pension sharing. The Family Law Act 1996 amended the Pensions Act 1995 so as to enable a court to capitalise and split pension rights at the time of divorce, enabling separate pension funds to be established for each former spouse. Due to difficulties with implementation, these provisions were replaced by the Welfare Reform and Pensions Act 1999 (see MCA 1973, ss. 24B–24D and 25B–25D). Where a petition for divorce is issued on or after 1 December 2000, the pension rights of either spouse can be valued, and a court can make a pension sharing order. The pension is valued by the CETV (cash equivalent transfer value) method and the order will specify the percentage of the value of the rights to be transferred. These provisions do not apply to every type of pension, and other alternatives such as pension attachment orders will remain. For more detailed comment on pension sharing, see 'A Practitioner's Guide to Pension Sharing' [2000] Fam Law 489, 543, 914.

The appropriate steps to take in considering pension rights are:

- Pension rights should always be investigated. Both spouses may have pension rights, and one spouse may have more than one potential pension. Information as to pension rights must be provided on Form E. The procedure to be followed is set out in FPR 1991, r. 2.20.

- If the pension rights are likely to have any great value they should be valued. Valuation may not be easy and may require expert advice. On the method of valuation note the Divorce (Pensions) Regulations 1996, providing for a cash equivalent transfer value (CETV).

- The terms of the pension should also be investigated to discover what payments may be made, when they would start, and whether there are any options under the scheme.

If one spouse has pension rights of some value you need to put this into the context of the case. How old are the parties? How long were they married? What other assets are available for making financial provision on divorce? Note that rights that will not accrue for at least ten years will generally be ignored (*Roberts* v *Roberts* [1986] 1 WLR 437). Only pension rights accruing while the couple were together will be taken into account (*H* v *H (Financial Provision)* [1993] 2 FLR 335).

If the pension rights have value, the marriage has been reasonably long, and the pension rights are likely to accrue within the next ten years or so, the current options for dealing with pension rights are:

(a) The financial provision ordered on divorce can take pension rights into account in a general way, for example transferring the matrimonial home to the wife to balance the wealth of a husband who has substantial accrued pension rights.

(b) An order can be made to take effect in the future (*Legrove* v *Legrove* [1994] 2 FLR 119 and *Jones* v *Jones*, unreported, 29 October 1998). For example a husband may be ordered to pay a lump sum to his former wife as and when he receives a lump sum on retirement, though there is a danger that the husband might die before he retires, and such an order will not necessarily be easy to enforce (*Hudson* v *Hudson* [1995] Fam Law 550).

(c) The attachment provisions outlined above may be used, provided the petition was filed after 1 July 1996. On the working of these provisions, see *T* v *T (Financial Relief: Pensions)* [1998] 1 FLR 1072 and *Burrow* v *Burrow* [1999] 1 FLR 508.

(d) A decision on pension rights cannot be delayed for several years to see what will happen (*Gibson* v *Archibald* [1989] 1 WLR 123).

(e) A pension fund may be seen as a marriage settlement from which provision can be ordered (*Brooks* v *Brooks* [1995] 2 FLR 13).

(f) The terms of the pension may allow for some provision to be made, for example by having the former spouse named as being entitled to some specific provision.

(g) The provision of a proper pension may be part of procedural or financial negotiations (*K* v *K (Financial Relief: Widow's Pension)* [1997] 1 FLR 35).

(h) Pension sharing will probably become the option of choice for divorces commenced after 1 December 2000 where one spouse has significant pension rights and the other does not. It is important to watch for case law and comment on how the new powers are being interpreted by the courts.

For further detail, see David Salter (Ed.), *Pensions and Insurance on Family Breakdown*, 2nd edn.

5.4 Bases for Provision

5.4.1 INTRODUCTION

An identification and balancing of the relevant factors in the case must finally be brought into focus in deciding on an overall basis for provision. The fact that the statutory powers to make orders and to take factors into account are wide may seem to provide a bewildering array of possibilities, but for every case some coherent solution must be found. This requires the development of professional expertise, and gives scope for you to build a case.

There are some statutory guidelines for finding an overall basis, in that the needs of any children should be put first, and the court should see if a clean break is possible. If neither of these points provides a complete answer then one of the factors in the case may be so important that it overrides all others. The substantial body of case law gives guidance on finding an appropriate basis in a case.

The following notes offer a broad summary of possibilities rather than a comprehensive study. A basic overall guide for deciding on an appropriate basis can be found in **5.4.10**.

5.4.2 PUT THE NEEDS OF CHILDREN FIRST

The welfare of any children is stated by statute to be a first consideration (MCA 1973, s. 25). However, this does not mean that the children are entitled to be given outright assets belonging to their parents, but rather that general provision for the children should be taken into account in dividing the assets of the parents. The most common effect of this principle is that where there are young children, the matrimonial home will often be used to provide a home for them either by settling it or transferring it to the custodial parent.

Although stability in the life of children is important, the existence of children will not always mean that the matrimonial home is preserved. In some cases it will have to be sold to provide capital if there is no alternative. If the house is large, it may be argued that it should be sold and a smaller property purchased.

The welfare of children is also important in terms of income, and the Child Support Act 1991 now means that in practice payments of maintenance for children will need to take priority. This will inevitably have an effect on overall settlements, and may make it less likely that generous capital provision will be made if high income payments cannot be avoided.

5.4.3 THE CLEAN BREAK

Based on earlier case law, the objective of trying to achieve a clean break between spouses on divorce was made statutory in 1984, when s. 25A was inserted into MCA 1973:

> *(1)   Where on or after the grant of a decree of divorce or nullity of marriage the court decides to exercise its powers under section 23(1)(a), (b) or (c), 24 or 24A ... in favour of a party to the marriage, it shall be the duty of the court to consider whether it would be appropriate so to exercise those powers that the financial obligations of each party towards the other will be terminated as soon after the grant of the decree as the court considers just and reasonable.*
> *(2)   Where the court decides in such a case to make a periodical payments or secured periodical payments order in favour of a party to the marriage, the court shall in particular consider whether it would be appropriate to require those payments to be made or secured only for such term as would in the opinion of the court be sufficient to enable the party in whose favour the order is made to adjust without undue hardship to the termination of his or her financial dependence on the other party.*

(3) Where on or after the grant of a decree of divorce or nullity of marriage an application is made by a party to the marriage for a periodical payments or secured periodical payments order in his or her favour, then, if the court considers that no continuing obligation should be imposed on either party to make or secure periodical payments in favour of the other, the court may dismiss the application with a direction that the applicant shall not be entitled to make any further application in relation to that marriage for an order under section 23(1)(a) or (b) ...

The idea of the clean break is that financial resources should be divided once and for all between the spouses, leaving no further obligations between them, and leaving each free to start a new life (see, for example, *S* v *S* [1986] Fam 189). This can usually only be achieved if there are sufficient available assets to satisfy the reasonable claims of the applicant, and if both spouses have such income or earning potential that maintenance payments will not be necessary. For example, a clean break may be achieved by transferring a matrimonial home to a wife and dismissing her claims to maintenance, provided that she can support herself (*Hanlon* v *Hanlon* [1978] 1 WLR 592).

There has been some dispute about whether there can be a clean break where there are children (*Dipper* v *Dipper* [1981] Fam 31), but this is largely semantic. There cannot be an absolute clean break in such a case because of the primacy of the needs of the children, who will normally require continuing maintenance, but there may still be a clean break as between the *parents* if the available assets so permit (*Suter* v *Suter* [1987] Fam 111). However, the court may be slow to dismiss finally and permanently all maintenance claims of a custodial parent (*Mortimer* v *de Mortimer-Griffin* [1986] 2 FLR 315), especially if his or her earning capacity has been negatively affected by parenthood (*C* v *C (Financial Relief: Short Marriage)* [1997] 2 FLR 27).

In reviewing the possibilities for a clean break one must be realistic. The objective is not to impose a clean break at any cost, but simply to see if one is possible. Even if the couple do own assets such as their home there may be difficulties in achieving a clean break. Transferring the home to one spouse may be unfair if it is the sole capital asset owned by the parties, so that unless one spouse can afford to buy out the interest of the other, the home may have to be sold and the proceeds divided, or the home settled. Note that there may be practical problems in trying to achieve a clean break, if for example there is a joint endowment mortgage.

In any event, a clean break must be seen in a practical context. In broad terms, both spouses will need somewhere to live and enough money to live on. If one spouse is not able to earn enough to be self-supporting, due to lack of qualifications, caring for children, age or illness, then a clean break will not normally be possible. An important question here is the extent to which a wife (or husband!) who has stayed at home can be expected to go out to work. It is clear that a relatively young and sufficiently qualified woman will normally be expected to find suitable work, but a woman with young children to care for will not usually be expected to work, nor will an older woman who has not worked for many years and who does not have appropriate qualifications, unless it can be shown that there are suitable positions available.

The question is one of realistic prospects in the light of qualifications, experience, age, the extent to which a career has been interrupted, the local job market, and any prospects for training or retraining available. Even if a spouse can find work, there is a question of how much he or she can be reasonably expected to earn. In *Leadbeater* v *Leadbeater* [1985] FLR 789 it was held that it was not reasonable to expect a wife aged 47 who had not worked for some years to learn modern office skills to support herself, though she might be expected to increase her income as a receptionist by working more hours. In *M* v *M (Financial Provision)* [1987] 2 FLR 1 the husband earned about £60,000 a year, but it was held that the wife could only earn £6,000 a year at most, so that continuing maintenance would be required.

To illustrate where a clean break has been held to be possible:

(a) *Minton* v *Minton* [1979] AC 593. House transferred to wife as basis for clean break.

(b) *S* v *S* [1987] 1 WLR 382. Husband's liability to pay continuing maintenance could be ended if he could afford to pay the wife a sufficiently large lump sum to compensate for loss of it.

(c) *Ashley* v *Blackman* [1988] Fam 85. There could be a clean break where the husband had remarried with two children and was living on only £6,700, where the former wife was schizophrenic and living on State benefits, as there was no alternative, and no additional hardship to the wife.

(d) *Duxbury* v *Duxbury* [1987] 1 FLR 7. There could be a clean break on the basis of the wife's reasonable needs where she was cohabiting.

See also *F* v *F (Duxbury Calculation: Rate of Return)* [1996] Fam Law 467) and 'Duxbury — the Future' [1998] Fam Law 741 and 'Is *Duxbury* the Answer' [1999] Fam Law 766.

To illustrate where a clean break has not been held to be possible:

(a) *Whiting* v *Whiting* [1988] 1 WLR 565. There was no obligation on the court to impose a clean break. Although the husband was redundant, his wife's claims should not be entirely dismissed, she should be left with a back stop for the future.

(b) *M* v *M* [1987] 2 FLR 1. No clean break where the wife was 47 and would only be able to work to support herself for a few years.

(c) *Atkinson* v *Atkinson* [1988] Fam 93. There could be no clean break although the wife was cohabiting as there was no evidence maintenance payments could be ended without hardship to her.

(d) *Hepburn* v *Hepburn* [1989] 1 FLR 373. It would be wrong to force a clean break on woman who was cohabiting. She should not be forced to remarry, but should be left with a nominal order.

(e) *Boylan* v *Boylan* [1988] 1 FLR 282. A lump sum can only buy out a wife's claims if it is sufficient. Here it was not, so continuing maintenance was required.

It is vital to appreciate, and to make it clear to the client, that a clean break will, apart from exceptional circumstances, make a permanent *end* to all the client's claims for provision (see *Hewitson* v *Hewitson* [1995] 1 All ER 472). Contrast this with a nominal maintenance order, which can be varied if circumstances change. Clean break orders are not susceptible to variation. Appeals or applications for further provision will only be possible in cases of fraud or the like. This will be an advantage for the person against whom provision is sought, but it must be considered seriously by the spouse seeking provision.

As a possible alternative to an immediate clean break, the court is encouraged to consider whether continuing obligations might be ended after a period of time. This may be appropriate where a spouse needs time to adjust, to find or to train for work, or to care for children until they are older. Such a delayed clean break can only be achieved where realistically possible and it is important to draft it with care (*G* v *G* [1997] 1 FLR 368). To give some examples:

(a) *Attar* v *Attar (No. 2)* [1985] FLR 653. Wife awarded maintenance for two years to allow readjustment.

(b) *C* v *C* [1989] 1 FLR 11. In a case where both spouses were reasonably well off, the wife was awarded a lump sum of £116,000 and maintenance for five years.

(c) *Waterman* v *Waterman* [1989] 1 FLR 380. After a relatively short marriage, the wife was awarded maintenance for five years, but as there was a child, her right to reapply at the end of that time was not barred.

(d) *Barrett* v *Barrett* [1988] 2 FLR 516. There is no presumption that maintenance should end as soon as possible. It is wrong to set a specific date for maintenance to end if the wife may not be able to find work. A time limit may be extended if the wife has not had time to adjust (*Flavell* v *Flavell* [1997] 1 FLR 353).

5.4.4 PRINCIPLES OF EQUALITY AND REASONABLE NEEDS

Whether there is a clean break or continuing provision, there needs to be some basis for assessing how assets held during marriage should be apportioned on divorce. In some circumstances one key factor dictates the outcome, for example if the couple are poor (see **5.4.6**), the marriage has been very short (**5.4.7**), or there has been serious misconduct by one spouse (**5.4.8**). For the case with no strong factors of this kind the approach has varied over the years.

After the passing of the MCA 1973, which conferred wide discretionary powers, the first major case to deal generally with how discretion should be exercised was *Wachtel* v *Wachtel* [1973] Fam 72. This case proposed the use of the 'one-third rule', the rationale being that if one spouse was expected to make long-term provision for another it might be unfair to take away as much as half of all capital and income and that one-third provided a more reasonable long-term basis. The intention of the one-third rule was that the spouse claiming provision should be ordered such provision as would result in his or her getting one-third of the joint capital and one-third of the joint income. As a simplistic example, if a husband earned £36,000 a year and his wife £6,000, the joint income would be £42,000. One-third of this would be £14,000, and as the wife was already earning £6,000 she would get an order for £8,000 a year. If the husband also had capital of £60,000 she would be awarded £20,000 as a capital payment.

The 'one-third rule' was really a starting point rather than a rule as such, and it should be emphasised that it was intended primarily for the case where one spouse 'had' significantly more assets than the other and where the order would be long-term. Where there is a clean break and/or where both spouses have significant assets, equality of division has always been seen as potentially more appropriate (*Burgess* v *Burgess* [1996] 2 FLR 34). The 'one-third rule' rule was criticised and held to be inappropriate in various cases in the 1980s and 1990s, and as it has increasingly become the norm for both spouses to work and to have some capital, it has fallen into disuse.

A principle that partly replaced the 'one-third rule', at least for cases where there is a significant level of income and capital, was that of seeking to meet the applicant's reasonable needs. However, there are many situations where there is insufficient money to meet all 'reasonable needs', or where such a principle is inappropriate as both spouses have built up and have good claims to income and capital. The case of *Conran* v *Conran* [1997] 2 FLR 615 illustrates the problems of simply seeking to meet reasonable needs.

There has over the years been some resistance to adopting a principle of equality of treatment, especially where wealth had been built up by or was being earned by one spouse rather than both spouses. However, there has been a clear shift in the recent case of *White* v *White* [2001] 1 All ER 1. In this case the House of Lords said that before making an award a judge should check tentative views against a yardstick of equality of division, and should depart from equality of division only if there was a good reason for doing so. In brief, the spouses in that case had been married for over 30 years and had two adult children. Throughout their marriage they had built up a successful dairy farm that had come to be worth £3.5 million, and their overall wealth was £4.6 million. At first instance it was held that the wife's reasonable needs would be met by her having £980,000 of the joint assets (about one-fifth). The Court of Appeal increased the wife's share to £1.5 million (about two-fifths) and both spouses appealed. The House of Lords upheld the decision of the Court of Appeal on the basis that the efforts of both spouses (including the wife's role in maintaining the household) had built up the business and there was no reason why the wife should be limited to her 'reasonable needs' with the husband keeping the excess. It was relevant to the shares that the father's family had contributed to the business too.

Equality will now be the starting point where both spouses, even if in their own ways, have assisted in accumulating assets, but there may well be factors justifying a departure from an equal division. On the interpretation of *White* by the courts, see *Dharamshi* v *Dharamshi* [2001] 1 FLR 736, *D* v *D* (*Lump Sum: Adjournment of Application*) [2001] 1 FLR 633 and *Cowan* v *Cowan* [2001] 2 FLR 192. For comment, see 'White v White — bringing s. 25 back to the people' [2001] Fam Law 24. It is likely that a body of case law will build up concerning the circumstances in which it is appropriate to depart from a principle of equality.

5.4.5 THE RICH COUPLE

White v *White* [2001] 1 All ER 1, of course, is a rich couples case. In such cases the 'ceiling' of reasonable needs has been lifted by *White*. So too, in theory anyway, has the discrimination between wealth creating work and 'homely management' of the house and children. In *Dharamshi* v *Dharamshi* (where the family business was worth £4.5 million gross) some departure from equality was justified by the wife's retention of the matrimonial home and the support her husband's family gave to the business.

It will generally be easier to achieve a clean break where there are substantial assets, but continuing maintenance may be ordered, for example, where it is not reasonable to expect the claimant spouse to go out to work. An alternative may be for a sufficiently large lump sum to be ordered to buy out the right to continuing maintenance. On the need for adequate information in a 'bigamy' case, see *W* v *W* (*Ancillary Relief: Practice*) [2000] Fam Law 473.

5.4.6 THE POOR COUPLE

There are sadly many cases where the joint assets of the spouses are not sufficient to provide properly for both. Where the money that has managed to finance one household is split there may simply not be enough to go round. There may not be an easy solution in such cases, and you will need a particularly practical understanding of the problems that such a couple may face, and a thorough understanding of the social security benefit system. This knowledge will need to be both detailed and up-to-date. Changes have taken place over recent years, including tightening up the possibility of claiming payments from a 'liable relative': see the Social Security Act 1990.

It is a clear principle that one spouse cannot normally expect the State to take over the expense of caring for the other spouse, as that is a legal liability of the spouse. However, it would clearly be unreasonable and illogical to order a spouse to pay maintenance if that would put the payer below subsistence level, as the effect would simply be that the payer would be in need of State benefit himself (*Shallow* v *Shallow* [1979] Fam 1). Therefore, a maintenance order should not normally be made if its effect would be to reduce the payer below subsistence level (*Barnes* v *Barnes* [1972] 1 WLR 1381). Thus in a case where joint resources are so low that it is inevitable that one spouse will have to rely on State benefits, it may be appropriate that a nominal order or no order be made for maintenance, and the claimant spouse be left to rely on State benefits.

Where resources are limited, the 'net-effect' approach is often used in considering maintenance payments. This is based on the cases of *Furniss* v *Furniss* [1981] 3 FLR 46 and *Stockford* v *Stockford* [1981] 3 FLR 58. The point is to calculate as accurately as possible how much the payer can afford to pay towards the maintenance of the other spouse in any case where the need for financial provision may outweigh the available resources. Attention is centred on the sum each party will have left to live on. The object is to ensure that the payer's net income (after deductions, including the maintenance payable to the spouse) is not reduced below subsistence level (that is, the income needs of the payer's new household as indicated by the appropriate income support level and the cost of their accommodation).

There is no single set method for making this calculation, which can be set out in slightly different ways, but the broad stages are:

(a)   Select a 'hypothetical order' for the maintenance of the claimant. This is done by intelligent guesswork, considering the facts of the case. If all else fails, try the one-third approach.

(b)   Calculate the gross income of the payer and the recipient. For this, assume the hypothetical order passes from the payer to the claimant.

(c)   Calculate the net income the payer and the claimant would have if the order were made, taking into account tax payable, and National Insurance and pension contributions.

(d)   Compare the net income each would have with the income support levels each household could claim.

(e)   If there is a disparity, try adjusting the hypothetical order and recalculating. If the payer is still above the income support level he could pay more; if he is reduced below it, he should pay less.

Where there are children, note that a CSA calculation will have to be made first. If the payer is not well off this may well leave little or nothing for any additional maintenance for the caring spouse.

5.4.7   THE SHORT MARRIAGE

If a marriage is short then this may be an overriding factor which in effect dictates the whole basis for provision. After a very short marriage (lasting weeks), there may be no provision at all (although a brief marriage can be debilitating, see *C v C (Financial Relief: Short Marriage)* [1997] 2 FLR 27). After a marriage lasting months, provision is likely to be on the basis of what the applicant has lost by the marriage. If the marriage is relatively short (in terms of years), provision might be on the low side of what might otherwise be reasonable. See also **5.3.3.6**.

5.4.8   CONDUCT

Conduct has to be exceptional to be relevant. If conduct is very bad, this may be an overriding factor which results in little or no financial provision being ordered. Otherwise, and more usually, poor conduct may have the effect of keeping the provision ordered to the low side of what might otherwise be reasonable. See **5.3.3.9**.

5.4.9   SPECIAL CIRCUMSTANCES AND ASSETS

The facts of the individual case may provide some special circumstance in the position of either spouse, or with regard to the assets available to make provision, which may inevitably have some practical effect on the basis on which financial provision can be ordered.

One type of asset that may require special consideration is a business or an interest in a business. If either or both spouses are involved in the running of a business there may be complex problems in deciding to what extent the business should be taken into account, in deciding how the business should be valued, and in deciding how provision might be made from a business, as it may be difficult to extract money from a business without prejudicing its chances of success. Expert assistance may well be required in dealing with accounts, taxation, the marketability of shares, and future projections for business success. For recent examples, see *Mubarak v Mubarak* [2001] 1 FLR 673 and *A v A* [2000] Fam Law 470.

It is difficult to detect a coherent policy in this area — and every case is different. *White v White* says equality should be the starting point. It is clear that a spouse who has actually helped to build up and run a business can claim some share of it (*Nixon v Nixon* [1969] 1 WLR 1676). Indeed in such circumstances that spouse may well have a legal interest independent of any claim on divorce. Other cases have also held that the value of a business should be taken into account in assessing the overall level of entitlement (for example, *Trippas v Trippas* [1973] Fam 134; *Bullock v Bullock* [1986] 1 FLR 372).

However, there may be compelling reasons why the value of a business should not be fully taken into account (for example, *Potter v Potter* [1982] 1 WLR 1255; *Dew v Dew* [1986] 2 FLR 341). The difficulties of awarding financial provision from an operating business is one, as in *P v P (Financial Provision: Lump Sum)* [1978] 1 WLR 483, where it was said that money invested in a business was very different from free capital. In *Burgess v Burgess* [1986] Fam 155, it was said that money needed to develop a business could not be used for financial provision. It seems that even if a spouse already has a shareholding in a family company, he or she may not be entitled to have the full value of those shares on divorce, but might rather be awarded a substantial lump sum in lieu (*P v P* [1989] 2 FLR 241).

5.4.10 DECIDING ON THE APPROPRIATE BASIS

An appropriate overall basis must be chosen for each case. There is no easy way to make this decision. The suggestions made in this section are not comprehensive, and they can overlap, or even conflict in a case. As a very simple general guide:

(a) If there are young children, their needs must be central to the overall package. Depending on the assets available, this may require that the home be transferred or settled. Once sufficient provision for the children is made, it may be possible to achieve a clean break between the parents, or it may be necessary to have continuing provision for the custodial spouse, especially while children are young. A nominal maintenance order (e.g. 5p per annum) can feel rather like a clean break (although it certainly is *not* one), but leaves options open if relevant circumstances change.

(b) If there are no children, the primary objective will be to achieve a clean break, if this is possible with the assets available. A clean break cannot be achieved if it is not realistic for a claimant spouse to be self-supporting.

(c) If any factor clearly dominates the case, such as the shortness of the marriage or very bad conduct, this may determine the overall basis for provision.

(d) As regards level of provision, the principle of equality or the reasonable needs of the spouse should provide a starting point.

(e) In any event, whatever broad starting-point is appropriate, all the factors can go into the balance in deciding the overall package.

There will not always be a single appropriate basis for a case. There may be alternatives, for example, between a clean break and continuing provision. If there are, the options should be fully discussed with the client.

Note that pre-nuptial agreements are not binding in English law, although they are enforceable in a number of other jurisdictions (*C v C (Divorce: Stay of English Proceedings)* [2001] 1 FLR 624). Like separation agreements, however, they may be taken into account if relevant, see e.g. *G v G* [2000] 2 FLR 18.

5.4.11 THE OVERALL PACKAGE

Once a suitable overall basis for provision has been identified, and the relevant factors assessed, the details of the overall package must be considered, balancing capital provision, income provision, provision for children etc. *The interrelation of all the elements of a package must be considered.* For example, if a spouse gets a capital asset, such as a house, will he or she have sufficient income to pay for it and maintain it? Alternatively, if a spouse has to borrow money to pay a lump sum, the effect of the repayments on his or her own income and the income available to pay maintenance must be considered.

In many cases, where the couple own their own home, that will be central to the package, as it will be the main asset they own. Deciding what will happen to the home will often involve not only deciding on ownership, but also looking at who should pay the mortgage, pay for repairs, pay the outgoings and so forth. Although the court does not have specific powers to make orders on all these details, they may be taken into account in deciding on the appropriate figure for maintenance, or might be the subject of undertakings in the final order. In *Teschner* v *Teschner* [1985] FLR 627 it was held that a wife could not be ordered to repair a home, but the home could be transferred to her on the basis that she was then likely to make the repairs as that would be in her own interests.

A vital starting-point in considering what should happen to the home is checking whether the house is in a sole name or joint names, what its value is, what mortgage attaches to it, and who has made mortgage or other payments in respect of the house.

To outline the main possibilities for the home:

(a) The house may simply be sold, especially if there is to be a clean break. Consideration should be given to the share of the proceeds each spouse will get (noting that it is generally better to do this in terms of proportionate shares rather than set figures, in case the expected value is not realised). Sale may not be a fair option if a spouse is old or ill, or may have trouble finding alternative accommodation (*Greenham* v *Greenham* [1989] 1 FLR 105). A clear period for effecting the sale should be set, and any possible difficulties in selling considered. Remember that the costs of sale need to be taken into account.

(b) The home may be left in or transferred into the name of one spouse only. Again this may form the basis for a clean break, and it should help to avoid continuing problems about paying for repairs, and possible future tax liability. However, if the home is the sole capital asset of the parties, it may simply be unfair for one spouse to get the full value, depriving the other spouse of all his or her capital. In such a case, some sort of charge or trust may be fairer.

(c) The home may be settled, especially if it is needed as a home for the children. This may be an advantage for the custodial spouse, but ties up the interest of the other spouse. Great care must be given to deciding the terms of the settlement, especially what interest each is to have in the house, and when it might be sold. Again, proportionate shares are better than set figures. As general examples of such trusts:

(i) *Mesher* v *Mesher* [1980] 1 All ER 126. Home settled to be sold when the children were 18 or left full-time education. The wife to pay the rates and the spouses to pay half the mortgage each. Each spouse to have a half share in the proceeds of sale.

(ii) *Harvey* v *Harvey* [1982] Fam 83. Home settled, not to be sold until the wife died or remarried. On sale, the wife to get two thirds of the proceeds of sale and the husband one third. Once the mortgage was paid off, the wife to pay the husband an occupation rent.

(iii) *Martin* v *Martin* [1978] Fam 12. No children, husband had alternative accommodation. Home settled, not to be sold while the wife was unmarried and lived in it. Each spouse to get half of the proceeds on sale.

(d) As an alternative to settlement, the home may be put into the name of one spouse, subject to a charge in favour of the other — known as a 'charge back' (see, for example, *Dunford* v *Dunford* [1980] 1 WLR 5). Consider whether the charge should be proportionate or a set figure, and when it should be realisable.

(e) If the home is not owned but is rented, then, unless both spouses are to move out, consider what names are on the lease, and whether there may be a possibility, if appropriate, of transferring the lease into another name.

5.4.12 BEING REALISTIC

Every aspect of the overall package must be checked to ensure that it 'works'. It must be realistic as regards resources available for payments, realistic as to needs, and realistic in terms of what each spouse has left to live on. Check that it is adequate and/or fair for the claimant and affordable by the payer.

Just as you find out full details of the resources each has before the application is made, you should look at the precise position that the client will be left in if the suggested provision is ordered. You should do the arithmetic and make it clear to the client what he or she will have in income and capital terms, so that future plans can be made.

Look ahead as far as possible. It is important to bear in mind what changes in the client's position are reasonably foreseeable, and to make sure that the provision made does provide for the future as far as is reasonably possible. For example, if a house is settled, consider what position the spouses might be left in when it is sold, looking at what their ages and resources are likely to be then.

5.4.13 TAXATION AND BENEFITS

In doing the arithmetic, one is not simply adding up income and capital. Any potential relevance of State benefits must be taken into account and explained to the client. It has been made clear by the courts that it is also part of the barrister's duty in every case to calculate tax implications and explain them to the client (see, for example, *Coleman* v *Wheeler* [1981] 2 FLR 99).

The principles for the taxation of maintenance are outlined in **Chapter 9**. The income tax effects for the payer and the recipient of maintenance should be calculated and explained to them.

The real possibilities of a charge to capital gains tax should never be ignored on divorce, especially if the couple are relatively wealthy (see *Aspden* v *Hildesley* [1982] 1 WLR 264 and *M* v *M* [1988] 1 FLR 389). The possibility of future liability to capital gains tax where a house is settled is also important, as the spouse who is not living in the home will have no exemption from tax when the house is sold.

5.5 Procedure for Ancillary Financial Relief

5.5.1 INFORMATION ABOUT YOUR CLIENT'S POSITION

Getting detailed information about the client's financial position is very important. This will involve careful investigation, clarity of thought, and realism as to what information may be available. It is often not sufficient simply to ask the client general questions — many clients will not realise what is relevant. Counsel must be aware of all the details that may be required. The most successful financial provision application will be that which is based on the soundest preparation.

The first source of information for the barrister will be the brief, which is likely to include some form of statement of the client's means. The amount of detail available initially will vary considerably, depending on the stage at which the barrister is briefed and the amount of preparatory work which the solicitor has done. It is, however, unlikely that the statement provided in the brief will be complete, as the client may well not have supplied full information to the solicitor, and the solicitor may well leave it to counsel to suggest what further information should be sought.

Whatever information is supplied in the initial brief must be carefully analysed. What is there must be sorted out, and any gaps or implications that need to be clarified must be identified. A list of further information that will be required from the solicitor, from the client, and from any other sources should be drawn up.

Depending on the complexity of the case, the next stage may be either a telephone call to the solicitor seeking further information, the arranging of a conference with the client, or the writing of an opinion on the case. In any event the following general points will apply.

Get the standpoint of your client clear: is your client seeking provision or trying to resist an application for provision? What are the client's objectives, and which of the objectives are most important? Do not automatically assume that your client will wish to get as much as possible, or will wish to pay as little as possible. Many spouses are prepared to make reasonable provision, especially for children. Is one particular asset of particular importance to the client? Does your client want to stay in the matrimonial home or move? In considering objectives, be aware of the effects of emotion. One spouse may want an asset as a matter of status or spite rather than of objective need. While the barrister should seek to fulfil the client's objectives, it may sometimes be necessary to talk to the client about what is reasonable.

Try to get a clear view, with actual or possible values, of the assets that your client has. As a basic checklist:

Income

Employment (including wages, commission etc.)	£
Value of fringe benefits	£
Any other work or business	£
State benefits	£
Pensions	£
Unearned income (e.g., dividends, interest)	£
Income regularly provided from another source (e.g., from a cohabitee)	£
From any other source	£
Total	£

Expenditure

Mortgage repayments or rent	£
Other costs of the home, e.g., water rate, repairs	£
Cost of services, electricity, gas, telephone	£
Council tax	£
Food	£
Clothes	£
Regular hire-purchase and credit sale payments	£
Costs and expenses of work or business	£
Cost of holidays	£
Other regular obligations (e.g., supporting a third party)	£
Any other expenses	£
Total	£

Ensure that all income or expenditure figures relate to the same period, for example, to the same calendar year or financial year, and all figures are annual, monthly or weekly.

Capital
Value of home (or share of home)	£
Savings	£
Shares	£
Other investments	£
Household goods, furniture etc.	£
Car	£
Other capital assets (e.g., jewellery)	£

Total £

Debts (liabilities not covered by expenditure)
Balance due on credit card	£
Bank loan	£

Total £

Make sure that a client gives a current rather than a historical value. In considering the matrimonial home, be clear who owns it and what mortgage may be attached to it, and perhaps whether a non-owner spouse may already have an equitable claim to a share in it. If either or both spouses have interests in a business, the valuation of the business may present particular problems, especially if it is a small business. Such points as the transferability of the shares in an unquoted company, or the value of goodwill due to the involvement of the spouse may need to be considered.

Separate income and capital liabilities so that you can see clearly if the client can afford his or her current lifestyle, or has any money to spare.

For all assets and liabilities do not just ask for figures, but get written verification where possible. Not only may this be required as proof when the matter comes on for hearing, but some clients do make mistakes or overlook points in the replies they give. Ask for pay slips, bank statements, mortgage statements, receipts, bills, accounts, building society statements etc. Be realistic about what records the client may or may not have but anticipate the documents which will have to be disclosed. In some cases, copies may be available where originals have been lost, for example, in the case of bank statements. Also be realistic about the amount of paperwork collected, bearing costs in mind.

Do not only get figures for each item, also consider practical aspects. Could an asset be sold easily or not? Are there any important points regarding the history of the asset? Could an asset be used as security for a loan or not? Does an asset have particular sentimental value to one spouse?

In taking this wide and realistic view, a knowledge of accounts, company law, partnership law, insolvency, revenue law, etc. will be valuable where appropriate.

5.5.2 THE USE OF FINANCIAL SCHEDULES

Financial schedules are a vital part of both the preparation and presentation of a case. They summarise the relevant figures in an accessible form, and help you, the client and the court focus on the implications of the orders sought. Ensure that they are up-to-date before use in court and that your opponent and the judge have copies.

There is no single format for preparing a schedule — in practice you will be able to see what other practitioners do and form a view as to what is most effective — but in general the schedule would try to do the following:

(a) Summarise the current position as to income, expenditure and capital of your client in so far as it is relevant to the application under consideration (e.g., if you are applying for maintenance pending suit you do not need a full summary of the capital position, though it might be relevant to bring in capital that is available to meet immediate needs).

(b) Summarise the proposed position as to income, expenditure and capital that your client will be in if the order sought is made (which needs to show how this will put your client into a satisfactory position if you are applying for the order, and how this will put your client into an untenable position if you are resisting an application for an unrealistic order).

(c) It is useful to have a format that can be used flexibly, so that for example it is easy to work out what the effect would be if an order £10 per week less than that sought were made, etc.

The following sort of format might be useful to support the case of an applicant:

Schedule of income and expenditure

The position of the applicant

Current position
Income

Employment		£	per month
Payments from respondent		£	per month
Child benefit		£	per month
Etc.			
	Total	£	

Expenditure

See paragraph of applicant's affidavit for details	£	per month

Balance

This shows a shortfall of	£	per month

Proposed position
Income

Employment	£	per month
Child benefit	£	per month
Increased payment by respondent	£	per month

Expenditure
(This might be the same as the existing position)
(Alternatively a whole new list of expenditure may
    need to be provided, if for example the applicant
    proposes to move house)

Balance

This shows a small surplus of	£	per month

Other liabilities of the applicant
(Might for example summarise sums owed on credit cards, loans taken out, and sums required to meet immediate needs, e.g., car repairs.)

Other resources available to the applicant
(Might for example summarise savings, cash balance at bank, etc.)

The position of the respondent

Monthly income	Total	£
Monthly expenditure	Total	£
Surplus per month	Total	£

Other resources available to the respondent

You would do the same sort of thing with property (e.g. the matrimonial home), other capital etc.

5.5.3 THE NEW RULES

The objectives of the new rules are to reduce delay, facilitate settlements, provide the court with much greater control over the conduct of proceedings and so deliver a more cost effective service. If that all sounds very familiar, then you will appreciate that these are the identical considerations which lay behind the recent changes to the rules of procedure in the mainstream civil courts. Although family practice is specifically excluded from the ambit of the new Civil Procedure Rules 1998 (which is why some of the 'old' terminology survives), many of the civil reforms were in fact modelled on features of practice in the family courts — and vice versa. The current system was 'piloted' in several courts before going nationwide (in updated and further Woolf-style) in June 2000.

5.5.3.1 Characteristics of the system
The main features of the ancillary relief procedure are:

- The primacy of the overriding objective (adapted entirely from the Civil Procedure Rules 1998 (CPR)).

- A pre-action protocol.

- Strict timetable for exchange of information and hearing dates.

- Parties exchange sworn statements of financial information in prescribed Form E (see **Appendix D**). This is intended to take the 'heat' out of the process which is a by-product of the reactive nature of the sequential exchange of affidavits which occurred traditionally. Some think it cuts the heart out of the process as well — but there is still scope for drafting skills.

- Curbs on unnecessary and time-consuming discovery requests. Form E is detailed and thorough and requires several types of documents to accompany it. Parties are discouraged from disclosing (or seeking disclosure of) additional information.

- Use of 'appointments' at pre-ordained stages to ensure that the issues in dispute are identified early on and to facilitate focussed attempts to reach agreement as early as possible.

- Use of statements of costs at each stage to ensure that everyone (including the court) is aware of the mounting litigation costs.

5.5.4 THE TIMETABLE: PROCEDURE AND PRACTICE

The ancillary relief pre-action protocol was adapted entirely from the CPR. It is set out at the end of **Appendix D** and, although it is largely addressed to solicitors, you should familiarise yourself with its content. Note, however, that not all cases will be amenable to attempts to resolve the matter pre-action. Where, for example, disclosure is at issue or the parties are at odds, it may be more appropriate to proceed directly to a court timetable and court management (para. 2.2).

When pursuing a claim, the procedural timetable is essentially divided into three parts.

5.5.4.1 Stage one: Application to first appointment
This is the initial phase, focusing on early disclosure and getting a general 'handle' on the case after an application has been made. Application is made in Form A. When this is filed, the court will list a first appointment between 12 and 14 weeks from the date of filing. The notice of first appointment (Form C) is served by the court on the respondent, along with a copy of the application. Once the date of the first appointment has been fixed, it can be changed only with the permission of the court.

Before the first appointment, five things should happen (r. 2.61B):

(a) Simultaneous exchange of financial information on Form E (see specimen in **Appendix D**). This must occur not less than 35 days before the first appointment. This rather lengthy standard form replaces the narrative affidavit of yesteryear. With it, quite intentionally, has gone a lot of the emotion as well as the lottery involved in finding the lawyers with the best (or better) drafting skills. The overriding objective seeks to ensure that the parties are kept, so far as possible, on an equal footing — and standard forms is one way of achieving that. In any case, Form E contains several boxes inviting comment on standard of living and conduct, so all is not lost for drafters.

Designated documents must be annexed to the form. All must be filed and served on the other side. Exchange of the forms etc. is to occur at the same time, which is sometimes easier said than done.

Counsel will not often be asked to assist with completing this financial statement. If you are, useful advice can be found in *Ancillary Relief: A Guide to the New Rules* by Nicholas Mostyn QC and John Nicholson (Butterworths, 2000).

(b) No later than 14 days before the first appointment, the following documents must be filed and served:

(i) A concise statement of issues in the case. This should set out clearly and succinctly what the areas of dispute are. The idea is to help narrow the issues. In the Cutforth case, for example, the dispute over the matrimonial home might be described like this:

ISSUE	APPLICANT'S CASE	RESPONDENT'S CASE
Housing	The applicant should remain in the family home. She needs four bedrooms and the chidren need continuity. She cannot buy other suitable accommodation near the children's school for less than the value of the family home.	The family home should be sold. A three bedroom house, of the type illustrated in the particulars annexed to the respondent's Form E, could be purchased with some of the proceeds; thus releasing about £50,000 for his housing needs.

(ii) A chronology. There may be scope for inserting a bit of 'colour' here.

(iii) Either a questionnaire, indicating what further disclosure is needed and why, or a statement confirming that no further information is required.

(c) No later than 14 days before the first appointment, both sides should file and serve a notice indicating whether they are in a position to use some or all of the first appointment as a Financial Dispute Resolution (FDR) hearing (see below).

(d) No later than 14 days before the first appointment, the applicant must file and serve on the respondent confirmation that relevant notice provisions have been complied with (e.g., notice to mortgagors, pension funds etc.).

(e) Each side must come to the first appointment with an estimate of costs (on Form H) up to that point.

5.5.4.2 Stage two: The first appointment to the FDR

Counsel is often instructed to attend on the first appointment. Both parties must do so, unless they are excused by the court. The appointment is usually listed for 30 minutes and it should not be adjourned or vacated unless there is a good reason. Non-service or late service of the other side's Form E (see **Appendix D**) could constitute a good reason for an adjournment. You or your instructing solicitors will have prepared and served the documents set out above. Confirmation that the trustees or managers of a pension scheme have been served if seeking relief under MCA 1973, s. 25B or 25C, and confirmation that the mortgagees have been served, should also be filed.

The District Judge determines the extent to which any questionnaire filed shall be answered and what documents required shall be produced. He can also order a valuation of a pension to be obtained.

The District Judge may be reluctant to order expert evidence at this stage. Note that such evidence should be provided by a single joint expert where possible. In fact, family law has been the pioneer in this regard (where do you think the CPR got the idea?) — welfare reports in Children Act cases, for example, have long been provided by a single expert. This tendency has now been given further impetus in the *President's Practice Direction on Ancillary Relief Procedure* of 25 May 2000.

Rule 2.61D states that 'the first appointment must be conducted with the objective of defining the issues and saving costs', so protracted and indiscriminate disclosure is actively encouraged. A party is only 'entitled' to further disclosure if it has been ordered at the first appointment or with leave of the court (r. 2.61D(3)). Remember that the District Judge will be thinking in terms of the need to identify the real issues and keep costs down. For these reasons you will not necessarily obtain all that you request unless you have prepared cogent reasons for disclosure. Voluntary disclosure happens in practice and advanced disclosure is now part of the pre-action protocol.

The District Judge will give directions as to the valuation of assets, obtaining and exchanging experts' evidence and any evidence sought to be adduced by each party, and as to any chronologies or schedules to be filed by each party. He can also order a valuation of a pension to be obtained.

Procedure varies slightly from court to court. Applicants usually open, giving reasons for the directions they seek and the other side responds in kind. Remember that requests will need to be justified by reference to the overriding objective.

If it appears that agreement between the parties may be possible at this stage, the first appointment can be 'converted' into a FDR (see below), in which case any discussion about further disclosure or evidence would await the success or failure of the attempt to settle. In the overwhelming majority of cases, however, the judge will fix an FDR, although a further directions hearing might be ordered in exceptional circumstances (e.g., a party failed to file a Form E). If an FDR, which is effectively court monitored conciliation, seems a waste of time, a date for a final hearing can be fixed at this stage. As can a date for the hearing of an application for an interim order.

An application may be made for maintenance pending suit. If you are applying for maintenance pending suit then notify the court to request a longer hearing.

At the FDR appointment
The purpose of the FDR is described as 'discussion and negotiation' (r. 2.61E(1)). It is important to arrive early and again, unless the court orders otherwise, both parties must attend the FDR. Legal representatives are expected to have a full working knowledge of the case so that the opportunity for settlement is not wasted. Not later than seven days before the FDR appointment the applicant will have filed details of all offers and proposals and responses to them.

At the appointment you should use your best endeavours to reach an agreement. Be prepared to open the case to the District Judge. It is essential to have prepared a schedule of assets, liabilities, income and outgoings. You must be prepared to make brief submissions in support of the orders you seek. The District Judge should point out to either party any argument or expectation which he considers unrealistic. If you reach an agreement you should be ready to draw up a consent order for the District Judge to make at the hearing or submit after the hearing for his consideration. If you are close to agreement but need more time the District Judge can give you more time, fix another date for a further FDR or the FDR can be adjourned for out of court mediation. If there is no agreement the proceedings are usually listed for a final hearing. You should then collect all documents containing offers, proposals and responses. The appointment is without prejudice and none of these documents should stay on the court file.

In the recent case of *W v W (Ancillary Relief: Practice)*, *The Times*, 15 March 2000, it was suggested that if, at the FDR, it is clear that the case is 'going to fight', the FDR judge may order 'narrative affidavits' to be filed if this would help 'illuminate' the conduct and contributions of each party.

Note that the judge who hears the FDR is not permitted to have any further dealings with the case, except to hold further FDR appointments or grant consent orders.

The FDR appointment is a significant innovation and it is important to explain to your client just what it is all about and what may or may not happen. In their book (see above), Nicholas Mostyn and John Nicholson set out some useful do's and don'ts as you and your clients approach the FDR, including being very clear about what your 'bottom line' is so that you do not lose sight of it in the heat of negotiation.

5.5.4.3 Information about the other side

Generally

Your client's claim for financial provision, or resistance to such a claim, can only be fully considered in the overall context of the income and capital available to both sides. Ideally, you need to know as much about the assets of the other side as you do about your own client's assets. Realistically, it may not always be easy to get such information if the other side is being obstructive.

Initially, you will ask your own client what he or she knows about his or her spouse's assets. Even if your client has little detailed knowledge, he or she may have a general idea what the spouse earns and owns, or at least be able to suggest points to be pursued. This source of information may be inaccurate, may have an emotional rather than an objective basis, and may well include conjecture and hearsay. But it may at least suggest some starting-points; and eventually, a useful basis of comparison.

The next source of information is of course the financial statement provided by the other side. As already suggested, you should go through this with your client, checking it for inaccuracies and omissions. Where the information is vague or incomplete, appropriate steps should be taken, either by way of asking for Form E to be completed or seeking additional information by way of questionnaire. Only ask for information you really need from the other side; questionnaires are not the place for scoring tactical points.

Questionnaires

As with the mainstream courts, one of the aims of the new rules was to put an end to cases getting bogged down in endless, expensive and often overwhelming requests for disclosure. This has been achieved in two ways. First, several of the sorts of documents routinely requested by parties in the past, are required to be annexed to their Form E financial statements. These include:

(a) Any recent valuations of the matrimonial home.

(b) The last 12 months' bank statements for all accounts listed.

(c) Surrender value quotations of all life insurance policies.

(d) The last two years' accounts of any business in which the other party has an interest.

(e) Last three payslips, and most recent P60.

(f) The last two years' accounts for any self-employment, or any relevant partnership.

(g) A valuation of pension rights if these are available.

A curious omission is credit card statements, so this will remain a typical request in the questionnaire, as will the disclosure of any of the above documents which were not annexed with Form E when it was served and filed.

Secondly, requests for further disclosure will not be granted if it would not further the overriding objective. Questionnaires must ask for what is necessary, but every request must be related to an issue in the case and, crucially, be proportionate.

By way of example, some of Mrs Cutforth's requests, for example, might sound like this:

Cutforth v *Cutforth* — Applicant's Questionnaire and Request for Documents

1. The Respondent states in his Form E that Jactrad Ltd 'has few assets and negligible income' but he failed to annex the last 2 years' accounts as required. Please provide a copy of these accounts, plus any documentary evidence relating to the ownership of shares in and value of the company. Please provide any draft accounts in respect of the period since the last prepared accounts.

2. The Respondent refers in his Form E to monthly payments on the matrimonial home which appear to exceed the mortgage. Please disclose the most recent mortgage statement (as should have been annexed to Form E).

3. The Respondent says he cannot afford the Applicant's stated needs, but does not make clear on what he spends his income. Please provide a schedule of all credit, charge and store cards held by him during the last 12 months, whether in his sole name, joint names, or upon which he has signing rights, together with copy statements for the like period.

The court does have powers to make more draconian orders regarding disclosure, where that is deemed necessary and proportionate. These include search orders and freezing orders, the setting aside of transactions intended to defeat or reduce a proper claim for financial provision (MCA 1973, s. 37, see **Appendix C**) or even imprisonment (*Lightfoot* v *Lightfoot* [1989] 1 FLR 414). None of these, of course, would be undertaken lightly.

If a spouse fails to provide information when an order is made, there are various implications:

(a) A party who fails to make proper disclosure can be ordered to pay costs occasioned by that failure (*P* v *P (Financial Relief: Non-disclosure)* [1994] 2 FLR 381).

(b) A party who fails to produce documents may be imprisoned for contempt if appropriate, but only as a last resort (see *Bluffield* v *Curtis* [1988] 1 FLR 170).

(c) A party who is very obstructive in providing information may be penalised in the order made (see *Mason* v *Mason* [1986] 2 FLR 212).

5.5.4.4 Analysis of evidence

Whenever, and however, disclosure of financial evidence is made, it is imperative to analyse the information carefully and cross-check it with assertions made by the disclosing party.

When you look at payslips, for example, check that they support the figure presented in Form E. Compare them with the P60.

When going through bank statements, it is important to look out for regular payments which suggest a source of income which has not been disclosed. Alternatively, a statement might reveal a bank account, pension, savings account or life assurance policy which has not been disclosed. Check transfers to other bank accounts and regular direct debits or standing orders. For example, see the sample bank statement below.

Example of bank statement

HAPPY BANK

Statement of Account   **IM 1X 05**
Sheet No. 6

Account Number: 0432366
FABIO JONES

Sort Code: 30–20–10

MR FABIO JONES
10 FRANK DRIVE
HARWICK
HA1 111

Telephone: 01473 111 222
Facsimile: 01473 111 333

All entries to 30 AUG 01 inclusive are complete

When overdrawn marked OD

Date	Particulars	Payments		Receipts		Balance	
2001	Opening Balance					2153	51
1 AUG	ST MARYS STREET C/P 3	100	00			2053	51
7 AUG	000073	152	37				
	000075	500	00				
	ST MARYS STREET C/P 3						
	DATE OF WITHDRAWAL						
	05 AUG	100	00				
	ST MARYS STREET C/P 3						
	DATE OF WITHDRAWAL						
	06 AUG	20	00			1281	14
8 AUG	SOLIHULL C/P 3	60	00			1221	14
10 AUG	NET CREDIT INTEREST						
	GROSS £0.24						
	TAX PAID £0.06					18	
	000076	400	00			821	32
14 AUG	000077	10	94			810	38
15 AUG	MARK STREET C/P 3	20	00				
	SCOTTISH WIDOWS D/D	44	10			746	28
21 AUG	TRANSFER	172	08			574	20
23 AUG	000007	15	35			558	85
24 AUG	000002	120	50				
	000005	100	00			298	35
	POUND STREET C/P 3						
	DATE OF WITHDRAWAL	40	00				
25 AUG	23 AUG			500	00		
	SUNDRY CREDIT 500072						
	000078	22	03			776	32
29 AUG	500073			100	00		
	000004	17	63				
	000006	150	00			708	69
30 AUG	000079	16	27			692	42
	TOTAL PAYMENTS/RECEIPTS	**2061**	**27**	**600**	**18**		

The items and balance shown should be verified. Any interest rates shown are the rates in force only on the date shown. Details of all other rates and calculations of any interest charged are available on request to your branch.

Reading the bank statements and credit card statements can give clues as to the standard of living of that party, e.g., look out for frequent holidays and restaurant bills when a party is pleading poverty.

When you look at business accounts, look at the balance sheet carefully. Look out for benefits a party receives through the business, e.g., entertainment, motor expenses and director's loan accounts and drawings. Also, look at the tax returns and see if they are consistent with the accounts.

5.5.4.5 Conferences

At an appropriate point, there should be a conference with the client. A conference may take place at a very early stage, perhaps even before the divorce proceedings are commenced, if there is a need to discuss what the client hopes to achieve, or if the facts of the case are complex, or if there are substantial assets. In any case, conferences may be needed at the various procedural staging posts, e.g., before Form E is filed (if Counsel is asked to draft this); before the first appointment; before any FDR appointments and; if no agreement is reached, before the final hearing. Earlier conferences will focus on aspirations and evidence; later ones, on priorities, reality, tactics and possibilities of settlement.

It goes without saying, therefore, that good conference skills are important in this context. Getting full information from the client will take great care, and perhaps some diplomacy! You will also need to give clear and practical advice. Special skill will be needed to deal with the emotional reactions of clients, and the effect that such feelings may have on their perspective. Reality can be a bitter pill to swallow.

5.5.4.6 An opinion

General points

Counsel may be asked to provide an opinion at any stage, but the main possibilities are (a) that an opinion may be sought at an early stage when there is little detail of the financial position but the client wants general advice, or (b) that an opinion or a further opinion may be sought at a later stage when more detailed figures are available. Counsel may be asked to deal with overall entitlement or with particular issues.

The following general checklist for the contents of an opinion dealing with financial provision will of course need to be fully adapted for each individual case. The opinion should:

(a) Show clear appreciation of the standpoint and objectives of the client, and of any particular concerns that the client has.

(b) Identify clearly the factors in the case which favour the client.

(c) Identify clearly the factors in the case which weaken the client's case or favour the other side.

(d) Advise clearly on the likely basis or alternative possible bases for provision.

(e) Deal clearly and comprehensively with the resources and assets that are available.

(f) Use the available figures to practical effect. Be specific.

(g) Advise clearly on further information or figures that should be sought.

(h) Ensure that a summary of clear, practical advice is provided.

In essence, it is vital to be clear, practical and thorough. Do not generalise about statutory provisions and the options available, or deal superficially with figures.

Notice of [Intention to Proceed With] an Application for Ancillary Relief

In the	Oxford
*[County Court] *[Principal Registry of the Family Division]	
Case No. *Always quote this*	O1 D 288
Applicant's Solicitor's reference	F\213\CR
Respondent's Solicitor's reference	M\DR\511

(* delete as appropriate)

Respondents (Solicitor(s)) name and address

CHARLES & DICKINS
72 Spire Mews
Oxford
Postcode OX1 2LJ

The marriage of Sandra Anne Cutforth and James Andrew Cutforth

Take Notice that

Delete as appropriate. the Applicant intends: *~~to apply to the Court for~~
*to proceed with the application in the [petition][~~answer~~] for
*~~to apply to vary;~~

☑ an order for maintenance pending suit   ☑ a periodical payments order
☑ a secured provision order   ☑ a lump sum order
☑ a property adjustment order (please provide address)   ☑ an order under Section 24B, 25B or 25C of the Act of 1973

If an application is made for any periodical payments or secured periodical payments for children:

● and there is a written agreement made before 5 April 1993 about maintenance for the benefit of children, **tick this box** ☐

● and there is a written agreement made on or after 5 April 1993 about maintenance for the benefit of children, **tick this box** ☐

● but there is no agreement, tick any of the boxes below to show if you are applying for payment:

☐ for a stepchild or stepchildren
☐ in addition to child support maintenance already paid under a Child Support Agency assessment
☐ to meet expenses arising from a child's disability
☐ to meet expenses incurred by a child in being educated or training for work
☐ when either the child or the person with care of the child or the absent parent of the child is not habitually resident in the United Kingdom
☐ other (please state)

Signed: Todd, Fisher, Burton + Co. Dated: 18.12.2001

[~~Applicant~~/Solicitor for the Applicant]

The Court Office at

is open between 10 am and 4 pm (4.30pm at the Principal Registry of the Family Division) Monday to Friday. When corresponding with the court, please address forms or letters to the Court Manager and quote the case number. If you do not do so, your correspondence may be returned.

Form A Notice of [Intention to Proceed With] an Application for Ancillary Relief

Notice of a First Appointment

In the	
Oxford	**County Court**
Case No. *Always quote this*	07 D 288
Applicant's Solicitor's reference	F/213/CR
Respondent's Solicitor's reference	M/DR/511

The marriage of *SANDRA ANNE* CUTFORTH and *JAMES ANDREW* CUTFORTH

Take Notice that

By [*4.2.02*] you must file with the Court a statement which gives full details of your property and income. You must sign and swear the statement. At the same time each party must exchange a copy of the statement with the [legal representative of the] other party. You must use the standard form of statement (Form E) which you may obtain from the Court office.

By [*8.3.02*] you must send to the Court and to the [legal representative of the] other party:

- a concise statement of the apparent issues between yourself and the other party
- a questionnaire setting out the further information and documents you require from the other party
- a Notice in Form G

The First Appointment will be heard by

(the district judge in chambers) at *Oxford County Court*

on *22 March* 2002

at *2* [a.m.][p.m.]

The probable length of the hearing is *30 Minutes*

You and your legal representative, if you have one, must attend the appointment. At the appointment you must provide the Court with a written estimate (in Form H) of any legal costs which you have incurred. Non-compliance may render you liable to costs penalties.

The court office at

is open between 10 am and 4 pm Monday to Friday. When corresponding with the court, please address forms or letters to the Court Manager and quote the case number. If you do not do so, your correspondence may be returned.

Example opinion

CUTFORTH v CUTFORTH

OPINION

1. I am asked to advise the Petitioner, Sandra Cutforth, with regard to her application for financial provision on divorce. She has made the usual global application in the Petition. In particular she seeks ownership of the former matrimonial home, a lump sum payment sufficient to enable her to purchase a car and pay off her current credit card bill as well as sufficient income to maintain, for herself and her children, the standard of living enjoyed during the marriage. She has also applied for maintenance pending suit.

2. In brief, although several of the s. 25 factors favour Mrs Cutforth, I take the view that she will not be able to 'have it all'. The court will effect a 'clean break' whenever, and as soon as, possible. In this context Mrs Cutforth may have to choose between, on the one hand, early financial independence in exchange for the larger share of the matrimonial property and, on the other, sharing the latter more equally in exchange for regular maintenance until she and the children adjust to the new circumstances.

3. This is, of necessity, a provisional view because there is still important information which needs to be gathered, especially as regards the value of the family assets. Until I have these details, I cannot advise more conclusively.

Background

4. The parties married in 1992. Mrs Cutforth is 34 years old; Mr Cutforth is 40. They have two children, Damian (now aged 8) and Gemma (now aged 6). The parties separated in May 2001, Mr Cutforth having been ordered to vacate the matrimonial home. The children remain there with their mother. Decree nisi has been granted; perhaps instructing solicitors could confirm whether decree absolute has followed.

5. Following some rather acrimonious pre-action discussion, Form A was issued by Mrs Cutforth on 18 December 2001. Both parties have filed Form E statements. The first appointment is listed for 22 March 2002, where the further information required from Mr Cutforth mentioned below should, if not forthcoming before that time, be sought.

Needs of children

6. In exercising their powers, the court will treat the welfare of the children as the first consideration. I assume there is no dispute about the children living with their mother or about their having reasonable contact with their father. Mr Cutforth currently pays £120 per week to his wife — she says it is for the two children, but he describes it in his Form E as 'maintenance for petitioner'. These, of course, are two entirely different things. Assuming the money is intended as child support, it seems that a CSA assessment would be closer to £80 per week per child (i.e., £160 per week). Could Instructing Solicitors please confirm this figure. Mrs Cutforth is not obliged to make a CSA application, and the wheels of that organisation turn slowly, but were Mr Cutforth not willing to match a figure which the CSA would order, then it would be advisable for her to make an application. In the meantime, the court could make an order in similar terms to that expected from the CSA. Perhaps the matter could, as a first step, be taken up with Mr Cutforth's solicitors. There is also no mention of who will be responsible for any school fees (it seems one of the children will soon attend boarding school). This can be catered for in a court order, but it is not clear what the parties intend. If Mr Cutforth is to pay for this, it would add a significant amount to his outgoings.

7. The children are likely to remain with Mrs Cutforth for the foreseeable future and they will need a suitable home for the period of their continued dependency. Mrs Cutforth would like to remain in the former matrimonial home, which is a four bedroom semi-detached

property. The advantages for the children of her doing so are clear, i.e., continuity and a sense of security. However, there is some question as to whether the property may be bigger than they need (as Mr Cutforth claims) and whether suitable alternative housing in the same neighbourhood is affordable (Mrs Cutforth says it is not). Perhaps Mrs Cutforth could collect particulars of (and see) some three and four bedroom properties in the area to help resolve this point.

8. The parties also take very different views of the value of the former matrimonial home: Mrs Cutforth estimates it to be about £150,000 whereas Mr Cutforth puts it at £200,000. Clearly this discrepancy needs to be resolved, so it is vital to get an agreed, up-to-date assessment. As a matter of priority, could those instructing please invite the respondent's solicitors to agree a valuer to carry out a valuation as soon as possible.

9. Mr Cutforth discloses an outstanding mortgage on the matrimonial home of £50,000. He also says in his Form E that he pays £450 per month 'on the property' — a figure exceeding that monthly mortgage repayments of £312.75. Mrs Cutforth says Mr Cutforth also pays all the outgoings on the property, so perhaps his figure of £450 per month includes this other expenditure, but this needs clarifying. The figure seems rather high. Accurate information as to the costs of Mrs Cutforth's remaining in the house is critical to her application for a transfer of the property to her name. It is unlikely that the court would make an outright transfer to her if she were unable to afford to live there.

Parties needs, resources etc.

10. At present, Mrs Cutforth apparently has a monthly income (including Mr Cutforth's payments to her) of £715 to meet current monthly expenses in excess of £695. Although Mr Cutforth pays all of the outgoings on the house, she still struggles to maintain the standard of living the family enjoyed during the marriage, and has found herself falling into debt. She also says she needs a car and looks to Mr Cutforth to meet these needs.

11. Mrs Cutforth's income would, of course, increase by £173 per month were child maintenance increased by £20 per child per week. In addition, there remains the question of her earning capacity, cited by Mr Cutforth under Part 4 of his Form E. At present she is working part-time as a receptionist at a small local toy factory but as she herself says, the pay is inadequate to meet her needs. Mrs Cutforth has a good degree in languages and prior to her marriage had a well-paid job with good career prospects. Not surprisingly, Mr Cutforth is therefore claiming that she is not exploiting her full earning potential, and this is likely to be an important issue in the case. Could Instructing Solicitors get from Mrs Cutforth further information on this point. What are her qualifications? What jobs might be open to her as an interpreter? How much do such jobs pay? Could she take a course to up-date her skills or increase her job prospects?

12. The court will only expect Mrs Cutforth to act reasonably. It may, for example, be the case that while the children are young she has to work locally and could not take on work as an interpreter because this involves long hours and a substantial amount of travel. Clearly, if Mrs Cutforth can only earn what she earns now, this will support her claim for mainten-ance for herself. On the other hand, if she could earn more, the court will take this into account in any decision it might make. In that case, it would be more realistic to argue that she should get the house as she will then be in a position to meet the outgoings on it. What are Mrs Cutforth's views on this?

13. Certainly it would seem that to cover the existing mortgage and other out-goings on the house would cost at least £1,000 per month. Increased child maintenance would obviously assist but even taking that into account (and query the boarding school factor) Mrs Cutforth would, on present figures, need at least an additional £110 per month to make ends meet were she to get the house outright.

14. There is also the added complication of Mr Redmond. Mr Cutforth claims that Mrs Cutforth's relationship with Mr Redmond should be taken into account in determining her ancillary relief application. It seems that while Mrs Cutforth has formed a relationship with

Mr Redmond it does not have the hallmarks of permanent co-habitation. Mrs Cutforth says that he stays the night occasionally and pays for occasional meals and family entertainment, but makes no direct contribution to the running of the household. She is non-committal about the future of the relationship. On this basis, it would seem that the relationship with Mr Redmond is not relevant to the outcome of Mrs Cutforth's application. If, on the other hand, the overnight stays were to become a regular event, they would become cogent evidence of cohabitation and it would be taken for granted that Mr Redwood contributes to the expenses of the household in which he lives. Mrs Cutforth should confirm that no such contributions are being made (or intended). It might reassure Mr Cutforth (who felt strongly enough to cite Mr Redmond as a party to the divorce) to know that any agreement between him and Mrs Cutforth could be upset were the situation to have been shown to be otherwise. Instructing Solicitors will no doubt bear this in mind and advise Mrs Cutforth of the effects of remarriage should this be relevant.

15.   Mr Cutforth says he has a monthly income of about £2,000 to meet current expenses of about £1,520. His expenses would obviously increase with larger child maintenance payments. They would also be apt to increase if he purchases a property for himself to live in, although for these purposes he should be able to make use of some or all of the payments he makes now in respect of the matrimonial home.

16.   It would seem that in addition to other fringe benefits from his employment, Mr Cutforth has earned various bonuses over the years. It seems likely that these might continue and details should be sought. As to the loan opportunities available to Mr Cutforth referred to by Mrs Cutforth, there is some doubt as to whether Mr Cutforth could qualify because he may leave this employment in the next couple of years.

17.   As to capital resources, although the former matrimonial home is registered in Mr Cutforth's sole name, Mrs Cutforth undoubtedly has an equitable interest in it. She apparently put £10,000 towards adding a conservatory (although Mr Cutforth describes this contribution somewhat less generously), but in any event may be taken to be up to 50% entitled if, as seems likely, her contributions to the family over the years assisted Mr Cutforth in making the mortgage repayments. It was apparently agreed, after all, that she gave up a promising career to look after the children. Until I have the information on the value of the property, however, it is impossible to put an accurate value on the parties' existing share in what appears to be the major matrimonial asset.

18.   In addition, Mrs Cutforth has £10,000 in savings and £15,000 worth of furniture which she inherited from her parents. As to the value of Jactrad Ltd, there is a dispute between the parties. According to Mr Cutforth, this is a company of few assets but this needs to be clarified. Mr Cutforth's Form E indicates that the accounts of the business will follow. If they do not, they should be sought at the First Appointment. If the company turns out to be of value, then clearly this will improve Mrs Cutforth's prospects as regards her capital claims. There is, perhaps, a curious lack of disclosure by Mr Cutforth of any other capital assets — does this accord with Mrs Cutforth's memory?

19.   I have very little detail on Mr Cutforth's housing needs. At present he lives in modest rented accommodation, but the court will want if possible to leave him with sufficient resources to buy suitable accommodation. This would require him to have enough capital for a deposit and sufficient income for mortgage repayments. He will need a property suitable for having the children for overnight stays (i.e., at least two bedrooms). Costs of such properties need to be investigated. If he could borrow money on favourable terms from his employer, then this would be relevant to his purchasing ability, as would his being relieved of mortgage payments on the former matrimonial home. Details of the loan scheme should be requested.

Other factors

20.   Although the marriage was not especially long, the court will undoubtedly recognise that Mrs Cutforth has made, and will continue to make, substantial contributions to the family in assuming the primary care of the children. There is also a clear disparity in income and earning capacity between the parties — Mrs Cutforth has been economically handicapped by her withdrawal from the labour market for some ten years. Mr Cutforth suggests that his wife was less than energetic in helping to build up Jactrad Ltd, which he says was

intended as a family enterprise. These allegations strike me as too vague to amount to conduct that would be relevant to Mrs Cutforth's application for financial provision, but it would be useful to have her reaction to them. The standard of living enjoyed during the marriage seems to have been a comfortable one — usually divorce requires both sides to make adjustments in this regard and the court will be alert to the need to ensure the financial burdens are shared as equally as possible. Given the parties' ages and the length of marriage, I doubt that the Court would ascribe much value to loss of pension rights in this case, but a degree of setting off may well take place. 'Pension sharing', however, is now an option.

21.   Having said all of that, the outcome of this case depends very much on what we find out about the value of the family's capital assets and the costs of alternative housing. The court would be very slow to deprive Mr Cutforth of all of his interest in the matrimonial home, unless he is able to raise or has access to other capital for housing purposes. Nor would it, in my view, give Mrs Cutforth the house were she unable to meet the outgoings herself: an outright transfer would be part of a clean break package. The property has a relatively small mortgage and if acquiring it is Mrs Cutforth's highest priority, then she should look carefully at the opportunities for exploiting her earning potential. She may not need that much more to meet the outgoings. She must also be clear that a clean break means forgoing any future financial claim (for herself) on Mr Cutforth.

22.   If Mrs Cutforth needs time to adjust to the change, then it may be possible to argue that she should be paid maintenance for two to three years while she gets back on her feet financially. Given that she is earning about £6,000, and Mr Cutforth is earning about £35,000, the one-third guideline would produce a figure in the region of £7,000 p.a. by way of periodical payments. This outcome would further jeopardise her claim to the whole house because it would tie up Mr Cutforth's income. Unless he has capital that he has not disclosed, such a deferred clean break package would, in my view, almost ensure that Mr Cutforth keeps a share in the former matrimonial home. This could take the form of the proceeds of an immediate sale or a charge-back or settlement. The two latter would mean that Mrs Cutforth could stay in the property, but would have less capital from it when it was sold after the children were grown. Given Mrs Cutforth's age and educational qualifications, and the fact that the court is directed by statute to achieve a clean break wherever possible, spousal maintenance for an indefinite period is not a realistic option. The court will take the view, and it is no doubt the case, that the sooner the parties achieve a financial clean break, the better.

23.   Whether and to what extent the lump sum payment will form part of the settlement package will again depend on the figures. On the face of it, Mrs Cutforth's need to have a car and pay her credit card bill is reasonable, as both partly relate to the care of the children. Indeed, if having a car would facilitate her realising her earning potential, this would give a boost to her claim. However, unless there is a source of capital from which Mr Cutforth could make such a payment, the court may decide that Mrs Cutforth should look to her own capital to meet some, if not all of these needs.

24.   Once the information I have identified is to hand, a clearer picture of the realistic possibilities will emerge. In summary, this includes:

- An agreed valuation of the matrimonial home.

- Prices of three and four bedroom properties in the area.

- More precise information on the nature and value of Jactrad Ltd.

- More precise information on Mr Cutforth's resources and expenditure.

- Confirmation of the projected CSA assessment.

- Mr Cutforth's views about meeting a CSA figure.

- Who will pay Damian's boarding school fees?

- Details of Mrs Cutforth's qualifications and employment prospects.

- Mrs Cutforth's views on her options.

In the meantime, given that Mrs Cutforth is falling into debt, the claim for maintenance pending suit should be pursued. The court should be notified that a longer appointment may be necessary for this purpose. The courts will award a reasonable amount to tide her over for the time being, but will not pre-judge the outcome of the main claim for financial provision. This should assist her to meet her immediate needs.

25. As soon as it is feasible, attempts should again be made to narrow the issues and agree an outcome with the other side. Neither party is publicly funded and, as always, it is important that costs should not be built-up unnecessarily. To the extent that agreement has not been reached, the First Appointment should help serve this purpose. At that time, a written estimate of costs should be provided to the court.

301 Gray's Inn Place Chambers

Sue D. Nym

11 February 2002

5.5.4.7 Negotiated settlements and Calderbank offers

It is important to try to negotiate agreed terms for financial provision. Leaving aside the impetus of the new rules, an agreed settlement offers many advantages for the spouses:

(a) Terms can be finely adjusted to the needs of a particular case.

(b) An agreement can include terms which a judge might not have power to order.

(c) An agreement gives the client more control over the outcome than going to court, subject to the wide powers of the judge or District Judge.

(d) Spouses are more likely to abide by an order they have agreed to.

(e) An agreed solution can save costs.

For more comment on the process and skills of negotiating a settlement, see the *Negotiation Manual*.

A move to try to negotiate an agreement is most likely to be formally made when sufficiently detailed information is available (e.g., after Form E's have been filed), although a suggestion that a settlement is desirable may be made at any stage (note the pre-action protocol). It is important to have a sufficiently thorough knowledge of the facts and figures of the case before trying to reach a settlement, as once the settlement is agreed an appeal or an application for further provision may be impossible. In preparing for a negotiation, you must have a *clear view* of what the client wants, and the parameters of the *most* and the *least* that the client might reasonably get and be prepared to accept.

A written offer of a settlement can be made at any time in order to try and save costs (*Calderbank* v *Calderbank* [1976] Fam 93) and see r. 2.69. Such a written offer is made by letter and is called a 'Calderbank offer'. It is quite an art to try to judge an offer that would interest the other side but which is not too generous. The letter should be headed without prejudice, but should reserve the right to refer to it at trial as regards the cost order if the other side does not get more than is offered. Because of the possible costs implications, Calderbank offers must be considered carefully.

Because the negotiated settlement will usually end all the client's claims it cannot be stressed too strongly that the terms must be clear and comprehensive. The terms must also be clearly explained to the client. On the operation of an offer, see *Butcher* v *Wolfe and Wolfe* [1999] 1 FLR 334.

5.5.4.8 Stage three: The final hearing

For cases which do not settle, the finale comes in the final hearing.

Preparation

Certain matters must be given particular attention when preparing for the hearing.

(a) *Bundles.* A bundle of documents relevant to both parties' cases should be prepared by the applicant for the hearing and properly indexed and paginated: *Practice Direction (Family Proceedings: Court Bundles)* [2000] 1 FLR 563.

The trial bundles must now be divided into separate sections, namely:

(i) applications and orders,

(ii) statements and affidavits,

(iii) experts and other reports,

(iv) other documents.

Bearing in mind that each case is different, the sorts of documents which might typically be relevant and so be included in the bundle would be:

- pay slips;

- relevant P60 forms;

- business accounts (if either party is self-employed or a director of a small company);

- bank and building society statements (going back over an informative but not excessive period);

- investment details;

- pension details;

- insurance policy details;

- credit card statements (going back over an informative but not excessive period);

- property valuations;

- mortgage redemption figure.

At the beginning of the bundle should be:

(i) a one-page summary of the background to the case,

(ii) statement of issues,

(iii) summary of orders/directions sought by each party,

(iv)   a chronology (if a final hearing or the summary of background in insufficient),

(v)   skeleton arguments as appropriate (see *Drafting Manual*, **Chapter 24**.)

The applicant should seek to agree the bundle with the respondent. The bundle should be lodged at least two clear days before the relevant hearing.

(b)   *The issues in dispute.* Continue to review the evidence carefully so that you do not waste time on matters which are agreed, but are able to deal effectively with areas in dispute. Decide in advance how relevant facts will be proved. Consider what evidence may be needed to support relevant allegations, e.g., regarding costs of alternative accommodation (estate agents), availability of (re)mortgage lender, availability of council housing (local authority). Plan any cross-examination so that it will be focussed and efficient. You must also have a clear and accurate view of the range of possible outcomes. A Statement of Issues and Open Statements will have been filed. Calderbank offers may have been made (but should not be revealed to the court until costs are considered!). Ancillary relief cases often settle at the door of the court and so right up to the very last minute you need to be able to recognise and make acceptable offers of compromise.

(c)   *Calderbank offers.* If you have not made a Calderbank offer, consider whether you ought to do so. You must be clear about the potential costs implications of making and/or not accepting a Calderbank offer.

(d)   *Tax considerations.* It is important to calculate in advance (so far as this is possible) the likely tax implications for all parties of any order sought. In some courts, District Judges require such calculations to be agreed between the parties.

(e)   *Benefit considerations.* Similarly, if any party is in receipt of any State benefits, it is important to consider in advance the effect that any order may have on entitlement or to the amount of such benefit.

(f)   *Child Support Agency.* If there are children in respect of whom a CSA assessment will or may be made, an estimate of the level of the amount of such payment ought to be made and included in the bundle.

(g)   *Schedules.* A schedule summarising your client's income/assets and outgoings/liabilities as at the date of the hearing should be prepared — for your use as well as the courts (see **5.5.2**). Not only will it concentrate your own mind on the realistic possibilities, it will help the District Judge/judge to have this information available 'at a glance'.

(h)   *Costs estimates.* Each party should prepare an estimate of costs, including an estimate of costs to date, an estimate of the anticipated costs of the hearing and any anticipated consequential costs such as costs of sale, purchase or re-mortgage of any property (see *Practice Direction (Family Division: Costs)* [1988] 2 All ER 63 and FPR 1991, r. 2.61F(1) (as amended)). This information could affect the final outcome as well as the order for costs at the end of the day. It is particularly important in publicly-funded cases, where the effect of the statutory charge must be borne in mind at all times (see **5.5.6**).

The hearing
The hearing usually takes place before a District Judge (except in very complex cases when it may be heard by a judge). Even if the parties have agreed terms for provision, these should be referred to the District Judge for the court's approval, with sufficient information as to the resources of the parties. Hearings traditionally take place in private, although this may be challenged under the European Convention on Human Rights.

It is usual for the parties to attend the hearing to give oral evidence, as the other side will wish to cross-examine them. Others may also be asked to attend to give evidence, for example, expert valuers if a valuation is not agreed. The basic evidence of the parties' means will be contained in Form E, but the District Judge or judge has a discretion over the evidence received.

Some District Judges set their own procedural agendas (e.g., by inviting discussion on a provisional view he or she has taken on the papers), but many require proceedings to run as follows:

Counsel for the applicant (whether this is the petitioner or respondent to the divorce proceedings) will, as a general rule, open. Where there are cross applications, the convention is that the first in time proceeds first, but if logic or convenience suggests otherwise, a different order may be adopted by agreement and with the leave of the court. The party opening has the advantage of the first and last word.

The applicant's opening
Ensure that the District Judge has all relevant documents, including the chronology, any schedules and, in more complex cases, a skeleton opening.

In the opening, you should:

- Introduce yourself and the other advocates, indicating who is appearing on behalf of whom.

- Outline briefly the nature of the application, referring to any relevant dates and application forms.

- Give a brief outline of the background to the case (i.e., names and ages of parties, date of marriage, names and dates of birth of children etc.) referring to any chronology which has been filed. This puts the application into context, but should not be over long. In particular, remember that marital conduct (or misconduct!) is usually not relevant to applications for financial provision and so should not be emphasised. Any attempt to make capital out of the behaviour of the other party (unless it is relevant) is likely to backfire.

- Set out the parties' financial position, using your schedule. Refer as necessary to any relevant documents in the agreed bundle (e.g., revaluation of matrimonial home).

- Summarise the evidence you intend to call, making reference to the more important paragraphs in the written evidence, reports etc. Check, as you go along, that the District Judge has all of the documents to which reference will be made.

- Indicate whether agreement has been reached on any issue.

- Tell the District Judge what order your client is seeking and why, indicating briefly the factors under **MCA 1973, s. 25**, on which you rely. For example, the children reside with the applicant, they need to be housed and, you are resisting sale of the former matrimonial home because the respondent is adequately housed. And whilst the respondent's share in the equity will be tied by way of a charge, this is justified because of the contributions the applicant made, and will continue to make, to the welfare of the family and her reduced earning capacity. If appropriate, outline any points of law, making brief references to any skeleton argument and/or authorities to be cited.

- Lastly, give a costs estimate of each of the parties.

Ensure that the District Judge has had or is given the opportunity to read the statements, reports etc. Even if the District Judge has read the file before you open your case, you should still summarise the main issues and deal with the matters above. However, do so *briefly* — be as concise and to the point as possible. In particular, be receptive to any hints the District Judge gives you that he or she has understood the point being made (and would like you to move on to the next one).

At the end of the opening (and once the District Judge has read the file) indicate that, unless the court wishes to hear further on any preliminary matter, you propose to proceed to the evidence.

The applicant's evidence

As a general proposition, Form E and other disclosed documents will contain all the relevant information. It will not normally be necessary (or desirable) to read or repeat this wholesale to the court. Keep the oral evidence succinct and to the point.

The evidence of the applicant will usually be tendered first but other witnesses may be taken first, for convenience sake.

Where the witness has sworn a statement and is then called upon to give oral evidence, this must be given on oath or affirmation. Get the witness to state his or her name and address and confirm that the contents of the relevant statement were correct at the time of swearing. Examination-in-chief is now limited to:

- updating the witness's evidence, if there has been a change in circumstances;

- allowing the witness to expand on issues in dispute — for example, why the applicant can only work part-time when the other party says he can work full-time; or why the alternative properties suggested by the respondent are not suitable (a good tip, in this context, is to advise the client to go and look at the properties which have been put forward by the other side); and

- allowing the applicant to say what order is being sought from the court and how that order would meet his needs.

Cross-examination will then follow. Keep it polite and purposeful. Discursive or discourteous cross-examination is counter-productive and should be avoided. Common areas of cross-examination of a party include: questions on bank statements; questions on lifestyle and expenditure; questions on rehousing; questions on co-habitees and their contributions to the household.

Any re-examination should be kept very brief. Remember only to use re-examination to clarify matters arising out of the cross-examination.

After cross-examination and (if appropriate) re-examination of the applicant, each succeeding witness will be called and dealt with in the same way. In the unlikely event that a witness is called to give oral evidence without first having sworn a statement, then all of that witness's evidence will have to be brought out in examination-in-chief and tested in cross-examination in accordance with general principles.

After all of the evidence for the applicant has been called, indicate to the court that the applicant's case is closed.

The respondent's case

As with any conventional civil case, the respondent is not entitled, as of right, to an opening speech. Otherwise, the respondent's case should be presented in the same way as the applicant's case.

Closing speeches

It is usual for the applicant who opened the hearing to make the final speech, preceded by the other party. However, the court has a wide discretion as to the order of speeches and the District Judge/judge may determine, or the parties (with the court's permission) may agree, a different order.

Your closing speech should, in short, attempt to persuade the court to make the order your client seeks. This should be done by reference to the relevant *facts* as disclosed by the evidence, and in particular to those factors under **MCA 1973, s. 25**, which support your case. Be practical and realistic. Demonstrate, by use of the relevant figures, how the order would work *in practice* (from both the applicant and respondent's perspective). It is rarely relevant what happened in some other case, but any pertinent law should be cited. Use common sense and keep your closing speech focussed.

Counsel should not, of course, go over ground that was covered in an opening speech. Do not be tempted to regurgitate all of the evidence the District Judge has just heard — simply highlight the important points. If you have omitted, or not had the opportunity to give an up-to-date costs estimate, do so in your closing speech.

Costs

Once judgment has been given, there will follow argument on costs. Refer to any Calderbank correspondence. Remember to ask for a detailed assessment of costs and also, if necessary, for a declaration pursuant to the Community Legal Service (Financial) Regulations 2000, reg. 52, which allows postponement of the legal aid charge against a property if applicable (see **5.5.6**). You will also need to ask for a certificate for counsel.

Court order

Having made his decision, it is possible that the District Judge will ask the parties to draw up the terms of the order to be referred back to the judge or District Judge for approval. If appropriate, the court may refer the order for financial provision to conveyancing counsel, if the order involves complexities in securing payments or in a property adjustment order (MCA 1973, s. 30). This is very rare.

5.5.5 COSTS

Keeping track of and controlling the costs of securing a financial provision order is very much part of the ethos of the new procedure. Parties are kept informed about the costs of the litigation as the case progresses while the overriding objective and active case management means that costs are kept proportionate. After all, whichever spouse pays the costs, the amount will effectively reduce the total available family resources.

The award of costs at the end of the case is at the discretion of the judge or District Judge. Although costs may follow the event (subject to an appropriate Calderbank offer), in family cases the court has an especially wide discretion where the assets are limited, or where one or other party is publicly funded, or where it is impracticable to make an order for costs. It may simply be too difficult to say who 'won'! The most common order is no order as to costs (i.e., each party bears his or her own costs).

The rules attempt to preserve the basic *Calderbank* principle (the family equivalent of a Part 36 payment into court) with refinements aimed at rewarding parties who win more than both they and their opponent offered, as well as punishing those who did not accept acceptable offers. The complexity of these rules, which are not without their problems and detractors, is beyond the scope of this Manual, but a useful résumé may be found in Mostyn and Nicholson's *Guide to the New Rules*.

Where there is a consent order, the payment of costs should also be agreed.

Note the possibility that a lawyer may be liable for a wasted costs order (*C* v *C (Wasted Costs Order)* [1994] 2 FLR 34 and *Ridehaugh* v *Horsefield* [1994] 2 FLR 194).

5.5.6 PUBLIC FUNDING

One or both of the spouses may have the assistance of public funding. Although being publicly funded is prima facie an advantage to the client, potential problems regarding the statutory charge must be kept in mind, and explained to the client (see *Singer* v

Sharegin [1984] FLR 114). This arises under Access to Justice Act 1999, s. 10(7), imposing a first charge in respect of the costs of the action on any property 'recovered or preserved' in the proceedings. The charge can attach to any property that is in issue in the proceedings, not just property which changes hands (*Hanlon* v *Law Society* [1981] AC 124). The charge can arise even if the claim for provision is settled (*Curling* v *Law Society* [1985] 1 WLR 470).

The problems of the charge may be seen whenever a capital lump sum is recovered, as the charge can then be put into effect immediately, even if the lump sum is awarded in lieu of continuing maintenance (*Stewart* v *Law Society* [1987] 1 FLR 223). The same could happen if the lump sum were awarded for the purchase of a house (*Simpson* v *Law Society* [1987] AC 861), but it is now provided that if a lump sum is specifically ordered for the purchase of a house, the charge (registered against the property) can be postponed until that house is sold. If a house is sold, costs can be enforced from the proceeds (*Chaggar* v *Chaggar* [1996] 1 FLR 450).

In many cases the major asset is the matrimonial home, which may need to be preserved as a home for a spouse and for children. In appreciation of this, where the matrimonial home or an interest in it is transferred on divorce, the statutory charge can be postponed until the home is sold. It is also possible for the charge to be transferred from one house to another if the spouse moves. This is clearly an advantage, but where a charge is postponed, interest will now accrue on the charge.

There are various ways of keeping the potential effects of a charge to a minimum:

(a) The first £2,500 of property is exempt from the charge (Community Legal Service (Financial) Regulations 2000, reg. 44).

(b) All reasonable efforts (by the parties and the courts) should be made to keep costs down as the case progresses.

(c) Efforts should be made to reach a reasonable settlement rather than pursue the matter to trial and build up costs.

(d) If your client is publicly funded, try to get an order or agreement that the other side will pay the costs, if they can afford to do so. Ask for this after the hearing if appropriate.

(e) Orders for periodical payments to a spouse will not be caught by the charge, nor will any provision ordered for children.

(f) Try to keep the property that is **in issue** in a case to the minimum.

(g) If there will inevitably be a charge, try to ensure that it attaches to a home and can therefore be postponed, though note that this option is not so attractive now that interest is payable on the charge.

Clearly the effects of any charge must be taken into account in agreeing provision. The approach taken by the courts is not entirely clear. It has been said that a judge should take the effects of a charge into account when ordering provision (*Simmons* v *Simmons* [1984] Fam 17). However, it has more recently been suggested that a judge should not do so (*Collins* v *Collins* [1987] 1 FLR 226).

Note also that the principles and provisions relating to possible costs orders against funded parties and against the Community Legal Service Fund itself apply to family law cases where relevant.

5.5.7   **TACTICS**

Tactics in the negative sense (e.g., delaying tactics) have been largely eliminated by the new rules. But there are still lots of positive tactical decisions to be made, from how things are worded to offers put and concessions made in negotiations.

Be aware of other factors that may be tied in with a financial provision application. For example, one spouse may be prepared to consent to a divorce under MCA 1973, s. 1(2)(d) (that is, two years' separation and consent) if the other is prepared to make some financial concession. As a different example, a dispute over the custody of children may be tied in with an application for financial provision where the spouse who gets custody is likely to have a better claim to stay in the matrimonial home.

An understanding of the relationship between the spouses can also help you in doing the best for the client. Emotional strain can cloud the judgment of some divorcing couples, but others will be able to behave reasonably to each other, and will wish to achieve a fair solution. Few couples want to see their children suffer unnecessarily. The relationship between the parties may be critical to getting information and in reaching a solution.

As so many cases result in agreed orders, effective negotiation skills are clearly important. Even if a consensual outcome is likely, there are still decisions to be made as to which side should make the first offer, what precisely they should offer, and when.

5.6 Orders and Consent Orders

5.6.1 ORDERS

The order for provision will be made by the judge or District Judge, or by the magistrates as appropriate. The order should be sufficiently detailed to provide not only for the amount to be paid, but when payments are to start, at what intervals maintenance is to be paid etc.

The importance of reaching a consensual order has been strongly underlined in the changes to the procedure for seeking financial provision. The overriding objective in the FPR 1991 (as amended) r. 2.51B provides that active case management should help the parties to settle the whole or part of the case and encourage the parties to use mediation where appropriate. For the FDR appointment, r. 2.61E provides that details of all offers and responses should be filed, and that at the appointment parties should use their best endeavours to reach agreement on all matters in issue, with the express possibility of a consent order being made at the end of the hearing. Rule 2.69 has been changed to make it clear that a party who does not accept a reasonable offer is at risk as to costs.

To increase the emphasis on settlement still further, Form E requires that from the start both parties provide reasonably detailed information and set out the orders they are seeking. Rule 2.69E provides for updated open proposals shortly before the final hearing:

> *(1) Not less than 14 days before the date fixed for the final hearing of an application for ancillary relief, the applicant must (unless the court directs otherwise) file with the court and serve on the respondent an open statement which sets out concise details, including the amounts involved, of the orders which he proposes to ask the court to make.*
> *(2) Not more than 7 days after the service of a statement under paragraph (1), the respondent must file with the court and serve on the applicant an open statement which sets out concise details, including the amounts involved, of the orders which he proposes to ask the court to make.*

5.6.2 POWERS TO MAKE CONSENT ORDERS

The judge or District Judge hearing an application for financial provision on divorce has an inherent power to make an order in terms suggested by the parties.

The new procedure makes it possible for a consent order to be made at a first hearing in a straightforward case, and does all it can to encourage a consent order by the end of the FDR appointment through the clarification of issues and offers.

Note that a consent order can only be made after a decree nisi (*Pounds* v *Pounds* [1994] 1 FLR 775), and that orders relating to capital can only became effective after decree absolute. This may need to be taken into account if drafting at an early stage.

5.6.3 THE ROLE OF THE CONSENT ORDER

Although negotiations for financial relief are common, a settlement must never be seen as an easy way out. The settlement should be based on full information just as much as a court order would be.

It is vital that the lawyer and the client keep at the front of their minds that, save in exceptional circumstances, it will form a final settlement of all claims. Any application for variation or further provision, or any appeal will normally not be possible. In *H* v *B* [1987] 1 WLR 113 it was held that once a spouse has agreed to a consent order, he or she cannot seek further provision. There is a duty to make full disclosure in carrying out negotiations for a consent order, or the order may be undermined (*Livesey* v *Jenkins* [1985] AC 424).

The terms of a consent order must be clearly explained to the client. Although an agreement may have advantages, there should be no undue pressure on a client to accept terms, particularly bearing in mind that the spouse may be very emotional at the time of a divorce (*Tommey* v *Tommey* [1983] Fam 15). As always, you must act within the client's instructions in negotiating. Note the exceptional case of *Dutfield* v *Gilbert H. Stephens & Sons* [1988] Fam Law 473, where a wife sought a quick divorce settlement but later sued her solicitors for not thoroughly investigating her husband's assets. It was held that she failed as her solicitors had acted within her instructions. Note that it is no defence to a claim for negligence against a lawyer that a court has approved a consent order (*B* v *Miller & Co.* [1996] 2 FLR 23).

5.6.4 DRAFTING A CONSENT ORDER

The draft consent order must be clear, comprehensive and accurate (*Dinch* v *Dinch* [1987] 1 WLR 252). Judges have frequently criticised poor drafting in this area, as in the case of *Dinch* itself, in which Lord Oliver of Aylmerton said:

> The appeal is yet another example of the unhappy results flowing from the failure to which I ventured to draw attention in *Sandford* v *Sandford* [1986] 1 FLR 412 to take sufficient care in the drafting of consent orders in matrimonial proceedings to define with precision exactly what the parties were intending to do in relation to the disposal of the petitioner's claims for ancillary relief so as to avoid any future misunderstanding as to whether those claims, or any of them, were or were not to be kept alive. The hardship and injustice that such failure inevitably causes, particularly in cases where one or both parties are legally aided and the only substantial asset consists of the family home, are so glaring in the instant case that I feel impelled once again to stress in the most emphatic terms that it is in all cases the imperative professional duty of those invested with the task of advising the parties to these unfortunate disputes to consider with due care the impact which any terms that they agree on behalf of the clients have and are intended to have upon any outstanding application for ancillary relief and to ensure that such appropriate provision is inserted in any consent order made as will leave no room for any future doubt or misunderstanding or saddle the parties with the wasteful burden of wholly unnecessary costs. It is, of course, also the duty of any court called upon to make such a consent order to consider for itself, before the order is drawn up and entered, the jurisdiction which it is being called upon to exercise and to make clear what claims for ancillary relief are being finally disposed of. I would, however, like to emphasise that the primary duty in this regard must lie upon those concerned with the negotiation and drafting of the terms of the order and that any failure to fulfil such duty occurring hereafter cannot be excused simply by reference to some inadvertent lack of vigilance on the part of the court or its officers in passing the order in a form which the parties have approved.

The vital importance of absolute accuracy in drafting is illustrated by *Richardson* v *Richardson* [1994] 1 FLR 286. It was recorded in the consent order that maintenance for a wife should continue at the rate of £8,000 for three years. Shortly before the end of the three-year period, the wife applied to increase the amount payable and to extend the period of the order. It was held that this could be done as nothing in the wording of the consent order prevented this. Precise wording may be vital for many purposes, e.g., possible tax relief (*Billingham* v *John* [1998] Fam Law 175). See also *B* v *B (Consent Order: Variation)* [1995] FLR 9, *L* v *L (Lump Sum: Interest)* [1994] 2 FLR 324 and *Richardson* v *Richardson (No. 2)* [1997] Fam Law 14.

Once terms are agreed, the draft order may be prepared by lawyers for both sides acting together, or may be prepared by the lawyer for one side and then sent to the other for amendment and approval.

The draft must follow the formal structure of a court order, illustrated in the example.

It is important to note that in addition to including orders, the order can include undertakings. It is important to decide which of the agreed terms can and should be orders and which could usefully be added as undertakings. Each item agreed should be set out in a separate paragraph. The possible problems of failing to draft in sufficient detail were illustrated in *Rooker* v *Rooker* [1988] 1 FLR 219, where there was a consent order that the home be sold, but the husband failed to sell for two years. It was held that the wife could get no compensation for this delay, and it would have been better if the original order had been drafted to protect her.

Adequate flexibility is also important. In *Masefield* v *Alexander* [1995] 1 FLR 100 it was only on appeal that a husband escaped difficulties brought about by a strict time limit in the order, and in *N* v *N (Valuation: Charge-Back Order)* [1996] 1 FLR 361 the husband found that he could not escape problems arising from a specific valuation clause.

Everything that is agreed by the parties should normally be included as an order or undertaking. Although it might be argued that an agreed term could be enforced even if it is not in the order, any omission may lead to real difficulties in enforcement (see *Edgar* v *Edgar* [1980] 1 WLR 1410 and *Brown* v *Brown* [1980] 1 FLR 322).

5.6.5 ORDERS

The court can only order those things which it has the power to order (MCA 1973, ss. 23 and 24).

As a basic checklist for what might be ordered:

(a) Maintenance for a spouse. How much? At what intervals (weekly, monthly)? When should payments start? Should payments be for a set period? Should any provision for review be built in? Even if there is no substantial order for maintenance, should a nominal order be included? On potential problems here see *Richardson* v *Richardson (No. 2)* [1997] Fam Law 14 and *Flavell* v *Flavell* [1997] Fam Law 211.

(b) Maintenance for children. Is any order necessary, or will this be dealt with by the Child Support Agency? How much? At what intervals? When should it start? Should it be payable to the child or the custodial parent?

    (i) Lump sum. If a lump sum is to be paid, how much? When? Payable by instalments? Any penalty if it is not paid on time? Interest?

    (ii) Sale of the home. If the home is to be sold, consider providing a time-limit linked with a penalty for delay. How should the proceeds be divided?

    (iii) Settlement of the home. Be very clear about the terms of settlement. When should the home be sold? Should there be any options for time of sale? How should the proceeds be divided? Who should occupy the home?

(iv) Transfer of property. Precisely what is to be transferred? When? Any penalty for failure to comply?

(v) Dismissing claims. Should the court be asked to dismiss any further possible claims by a spouse? It is especially important to consider this where there is to be a clean break. For example, the possibility of claims for maintenance in the future, and the possibility of claims for provision from the estate of the spouse on death may be dismissed.

(vi) Costs. Who should pay? What costs should they pay? The order may need to be detailed or some costs may not be covered (*Wallace* v *Brian Gale & Associates, The Times*, 5 March 1998). It is important to take the new rules on costs fully into account, see 'Ancillary Relief: the New Costs Rules' [2000] Fam Law 326 and 850.

(vii) Liberty to apply. This can be given to allow the parties to return to court if there are any difficulties in enforcing the order.

If orders are required in respect of the children the practice is that they should be separately recorded on the appropriate form. Care is needed if a decision on any application is adjourned (*D* v *D (Lump Sum Order: Adjournment of Application)* [2001] Fam Law 254).

5.6.6 UNDERTAKINGS

Undertakings are not an essential element of a consent order. In a relatively straight-forward case no undertakings may be required. However, the undertaking is an extremely useful and flexible way of adding extra details to an order. The point is that the court can only actually order those things which it has the power to order by statute, which includes the items outlined in **5.6.5**. If the parties wish to agree to further details, such as one party allowing something to be done, or one party making specific payments, this cannot be directly ordered by the court, but may be the subject of an undertaking. For example, in *Milne* v *Milne* [1981] 2 FLR 286 it was held that a party could not be ordered to take out a mortgage or an insurance policy, but these matters could be the subjects of undertakings.

The status of an undertaking must be appreciated. As it is not an order, it cannot be directly enforced as such. It is rather an undertaking given to the judge, and therefore any breach would be a contempt of court, and could be treated as such, for example, by the imposition of a fine or a term of imprisonment. Because of possible enforcement problems, if something could be ordered, it is better that it be the subject of an order rather than an undertaking. On enforcing undertakings, see *Symmons* v *Symmons* [1993] Fam Law 135.

Note that undertakings cannot be used in magistrates' courts as there is no possibility of enforcement through contempt of court.

5.6.7 SAMPLE CONSENT ORDERS

The following sample orders are intended to cover all the most common types of financial provision, and to illustrate possible variations in drafting style. All the samples are loosely related to the facts used in the affidavits and opinion in this chapter, but they are not solely based on those facts so that it is possible to illustrate a variety of scenarios. Note that if child maintenance is being left entirely to a Child Support Agency assessment it does not need to be referred to at all in the order.

Further sample paragraphs are provided at the end of the full sample orders. For further examples, see *Practical Matrimonial Precedents*, a loose-leaf publication (Sweet & Maxwell), and in particular, the supplement 'At Court — Ancillary Relief and Precedents'.

CONSENT ORDER PROVIDING FOR A CLEAN BREAK BASED ON A TRANSFER OF PROPERTY ORDER, AND ORDERING CHILD MAINTENANCE BY CONSENT

IN THE OXFORD COUNTY COURT   01 D   No. 288

BETWEEN   SANDRA ANNE CUTFORTH   Petitioner

and

JAMES ANDREW CUTFORTH   Respondent

and

JUSTIN REDMOND   Party Cited

Upon hearing counsel for the Petitioner and for the Respondent (*if settled in court*)

And upon it being agreed between the parties that the provisions of this order are accepted in full and final settlement of all financial claims made by each against the other for themselves under the Matrimonial Causes Act 1973 and the Married Women's Property Act 1882 as amended

And upon the parties declaring that the provision made in this order fulfils the Respondent's responsibilities to the children of the family (and in consequence it being further agreed that the Petitioner will not apply for the revocation of the order for periodical payments made for the children)

And upon the Petitioner undertaking as from the date of the transfer of property to her referred to below:

(1)   To pay or cause to be paid the mortgage to the Bland Building Society (number 123456) and all other liabilities relating to the property known as 13 Jasmine Close, Oxford, Oxfordshire.

(2)   To use her best endeavours to procure the release of the Respondent from any liability under the mortgage in favour of the Bland Building Society and in any event to indemnify the Respondent against all such liability.

And upon the Respondent undertaking:

(1)   To pay or cause to be paid all payments due under the mortgage and collateral endowment premiums relating to the property up to the date that he transfers his legal and beneficial interest to the Petitioner.

(And subject to the Decree Nisi being made absolute)

By consent it is ordered:

(1)   The Respondent do within 28 days of the date of this order transfer all his legal estate and beneficial interest in the property known as 13 Jasmine Road, Oxford, Oxfordshire to the Petitioner, subject to the existing mortgage in favour of the Bland Building Society but otherwise free from encumbrance.

(2)   The Respondent do within one month of the date of this order pay or cause to be paid to the Petitioner a lump sum of £10,000, the sum to carry interest at the rate of 10% per annum if it is not paid by the due date.

(3) The Respondent do pay periodical payments to the Petitioner for the benefit of the children of the family, Damian John Cutforth and Gemma Jane Cutforth at a rate of £40 per week in respect of each child, the first payments to be made on 1 June 2000, and the payments to last until each child respectively attains the age of 17 years or ceases full-time education (whichever is the later) or until further order.

(4) Upon compliance with paragraphs 1 and 2 of this order and upon compliance by the Respondent with his undertaking, the Petitioner's and the Respondent's claims for financial provision and property adjustment orders do stand dismissed, and it is directed that neither party shall be entitled to apply to the court thereafter for an order under s. 23(1)(a) or (b) of the Matrimonial Causes Act 1973 as amended.

(5) Pursuant to the Inheritance (Provision for Family and Dependants) Act 1975, s. 15, the court considering it just so to order, neither the Petitioner nor the Respondent shall be entitled on the death of the other to apply for an order under s. 2 of that Act.

(6) There be no order as to costs (save assessment of the Petitioner's costs). It is certified for the purposes of the Community Legal Service (Financial) Regulations 2000, reg. 52, that the property at 13 Jasmine Road, Oxford, Oxfordshire has been preserved/recovered for the Petitioner for the use as a home for herself or her dependants.

(7) Liberty to both parties to apply.

Dated etc.

[handwritten marginal note: LSC will put charge on property for when its sold. This accrues interest.]

CONSENT ORDER PROVIDING FOR A CLEAN BREAK BASED ON A SALE OF PROPERTY, AND ORDERING ADDITIONAL CHILD MAINTENANCE

IN THE OXFORD COUNTY COURT	01 D	No. 288

BETWEEN   SANDRA ANNE CUTFORTH   Petitioner

and

JAMES ANDREW CUTFORTH   Respondent

and

JUSTIN REDMOND   Party Cited

Upon hearing Counsel for the Petitioner and for the Respondent

Upon the parties agreeing that the contents of the former matrimonial home are the absolute property of the Petitioner.

And upon the parties further agreeing that the Respondent shall pay the school fees ordered below directly to the headmaster/bursar of the school, and the receipt of that payee shall be sufficient discharge.

Whereas an assessment has been made under the Child Support Act 1991 in respect of the children of the family and the Court is satisfied that additional payments in respect of the children are appropriate, by consent it is ordered:

(1)   The property known as 13 Jasmine Road, Oxford, Oxfordshire be placed on the market for sale forthwith and upon sale the net proceeds of sale be divided between the Petitioner and the Respondent as to two thirds the Petitioner and one third the Respondent. The term net proceeds of sale shall mean the gross sale price less the amount outstanding in respect of the mortgage in favour of Bland Building Society and the legal costs and estate agent charges in respect of sale.

(2)   The Respondent do pay or cause to be paid for the benefit of the children of the family Damian John Cutforth and Gemma Jane Cutforth periodical payments at the rate of £80 per month each, the first payment to be made in the month following the making of this order until they shall each respectively achieve the age of 17 years, or cease full-time education or further order.

(3)   As from   , the Respondent do pay or cause to be paid to the Petitioner for the benefit of Damian John Cutforth until such time as he shall cease secondary education or until further order periodical payments of an amount equivalent to the school fees, including reasonable extras, at the school the child shall from time to time attend by way of three payments on   ,   , and

(4)   Upon compliance by the parties with paragraph 1, all the claims of both the Petitioner and the Respondent against the other for financial provision and property adjustment orders pursuant to the Matrimonial Causes Act 1973 as amended and the Married Women's Property Act 1882 shall stand dismissed, and it is further directed that neither party shall be entitled to make further application in relation to the marriage for an order under s. 23(1)(a) or (b) of the Matrimonial Causes Act 1973.

(5)   Upon compliance by the parties with paragraph 1, it is directed, the Court considering it just to do so, that neither party shall be entitled on the death of the other party to apply for an order for themseleves under s. 2 of the Inheritance (Provision for Family and Dependants) Act 1975 against the estate of the other.

(6)   No order as to costs.

(7)   Liberty to both parties to apply.

Dated etc.

CONSENT ORDER PROVIDING FOR CONTINUING PERIODICAL PAYMENTS TO THE PETITIONER AND MAKING PROVISION FOR WHAT WILL HAPPEN IF THERE IS A LATER APPLICATION TO THE CSA AND THE MATRIMONIAL HOME BEING HELD ON DEFERRED TRUST OF LAND

IN THE OXFORD COUNTY COURT		01 D	No. 288

BETWEEN   SANDRA ANNE CUTFORTH   <u>Petitioner</u>

and

JAMES ANDREW CUTFORTH   <u>Respondent</u>

and

JUSTIN REDMOND   <u>Party Cited</u>

Upon hearing Counsel for the Petitioner and for the Respondent

And upon the Petitioner undertaking to pay or cause to be paid as from the date of this order, all monies which shall become payable in respect of the mortgage of the former matrimonial home known as 13 Jasmine Road, Oxford, Oxfordshire and the building insurance premium, the water rates and the council tax on the property.

Whereas it has been agreed that the provision made in this order fulfils the Respondent's responsibilities to the children Damian John Cutforth and Gemma Jane Cutforth, and in consequence it is also declared:

(1) that the Petitioner will not apply for the revocation of this order for periodical payments for the children

(2) that in the event of an assessment being made under the Child Support Act 1991 in respect of either of the children, the sums referred to in paragraph (1)(b) below shall be reduced pro tanto by any sums payable as child support maintenance in respect of the children

By consent it is ordered:

(1) The Respondent do pay or cause to be paid to the Petitioner from 1 June 2000 periodical payments for the following amounts, payable monthly in advance

(a) for herself during their joint lives or until the Petitioner shall remarry or until further order at the rate of £5,000 per annum

(b) for the benefit of each of the children, at the rate of £2,500 per annum, until such time as they shall respectively attain the age of 17 years, or shall cease full-time education or training (whichever shall be the later) or until further order.

(2) The Respondent do forthwith transfer into the joint names of himself and the Petitioner the property known as 13 Jasmine Road, Oxford, Oxfordshire, to be held by the Petitioner and the Respondent upon trust for themselves as beneficial tenants in common in equal shares, on condition that the property shall not be sold until the earliest of the following events:

(i)   the death of the Petitioner;

(ii)   the remarriage or cohabitation for a period in excess of 6 months of the Petitioner;

(iii)   until the children of the family shall both have attained the age of 18 years or ceased full-time education (whichever is later).

(3)   The Petitioner do forthwith transfer to the Respondent all legal and beneficial interest in the Peugeot 206 car registration number D 123 XYZ

(4)   The Respondent do pay the Petitioner's costs on an indemnity basis, to be taxed if not agreed, including the costs of negotiation.

(5)   Liberty to both parties to apply as to the implementation of this order.

5.6.8   EXAMPLES OF UNDERTAKINGS THAT MAY BE INCLUDED IN A CONSENT ORDER

The following are examples of possible undertakings in a consent order:

(1)   To invest the net proceeds of sale of the property at 7 Acacia Avenue, Brentwood, Essex, in the purchase of a freehold dwelling-house for the sole use and occupation of the Petitioner.

(2)   To permit the Petitioner to reside in the property free of rent during her lifetime until remarriage.

(3)   Not to sell, charge or otherwise dispose of the property without the prior consent of the Petitioner in writing.

(4)   Not to cause, allow or permit the child of the family Ernest Alan to meet or otherwise come into contact with John Smith.

(5)   To attend a one-year full-time course of training in word processing.

(6)   To allow the child of the family Sarah Alice to attend the Dame Alice Ward Preparatory School, Godalming, Surrey between the ages of 7 and 13 years, should she succeed in obtaining a place at the above named school.

(7)   To sign and deliver within 7 days of this order an irrevocable instruction to the trustees of the pension fund to pay to the Respondent a full widow's pension in the event he predecease her, provided at such time she has not remarried.

(8)   To use her best endeavours to secure the release of the Respondent from his covenants under the mortgage account no. 123 with the Blank Building Society secured on 7 Acacia Avenue, Brentwood, Essex and, in any event, to indemnify the Respondent from all liability under it.

5.6.9   ALTERNATIVE ORDERS

The following are examples of possible orders in a consent order:

(1)   The Respondent do pay periodical payments to the Petitioner at the rate of £25 per week for a period of three years commencing 1 April 2000 (and it is directed pursuant to MCA 1973 that the Petitioner shall not be entitled to apply for any extension of the period of three years).

(2)   The Respondent do pay to the Petitioner a lump sum of £30,000 payable by six equal instalments of £5,000 on 1 February and 1 July in each year commencing on 1 February 2000.

(3) The Respondent do forthwith place the property known as 99 Sycamore Drive, Slough on the market for sale at a price to be agreed between the parties or by the court. Upon sale the net proceeds of sale to be divided between the Petitioner and the Respondent in the proportion three fifths to the Respondent and two fifths to the Petitioner.

(4) The Petitioner do transfer to the Respondent all her interest in the property known as 77 Yuppie Towers, Isle of Dogs, London, subject to the mortgage but otherwise free from encumbrances.

(5) The matrimonial home be charged with payment to the husband of 25% of the net proceeds of sale upon voluntary sale or on the death of the Petitioner. [Remember to define net proceeds of sale.]

(6) The Petitioner's claim for a property adjustment order to stand dismissed.

(7) The Respondent shall not on the death of the Petitioner be entitled to apply for an order under section 2 of the Inheritance (Provision for Family and Dependants) Act 1975, the court considering it just so to order.

(8) The Respondent shall pay or cause to be paid periodical payments for the Petitioner and the child of the family to be made in the global sum of £200 per month, payable monthly in advance. For so long as the Respondent is under an obligation to maintain the child the £200 shall be apportioned so that the amount payable in respect of the child is equal to such sum as the Respondent has to pay under any assessment made under the Child Support Act 1991.

5.7 Enforcement of Orders

5.7.1 THE IMPORTANCE OF ENFORCEMENT

The detailed possibilities for enforcing orders must be researched if necessary. These notes merely give a general guide.

The most important point is that many possible enforcement problems can and should be avoided. In a family provision case, any problems with enforcement are often foreseeable, due to the assets involved, the attitude of one or both spouses, or the circumstances of the case. Going back to the court for enforcement will itself cost money and cause stress, so any need to return to court should be avoided if at all possible.

As suggestions for avoiding or alleviating enforcement problems:

(a) If the spouses can agree the details of provision they are more likely to abide by them, so a negotiated settlement should be reached where possible.

(b) The precise effects of an order should be explained to the client to avoid any misunderstanding.

(c) The details of every order must be carefully drafted to avoid ambiguities and omissions that may cause problems.

(d) Some provision for enforcement may be included in an order, for example, by providing a penalty lump sum if something is not done by a set date, or only dismissing a spouse's claims once the other spouse has fulfilled a term (but avoid doing this if it would simply make the order more complex, or be irritating rather than productive).

(e) If there are any options in making provision, consider whether one may be easier to enforce than another.

As an obvious practical point, once an order is made the solicitor should if appropriate check with the client that steps ordered are being taken, and should take action quickly if there is any delay or difficulty. Delay in enforcement may of itself cause problems, if, for example, the capital value of property alters, or arrears of maintenance accumulate and therefore have to be remitted.

Enforcement is primarily a matter of returning to court once there has been some default on an existing obligation, but because of the delays and difficulties this can cause, the powers of the High Court and of the county court when making a maintenance order have been extended by the Maintenance Enforcement Act 1991, s. 1. These courts may now order that payments be made by standing order or some similar method, and may order the payer to open a bank account for this purpose. It is now also possible to make an attachment of earnings order when making the maintenance order rather than waiting for a default in payment.

5.7.2   MODES OF ENFORCEMENT

An appropriate mode of enforcement must be chosen, depending on the type of order breached, and the form of the breach. Procedural points relating to enforcement must be kept in mind, for example, if an order is not made in a magistrates' court it can be enforced there if it is registered there (Maintenance Orders Act 1958).

5.7.2.1   Attachment of earnings
An order can be sought to get maintenance paid directly from an individual's salary to the recipient under the Attachment of Earnings Act 1971. This Act has been amended by the Maintenance Enforcement Act 1991, primarily to allow orders to be made at the same time as a maintenance order is made. This can be useful, but only if the payer is in steady employment.

5.7.2.2   General civil remedies
Many forms of enforcement for civil claims are appropriate in a family case, for example, a charging order, a writ of *fieri facias*, garnishee proceedings or a judgment summons, see the **Civil Litigation Manual, Chapter 38**. See, for example, *Gandolfo* v *Gandolfo* [1981] QB 359. The appropriateness of such proceedings must be properly considered, see, for example, *Clark* v *Clark* [1989] 1 FLR 174 where lawyers were criticised for seeking sequestration where the resulting funds did not cover costs, let alone the sum due.

5.7.2.3   Imprisonment
This is a last resort, which will not generally be available or be used for a simple failure to pay. However, it may be a possibility where a spouse has flouted court orders and is therefore in contempt of court, as in *Lightfoot* v *Lightfoot* [1989] 1 FLR 414.

5.7.2.4   The international element and reciprocal enforcement procedures
If a spouse lives or moves abroad, the possibilities for registering and enforcing an order in the country in question will have to be researched.

5.8   Returning to Court: Appeal and Variation

5.8.1   CONTEXT

A spouse may appeal against an order or, if appropriate, seek a variation or further provision. However, there are limits and difficulties in returning to court which must not be overlooked in considering the original order.

The different possibilities for returning to court should be clearly distinguished and the correct option chosen for each case:

(a)   Returning to the court which made the order. This may be done without commencing new proceedings, but generally only to clarify the terms of the order made, not to make any radical alteration or addition. To allow the parties to return to the court if necessary, 'liberty to apply' may be added to an order.

(b) Appeal. On normal principles, an appeal will lie to challenge an order made if there is cause.

(c) Variation. If there is a later change of circumstances, a party may apply to court to vary the original order.

(d) Additional orders. A further order may be sought in some circumstances. For example, the powers of the court on divorce under MCA 1973, ss. 23 and 24, may be exercised on divorce or at any time thereafter. Note, however, that a court will be slow to add to an existing order without good reason, especially if the existing order was made by consent and was intended to end all claims.

It may be possible to vary or add to an order without actually returning to court. This may be done either if the terms of the original order allow for variation without return to court, or if the parties agree to a variation by consent.

Problems arise particularly in the case of a consent order, where the court will be very slow to allow an appeal or order extra provision where the parties have agreed provision, and in the case of a clean break, where the court will be slow to undermine the clean break by making a further order.

There are in practice a variety of procedural options for the route by which a case can be returned to court for appeal or variation, and a variety of overlapping factors relevant to whether an appeal or variation may be granted. Calls for a more unified procedural approach have increased over recent years (see, for example, the case of *Benson* v *Benson* [1996] 1 FLR 692). For a useful summary, see D. Burrows, 'Appeals and Applications to set Aside' [2000] Fam Law 428.

5.8.2   APPEAL

An appeal might be based on the factors taken into account by the court, the basis chosen for provision, or some detail in the order. An appeal might also be based on some factor undermining the order, such as fraud, mistake, or incomplete disclosure. On the problem of procedure on appeal, see *Benson* v *Benson* [1996] 1 FLR 692.

In the case of a consent order, the possibilities for appeal are very limited. A party who has agreed to an order will rarely be allowed simply to change his or her mind, or the finality of consent orders would be in doubt. To illustrate the problems in appealing from a consent order:

(a) *Simister* v *Simister* [1986] 1 WLR 1463. As a husband had agreed that his wife should get one third of his salary as maintenance he could not appeal against that.

(b) *Barber* v *Barber* [1987] Fam Law 125. As a wife knew of her husband's pension rights when she agreed to provision, she could not appeal to get further provision in respect of those pension rights.

(c) *Cook* v *Cook* [1988] 1 FLR 521. As it was agreed that the wife should get the home, the fact that she was cohabiting with another man did not undermine this agreement. Conversely if a wife agrees to leave on cohabitation, that is enforceable (*Omeilan* v *Omeilan* [1996] 2 FLR 306).

(d) *Cornick* v *Cornick* [1995] 2 FLR 490, *Harris* v *Manahan* [1997] 1 FLR 205. A dramatic change in the value of property, if at all foreseeable, cannot be a basis for an appeal. However, an appeal will be allowed if one party has knowingly misled the other (*Middleton* v *Middleton* [1998] 2 FLR 821).

(e) *Xydhias* v *Xydhias*, *The Times*, 3 January 1999. Once an agreement is made it is enforceable, even if not yet in the form of an order.

An appeal has only been allowed in the case of a consent order where the order has been undermined by a procedural irregularity or by serious misconduct such as fraud or mistake. For example:

(a) *Munks* v *Munks* [1985] FLR 576. It was held that there could be an appeal where the consent order was made before decree nisi as this was a procedural irregularity.

(b) *Redmond* v *Redmond* [1986] 2 FLR 173. A wife was allowed to appeal when she agreed to provision on the basis that her husband would not apply for redundancy, but he later did so apply.

(c) *Campbell* v *Campbell* [1997] FLR 609. The consent order was so poorly drafted as to be contradictory so the case was reopened. See also *Standley* v *Stewkesbury* [1998] 2 FLR 610. The wording of the order was held not to reflect the real agreement.

(d) *Hill* v *Hill* [1998] FLR 198. The original agreement was not comprehensive, so a further application could be made.

5.8.3 VARIATION

It is possible to seek the modification of an order for a lump sum or a property adjustment order, but the court will be slow to vary such orders without good reason (*Carson* v *Carson* [1983] 1 WLR 285). Note that the court has no power to make more than one order for payment of a lump sum or a property adjustment order. It is much more likely that an application to vary will relate to a maintenance order (MCA 1973, s. 31), usually because the means of one of the parties have changed, or the passage of time has eroded the value of the order. A variation may alter the term of payment as well as the amount. An order for one form of provision will rarely be varied to provide a different form of provision, but this may be done, for example, to replace periodical payments with a single lump sum.

In deciding whether a variation should be ordered, the court will consider any material change respecting either party since the order was made. This will often primarily consist of reviewing changes in financial resources, and therefore resources should be fully investigated as they would be before an initial application. The court will also take into account any change in other factors that are relevant to provision. The court might consider, for example, whether one of the spouses is now cohabiting and therefore has extra resources or liabilities.

If there has been a material change then the court will reassess financial provision to decide what is now appropriate, taking into account all the factors it would take into account on an original application.

As with an appeal, it will be difficult for a party to seek a variation of an order to which he or she has consented. It is possible to apply (*Jessel* v *Jessel* [1979] 1 WLR 1148) but the court will be slow to order the variation without good reason. In *T* v *T* [1988] 1 FLR 480 there was a consent order for provision for a wife to last until she married or her husband retired. When her husband did retire it was held that she could not have these terms varied to provide extra provision. If claims for financial provision have been dismissed, it will not be possible to seek a variation to get provision (*De Lasala* v *De Lasala* [1980] AC 546). On a variation linked to a clean break, see *Jones* v *Jones* [2000] Fam Law 607.

Variation may be possible if the welfare of a child is at stake (*N* v *N (Consent order: Variation)* [1993] 2 FLR 868).

Some limited relief may be available in exceptional circumstances. In *Thwaite* v *Thwaite* [1982] Fam 1 it was held that although the consent order could not be varied, the court would refuse to enforce it in favour of a party who had not complied with its terms.

5.8.4   PROFESSIONAL NEGLIGENCE

If other routes fail, the client may feel driven to blame the lawyers for an unsatisfactory divorce settlement. There has been a recent spate of cases in this area, and at the time of writing the position is not entirely clear. One can only say that the lawyer should ensure that a client is fully advised of the terms and implications of any settlement, including any possible drawbacks, and that the client is aware of options and takes informed personal decisions.

In *Kelley* v *Corston* [1998] 1 FLR 986 a barrister advised a client to accept a door of the court settlement, but she then complained that the settlement left her unable to fund the mortgage on her home. It was held that the barrister was immune from proceedings, either because actions at the door of the court were immune in the same way as actions in court, or because the settlement had been approved by the judge. This area of law was further considered in other cases that were consolidated for hearing in the House of Lords with a decision reported as *Hall and Co.* v *Simons* [2000] 2 FLR 545. In summary it is clear that advice given before a hearing will not necessarily be immune from legal action. This makes it more important than ever that clear and accurate advice is given as regards what financial relief may be awarded on divorce, and what might be offered or accepted by way of settlement.

See 'Professional Negligence Claims arising out of Consent Orders in Family Proceedings' [1999] Fam Law 773.

SIX

FINANCIAL PROVISION FOR CHILDREN

6.1   Introduction

These materials do not seek to do more than provide an introduction to the principles in this area. If further research is required for a case a variety of useful and practical books are available, for example *Child Maintenance: The new law* by Roger Bird, Family Law, and the *Child Support Handbook*, by Emma Knights and Simon Cox published by the Child Poverty Action Group.

Although the calculation of child maintenance is now primarily the responsibility of an independent agency it is vital that any lawyer working in the family law field be familiar with how the system works, with the appropriate terminology, and with the continuing role of the court in certain circumstances. This can be an area of some difficulty for practitioners:

- The inter-relation between the powers of the court and of the Child Support Agency (CSA) is not a simple one.

- An application to the CSA cannot be made while the parents live together, and once an application is made it may take some time to process. This means that the practitioner often has to guess at what the maintenance figure will be when advising a client.

- Areas for negotiation for financial provision can be narrowed by the existence of the CSA, because it may be difficult or impossible to exclude the Agency from jurisdiction in a case, and therefore financial provision may have to be structured round what the CSA orders.

- The formula for calculating child maintenance has little flexibility, and may appear to operate harshly in some cases.

It is well known that in practice the CSA has been quite heavily criticised. The Child Support Act 1991 was not perceived to be fair in a number of ways, e.g., in failing to make any allowance for existing financial settlements or for various types of expenses. A number of these original criticisms have been addressed by the introduction of the departures system and by amendments to rules, but other problems remain. The workload of the CSA is high, and its reputation for administrative efficiency and accuracy has not been high. Substantial efforts have been made to address criticisms and improve accuracy, but it remains the case that there are administrative problems, and the date on which the Agency will take on all child support cases has been put off indefinitely. Significant modifications to the system for calculating CSA payments have been made by the Child Support, Pensions and Social Security Act 2000. In particular, a flat rate proportion of income will become payable to children (15% for one child, 20% for two and 25% for three or more children). While this approach is simpler to understand than the former complex formula, it makes few concessions to individual circumstances. At the time of writing it is not clear when the new formula will be in force, but it is suggested that it may be April 2002 for new cases. This legislation also introduced tougher penalties for non-payment, including perhaps not entirely logically, disqualification from driving.

6.2 The Child Support Agency

6.2.1 THE ROLE OF THE CHILD SUPPORT AGENCY

The theory behind the Child Support Act 1991 (which came into force on 5 April 1993) is that parents should take proper financial responsibility for their children. Child support payments should be set at a realistic and reasonably uniform level by the use of a standard formula for calculation. A special agency, the Child Support Agency was set up to gather relevant information, make calculations using a set formula, and to assist in the enforcement of payments due.

Where the CSA has jurisdiction, the courts no longer have power to award maintenance for children. Essentially, the CSA has jurisdiction where there is a 'parent with care', an 'absent parent' and a 'qualifying child' within the United Kingdom. In such circumstances either parent can apply to the CSA for a maintenance assessment to be made, and the parent with care must do so if he or she is in receipt of income support, family credit or disability working allowance. If an application is made, the CSA will send out maintenance assessment forms for both parents to complete. Once the forms are returned, the CSA calculates the maintenance payable as set out below.

A number of cases have made it clear that because the CSA is an independent agency it is outside the court system, and there can for example be no appeal to a court (*Secretary of State for Social Security* v *Shotton* [1996] Fam Law 189).

The role of the CSA is still evolving. It was originally planned that all child maintenance would be dealt with by the CSA by 1997, but for various reasons this date has been put off indefinitely.

6.2.2 THE FORMULA FOR ASSESSING WHAT IS PAYABLE

Once the provisions of the Child Support, Pensions and Social Security Act 2000 come into force the more complex formula that follows will be replaced by a simple proportion of income as follows: for one child 15%, for two children 20% and for three or more 25%. This will be easier to understand, but the lack of flexibility will undoubtedly attract criticism. There will no doubt also continue to be questions about what income should be apportioned. For more detailed comment, see 'Child Support — The New Formula' [2000] Fam Law 820.

As for the formula currently used, in practice a personal computer package is often used to make calculations (for example 'Child's Pay' which is produced and marketed by the Family Law Bar Association or the Child Support Calculation Pack).

The basic stages for making the calculation are:

(a) The 'maintenance requirement' is calculated. This gives the total figure that should ideally be available to maintain the child(ren) in question. It is composed of a set figure for each child plus a 'family premium', depending on the age of each child. Child benefit payable is deducted.

(b) It is then decided how the 'maintenance requirement' should be met. A separate calculation is made for each parent:

(i) The 'assessable income' is calculated. This includes net income from all sources, plus any family credit received.

(ii) From this, 'exempt income' is deducted. This includes a set figure to be deducted for each adult and child living in the payer's house, and a deduction for housing costs.

(iii) The 'maintenance assessment' is then calculated. Essentially the figure from (ii) is deducted from the figure from (i). If only the absent parent has assessable income then one-half of the remaining assessable income to make up the figure of the maintenance requirement must be paid as child maintenance. If the absent parent has assessable income above this amount, up to one-quarter of the remainder must also be paid, up to a ceiling figure which at the time of writing is £8,980. If both parents have assessable income then each must pay an appropriate proportion of the maintenance assessment. If the child lives for part of the year with each parent then the amount payable can be apportioned.

(iv) The maintenance assessment must not reduce a parent's income below the 'protected income' level. Essentially this means that no-one should be reduced below the level of income support. An absent parent will not normally be assessed to pay more than 30 per cent of his or her net income in child maintenance payments.

Payments can be ordered to be paid direct to the parent caring for the child or through the Agency. The Agency has powers to enforce orders. It will play a role in tracing an absent parent, and will then generally use enforcement possibilities, such as attachment of earnings, that are already in force. There is also provision for the review of orders every two years.

Although it is the responsibility of the Child Support Agency to make calculations, a lawyer may need to make a calculation of what the CSA might order, for example in advising a client before the couple have separated what sort of figure might be payable in respect of a child, or in advising the court what the CSA might order as a comparison to what is being sought in varying an existing court order.

Note that changes in benefit levels and changes in regulations can mean that any sample calculation can become out of date quite quickly. If you actually need to make a calculation you should ensure that you are using fully up-to-date information as to the elements of the calculation and the level of benefits. This may be obtained through an up-to-date book, or through an updated version of one of the software packages that is available to assist in the making of calculations.

6.2.3 THE DEPARTURES SYSTEM

The child support legislation has been constantly criticised, for example because it made no allowance for pre-existing settlements (*Crozier* v *Crozier* [1994] 1 FLR 126). For other problems, see *B* v *M* [1994] 1 FLR 342, *Mawson* v *Mawson* [1995] Fam Law 9 and *Smith* v *McInerney* [1995] Fam Law 10. This has resulted in some substantial changes.

The Child Support and Income Support (Amendment) Regulations 1995 provided for an extra 'broad brush' allowance to be available on application by an absent parent who had transferred property worth more than £5,000 to the parent with care before April 1993. It is necessary to provide evidence of the transfer, and only the net value transferred is taken into account. It is assumed that each spouse was entitled to a half share in property, so that only value transferred in excess of the half share will count. Where the value transferred does exceed £5,000 an allowance for exempt income will be made (thus reducing the maintenance assessment) in the following bands:

£ 5,000 — £10,000	£20 per week
£10,000 — £25,000	£40 per week
£25,000 plus	£60 per week

The Child Support Act 1995 provides for a more detailed system of 'departures' where a maintenance agreement or a capital settlement was made before April 1993, where specific costs have not been taken into account in the statutory formula and it seems fair to allow a departure, or where the formula has produced an unrealistically low assessment. It is intended that departures will only be allowed in a small minority of cases, but it remains to be seen if this will be the case in practice. The departures system was piloted in South East England, and came into force generally in December 1996. In outline, once maintenance has been assessed, either parent can apply to the CSA for a departure. The effect of a departure is to allow an additional figure to be taken into account when calculating assessable income. The procedure involves completing a form and supplying appropriate supporting documentation. A departure might be sought in the following circumstances:

- If specific additional costs of the parent are not taken into account by the set formula, e.g., costs arising from disability, or debts arising from the former relationship. For a departure it will be necessary to show that the applicant will face hardship in being unable to support himself or herself and any new family if the formula is applied strictly, and it must be fair to both parents to allow the departure.

- If a parent with care can show that the use of the formula has produced an unrealistically low assessment, for example because the wealth of the absent parent has been misrepresented.

- If a maintenance agreement was made before April 1993, an absent parent can apply for a departure to take into account new commitments made on the basis that maintenance had been finally settled by that agreement, from which it would be unreasonable to expect the absent parent to withdraw, or to take into account relevant debts incurred before April 1993.

- If a capital/property settlement was made before April 1993 the applicant can apply for a departure without showing hardship if he or she can show a reasonable belief that there was a final settlement of liability, that child mainten-ance was at a lower level than it would otherwise have been as a result, and that the 'broad brush' approach is not adequate. It will need to be shown that it is fair to both parents to allow a departure.

6.3   The Powers of the Court

6.3.1   AREAS WHERE THE COURT RETAINS JURISDICTION

The powers of the court to order financial provision for children are unaffected by the Child Support Act 1991, save that the courts cannot exercise their powers where the CSA has jurisdiction (Child Support Act 1991, s. 8). Note that when the provisions of the Child Support, Pensions and Social Security Act 2000 come into force, a court order will only prevent an application to the CSA for a period of one year.

The main circumstances in which a court can still make an order are:

(a) If the CSA does not have jurisdiction, for example because one of the parents is not habitually resident within the UK.

(b) If the child is not the natural or adopted child of both parties to the marriage but is, for example, a step-child.

(c) If the child is aged 17–19 and is not still in full-time education, or if the child is aged over 19 (but there do need to be special circumstances for an order to be made once a child is of age).

(d) If the parent is rich, so that an order *in addition* to the CSA award is appropriate.

(e) If the order is for school fees.

(f) If the child is disabled or blind and therefore has special needs in addition to normal maintenance.

(g) If the order is for a lump sum or property adjustment, rather than for maintenance. See, for example, *Re G (Children Act 1989, sch. 1)* [1996] 2 FLR 171 and *Phillips* v *Pearce* [1996] 2 FLR 230.

6.3.2 OVERLAP BETWEEN THE COURTS AND THE CSA

It was originally envisaged that all cases would be within the jurisdiction of the CSA by 1996. Due to a variety of practical problems this date has now been put off indefinitely. Essentially the position is as follows:

(a) If the parent with care of a child is in receipt of benefit he or she can be required to apply to the CSA for an assessment, and will normally be so required unless there is domestic violence in the case. If there is any existing agreement or order it will stay in effect until an assessment has been made, but once an assessment has been made it will become ineffective.

(b) If the parent with care of a child is not in receipt of benefit he or she can apply to the CSA for an assessment, but does not have to do so.

    (i) It may be attractive to apply if an assessment might lead to a high figure being payable, but the application might antagonise the absent parent, and this needs careful consideration in advising on or carrying out a negotiation.

    (ii) If there is an existing court order it will stay in force and can be varied or revoked. It will not necessarily be revoked simply to allow an application to be made to the CSA to get a higher award (*B* v *M (Child Support: Revocation of Order)* [1994] Fam Law 370). Existing orders will probably eventually be brought into the new system.

    (iii) If there is no existing court order then it is still possible for the court to make an order for maintenance, provided this is agreed by the parties and the order reflects a written agreement. This may be an attractive option if the couple wish to exclude the involvement of the CSA.

If maintenance for a child is set by agreement, or if an application is made to vary a court order, the figure that the CSA might award is relevant for the court to consider, but would not be decisive (*E* v *C* [1996] 1 FLR 472).

In any event the court can still make one of the orders set out in **6.3.1**.

6.3.3 WORDING AN ORDER FOR FINANCIAL PROVISION

It is important to word an order correctly, and where appropriate to put the order in context as regards the CSA. Try to foresee possible future developments rather than simply recording the current position. Do make sure that any precedents you use are up-to-date.

The main options are as follows:

(a) If the CSA has jurisdiction and makes an assessment then, of course, no court order is necessary. However, if a consent order for financial provision is made on divorce, it may still be useful to record (probably in the 'Whereas . . .' section of the order) that a CSA assessment is to meet the needs of the children.

(b) It is possible, and often advisable, to word an order to allow for the replacement of a court maintenance order by any payments ordered to be made under a future CSA assessment. Its effect should be to reduce the maintenance order, pound for pound, by the amount of any CSA assessment. See, e.g., the sample consent order at p. 101.

(c) If the court has jurisdiction because the parties are agreed and there is a written record of that agreement, or because an existing order is being amended, then the figure for maintenance can be ordered in a conventional way. However, it may help to clarify the situation if the order for maintenance or the 'Whereas . . .' section of the order records that the order is made on the basis that there will not be an application to the CSA.

(d) If the court is making an order that it has the power to make in any event, e.g., for school fees, the order can be worded in a conventional way. However, again it may help to clarify the situation to state whether or not the order is in addition to a CSA assessment.

(e) It may be that the spouses agree the financial provision for the children on one basis, but that basis changes. For example, provision may be agreed on the basis that both spouses are earning, but then the spouse with care may for some unforeseen reason become reliant upon State benefit and be forced to make an application to the CSA. If appropriate a consent order should allow for a change of this sort, for example making it clear that a maintenance order is ordered on the basis that there will be no application to the CSA.

On the interrelationship of CSA payments and court orders, see *AMS* v *Child Support Officer* [1998] 2 FLR 622 and *Dorney-Kingdom* v *Dorney-Kingdom* [2000] 3 FLR 20.

SEVEN

CHILDREN

7.1 Introduction

The law relating to children can now be found in the Children Act 1989 (CA 1989). The main rules governing jurisdiction and procedure are:

(a) in the magistrates' court, the Family Proceedings Courts (Children Act 1989) Rules 1991 (SI 1991 No. 1395) (FPCR 1991);

(b) in the county court and High Court, the Family Proceedings Rules 1991 (SI 1991 No. 1247) (FPR 1991); and

(c) in the domestic court the Family Proceedings Courts (Matrimonial Proceedings etc.) Rules 1991 (SI 1991 No. 1991) (FPC(MP)R 1991).

Forms have been introduced and must be used in all applications. Where no form is provided, then a written request should be made to the court.

Much of the philosophy underpinning the legislation is of non-intervention — a belief that, in the main, parents know best what is good for their children and will act in their children's best interests. It also provides for a unified structure of both law and jurisdiction, with concurrent jurisdiction and cases capable of being transferred from one court to another.

The Handbook of Best Practice in Children Act Cases (HMSO, June 1997) contains detailed guidance by the Children Act Advisory Committee.

The Human Rights Act 1998 also has an impact in child cases as it incorporates the European Convention on Human Rights directly into UK law. There are a number of areas where the 1998 Act is relevant in child cases. The Act imposes obligations on the State, both negative and positive, as well as applying to public authorities. The individual is, therefore, able either to bring proceedings directly against public authorities under the 1998 Act or rely on Convention rights in any legal proceedings. The most obvious areas in which the Act applies in child cases relate to unmarried fathers, same-sex couples, care plans, the enforcement of contact orders and the disclosure of information (see *TP and KM* v *United Kingdom (Application No. 28945/95)*, *The Times*, 31 May 2001). Where a local authority fails to act to protect children from abuse then Article 3 (inhuman and degrading treatment) can be used (see *Z and Others* v *United Kingdom (Application No. 29392/95*, *The Times*, 31 May 2001, where pecuniary damages were awarded for this breach under Article 13). There may well be other areas of relevance as the impact of the legislation begins to be felt.

7.2 Parental Responsibility (PR)

This concept makes clear that being a parent creates responsibilities rather than rights, and hence that these responsibilities exist whatever the state of the parents' relationship with each other. It emphasises the view that each will retain a (shared) continuing responsibility for the children. Where more than one person has parental responsibility for a child each of them is given power to act alone (CA 1989, s. 2(7)) unless each person with parental responsibility is by law required to give his or her consent, for example, to adoption. Parental responsibility can be shared by a range of people and with a local authority where the child is in care, and an order can be made even though the child was neither born nor is resident in the UK.

7.2.1 WHAT DOES PARENTAL RESPONSIBILITY MEAN?

The concept of parental responsibility replaces that of custody whilst incorporating into it much of the common law meaning of custody. The CA 1989, s. 3(1), states that parental responsibility encompasses 'all the rights, duties, powers, responsibilities and authority which by law a parent of a child has in relation to the child and his property'. At common law the meaning of custody has never been absolutely clear with most writers relying on the definition of it by Sachs LJ in *Hewer* v *Bryant* [1970] 1 QB 357 at p. 373:

> ... 'custody' ... embraces ... a 'bundle of powers'... These include power to control education, the choice of religion, and the administration of the infant's property. They include entitlement to veto the issue of a passport and to withhold consent to marriage. They include, also, both the personal power physically to control the infant until the years of discretion and the right ... to apply to the courts to exercise the powers of the Crown as *parens patriae.*

The 'bundle of powers' has often been described as a dwindling one because the more mature the child is the more difficult it is for a parent to justify exercising total power over him or her. A particular example of this can be seen in the discussion surrounding the power to control the medical treatment of a child (see *Gillick* v *West Norfolk & Wisbech Area Health Authority* [1986] AC 112).

The main difference is to make clear that there are responsibilities which automatically follow parenthood. The Children (Scotland) Act 1995 defines parental responsibility and included are such items as safeguarding and promoting the child's health, development and welfare, direction and guidance, the maintenance of personal relations and direct personal contact and to live with the child (see s. 1(1)).

7.2.2 WHO HAS PARENTAL RESPONSIBILITY?

Parental responsibility can be acquired in any of the following ways:

(a) *Automatic responsibility.* The CA 1989, s. 2, specifies that parents who were married to each other at the time of the child's birth each have parental responsibility, and that where the child's parents are not married to each other at that time the mother has parental responsibility.

Note, however, that a consultation is underway through the Lord Chancellor's Department aimed at reviewing the position of unwed parents in relation to their children. In *Soderback* v *Sweden* [1999] 1 FLR 250, the child was born to unmarried parents. The mother's husband applied to adopt the child of the former relationship. The natural father opposed the adoption and applied under Article 8 of the European Convention on Human Rights claiming a violation of his right to respect for family life. The Court held that the father's rights had not been violated under Article 8 because there had been infrequent and limited contact between him and the child. As there were very strong family ties between the husband and the child, the effect of the adoption on the father's relationship with the child would not be disproportionate and fell within the state's margin of appreciation. This case is an example of the State's positive obligation to further family life.

The European Convention on Human Rights has also been used by unmarried fathers. In *X, Y and Z* v *UK* [1995] 2 FLR 892 and *Keegan* v *Ireland* (1994) 18 EHRR 342 the court was asked to consider the meaning of family life (Article 8) and concluded that a number of factors would be relevant, including whether the couple lived together, the length of their relationship and whether they had demonstrated their commitment to each other by having children. See also *McMichael* v *UK* (1995) 20 EHRR 205. In *R (Montana)* v *Secretary of State for the Home Department* [2001] 1 WLR 552 (CA), it was held that the refusal by the Home Secretary to register the citizenship of a child whose father had an agreement to share parental responsibility with the Norwegian mother, with whom the child lived in Norway, was not in breach of Articles 8 (family life) and 14 (discrimination on grounds of sex) of the European Convention.

Equally, a same sex couple who have become parents through artificial insemination might also be able to use the Convention to claim equality with unmarried fathers.

There is a duty to consult in relation to any serious or long-term decisions affecting a child (*Re G* [1994] 2 FLR 192) which can be enforced through a s. 8 order.

(b) *By court order or agreement.* Where the father is not married to the mother when the child is born, the father can acquire parental responsibility either by order of the court, or by entering into an agreement with the mother to share responsibility. In *Re X (Parental Responsibility Agreement: Children in Care)* [2000] 1 FLR 517, it was held that when children are in care under a care order, the mother cannot enter into a parental responsibility agreement with the father of the child without the consent of the local authority. If paternity is disputed then it must be proved. The Parental Responsibility Agreement Regulations 1991 (SI 1991 No. 1478) provide for the form and manner for recording the existence of the agreement. A specific form is available from the county court. From January 1995 (SI 1994 No. 3157) applicants must take the completed form to the court where the clerk or officer authorised by the judge will witness the signature. Agreements must be registered in the Principal Registry. It should be noted that an agreement can be terminated by order of the court either on application by a person with parental responsibility or, with leave, by a child with sufficient understanding (CA 1989, s. 4(3) and (4)) (see *Re A* [1994] 2 FCR 709, CA).

It has been held that the decision as to whether or not to make an order should be based on the child's welfare as the paramount consideration (*Re G (a minor) (Parental Responsibility Order)* [1994] 1 FLR 504, and the making of the order should be better for the child than making no order at all. Factors which will be taken into account include the degree of commitment shown to the child, degree of attachment that exists, and the father's reasons for applying (see *Re H (No. 3)* [1991] Fam 151).

It is expressly provided that others may have some (but not full parental) responsibility for a child (see s. 3(4) and (5)). In particular, it is provided that a person who has the care of a child may do what is reasonable to safeguard and promote that child's welfare.

(c) *By appointment as a guardian on the death of a parent.* A guardian will only acquire parental responsibility if,

(i) appointed by the court when a child has no parent with parental responsibility (or where the only parent with a residence order has died);

(ii) appointed in writing (signed and dated) by a parent with parental responsibility, to act after his or her death;

(iii) appointed by a guardian to act in his or her place (see CA 1989, s. 5).

An appointment which is not a court appointment takes effect only when there is no parent with parental responsibility for the child. There are detailed provisions concerning revocation of the appointment (CA 1989, s. 6(1) to (4)), and the guardian can disclaim the appointment (CA 1989, s. 6(5) and (6)). The court can at any time terminate the appointment (CA 1989, s. 6(7)).

A person who has parental responsibility may not transfer that responsibility to another. However, he or she can arrange for the responsibility to be met by some other person acting on his or her behalf (including someone who has parental responsibility for that child) whilst remaining responsible for any failure by that delegatee to act (CA 1989, s. 2(9) to (11)).

7.3 Section 8 Orders

These replace the previous types of order (**7.24.1**). In certain respects the new orders necessarily replicate, at least to some extent, the old. It should be noted that these new orders have no impact on the existence of parental responsibility, which will continue except in the circumstances explained in **7.2.2**, although a person with parental responsibility must not act in a way which is incompatible with any order made under the Act.

7.3.1 TYPES OF SECTION 8 ORDER

Section 8 of the Children Act 1989 empowers the court to make, vary or discharge the following orders:

(a) *Contact order (CO).* This provides for all kinds of contact, including access and/or staying access, telephone calls, letters etc. including contact at contact centres (there is now a judicially approved protocol governing the operation of referrals to child contact centres). A contact order made in favour of a parent no longer living with his or her spouse and children will cease to have effect if the parents resume cohabitation for a period exceeding six months (CA 1989, s. 11(6)). Orders can be made *ex parte* or by consent, on written evidence or after oral hearing and in favour of any person.

Contact will not generally be refused between a child and its parent unless there are very clear reasons for so doing, for example, violence or the clearly expressed wishes of the child. In effect, therefore, there is a presumption of contact between parents and their children (see **7.4**). The same presumption does not apply as between children and their step-parents or grandparents.

Interim contact orders are possible but generally courts are cautious about making such orders. Courts can also, either upon application or of their own motion when making an adoption order or freeing a child for adoption, make a contact order, although courts will only with very good reason impose a contact order in the face of opposition from the adopters.

(b) *Residence order (RO).* This form of order specifies with whom the child is to live. A residence order can be made in favour of more than one person at a time, whether or not those persons are living together. *A v A* [1994] 1 FLR 669, shared residence order is rare and will be made only in unusual circumstances and where it would be of positive benefit to the child, e.g., where the child has a settled home with one parent and substantial contact with the other. A shared residence order has been used to enable an unmarried couple to in effect adopt a child by making an adoption order in favour of one party and a joint residence order in favour of both (see *Re AB, The Times*, 10 August 1995). The new order may define the time which the child is to spend with each person. If the parents who each have a residence order resume cohabitation for a period exceeding six months, the order will cease to have effect (CA 1989, s. 11(5)). Orders can be made *ex parte.*

If a residence order is made in favour of a father who is not married to the mother of the child and does not have parental responsibility, then that father must also be given by the order parental responsibility for the child (CA 1989, s. 12(1)). If a residence order is made in favour of a person without parental responsibility then that person will be given that responsibility (excluding the power to consent to adoption or free for adoption or appoint a guardian) for the duration of the order (CA 1989, s. 12(2) and (3)). A residence order gives no power to any person to change the child's surname, or to arrange for the child's removal from the jurisdiction for more than one month without the consent of all persons with parental responsibility or the leave of the court (although the court can include in the order general or specific leave to remove the child from the jurisdiction) (CA 1989, s. 13). In *Re K (Minor) (Residence Order)*, *The Times*, 8 January 1999, on an application by the mother for leave to remove the child from the jurisdiction the court found the mother to be untrustworthy (having refused to allow the father to visit his child at an earlier stage). There was therefore concern that the father would not be allowed to see his child and so it was appropriate to refuse the application and also to deny the mother's claim for residence although she was granted contact.

In *Payne* v *Payne* [2001] 2 WLR 1827 (CA), the court held that in relocation cases the rights of all the parties have to be balanced under Article 8 of the European Convention on Human Rights and any interference had to be both justified and proportionate. In this case the Convention did not affect the requirement to balance the factors influencing the operation of the paramountcy of the welfare principle. In such a case the courts have to balance the reasonable proposals and motivation of the parent wishing to relocate, the effects on the child of seriously interfering with the life of a custodial parent and the denial of contact to the absent parent.

Interim residence orders which last for a limited period are possible but should be strictly limited in time to avoid delay. Applications can be made *ex parte*, although only exceptionally (*Re G* [1993] 1 FLR 910), for example where a child has been snatched or is in some other immediate danger. In order to challenge an *ex parte* order it is necessary to apply for discharge or variation on notice.

(c) *Prohibited steps order (PSO)*. This form of order prevents a parent with parental responsibility from taking any step which is specified in the order without the prior consent of the court, e.g., taking the child out of the jurisdiction or changing the child's surname. A number of recent cases has considered the vexed question of changing children's surnames, in *Re PC (Change of Surname)* [1997] 2 FLR 730 it was held that where both parents have parental responsibility either may change the child's surname provided the other consents, although such consent need not be in writing. In *Dawson* v *Wearmouth* [1997] 2 FLR 629 the court held that an unmarried father could apply to have the child's surname changed to his own but the court had discretion to decide whether to grant the application which was of major significance to the welfare of the child. Here the mother's surname (that of her former husband and other children) was ordered to be retained by the child.

Where a residence order or care order is in place (CA 1989, ss. 13(1) and 33(7)), the child's surname cannot be changed without the written consent of every person having parental responsibility or the leave of the court. See *Practice Direction (Child: Change of Surname)* [1995] 1 FLR 458. Leave will only be granted in exceptional circumstances (*Re B (Change of Surname)* [1996] 1 FLR 791). See also *Re C (Minors) (Change of Surname)*, *The Times*, 8 December 1997 and *Re C (A Minor) Change of Surname*, *The Times*, 2 February 1998.

Ex parte applications possible; leave required in magistrates' courts (see FPCR 1991; FPR 1991). See *Nottingham CC* v *P* [1994] Fam 18. Here the local authority sought an *ex parte* order to oust the father from the family home where there was evidence of the possible sexual abuse of a daughter. The court found that the appropriate procedure here would have been through care. Otherwise the effect of the application if granted would have been a 'no contact order' when the authority had no power to apply for a contact order. In *Re H* [1995] 1 FLR 638 a prohibited steps order was made to prevent contact between the children and the mother's former cohabitant because of the possible risk to the children. To have made a 'no contact' order would effectively have put the mother under an obligation to prevent contact; the PSO was therefore the more sensible course.

(d) *Specific issue order (SIO).* This form of order directs the way in which a disagreement about a specific issue which has arisen or may arise in respect of any aspect of parental responsibility should be resolved, e.g., where those with parental responsibility do not agree on the form of education or religious upbringing which the child should have, the matter can be referred to the court for it to make a specific issue order but not to oust one parent from the home (*Nottingham CC* v *P* [1994] Fam 18). *Ex parte* applications possible; leave required in magistrates' courts. See *Camden LBC* v *R* [1993] 2 FLR 757. An application for the court to authorise the use of blood products on a child whose parents were Jehovah's Witnesses was successful. It was considered an appropriateuse of the court's powers under CA 1989, s. 8, in preference to wardship, since there was no wider issue concerning the future welfare of the child. A contested issue relating to emergency medical treatment in *Re O* [1993] 2 FLR 149, was thought better dealt with under the wardship jurisdiction, although an application to allow a sterilisation operation to be carried out on a mentally retarded girl could be authorised (see *Re HG* [1993] 1 FLR 587).

The court may not make a prohibited steps or specific issue order if the result envisaged could be obtained by making a residence or contact order. The court may not make a prohibited steps or specific issue order which in effect places a child in the care or under the supervision of a local authority, or which requires the child to be accommodated by or on behalf of the local authority, or confers power on a local authority to determine any issue on parental responsibility which has arisen or may arise.

A section 8 order may contain directions about how it is to be carried out, impose conditions on parents or other persons and specify when it is to come into effect and how long it is to last for, and any other provisions which the court thinks fit (CA 1989, s. 11(7)) (see *Re M, The Times*, 10 November 1993). In *Re E (Residence: Imposition of Conditions)* [1997] 2 FLR 638 a mother successfully appealed against the imposition of a condition requiring her to live at a specific address, the court taking the view that the issue of location of residence should have been determined through cross applications for residence and not through the imposition of conditions aimed at interfering with the ordinary rights of the custodial parent.

A section 8 order will be discharged by a care order (CA 1989, s. 91(2)).

7.3.2 SITUATIONS IN WHICH THE COURT CAN MAKE A SECTION 8 ORDER

Under CA 1989, s. 10, a section 8 order with respect to a child can be made in any family proceedings in which an issue arises with respect to the welfare of the child provided that the application is made by a person entitled to apply for such an order, or the court has granted leave to a person not so entitled to make such an application and if, in any event, the court considers that such an order should be made.

Equally, orders can be made in other proceedings on the application of a person entitled to make such an application or where the applicant has obtained the leave of the court.

7.3.3 WHAT ARE FAMILY PROCEEDINGS?

Family proceedings include any proceedings under the inherent jurisdiction of the High Court concerning children (excluding an application for leave made by a local authority) (i.e., wardship); proceedings under CA 1989, Parts I (general principles),

II (orders in respect of children in family proceedings) and IV (local authority support for children); and proceedings under MCA 1973 (divorce etc.), FLA 1996 (injunctions in domestic violence etc. cases), Adoption Act 1976 (adoption cases), FLA 1996 (applications in a magistrates' court for financial support or protection from domestic violence), FLA 1996 (applications concerning occupational rights in the matrimonial home) and Matrimonial and Family Proceedings Act 1984 (financial provision following divorce etc.), applications under s. 30 of the Human Fertilisation and Embryology Act 1990. See also *Practice Direction* [1995] 1 All ER 586.

7.3.4 WHO IS ENTITLED TO APPLY FOR A SECTION 8 ORDER?

Those entitled to apply for section 8 orders vary according to the nature of the order sought. For example, where a child is in the care of a local authority the only order which the court has power to make is a residence order (CA 1989, s. 9(1)). Once a child has reached the age of 16 the court has no power to make any section 8 order (except for discharge or variation) unless the circumstances are exceptional (CA 1989, s. 9(6)).

Those who can apply are:

(a) Parents or guardians and persons who have a residence order in respect of the child can apply for any section 8 order (CA 1989, s. 10(4)). This includes the unmarried father but not former parents whose child has been adopted. Parents can apply for leave on behalf of their child where the child is too young to do so on his or her own behalf, where this would enable the child to be represented within the legal aid scheme.

(b) (i) Any party to a marriage where the child is a 'child of the family' of that marriage. 'Child of the family' includes both the natural children of the parties to the marriage and step-children treated as a child of the family, excluding foster children.

(ii) any person with whom the child has been living for a period of at least three years (subject to CA 1989, s. 10(10)), and

(iii) other persons who have the consent of the person in whose favour a residence order has been made, or the consent of the local authority which has the child in its care, or the consent of each person with parental responsibility can apply for a *residence or contact order* (CA 1989, s. 10(5)). Local authorities *cannot* apply for or have such orders made in their favour.

(c) Other persons given standing by rules of court, which may prescribe the circumstances in which others can apply and the orders which can be sought.

(d) Those to whom the court has granted leave to apply. Application is in writing and a hearing will only be arranged if the grounds are not made out in the written application (see FPCR 1991; FPR 1991). Natural parents of an adopted child must seek leave (*Re S, The Times*, 8 March 1993), as must a child (see *Re C* [1994] 1 FLR 26, *Re SC* [1994] 1 FLR 96).

7.3.5 WHEN WILL THE COURT GRANT LEAVE TO APPLY FOR A SECTION 8 ORDER?

Factors which the court is required to take particularly into account in deciding whether or not leave should be given can be found in CA 1989, s. 10(9). Included are: the nature of the application, the applicant's connection with the child, the risk of harmful disruption to the child's life and, if the child is being cared for by the local authority, any plans which the authority has for the child's future and the wishes of the child's parents (see *Re A* [1992] Fam 182). This was an application by a former local authority foster mother for leave to apply for a residence order over her former foster child. It was held that courts are required to take into account the local authority's plans for the child (see CA 1989, s. 10(9)(d)(i)) which must be based on the duty to safeguard and promote the child's welfare. They should not determine the application for leave on the basis that the welfare of the child is the paramount consideration. However, s. 10(9) does not provide an exclusive list of the factors to be taken into account. The items are contained in the checklist in s. 1(3) so that the child's wishes may be taken into account and it has also been held that the court can have regard as to whether or not the substantive application has a chance of success (but not that it would be bound to succeed) (see *G* v *Kirklees MBC* [1993] 1 FLR 805 and *C* v *Salford CC* [1994] 2 FLR 926).

There is also concern that cases will involve too many parties and so where for example the interests of grandparents coincide absolutely with those of the parents there is no good reason to grant them leave to be separately represented (see *Re M (Sexual Abuse: Evidence)* [1993] 1 FLR 822).

Where a child is in the care of a local authority the courts will be circumspect about granting leave when, in effect, the purpose of the application is to act purely as a review of the local authority's decisions in respect of the child (see *Re M (PSO: Application of Leave)* [1993] 1 FLR 275).

If the application for leave is made by the child, then the court can only grant leave if satisfied that the child has sufficient understanding to make the proposed application (CA 1989, s. 10(8)). Such applications should be determined by the High Court (*Practice Direction (Applications by Children: Leave), Fam D* [1993] 1 WLR 313). The s. 10(9) guidelines do not apply to applications made by children; there has, however, been a conflict of opinion as to whether or not the welfare principle should be paramount (see *Re C* [1994] 1 FLR 26 and *Re SC* [1994] 1 FLR 96 at **7.3.4**, the latter case following the thinking of the Court of Appeal in *Re A and W (Minors)* [1992] 1 WLR 422, that an application for leave does not involve a decision about the future upbringing of the child). The current criterion which is taken into account is therefore the likelihood of the success of the application so as to avoid situations where the child is embarking on proceedings which are doomed to failure.

The court also has the power under CA 1989, s. 91(14) to restrict any person from making applications under the Act without leave. See *Re R* [1998] 1 FLR 149 for an example and *C* v *W* [1998] 1 FCR 618 where it was said that the power was not just for hopeless or fruitless applications, but also where a parent pursues litigation unreasonably and in a manner damaging to the interests of the child.

Foster-parents who have had the child *living with them* within the previous six months cannot apply for leave unless they have the consent of the local authority, they are related to the child or the child has lived with them for the past three years (CA 1989, s. 9(3) and (4)).

7.3.6 DURATION OF PARENTAL RESPONSIBILITY AND SECTION 8 ORDERS

Agreements and guardian appointments last until the child reaches the age of 17. Section 8 orders end when the child is 16, unless s. 9(6) of CA 1989 applies (i.e., the circumstances are exceptional). If s. 9(6) applies the order will end when the child is 18 (CA 1989, s. 91(11)).

7.3.7 ENFORCEMENT OF SECTION 8 ORDERS

See the Family Law Act 1986, s. 34 which empowers the court where an order has been disobeyed to make an order authorising an officer of the court or a police officer to take charge of the child and deliver that child to another. An *ex parte* order can also be sought under the inherent jurisdiction for the tipstaff to find and recover a child — it is not necessary to establish that the initial order has been disobeyed.

Otherwise the failure to obey an order of the court or undertaking to the court given in injunctive form is a contempt which can be punished by fine, imprisonment or sequestration of assets. It should be noted that those who conspire to encourage non-compliance with such orders may themselves be in contempt. If it is intended that this form of enforcement should be available then this could have an impact on the nature of the section 8 order applied for in the first place — it may be more sensible to use a PSO for example to prevent a change to the child's surname. Equally the form of the order as drafted for the court's approval must be clear and precise and orders for 'reasonable contact' would clearly not be enforceable in this way. See FPR 1991, r. 4.21A for procedure.

For orders made in the magistrates' court, see the Magistrates' Courts Act 1980, s. 63(3) which enables the court on application to fine or commit. Residence orders are specifically included within this power, see CA 1989, s. 14. The guiding procedure is to be found in FPCR 1991, r. 24.

Generally, committal orders are thought to be orders of last resort and are rarely imposed. But in *A v N (Committal: Refusal of Contact)* [1997] 1 FLR 533, a mother who had shown implacable hostility towards contact between the father and the child was committed to prison for flagrant breach of the court order requiring the child to have contact with the father. The court held that the child's welfare was a material consideration but not the paramount consideration and so even though the child would be affected by the imprisonment of the mother there was ultimately a limit as to what the court would endure by way of breaches of its orders. Although a county court judge has jurisdiction to proceed of his own motion with a committal order where the other party to the proceedings is not requesting committal, such a procedure is appropriate only in exceptional and urgent cases and as a last resort where all other remedies have been exhausted (*Re M (A Minor) (Contact Order: Committal)*, *The Times*, 31 December 1998).

7.4 The Welfare Principle

Children Act 1989, s. 1, states that the court should have regard to the child's welfare as the paramount consideration when determining any question relating to the child's upbringing or the administration of the child's property. The principle applies therefore to wardship proceedings, non-convention (that is, non-European and Hague Convention cases) child abduction cases and the exercise of the inherent jurisdiction in general. However, it does not apply in those cases described above, where the child's upbringing is not directly in issue, for example where the application is for leave to make an application under s. 8, or in restricting publications that might be harmful to a child nor in Adoption Act 1976 proceedings where the child's welfare is the first consideration. The welfare principle is made subject to the general non-interventionist principle that the court shall not make the order or any order *unless it considers that doing so would be better for the child than making no order at all*. This means that the court must be assured that there is actually some benefit to the child in making the order sought.

Unlike the previous law, where the only guidance on the application of the welfare principle was to be found in the case law, the new legislation provides a list of circumstances to which the court is directed to have particular regard when considering whether or not to make a section 8 order, or when deciding whether or not to make, vary or discharge a care or supervision order. See *Re H* [1994] 2 AC 212, the court held that the welfare of the child on whose behalf the application is made should have paramountcy in the proceedings. See also *F v Leeds CC* [1994] 2 FLR 60. The circumstances include:

(a) The ascertained wishes of the child, subject to the age of the child (i.e., what the child has said he or she wants to happen, if he or she is considered old enough or mature enough to reach such a decision) — not given priority (*Re J* [1992] Fam Law 229).

(b) The child's physical, emotional and educational needs (i.e., who can best provide for all the needs of the child). Issues such as with whom the child has a bonded relationship, the impact which an order is likely to have on the child's sense of security and the importance of maintaining the status quo are of importance here, as is knowing both parents (*Re R, The Times,* 29 March 1993).

(c) The likely effect of any change in the circumstances (e.g., if another adult is to be introduced into the child's life because one parent is to remarry or cohabit with someone new, a move to new accommodation or to a new school etc.). See *Re H, The Times,* 7 September 1992.

(d) The age, sex, ethnicity, background and any other characteristics of the child which the court thinks relevant. (In *Re B* [1998] 1 FLR 520 the court stated that there had been a major shift in expert opinion on the weight to be given to the ethnic background of children in residence cases, and so confirmed that two Nigerian boys could remain with their white foster mother who had cared for them since birth in accordance with the boys' vehemently expressed wishes.) It is often said that very young children and pubescent girls need their mothers most whilst growing boys need their fathers, although such views are not invariable principles and no legal presumption exists in favour of one or other parent. Other issues which may be relevant here relate to bringing up a child in circumstances that could be said to be slightly unusual and hence which might potentially affect the child's welfare, for example, where a parent belongs to a religious cult group or is a scientologist, or, where grandparents are seeking a section 8 order, their age may be a relevant consideration.

(e) Any harm which has been suffered or of which there is a risk (e.g., where a child has been neglected or physically or sexually abused or it is feared that there is a risk of such abuse).

(f) The ability of the parents or other relevant people to meet the child's needs (e.g., where the adult carer suffers from some disability which affects the care which he or she can offer this will be a relevant consideration). Lesbianism *per se* will not be seen as making a mother unfit to have the future care of her child (see *C v C* [1991] 1 FLR 223).

(g) The range of powers available to the court in the proceedings (i.e., whether it is right for the court to exercise its powers in a particular way).

In *Re N,* unreported, 27 July 1999, the House of Lords held that the Roman Catholic foster parents of a Downs Syndrome child born to orthodox Jewish parents could have a residence order made in their favour with reasonable contact to the child's natural parents. The House of Lords confirmed that the benefit to the child of continuing to be brought up by the foster parents, to whom she had become greatly attached, outweighed the benefit to her in being brought up as an orthodox Jew as she did not have the capacity to fully understand or appreciate her Jewish heritage. In effect, this case has added consideration of religious background to the checklist of matters to be taken into account when assessing the welfare principle.

A failure by the court in reaching a decision to run through the checklist may make it easier for a dissatisfied party to appeal against the decision, made on the grounds that the judge below was 'plainly wrong' (see *M v M* [1987] 2 FLR 146).

The general principle in disputed contact cases has been that the child has a basic right to know both its parents, but there are an increasing number of cases in which there have been cogent reasons why the child should be denied that opportunity. See *Re D* [1993] 2 FLR 1. In this case the cogent reason for denying access was the 'implacable hostility' to contact of both the mother and her parents with whom she and the child lived. In *Re D (Contact: Reasons for Refusal)* [1997] 2 FLR 314, the Court of Appeal held that implacable hostility could occur in cases where there were good reasons for that hostility as well as in cases where there were no good reasons for that hostility. In this case there were good reasons because of the violence of the father to the mother. In *Re L (A Child) (Contact: Domestic Violence)* [2001] 2 WLR 339, it was held that while there is no presumption against contact simply because of domestic violence, it was one factor amongst many which might offset the assumption in favour of contact when carrying out the balancing exercise under the welfare principle. Further, in interim contact applications, where allegations of domestic violence have yet to be adjudicated upon, the court should give particular consideration to the likelihood of harm, whether physical or emotional, if contact is granted or denied, and try to ensure that any risk to the child is minimised and the safety of the child and residential parent protected, during, before and after contact. The court further suggested that under Article 8(2) of the European Convention on Human Rights, the interests of the child must prevail where there is a serious conflict between the interests of the child and a parent. In all cases the power to order no contact or no direct contact should be exercised sparingly.

Section 11 of the Family Law Act 1996 also makes provision for the making of orders under the Children Act 1989 over children of the family (those under 16 or over that age but in respect of whom the court directs that the section should apply) where there are proceedings for divorce or separation. The concept of the welfare of the child being paramount applies, but in application of that concept the court is required to have particular regard to:

(a) the wishes of the child, having regard to its age;

(b) the conduct of the parties in relation to the upbringing of the child;

(c) the general principle that in the absence of evidence to the contrary, welfare will be best served by:

(i) regular contact with those who have parental responsibility and with members of the family;

(ii) maintenance of as good a relationship with the parents as possible;

(d) any risk attributable to:

(i) where and the persons with whom the child will reside;

(ii) any other arrangements for the care and upbringing of the child.

7.4.1 WELFARE REPORTS

In order to help the court make an informed decision about the welfare of the child, CA 1989, s. 7, empowers the court to seek expert evidence in the form of a written or oral welfare report (or ask the local authority to arrange for such a report to be made). In the past, such a report would have been compiled by somebody known as a 'court welfare officer'. In April 2001 the three branches of the welfare services (the Official Solicitors' Department, guardians *ad litem* and court welfare officers) were merged into one body known as the Courts and Family Court Advisory and Support Service (CAFCASS). Unless prepared by a local authority officer, the new title for those compiling court welfare reports is 'children and family reporter'. You may find practitioners using both/either titles while they adapt to the change.

The court can ask that such reports concentrate on certain specified matters or ask for a general report. The court can override legal professional privilege in proceedings and order disclosure of reports adverse to a party's interests if it is relevant to a determination (*Re R* [1993] 4 All ER 702).

7.5 Rules of Evidence

You should particularly note that the rules relating to the admissibility of hearsay evidence can be ignored by the court if it considers that any statement or evidence is relevant to any issue before the court (see Children (Admissibility of Hearsay Evidence) Order 1993 (SI 1993 No. 621)). Civil courts may thus admit hearsay evidence, such as evidence of interviews conducted by psychiatrists and social workers in which children disclose physical or sexual abuse (CA 1989, s. 96(3) to (5)). In civil proceedings before a juvenile court a statement made by a child (or by a person connected with, or having control of the child) that he has assaulted, neglected or ill-treated the child, or a statement in any report made by a children's guardian or by a local authority, is admissible in connection with any proceedings relating to the upbringing, maintenance or welfare of the child, regardless of whether or not it is also hearsay. The aim of these provisions is to overturn the decision of the Court of Appeal in *H v H (Minors) (Child Abuse: Evidence)* [1990] Fam 86. In *Re G* [1993] 2 FLR 293 it was suggested that the fundamental rules of evidence should only be relaxed in the most exceptional circumstances amounting to a serious threat to the welfare of the children. The Act also allows civil courts to accept unsworn evidence from young children if the court deems the child capable of understanding the duty to speak the truth and is of sufficient understanding (CA 1989, s. 96(2)(a) and (b)).

Section 98 of the Act removes the privilege against answering questions which might elicit incriminating replies in any proceedings relating to care, supervision or emergency protection. The witness is however protected against the criminal consequences of making a damaging admission but not in proceedings relating to contact and residence orders (see *Re K, The Independent,* 23 November 1993).

Each party must file written statements containing the major thrust of the oral evidence to be called at trial and copies of any documents which are to be relied upon, including experts' reports. See also *Re D, The Times,* 11 March 1998, as to abiding by Home Office Guidance on interviewing children on video.

Copies must be served on all parties to the proceedings (or their legal representatives) including the children's guardian or children and family reporter appointed by the court but is otherwise confidential (except that copies may be supplied to the Legal Services Commission). The timetable for compliance will be fixed at the directions hearing. Evidence which is not disclosed under these rules may not be adduced at trial without the leave of the court.

In *Re B* (1993) 143 NLJ 969, it was held that the Act gave no power to override legal and professional privilege (see also *Oxfordshire CC v M* [1994] 2 WLR 393). But compare the position in wardship under *Re A* [1991] 2 FLR 473. Statements made by either party in the course of conciliation meetings cannot be disclosed (*Re D, The Times,* 12 February 1993) unless there are exceptional circumstances suggesting serious future harm to the child.

A witness summons can be issued against a child but only if it would not be oppressive.

In *Re N, The Times,* 25 March 1996, it was held that where allegations of sexual abuse are made and expert evidence is admitted as hearsay evidence in relation to a videoed interview with the child, it was for the judge alone to decide whether or not the child was to be believed. Here the interview had been very pressured with leading questions being put to the child and so the father's application for contact was ordered to be reheard.

In *Re CB and JB (Child Abuse Evidence)* [1998] 2 FLR 211, it was held that experts' reports on the question of propensity to injure a child should not be routinely adduced in evidence. For the threshold criteria to be met all that is required is evidence that a child has been injured non-accidentally whilst in the parents' care.

In *Re CH* [1998] 1 FLR 402, the Court of Appeal said that it was undesirable to allow significant discussion about the future care of a child to be held in the judge's private room; rather, any such discussions should be held in private in the court room so that those discussions can be recorded and a transcript made.

7.6 Avoidance of Delay

One of the major criticisms of the operation of this area of the law has been the inordinate time that it has taken for cases finally to be resolved by order of the court. Delay in reaching a final decision in these important matters can be extremely damaging to the children concerned particularly since a child's sense of time is very different from that of an adult. Children can feel extremely insecure whilst waiting for a case to be resolved. In some cases, courts have been forced to give judicial authority to the *de facto* situation rather than risk the psychological damage which could result from moving the child.

The CA 1989, s. 11, attempts to deal with this problem by requiring the court to draw up a timetable and give directions to enable it to deal with the matter without delay. Rules have been made (FPR 1991, r. 4.14(2) or FPCR, r. 14(2)) to provide for directions appointments in all courts including the magistrates' courts. Attendance at the hearing is obligatory unless the court directs otherwise. Proceedings are conducted by the clerk in the magistrates' court and by the District Judge in the county court. The appointment will deal with the timetabling of the case, the appointment of a children's guardian or solicitor for the child, the submission of evidence, the preparation of welfare reports, the transfer and consolidation of proceedings, the service of documents and the attendance of the child at hearings. Directions can also be given about the order of speeches and evidence. Directions can be given of the court's own motion subject to the parties having been given notice and having the opportunity to make representations. Directions hearings tend to be oral hearings and parties can be required to attend. In the magistrates' court directions hearings are held by the clerk whose powers are very restricted.

Section 11(3) gives the court power to make what is, in effect, an interim section 8 order.

7.7 Orders for Financial Relief Attached to a Residence Order

These provisions can be found in sch. 1 of the CA 1989. Where a residence order is in force (or when it is to be varied or discharged) the court, at any time, can make, vary or discharge a periodical payments order or a lump-sum order (all courts), and secured periodical payments order, settlement order or property transfer order (county court and High Court only) made in favour of a child or in favour of the applicant for the benefit of the child.

Application can be made for a periodical payments order and/or lump-sum order by a person (whose parents are not living together as part of the same household) who (not having an order in his or her favour at the time he or she reached the age of 16) has reached the age of 18 and is continuing to receive education or training, or where there are special circumstances. This provision enables children to apply in their own right for maintenance provided that their parents are living apart.

Orders continue in force until the child's 17th birthday, unless the court thinks it right to specify a later date not beyond the child's 18th birthday. Orders may be extended beyond the child's 18th birthday if the child is in receipt of education or training, or there are special circumstances. There are a number of proposals for reform relating to pre-marital agreements and also to the division of property and capital on divorce. It is unclear at the time of writing when or if any of these proposals will affect the financial position of children.

In exercising its discretion the court is directed to have regard to the same matters which apply on divorce etc. (see **5.3**). Note also the effect of the Child Support Act 1991. The government has proposed changes to the current scheme suggesting that it be replaced by a simpler formula based on a fixed percentage of net income varied accordingly to the number of children.

7.8   Family Assistance Orders

In exceptional circumstances, with the consent of all the adult parties in the matter, under CA 1989, s. 16, the court can make a family assistance order. This requires a local authority or court welfare officer to advise, assist or befriend the person named in the order. A family assistance order remains in force for six months. The purpose of this provision is to replace the previous exceptional power to make a supervision order in family proceedings.

7.9   Role of the Local Authority

The aim of the legislation is to develop the concept of a 'voluntary partnership' between parents and State. However, where reasonable parental care is lacking, so that there is a risk of significant harm to the child, the local authority should decide whether to apply for a care order or seek to make up for the lack of care in some other way. It is now thought that a delayed application will not be in the interests of the child. Government guidance on the application of this part of the legislation is now provided in 'Working Together to Safeguard Children: a guide to inter-agency working to safeguard and promote the interests of children' and should be read in the light of 'Framework for the Assessment of Children in Need and Their Families' (April 2000) which gives detailed guidance on how local authorities should implement assessments of need. There is also guidance on preparing reports for court.

The Children (Leaving Care) Act 2000 amends the CA 1989, ss. 17, 20 and 22 to improve the position of children leaving care and to get local authorities to take on board their responsibilities to act as a parent. This new legislation increases the services which should be provided by local authorities. Failure to comply with these duties however is not actionable.

7.9.1   DUTY OF THE LOCAL AUTHORITY TO PROMOTE THE WELFARE OF CHILDREN

The CA 1989, s. 17, explains that every local authority has a duty to safeguard and promote the welfare of children in its area who are in need and, so far as is consistent with that duty, to promote the upbringing of such children by their families (a family for these purposes encompasses both those where one or more of the adult members has parental responsibility, and those with whom the child has been living: s. 17(10)). There is no common-law duty placed on local authorities to act as and apply the standard of care of a responsible parent in relation to protection from physical, psychiatric or psychological harm, providing appropriate education and home environment and placing in short and long-term foster care. However, the local authority can be liable vicariously for acts of social workers in carrying out the statutory duties of the local authority (see *Barrett* v *Enfield LBC* [1997] 3 All ER 171).

In the performance of this duty, local authorities are empowered, having regard to the means of the child and to the means of each parent, to give assistance in kind or, in exceptional circumstances, in cash. Cash payments may have to be repaid but not whilst the payee is in receipt of family credit or income support.

A child is in 'need' if he or she is unlikely to maintain a reasonable standard of health or development, or if his or her health or development is likely to be impaired or further impaired unless the local authority provides help, or if he or she is disabled (CA 1989, s. 17(10) and (11)).

Local authorities are also empowered (but not obliged) under the Act to provide such day care and after-school and holiday facilities as they consider appropriate, and are obliged to undertake annual reviews of the provision made (CA 1989, ss. 18 and 19).

7.9.2 DUTY TO PROVIDE ACCOMMODATION

Every local authority is required by s. 20 of the CA 1989 to provide accommodation for any child in their area who requires accommodation and is in need because there is no person who has parental responsibility for the child, or the child is lost or abandoned, or the person caring for the child is prevented from providing him or her with suitable accommodation or care for any reason whether permanently or temporarily. Local authorities are obliged to provide a roof over the head of a child who is in need of such support because his or her parents are not able or available to provide.

A local authority, under s. 20(3), may also provide accommodation for any child over the age of 16 if the welfare of the child is likely to be prejudiced if he or she is not provided with accommodation.

A local authority may not provide accommodation under s. 20 for a child if any person with parental responsibility for the child objects and is willing and able to provide or can arrange to provide accommodation for the child. This last provision overturns the problems which previously arose under the Child Care Act 1980, s. 2, when the return of a child received into care was sought. It is now clear that those with parental responsibility wishing to take back a child are entitled to do so and can remove the child from accommodation provided under s. 20 at any time. The only exceptions to this occur where the person with a residence order (who has the day-to-day responsibility for the child) agrees to the authority providing accommodation, or where the child is over the age of 16 and agrees to the authority providing accommodation.

A local authority has power to provide for a child who is provided for by someone with parental responsibility, or is over the age of 16 but under 21, if to do so would safeguard or promote the child's welfare.

In deciding how to exercise its powers under s. 20 the authority is required to have regard and give due consideration to the wishes of each child, subject to that child's age and understanding.

7.9.3 CHILDREN LOOKED AFTER BY THE LOCAL AUTHORITY

A child is looked after by a local authority if he or she is in the care of or provided with accommodation by the local authority (CA 1989, s. 22).

An authority must safeguard and promote the welfare of any child it is looking after and make available such use of services as appears reasonable where the child is being cared for by its parents. However, if there is a need to protect members of the public from serious injury this obligation is avoided and in these cases the Secretary of State will give directions with which the authority is obliged to comply (CA 1989, s. 22).

In deciding how to look after a child an authority is required (see the Arrangement for Placement of Children (General) Regulations 1991 (SI 1991 No. 1890)) to ascertain and give due consideration to the wishes of the child, parents, others with parental responsibility and any others whose wishes and feelings the authority considers relevant (for example, grandparents). The authority is also required to give due consideration to the child's religious persuasion, racial origin and cultural background in deciding how or what care to offer. This provision will enable a local authority to pay regard to any problems it can foresee in a child being cared for by a family from a different racial or cultural background from that of the child (CA 1989, s. 22). See *Re M* [1995] 2 WLR 302 on placing in secure accommodation.

An authority must, when looking after a child in its care, provide that child with accommodation (so far as is practicable near to his or her home and where the authority is providing accommodation for a sibling, with that sibling) and to maintain that child (CA 1989, s. 23). Accommodation can be provided by placing the child with his or her family, relative or other suitable person (paid or not), or placing the child in a community home, voluntary home, registered children's home, in a special home (CA

1989, s. 82(5)) or making such other arrangements as appear appropriate. Local authority foster parents do not include those who are also parents of the child, those with PR or those with an RO immediately before the care order was made for the child (see the Foster Placement (Children) Regulations 1991 (SI 1991 No. 910)).

7.9.4 DUTY TO PROVIDE ADVICE AND ASSISTANCE

This duty arises when a child under the age of 21 ceases to be looked after by the authority (see CA 1989, s. 24 for detailed provisions). See, however, *R v Lambeth LBC, ex parte Caddell, The Times*, 30 June 1997 for limitations once the child reaches 18.

7.9.5 USE OF SECURE ACCOMMODATION

See s. 25 of the CA 1989 for detailed provisions concerning children who have a history of absconding and are likely to suffer harm if they abscond, or are likely, if kept in non-secure accommodation, to injure themselves or others. The general principle is that the authority of a court is required if a child is to be kept in secure accommodation for more than a short period of time, the maximum periods of such confinement being specified by regulation. (See the Children (Secure Accommodation) Regulations 1991 (SI 1991 No. 1505).) See Guidance on Permissible Forms of Control in Children's Residential Care (DH) and the Children's Homes Regulations 1991, reg. 7. In *Re K (A Child) (Secure Accommodation Order: Right to Liberty)* [2001] 2 WLR 1141, it was held that a secure accommodation order could be granted even where the child was subject to an interim care order. There would also be no breach of Article 5 of the European Convention on Human Rights as the purpose of such an order is the deprivation of liberty and the order falls within the justification for such deprivation of liberty as being for the purposes of educational supervision.

7.9.6 REVIEW OF CASES INVOLVING CHILDREN LOOKED AFTER BY LOCAL AUTHORITIES

The Review of Children's Cases Regulations 1991 (SI 1991 No. 895) made under the CA 1989, s. 26, provide for the regular review of the case of each child who is being looked after by a local authority and encompass the manner of the review, the considerations to be taken into account, the time for review and frequency of review. The regulations may require the authority to seek the views of the child, his or her parents, those with parental responsibility and any other person who appears to be relevant; to consider whether to apply to discharge the order etc. and to notify the results of the review to the child, his or her parents, etc. In *R v Cornwall CC, ex parte L, The Times*, 25 November 1999, it was held that the authority could not put a blanket bar on the attendance of solicitors at case conferences and generally a parent's solicitor should be allowed to attend and participate unless it would undermine the purpose of the conference.

Local authorities are required to establish a procedure to enable any representations or complaints to be made to them. See Representations Procedure (Children) Regulations 1991 (SI 1991 No. 894) which also lay down a timetable and detail how matters are to be conducted.

There appears to be a view that, prior to any application for judicial review of a local authority's actions, the complaints procedure should be used. Where there has been genuine consultation, judicial review is unlikely to succeed (see *Re T* [1995] 1 FLR 159).

There is also now clear authority in *X v Bedfordshire CC* [1995] 3 WLR 152 for the proposition that a local authority owes no duty of care in respect of its duties under the CA 1989 such as would found a claim in damages. In *W v Essex CC and Another* [2000] 1 FCR 568 (HL), where there were very special circumstances, the parents succeeded in their claim against a local authority where they had fostered a child with known or suspected tendencies towards sexual abuse when they had specifically asked the authority to avoid such a placement. In the event the foster child had abused the children of the foster parents and the whole of the family were entitled to make a claim for psychiatric damage which, in consequence, was suffered.

7.10 Care and Supervision

7.10.1 IN WHAT PROCEEDINGS CAN AN APPLICATION BE MADE?

Application can be made specifically for a care or supervision order, or an application can be made in any family proceedings. In *Re RD, The Independent*, 22 March 1993, it was held that the protection of the child is the decisive factor, and so a care order will be made where this is necessary even if the authority's view is that a supervision order would provide the necessary protection. If, in family proceedings, a question arises in respect of the child's welfare such that it may be appropriate for the court to make a care or supervision order, the court may, under CA 1989, s. 37, direct the appropriate authority to investigate the child's circumstances. This ensures that such a case can be disposed of efficiently either by the authority taking over the application for care or supervision, or by the authority taking such steps as are necessary to avoid having to take proceedings to gain the care or supervision of the child. The investigating local authority is required to consider whether to apply for a care or supervision order (and if it decides not to, to inform the court of its reasons for not doing so), provide services or assistance to the family or take any other action in respect of the child which it considers appropriate. If the local authority does not apply for care or supervision, it is required to explain to the court what services are, or assistance is being or will be provided and any other action which has or is to be taken (including a decision to review the case at a later date). This information must be given to the court within eight weeks of the direction to investigate unless the court directs otherwise.

7.10.2 WHO CAN APPLY?

Application for a care or supervision order can be made by a local authority or an authorised person (which includes the NSPCC and any others authorised by the Secretary of State to bring such proceedings). Note that the police are now excluded. Where it is reasonably practicable to do so, an authorised person will be expected to consult with the local authority in whose area the child appears to be ordinarily resident. Application by an authorised person is not possible when the child is already the subject of an application, or is subject to a care or supervision order, or is provided with accommodation by or on behalf of a local authority (CA 1989, s. 31).

7.10.3 IN WHOSE FAVOUR CAN AN ORDER BE MADE?

Both care and supervision orders must designate the local authority into whose care or supervision the child is to be put. The designated authority must be the authority within whose area the child is ordinarily resident or the authority for the area in which the circumstances which led to the making of the order arose (CA 1989, s. 31).

7.10.4 GROUNDS FOR MAKING AN ORDER

These are detailed in s. 31(2) of the CA 1989 and require that the court is satisfied (*Re G* [1995] Fam 16) that:

(a) the child concerned is suffering, or is likely to suffer, significant harm (both the present and future tenses are used to avoid one of the problems which arose under the previous legislation); and

(b) the harm, or likelihood of harm, is attributable to:

(i) the care given to the child, or likely to be given to the child if the order were not made, not being what it would be reasonable to expect a parent to give to him (this definition attempts to prevent middle-class or uni-ethnic views about parenting being imposed on the population as a whole); or

(ii) the child's being beyond parental control (this follows the previous law and, in effect, allows a parent to 'divorce' his or her child).

These conditions are known as the threshold criteria and apply also to whether a child can be put on the 'at risk' register (*R* v *Hampshire CC, ex parte H, The Times*, 22 June 1998).

In *Lancashire CC* v *A* [2000] 1 FCR 509, the House of Lords held that the threshold conditions could be met where the court is satisfied that a child has suffered significant harm, even if it is impossible to say, where care is shared, as in this case between the parents and child minder, which of the carers had inflicted the injury. An attempt to use Article 8 (respect for family life) of the European Convention on Human Rights failed because the local authority had done no more than was reasonably necessary to further its legitimate aim of seeking to protect the child from further injury.

'Harm' is defined as ill-treatment or the impairment of health or development. 'Development' means physical, intellectual, emotional, social or behavioural development. 'Health' means physical or mental health. 'Ill-treatment' includes sexual abuse and forms of ill-treatment which are not physical. 'Significant' is not defined in the legislation and presumably its meaning will fall to be decided by the courts. *The Collins English Dictionary* defines 'significant' as 'important, notable or momentous', which suggests quite a high standard and could limit the use made of the care and supervision provisions in the legislation. It was hoped that courts would avoid a strict legalistic analysis of words used in legislation. So a flexible approach to the interpretation of s. 31 is intended. It follows the general principle which underlies this legislation that the situations in which the State should be able to interfere in the integrity of the family should be very carefully circumscribed and follows the recommendations made in the Butler-Sloss Inquiry into the Cleveland sex abuse cases. In *Re M (Care Order: Threshold Conditions)* [1994] 2 AC 424, the House of Lords laid down the appropriate approach as to the time at which it must be established whether or not the threshold criteria have been made out. This is the time at which the local authority initiates the proceedings, the moment immediately before the process of protection is put in place, not the date of the hearing by which time the authority may well have ensured that the child's welfare is being adequately provided.

In *Re H and R* [1996] 2 WLR 8 the court held that it must be satisfied as to the existence of facts on the balance of probabilities and then exercise its discretion as to whether or not the existence of those facts make it likely that the child will suffer significant harm. In *Re B (Split Hearing: Jurisdiction)* [2000] 1 FLR 334, it was held that under the County Courts Act 1984, s. 77, the Court of Appeal had power to review a split hearing in which at the first stage of establishing how and by whom a child had been injured, the court of first instance had erred. Only in exceptional cases can the court prefer the evidence of lay witnesses (that of the grandmother) over that of medical experts.

Once the threshold criteria have been fulfilled then the welfare of the child becomes the paramount consideration within the context of s. 1. The authority must put before the court its plans for the future care of the child (this is included in the form) and the court must be satisfied without a detailed investigation of every aspect of the future care of the child that these broadly secure the welfare of the child. In *Re D (Care: Natural Parent Presumption)* [1999] 1 FLR 134, the Court of Appeal considered whether there were any compelling factors which overrode the *prima facie* right of the child to be brought up by its surviving natural parent. Having considered the individual merits of the potential carers, the presumption remained with the natural parent and not with the grandparent who had the care of half-siblings to the child. The sibling relationship could be protected through contact and so was not a compelling factor which overrode the presumption.

The Human Rights Act 1998 can be used to challenge care plans put forward by a local authority and accepted by courts because, in effect, courts are devolving the decision-making process to the local authority. (See Article 8, and possibly Article 6, of the Convention which protects the right to a fair trial.)

Where there are no grounds, or if courts interpret their powers very restrictively, local authorities will not be able to turn to the wardship jurisdiction as a substitute for care proceedings. See also *Re M (No. 2)* [1994] 1 FLR 59.

7.10.5   AGE LIMITS

Application can be made in respect of children only when they are under the age of 17 or, if the child is married below the age of 17, the age limit becomes the age on marriage.

7.10.6   AVOIDANCE OF DELAY

The court is required to draw up a timetable and give such directions as may be necessary to ensure adherence to that timetable so that the application can be disposed of without delay, since it is recognised that delay may prejudice the welfare of the child. To encourage the speedy resolution of cases, rules of court have been made ensuring that the court keeps control of the timetable through directions given at the directions hearing. See *Re B, The Times*, 13 May 1998, for a discussion of the principles.

Courts should avoid as far as possible continuous adjournments or continuous interim care orders (see *Cheshire CC v P* [1993] 2 FLR 742). However, in *C v Solihull MBC* [1993] 1 FLR 290, Ward J suggested that a planned and purposeful delay may be useful:

> The court should consider all the facts and make a decision finally disposing of the case when all the facts are fully available. They need assessment results. To pass the responsibility to the local authority with a care order would be unfair to the parents with their only possible solution to apply for a residence order. There is a third course open, that the court keep control of the case, make interim arrangements and not make a decision until all the facts are available.

In *Buckingham CC v M* [1994] 2 FLR 506 the court made it clear that where a phased return of the child to its parents was considered appropriate there would be no other way for the court to control the return other than by using interim orders.

7.10.7   DURATION OF ORDERS

Orders last until the child is 18 unless brought to an end earlier (CA 1989, s. 91(12)).

7.10.8   CARE ORDERS

Once a care order is made the local authority is bound to receive and keep the child in its care whilst the order remains in force unless the application was made by an authorised person who did not consult the local authority in advance of making the application. In the latter case, the child must be kept in the care of the authorised person until the child is received into the care of the local authority.

7.10.8.1   Effect of a care order

The effect of a care order is to place parental responsibility in the local authority and to give the authority power to decide the extent to which a parent or guardian of the child can continue to meet his or her parental responsibility towards the child subject to any other enactment which may limit continuing parental responsibility. Parental responsibility will only be continued if the authority is satisfied that it is necessary to safeguard or promote the child's welfare. As with the previous law, the exercise of discretion by a local authority will be subject to judicial review if it can be established that the authority has acted unreasonably or maliciously — a very difficult burden to satisfy. A parent or guardian who has the care of a child who is subject to a care order is entitled to do what is necessary to safeguard and promote the child's welfare. See *Re B* [1993] Fam 301; *Kent CC v C* [1993] Fam 57.

The local authority's powers are limited in that it cannot decide that the child be brought up in a religious creed different from that which would have applied but for the order (see *Re N*, unreported, 27 July 1999), nor can it consent to adoption or free the child for adoption, nor can it appoint a guardian. During the currency of a care order the child may not become known by a new surname. In *Re J* [1993] 1 FCR 74 a child wanted to be known by the name of her foster parents, and unusually and exceptionally the court accepted that her natural parents should not be notified of the application. The child may not be removed from the jurisdiction (subject to CA 1989, s. 33(8)) without the written consent of all those with parental responsibility or the leave of the court. Those with serious convictions for child abuse can neither foster nor adopt children (see the Child (Protection from Offenders) (Miscellaneous Amendments) Regulations 1997 (SI 1997 No. 2308) and the sub-regulation inserted into the Foster Placement (Children) Regulations 1991 (SI 1991 No. 910), reg. 3(4A) and *Lincolnshire County Council* v *R-J and Others, X and Another Intervening* [1998] 2 FLR 110).

7.10.8.2 Effect of a care order on parental contact with the child

The basic principle is that the child should maintain contact with his or her parents and family, and so the legislation provides that the authority shall allow a child, who is subject to a care order, reasonable contact with his or her parents, guardian and/or any person who, before the care order, had a residence order in respect of that child. If necessary, application can be made to the court for an order, or an interim order can be made, allowing contact, including an application for such an order by a person who has obtained the leave of the court to apply. Applications can be made once only in every period of six months unless the leave of the court is obtained (CA 1989, s. 91(17)). An example of how the court looks at applications for contact to a child subject to a care order is *Re B* [1993] Fam 301, where it was said that contact must not be allowed to destablise or endanger or frustrate the arrangements planned for the child. These must command the greatest respect and consideration from the court but the court can require the authority to justify their long-term plans to the extent that those plans exclude contact with a parent. Where, however, parents are using the application for contact as in effect a further application to obtain the return of the child, the application is likely to meet with little success especially where the matter has already been fully considered. The authority or the child can apply to the court for an order that a named person should have such contact with the child as the court considers appropriate. This includes a power to authorise the authority to refuse contact to a named parent, guardian or person who had a residence order. These orders can be made when the court makes a care order or in any other family proceedings even if no application for such orders has been made.

In exercising its discretion to determine issues related to future contact the court should have regard to the child's welfare as paramount and to the long-term plans of the authority for the child's future and to the provisions of s. 1 (*West Glamorgan CC* v *P (No. 2)* [1992] 2 FCR 406; *Re S, The Independent,* 10 January 1994).

The authority has power to deny contact, including that granted under a contact order, if it is satisfied that this is necessary to safeguard or promote the welfare of the child and the refusal is urgent and does not last for more than seven days. The Contact with Children Regulations 1991 specify the steps which the authority must comply with when exercising these powers, the terms and conditions which should apply where the authority and person in relation to whom the order is made agree to depart from the terms of the order and the arrangements for notifying the variation or suspension of the original arrangements.

These orders can be made subject to such conditions as the court considers appropriate. In *Re SW, The Independent,* 1 March 1993, it was held that the court can, of its own motion, include a prohibition against contact with a parent, even though that parent has not had notice that further contact will be opposed.

7.10.9 SUPERVISION ORDERS

7.10.9.1 Duties of the supervisor

The supervisor must advise, assist and befriend the supervised child, take such steps as may be necessary to give effect to the order and, if the order is not complied with or is no longer thought to be necessary, consider whether to apply to the court for its variation or discharge.

7.10.9.2 Education supervision orders

These can be made on the application of any local authority in circumstances where a child (but not one who is in the care of the local authority) who is of compulsory school age is not being properly educated (that is, in receipt of efficient full-time education suitable to his or her age, ability or aptitude and any special educational needs he or she may have). For further details see CA 1989, s. 36.

7.10.9.3 Powers of a supervisor

Detailed provisions as to supervisors' powers can be found in CA 1989, sch. 3. See on extension of supervision order *Re A* [1995] 1 WLR 482, CA.

7.10.10 INTERIM ORDERS FOR CARE OR SUPERVISION

The court is empowered by s. 38 of CA 1989 to make an interim order if it reasonably believes that the grounds specified in s. 31(2) (see **7.10.4**) are likely to be made out. In *Hampshire CC v S* [1993] 1 FLR 559 the court made a number of observations indicating to magistrates the way in which they should deal with applications for interim orders: orders should be made to establish a holding position but avoiding delay for its own sake; if there is no time to consider the case properly, consider transferring laterally to a court which can make a full determination; avoid making findings as to disputed facts; seek to avoid changing the status quo, but if a substantial change in the situation is envisaged then to permit oral evidence limited to the issues which are essential to the interim stage and cross-examination of that evidence; they should have written advice of the guardian *ad litem* who should be available to give oral evidence where there is a substantial dispute between the parties; full compliance with the rules, in particular reading of the evidence prior to the hearing, making a full written record and the recording of the reasons for their decision and adjourn to the next day if there is not time to comply with these proceedings (as long as one of the justices can return on the next day to complete the formalities); reasons should be stated concisely summarising briefly the essential factual issues between the parties. The court also has power to give directions with regard to the carrying out of a medical examination, e.g., for an AIDS test, or psychiatric examination or to prevent such examinations or make them subject to court directions. Interim orders can be made in any proceedings for care or supervision and in family proceedings where the court has directed the local authority to mount an investigation into the circumstances of the child. They are intended to advantage neither side.

In *Re CH (Care or Interim Care Order)* [1998] 1 FLR 402, the court made a care order following the recommendation of the local authority in its care plan which cautiously favoured rehabilitation even though the guardian *ad litem* had recommended adoption. On appeal an interim care order was substituted because expert evidence on where the child should be placed was not available to the court and the court therefore did not have full evidence on which to make a definitive decision.

Where an application for a care or supervision order has been made and the court decides to make a residence order, the court must also make an interim supervision order unless the court is satisfied that the child's welfare will be satisfactorily guarded without such an order.

The duration of an interim order is strictly limited — see s. 38(4) for the detailed rules — and, in deciding its length, the court is directed to have regard to whether any party who was or might have been opposed to the making of the order was in a position to argue fully his or her case against the order. See *Re G* [1993] 2 FLR 406, where it was held that the practice of local authorities routinely seeking renewals of interim orders was to be discouraged. For a recent discussion of this area, see *W and B (Children); W (Children)* [2001] All ER (D) 285 (CA), where the court suggested that there remained 'a wide discretion to make interim care orders where the care plan seems inchoate or where the passage of a relatively brief period seems bound to see the fulfillment of some event or process vital to planning and deciding the future' (Thorpe LJ).

7.10.11 DISCHARGE AND VARIATION OF CARE AND SUPERVISION ORDERS

Under s. 39 of the CA 1989 application to the court for the discharge or variation of a care or supervision order can be made by the child, by any person with parental responsibility for the child or, where there is a care order, by the local authority designated in the order, or, where there is a supervision order, by the supervisor. A person with whom the child is living but who does not fall within the above list may apply for the variation of a supervision order where it imposes a requirement which affects that person.

The court can discharge a care order and substitute a supervision order and vice versa. The court is not required to have regard to the provisions specified in s. 31(2) in exercising this power but must have regard to the welfare principle contained in s. 1.

If the court makes a residence order this automatically discharges a care order (CA 1989, s. 91(1)).

When an application for discharge or substitution of care for supervision or vice versa has been made, no further application for any of these orders can be made without the leave of the court until six months have elapsed (CA 1989, s. 91(15)). Equally, s. 91(14) gives the court power to prevent any further applications for discharge being made by a parent without the leave of the court. Such an order can be unlimited as to time (within the children's minority) and need not be restricted to those cases where repeated applications have been made as the welfare principle applies, so where there are exceptional and extreme circumstances the court can exercise this power (see *Re P* [2000] 2 FLR 910).

7.11 Children's Guardians

Various amendments have been made by the Criminal Justice and Court Services Act 2000 which brought into being the Children and Family Court Advisory and Support Service (CAFCASS). This establishes a new public body which incorporates the work of the family court welfare services, the guardian *ad litem* and the reporting officer service and most of the children's work of the Official Solicitor's Department. New terminology now applies, such that guardians *ad litem* are 'children's guardians' and welfare officers are 'children and family reporters'. The general rule remains that the court shall (in certain specified proceedings (see CA 1989, s. 41(6)) always appoint a children's guardian unless it is satisfied that it is not necessary to do so in order to safeguard the child's interests (CA 1989, s. 41(1)).

CAFCASS Legal has taken over the functions of the Official Solicitor's Department in all family proceedings and may represent children in family proceedings held in either the High Court or county court, but not in the family proceedings court. CAFCASS Legal will accept cases where case law establishes a need for a child to be granted party status and to be legally represented. In broad terms, a member of CAFCASS Legal will be appointed only as a children's guardian where the case is exceptionally difficult, unusual or sensitive or where the Official Solicitor has previously acted for the child. The Official Solicitor's Department will still be available to act in cases where the child's welfare is not the subject of family proceedings or where CAFCASS has no longer the power to act because the child is over the age of 18 years.

7.12 Protection of Children

The Family Law Act 1996 (which came into force on 1 October 1997) requires the court to have regard when making an exclusion order or non-molestation order to whether any relevant child is likely to suffer significant harm attributable to the conduct of the respondent (s. 33(7)). It also provides that with the leave of the court a child can apply for an occupation order and/or non-molestation order (s. 43). Section 52 and sch. 6 amend the Children Act 1989, s. 38, so as to enable the court to attach to an interim care order an exclusion requirement where that would have the effect of preventing the child from suffering or being likely to suffer significant harm. See also *Practice Direction* [1998] 1 WLR 475 and *Practice Direction* [1998] 1 WLR 476.

7.12.1 EMERGENCY PROTECTION ORDERS (EPOs)

7.12.1.1 Application for an emergency protection order

Emergency protection orders under s. 44 of CA 1989 replace the place of safety orders which had been heavily criticised. The new procedure aims to protect children at risk whilst ensuring that parents (and any others with parental responsibility) have the opportunity to challenge the action being taken in the certitude that the matter will be resolved within a settled and limited time. The application can be made by anyone but must be made in the family proceedings courts and can be to a single justice; it cannot be transferred to a higher court. If the application arises out of a s. 37 direction to a local authority to investigate then the application is to the court which gave the s. 37 direction.

Orders can be made if, and only if, the court is satisfied that there is reasonable cause to believe that the child is likely to suffer significant harm if:

(a)   he is not removed to accommodation provided by or on behalf of the applicant; or

(b)   he does not remain in the place in which he is then being accommodated.

The order should either name the child or clearly describe him or her (CA 1989, s. 44(14)).

Where the court does not have adequate information as to the child's whereabouts but that information appears to be available to another person the court can, under s. 48 of CA 1989, include in the emergency protection order a provision requiring that person to disclose information about where the child is to the applicant. Self-incrimination is no excuse for failing to comply with such a provision in the order but any statement or admission made in complying with it is made inadmissible in any criminal proceedings except perjury.

An emergency protection order may, under s. 48(3), authorise the applicant to enter premises to search for the child and, if the court has reasonable cause to believe that there is another child on those premises with respect to whom an emergency protection order ought to be made, it may, under s. 48(4), order the applicant to search for that other child on those premises. An order under s. 48(4) can be converted into an emergency protection order if, having found the child on the premises, the applicant is satisfied that the grounds for making an emergency protection order are satisfied. The applicant should then notify the court. It is a criminal offence to obstruct any person using these powers of entry and search and is punishable by a fine (CA 1989, s. 48(7) and (8)).

A warrant may be issued authorising a constable to assist the applicant in entering and searching premises where the applicant has been prevented from entering and searching or is likely to be so prevented (CA 1989, s. 48(9) to (13)).

7.12.1.2 Effect of an emergency protection order

Whilst in force, an emergency protection order operates as a direction to any person who is in a position to do so to comply with any request to produce the child to the applicant; authorises the removal to and retention of the child at accommodation provided by the applicant and the prevention of the removal of the child from any hospital etc. in which the child was being accommodated immediately before the order was made, and it gives the applicant parental responsibility for the child.

7.12.1.3 Meaning of parental responsibility in this context

Parental responsibility in this context has a somewhat restricted meaning. It requires action to be taken only to the extent that is reasonably required to safeguard or promote the welfare of the child given the duration of the order. Regulations will be made setting out in more detail the action required by the applicant.

7.12.1.4 Directions which the court can give

Contact

The court can give such directions as it thinks fit on the making of an emergency protection order or at any time whilst it remains in force to govern the contact which is or is not to be allowed between the child and a named person subject to such conditions as the court deems appropriate.

Medical or psychiatric examination

The court can decide whether the child should be medically or psychiatrically examined and the nature and extent of any such examination, including an examination of the parents (*Re C* [1997] AC 489).

7.12.1.5 Variation

Rules of court prescribe who can apply to have an order varied (see Emergency Protection Order (Transfer of Responsibilites) Regulations 1991 (SI 1991 No. 1414)).

7.12.1.6 Powers of the applicant

The applicant can return the child or allow the child to be removed if it appears to him or her that it is safe to do so (CA 1989, s. 44(10)). Section 44(11) specifies to whom the child should be returned. Further action can be taken at any time by the applicant (CA 1989, s. 44(12)).

7.12.1.7 Effect of an emergency protection order on contact

The general rule is that the applicant should (subject to any directions given by the court) allow the child reasonable contact with his or her parents, any person with parental responsibility for him or her, any person with whom she or he was living before the making of the order, any person in whose favour a contact order is in force and any person acting on behalf of these persons (CA 1989, s. 44(13)).

7.12.1.8 Duration of an emergency protection order

An emergency protection order shall have effect for a period not exceeding *eight days* (CA 1989, s. 45(1)). There is special provision in s. 45(2) for the effect of public holidays. This period can be extended by a maximum period of seven days on application to the court once only (CA 1989, s. 45(4) to (6)). The power of the court to extend the order is strictly limited. It can do so only if it has reasonable cause to believe that the child concerned is likely to suffer significant harm if the order is not extended.

The length of an emergency protection order is much shorter than its predecessor, the place of safety order, and the limitation on extending even this short-term power is intended to meet many of the criticisms which were made about the previous law. State interference in the family is reduced in terms of the time for which a child can be removed from its family surroundings without the matter being fully investigated and, if risk is established, the matter coming to a full hearing if the authority think this is the best way of resolving the danger to the child.

7.12.1.9 Rules of evidence

It is made clear in s. 45(7) of CA 1989 that the court can take account of any statement or evidence given to the court which is, in the court's opinion, relevant whether or not it is hearsay. The court is also empowered to hear unsworn evidence from a child provided that it believes the child is capable of understanding the duty to speak the truth. See also s. 96 (**7.5** above). Generally it will be unusual for a court to make a witness summons against a child of 12 or younger. In *SCC v B* [2000] 1 FCR 536, it was held that the expert used by the father to defend criminal proceedings relating to child abuse could not be ordered to be disclosed. They were subject to legal professional privilege and the usual requirement of full and frank disclosure could not override privilege. In *Re B (Sexual Abuse: Expert Reports)* [2000] 2 FCR 8 (CA), the court held that although a single joint expert was to be preferred, in this case it was not appropriate as a court expert was required as compared with an expert involved in the psychiatric treatment of the child.

7.12.1.10 Discharge of an emergency protection order

In meeting some of the criticisms levelled at the previous law, the power to apply for the discharge of an emergency protection order has been introduced as a kind of appeal against the making of the order. However, there is no right of 'appeal' where an order has been refused (*Essex CC v F* [1993] 1 FLR 847).

The Family Proceedings Courts (Children Act 1989) Rules 1991 (SI 1991 No. 1395) specify the circumstances in which an application for discharge can be made by the child, a parent, any person with parental responsibility and any person with whom the child was living before the order was made. An application for discharge can be heard only once 72 hours have elapsed since the making of the order but, if the order has been extended, then the application can be heard immediately.

7.12.1.11 Appointment of a children's guardian

Section 41 of CA 1989 applies and so the general principle is that a children's guardian should always be appointed.

7.12.2 CHILD ASSESSMENT ORDERS (CAOs)

Where an authority wishes to satisfy itself about the health and well being of a child, a child assessment order may be made under s. 43 of CA 1989. It is intended to be available in circumstances where the evidence is not sufficient to warrant the making of an emergency protection order. Application for a child assessment order will be made *inter partes* (whereas an emergency protection order will usually be made *ex parte*). If, having heard all the evidence, the court takes the view that the case is more serious than it first appeared, it is empowered to make an emergency protection order rather than a child assessment order. Parental responsibility is retained by the parents throughout the period of the assessment. The assessment can be made by a family doctor in familiar surroundings. The assumption is that parents will be much more likely to cooperate with this kind of order. The order will enable the child to be removed from parental care for up to seven days in order for the assessment to be carried out. The grounds for making such an order are set out in s. 43(1) which provides that the court must be satisfied that:

(a) the applicant has reasonable cause to suspect that the child is suffering, or is likely to suffer, significant harm;

(b) an assessment of the child's health/development/treatment, is necessary to establish whether the child is suffering significant harm; and

(c) it is unlikely that an assessment could be satisfactorily made without such an order.

7.12.3 CHILDREN TAKEN INTO POLICE PROTECTION

7.12.3.1 Removal and accommodation of children by the police

Where a constable has reasonable cause to believe that a child would otherwise be likely to suffer significant harm, he may, under CA 1989, s. 46:

(a) remove the child to suitable accommodation and keep him there; or

(b) take such steps as are reasonable to ensure that the child's removal from any hospital, or other place, in which he is then being accommodated is prevented.

7.12.3.2 The constable's duties as regards the child and relevant local authorities

Once a child has been taken into police protection the constable is obliged to explain what has happened and what will happen and why it has happened, to the authority in whose area the child was found, the authority in whose area the child is ordinarily resident, and the child (if he or she is capable of understanding). The constable is also required to ensure that the case is investigated by the designated officer and to ensure that the child is finally accommodated by or on behalf of the local authority.

7.12.3.3 The constable's duties as regards the parents of the child

As soon as is reasonably practicable the constable is required to take steps to inform the child's parents, those with parental responsibility for the child, and any person with whom the child was living immediately prior to the action taken, of the steps taken, any further steps that may be taken and the reasons for acting.

7.12.3.4 Role of the designated officer

The designated officer is required to inquire into the case and, unless there is reasonable cause to believe that if the child were released, he or she would suffer significant harm, to release the child.

An application can be made by the officer for an emergency protection order whether the authority knows and approves or not. However, neither the constable nor officer has parental responsibility for the child. The officer is required to do what is reasonable in all the circumstances to safeguard and promote the child's welfare. The officer will also be responsible for deciding whether to allow contact with the child and the extent to which such contact is reasonable and in the child's best interests. Those who may be allowed contact are the child's parents, those with parental responsibility, any person with whom the child was living immediately before being taken into police protection, any person with a contact order and any person acting on behalf of any of these persons.

7.12.3.5 Role of the local authority

Where the child is being accommodated by the local authority, it is for the authority to decide whether to allow contact with the child and, if appropriate, its extent. In *Re W (A Minor) (Parental Contact: Prohibition), The Times*, 21 January 2000 (CA), the Court held that it had no power under CA 1989, s. 34(2), to prohibit a local authority into whose care a child had been placed from permitting parental contact with that child.

7.12.3.6 Duration of police protection

The maximum period for which any child can be held in police protection is 72 hours.

7.12.3.7 Duty to investigate

Where a local authority knows that a child is subject to an emergency protection order or police protection or has reasonable cause to suspect that a child living or found in its area is likely to suffer significant harm, the local authority should investigate to establish whether it should take any action to safeguard or promote the child's welfare. If it decides that no action to obtain an order is necessary it can nevertheless review the case at a later date. Section 47(3) of CA 1989 particularises what enquiries should be made and s. 47(9) to (11) what assistance should be given. The authority is required to take such steps as are reasonably practicable to obtain access to the child unless it already has sufficient information about the child and, if the authority is refused access to the child, it is required to apply for an emergency protection order, care order or supervision order unless satisfied that the child's welfare can be satisfactorily safeguarded without such an order.

7.13 Wardship and the Inherent Jurisdiction

Section 100 of CA 1989 provides that the wardship court (be it the High Court or some other court exercising the wardship jurisdiction) does not have the power to put children into the care or under the supervision of the local authority. Equally local authorities are no longer entitled to use the wardship jurisdiction without the prior leave of the court and leave will only be granted if the court is satisfied that the result which the local authority wishes to achieve could not be achieved through the making of any other order and there is reasonable cause to believe that if the inherent jurisdiction is not used the child is likely to suffer significant harm. See *Re J* (1992) 142 NLJ 1123, where the local authority sought leave for a court order for medical treatment of a girl suffering from anorexia nervosa. The court also has power to order that such a child can be detained in hospital until treatment is complete (*Re C* [1997] 2 FLR 180 and *Devon CC v S* [1994] 1 FLR 355). Courts have recommended that applications for AIDS tests on children should be made under the wardship jurisdiction.

This provision means that in effect the wardship jurisdiction is being used only by those who have no other means of seeking the court's help to protect a child, for example, for some non-therapeutic surgical intervention or to protect the child from publication of information which might be harmful to that child.

The procedure is by originating summons with an affidavit in support, and is immediate once issued so that no step can be taken without prior court permission. This is particularly useful for threatened child abduction.

In *Kelly v BBC* [2001] 2 WLR 253, it was held that the publication of information about a ward, was not of itself a contempt of court. The media did not need the permission of the court to interview a ward or to publish the results of such an interview where the interview did not raise any questions about the ward's upbringing and there was a clear public interest in broadcasting the interview which, if suppressed, would involve a derogation from the right to freedom of expression, guaranteed by Article 10 of the European Convention on Human Rights.

Likewise, the inherent jurisdiction is invoked by originating summons supported by affidavit, local authorities need the leave of the court. The power in wardship to protect children is probably greater (see *R v Central Television plc* [1994] Fam 192).

The courts will not interfere through either jurisdiction with the exercise of powers clearly vested in other bodies, e.g., local authorities, the immigration authorities, or to interfere with the normal criminal process, or to order a medical practitioner to treat a child in any manner contrary to his or her clinical judgment.

Local authorities can use the jurisdictions to help resolve issues which they have no power to deal with under their statutory powers and must seek leave to apply for the jurisdiction on the basis that they have not the powers they seek. Section 8 will often provide the powers they need under SIOs or PSOs.

The court can only exercise its jurisdiction where there is evidence that without it the child would suffer significant harm, for example the prevention or sanction of an abortion, medical treatment for an anorexic, sterilisation operations, the continuation of medical treatment and cases where there is no other way to prevent, for example, a paedophile having contact with children (see *Devon CC v S* [1994] 1 FLR 355).

7.14 The European Convention on Human Rights and the Human Rights Act 1998 and Judicial Review

Article 8 of the European Convention covering the protection of family life, can be used to review the removal of a child from its parents.

In *R v Portsmouth Hospitals NHS Trust, ex parte Glass* [1999] 2 FLR 905, the mother of a severely disabled child was denied a declaration from the court as to the course which doctors should take if any disagreements arose between them and the mother as to future treatment or withholding treatment. The Court of Appeal denied the declaration as the best interests of the child would be likely to vary according to the particular condition of the child at any given time. The Court suggested that judicial review should always be regarded as a procedure of last resort and, on the facts of this case, a number of possible applications would have been more appropriate (e.g., a section 8 specific issues order; wardship; or a declaration under the best interests procedure. However, in cases involving children, the last thing the court should be concerned about is whether the right procedure has been used and the court had sufficient powers to ensure that the right course was pursued in the best interests of the child.

7.15 International Custody Problems

If it is feared that an attempt may be made to remove a child improperly from the jurisdiction, the child may be made a ward of court or an injunction may be sought preventing the removal of the child.

It is possible for a parent who is worried about a possible improper removal of a child to give notice to the passport office to stop a passport being issued for the child without consent (*Practice Direction* [1973] 3 All ER 194 and *Practice Direction* [1977] 3 All ER 122). The Home Office will try to assist in preventing the illegal removal of a child from the jurisdiction if they are informed.

Because of the problems of international child abduction, the Hague Convention of Civil Aspects of International Child Abduction 1980 and the European Convention of Recognition and Enforcement of Decisions Concerning Custody of Children 1980, provide procedures for tracing a child and returning it, put into effect through the Child Abduction and Custody Act 1985. Under the Act, it is an offence to attempt to take a child from the UK without requisite consents. The Family Law Reform Act 1987 allows for orders made in one part of the UK to be directly enforceable in another part. If the child has been taken to a non-convention country there is little hope.

Where children are brought from a State which is not a signatory to either the European or Hague Conventions then the court is free to determine the case on its merits under the wardship jurisdiction, although the court will commonly have regard to the factors specified in the Hague Convention in reaching its decision. If the child is brought from a convention country then the provisions of the convention are applied instead of those of wardship, but the wardship will apply if the convention application fails.

The Hague Convention makes exceptional provision for the court to consider the welfare of children where the needs of the child require the court to take action other than the summary return to the country of habitual residence under Article 13 (see *Re M (Abduction: Psychological Harm)* [1997] 2 FLR 690). Where the foreign jurisdiction concerned does not take account of the child's welfare in its determinations as to the arrangements for the child's future, the court is justified in refusing return to the court of habitual residence (see *Re JA (Child Abduction: Non-Convention Country)* [1998] 1 FLR 231).

Children's views can be taken into account provided they are sufficiently mature and their views can therefore overturn the presumption of return (see *Re B (Abduction: Children's Objections)* [1998] 1 FLR 667). For these purposes separate representation is possible (see *Re S* [1997] 1 FLR 486).

For the situation in respect of unmarried fathers, see *Practice Note (Child Abduction and Custody Act 1985): Hague Convention: Applications for Return Orders by Unmarried Fathers* [1998] 1 FLR 491.

It is possible for the court in exercising its inherent jurisdiction to order that a father who had previously abducted one of his children should be required to keep his passport with his solicitors from where it was not to be released without either the order of the court or the consent of the mother (*Re A-K (Minors) (Foreign Passport: Jurisdiction)* [1997] 2 FLR 563).

An interesting development can be seen in *Re T (Staying in Contact in Non-Convention Country)* [1999] 1 FLR 262 where the court required undertakings to be given to apply for 'mirror orders' in Egypt to ensure the child's return from the father's home in Egypt. Egypt is not a party to the Hague Convention. The court emphasised the importance for children to be aware of their cultural identity.

In *Re E* [2000] Fam 62, the court underpinned the importance of the cultural background (unless there are exceptional circumstances, such as persecution or ethnic, sex or other discrimination) in assessing the welfare of the child. The Court of Appeal noted that it would be unrealistic to expect that child welfare would be equally understood and applied throughout the member States to the Hague Convention.

See also the Convention on Jurisdiction and Recognition and Enforcement in Certain Family Matters 1998, which regulates concurrent matrimonial proceedings in courts of different member States involving the same parties and allows for recognition and enforcement throughout the EU. In *Osman v Elasha* [2000] 2 WLR 1037 (CA), the Court, when making an order for the immediate return of a child to his habitual residence in a non-Convention country, should consider the welfare of the child as the paramount consideration. In this case, the welfare principle had to be considered in the light of Sudanese custom and culture, which applied Islamic law and which was familiar and acceptable to a practising Muslim family.

In *Re M* [1997] 1 FCR 109, a child who was habitually resident in Scotland but physically present in England, could be subject to the jurisdiction of the English court for the purposes of the court to implement a care plan.

7.16 Adoption

This is the process under which parental responsibility is permanently and irrevocably transferred from the natural parents. The procedure is governed by the Adoption Act 1976, although its replacement is making its way through Parliament (Adoption and Children Bill 2001). See also Adoption Agency Regulations 1983 and the Foster Placement (Children) Regulations 1991 (both as amended with effect from 31 January 2000); and the Adoption (Inter-country Aspects) Act 1999 which now prevents people from avoiding the local authority assessments and entry clearance by adopting abroad.

Applicants must be over 21 years of age and domiciled in the UK, Channel Islands or the Isle of Man. Single people may adopt; married couples may adopt, even if separated, but married people cannot adopt alone except in exceptional circumstances. A person remains single for these purposes even though he or she is actually part of a stable relationship, whether homosexual or heterosexual (*Re W* [1997] 3 FCR 650). The child must be placed with the adopters by an adoption agency unless there is a High Court order.

Where a child has not been placed by an adoption agency then the potential adopters must give notice of their intention to apply to adopt to the local authority so that it can investigate their suitability and make a report to the court. Those seeking a child through an agency will be assessed by that agency using a list of factors including: their health, lifestyle, relationship, age, etc. They will also be subject to police checks. An adoption panel will decide whether the adopters are suitable. The panel will then assess the suitability of the matching of applicants to child and report to the court.

If an adoption is contested then a children's guardian will be appointed.

The court will take into account the welfare of the child as the first consideration but this is not the paramount consideration. There have been many cases when the court has been forced to balance the welfare of the child against public policy interest, specifically immigration policy. The first stage in such cases is for the court to consider the motivation for making the application to adopt and only if it is clear that it was not intended to result only in British nationality can the court continue to the second stage of balancing public policy against the welfare of the child (*Re QS* [1997] 1 FCR 9). There are a number of inconsistent cases on this issue. In some cases, the courts have been concerned to ensure that the object of the adoption order is genuinely to transfer parental responsibility where the child concerned cannot be cared for by its natural parents and there will be no recourse to public funds for the child's support (see *Re RH* [1996] 2 FLR 187). In other cases, the court has been more concerned to ensure that the welfare test is applied specifically to the benefits arising from adoption and has expressly stated that in making this assessment the benefits arising from the attainment of British citizenship must not be taken in to account (see *Re B*, *The Times*, 16 March 1998). In yet other decisions, the court has been more concerned to establish whether or not the adoption is intended to underpin a genuine desire to create a family relationship in contrast with those whose main aim is to achieve a legal status, e.g., citizenship, and are therefore a sham or mere convenience (see *Re J* [1998] 1 FLR 225).

It is now increasingly common for some contact to be ordered to be maintained with the natural parent, although often this will be an order for indirect contact, and will not be at such a level as to destabilise the placement.

7.16.1 PARENTAL CONSENT

The consent of the parents of the child, or of the mother if the child is illegitimate, is required. The consent must be freely given, but it can be dispensed with by the court:

(a) If the parent or guardian cannot be found or is incapable of giving agreement.

(b) If he is withholding his consent unreasonably (this does not have to be culpable: *Re W* (An Infant) [1971] AC 682).

(c) If the parent or guardian has persistently failed without reasonable cause to discharge the parental duties in relation to the child.

(d) If the parent or guardian has abandoned or neglected the child.

(e) If he has persistently ill-treated the child.

(f) If he has seriously ill-treated the child.

7.16.2 FREEING FOR ADOPTION

This is the procedure whereby the consent to adoption can be obtained before the child is placed for adoption. The procedure is often used in cases where it is expected that the adoption itself will be contested. The child must be placed within 12 months of the order, and revocation of the freeing order is possible if there is no placement within that time.

7.16.3 PLACING THE CHILD FOR ADOPTION

There are strict rules regarding the placing of a child for adoption. The procedure is that a child will be freed for adoption by a court, on an application made by an adoption agency. The order freeing the child for adoption can be revoked if the child is not in fact adopted. A final adoption order can be made by a court, before which the adopters must have had the child living with them for a minimum period. The child must be at last 19 weeks old and have been with adopters for 13 weeks, or if the child was originally fostered, the child must be at least 12 months old and have spent at least 12 months with the adopters.

7.17 Surrogacy

The term surrogacy basically covers those situations where a woman agrees to have a baby for another couple, whether or not for payment. The law on this area is far from clear, but prima facie parental responsibility for the child will vest in the natural mother, not in the couple who hope to bring up the baby. Although the father can be given parental responsibility by agreement or by order of the court. See **7.2.2**. There is a substantial problem over whether any contract to hand the baby over should be enforceable. It seems doubtful that any contract to pay money for a child would be enforceable if the money were not paid voluntarily.

The welfare of the child would be paramount in any case coming to court. In the 'Baby Cotton' case — *Re C (a minor) (Wardship: Surrogacy)* [1985] FLR 846 — it was held that the 'parents' should take the child as the mother was quite happy to hand it over. Also, it seems that the 'parents' can adopt the child (*Adoption Application: Surrogacy AA 212/86, The Times*, 12 March 1987). However, if the natural mother wished to keep the child it seems unlikely that she would be prevented from doing so unless she was unsuitable.

Following the *Warnock Committee Report*, it is now an offence under the Surrogacy Arrangements Act 1985 to be involved in negotiating or making a surrogacy arrangement on a commercial basis, or to advertise to make such arrangements.

7.18 Procedure

7.18.1 CONDUCTING PROCEEDINGS

The Family Proceedings Courts (Children Act 1989) Rules 1991 (SI 1991 No. 1395) require the filing of written applications, witness statements, experts' reports, guardian *ad litem* reports and court welfare officer reports. Note the *Practice Notes on Court Bundles* [1994] 1 FLR 323. The timetable looks like this:

(a) Complete appropriate form.

(b) File form at court including copies for R.

(c) Court will fix date for directions hearing and endorse date on copies.

(d) A serves copies on R (time-limits for service set out in FPCR 1991, sch. 2, and FPR 1991, app. 3 — court can extend or abridge time — parties cannot extend by agreement).

(e) Application can be withdrawn only with agreement of the court.

(f) Section 8 applications and financial relief orders, R must file answer within 14 days of service. For other orders in the county court or High Court, R *may* file an answer.

(g) *Ex parte* orders must be served within 48 hours unless the court grants an extension.

Note that it is important in cases concerning physical or sexual abuse for provision to be made for factual issues to be determined at a preliminary stage. Experts could meet before the full hearing, be jointly briefed as to the issues, and be provided with itemised documentation. Good practice, as proposed by the Children Act Advisory Committee, allows for meetings to take place at an early stage and for a schedule to be prepared for the court identifying areas of agreement and discord thereby allowing the early hearing of factual matters. See *Re S* [1996] 3 FLR 578.

7.18.2 WHO HAS JURISDICTION?

See Children (Allocation of Proceedings) Order 1991 (SI 1991 No. 1677) (as amended, SI 1994 No. 2164). All public law cases (care, supervision EPOs) must be commenced in the magistrates' court. Cases (except EPOs) must be commenced in the magistrates' court. Cases (except EPOs) can be transferred to the county court at any time if:

(a) They are of exceptional gravity, importance or complexity, e.g., conflicts in evidence, novel or difficult points of law or questions of general public interest.

(b) They should be consolidated with pending proceedings.

(c) The matter is urgent and no other magistrates' court can take the case.

If an application for transfer is refused, a nominated care District Judge can reconsider the matter. Transfer will be to a 'care centre' county court. On receipt of the file the District Judge must give directions including the possibility of transferring to the High Court if:

(a) The proceedings are appropriate for determination in the High Court.

(b) Transfer would be in the interests of the child.

HIV tests should always be heard by High Court, see *Re X* [1994] 2 FLR 116.

Transfer back to the magistrates' court is possible provided that the views of the justices' clerk have been obtained, subject to appeal to a circuit judge.

There is some concern that magistrates have been less than willing to transfer appropriate cases.

In private law matters (section 8 cases etc.), proceedings can be commenced in any court with jurisdiction, namely, magistrates' court, county court or High Court. Magistrates may transfer to the county court if they feel that that is the more appropriate forum, and county courts can transfer to the High Court if that is considered the more appropriate forum. Proceedings in the county court and High Court are governed by the Family Proceedings Rules 1991 (SI 1991 No. 1247) as amended by SI 1991 No. 2113), *Practice Direction* [1995] 1 All ER 586, see also *Practice Direction (Family Division: Family Proceedings) (Allocation to Judiciary)* [1997] 2 FLR 780.

7.18.3 ARRANGEMENTS IN THE COUNTY COURT

County courts are now categorised as centres; there are divorce centres, family hearing centres and care centres. The jurisdiction of each centre is limited.

7.18.4 WITNESS STATEMENTS IN SUPPORT OF CHILDREN APPLICATIONS

Each party is required to file and serve written statements of the oral evidence (and copies of any documentary evidence) which he or she intends to adduce at the hearing. Such statements should be dated and include a declaration that the maker believes the contents to be true. However, because emotions are apt to run high, and in the interest of the parties coming to a sensible agreement on the care of their children without resort to the court, no documents should be filed or served in a section 8 case until the court gives leave, i.e., when it becomes apparent there will in fact have to be a hearing. At the hearing, no party may adduce evidence or seek to rely on a document which has not been disclosed in advance to the other side, unless the court gives permission.

The statements of the parties in section 8 cases should be drafted with particular care. The court will read them in advance of the hearing and will quite naturally form an initial view of the case which could have a significant impact on the outcome. You would never, of course, manufacture evidence, but (as with all witness statements/affidavits) you want to put what evidence there is in as favourable a light as possible. Therefore, such statements should be relevant, readable — and persuasive.

The following is a general checklist for the possible contents of a statement in support of an application for a residence order.

(a) The reason for the application.

(b) A very brief introductory history of the marriage/relationship between the parents, including the roles of the parents in the caring of the children.

(c) If the spouses or parties have already separated, an explanation of the children's circumstances since then, including information about contact with the absent parent. The aim is to put the application into context; it should not be treated as an opportunity to rehearse the reasons for the breakdown of the marriage.

(d) The present situation of the children, including appropriate details of where they are living, where they are going to school, their daily care and routine.

(e) The witness's views as to the children's needs, and, depending on the perspective of the client, what is right or wrong with the existing arrangements for the child. This should not become a catalogue of petty grievances against the other party. The court will not be well disposed towards an applicant who displays a retributive streak towards the other parent. It may give the impression that the applicant is more interested in exacting revenge than in the interests of the children. Genuine concerns, however, should be clearly articulated and explained.

(f) Appropriate details (e.g., as to housing and schooling) of the proposed arrangements for the child if the applicant is awarded a residence order. Get as much information as possible (e.g., the school the children will attend, whether they have a place, how will they get there etc.). Suitability and stability are the hallmarks of a successful section 8 application.

(g) Appropriate details of any new partner the spouse may have who will come into contact with the child and their relationship with the child.

(h) Appropriate details of any relative or other person who may help to care for the child, especially if the spouse seeking a residence order will be working.

(i) Anything special about the child, e.g., disability or persistent illness.

(j) History of parental contact and proposals to allow the other parent contact. It will obviously help an applicant for a residence order if he or she has had regular, prolonged and happy contact with the children. Equally, a parent seeking residence who displays an unco-operative or disruptive attitude towards contact with the other parent (without compelling reasons) will only turn the court against the application.

(k) A summary of the order sought.

7.18.5 PROCEDURE IN PRIVATE LAW CHILDREN CASES

At the Directions hearing you need to be clear about whether you want a welfare report to be prepared for the court. A welfare report may only be ordered pursuant to s. 7 of CA 1989, i.e., when a court 'considering any question with respect to a child under the Act 'requires a report' of relevant matters relating to the welfare of that child. In practice, reports are ordered in most residence and contact cases. However, if the court does not automatically order a report and you believe that one would assist your case then you should be prepared to make submissions for one.

A children and family reporter (previously known as a court welfare officer) is a prime example of a single, court appointed expert who will visit the parties in their homes, with and without the children present. In addition, he or she will make any other relevant investigations by, for example, visiting the children's school, talking with other relatives/carers, consulting the family GP. When you get a copy of the report, read it carefully — its recommendations are extremely important. If the children and family reporter's recommendations are against you, the chances of succeeding in an application (especially for residence) are in most cases dramatically reduced. Having said that, he or she can misunderstand a conversation or misconstrue an event (and on occasion you may feel the approach taken is unsound) so always check to see what aspects of the report need clarification or testing in cross-examination.

Once you have read the report you need to check whether the child and family reporter will be attending if you wish to cross-examine on matters of importance. He or she will often give evidence-in-chief and be cross-examined by both parties at the beginning of the hearing (after counsel for the applicant has opened). Occasionally, however, it may be desirable for the reporter to hear the parties giving evidence first.

Other expert evidence (e.g., to counteract the court appointed expert's views) may only be called with the permission of the court. See generally the Children Act Advisory Committee's *Handbook of Best Practice in Children Act Cases* and *Re A (Family Proceedings: Expert Witnesses)* [2001] 1 FLR 723 regarding the instructing of experts in family proceedings.

At the hearing itself, held in private, the court may give directions as to the order of witnesses and speeches. Generally speaking, counsel for the applicant opens, calls witnesses who have sworn statements in favour of his or her case, examines the witness where appropriate and tenders the witness for cross-examination by counsel for the respondent. Then examination and cross-examination of the respondent's witnesses takes place. Counsel for the respondent closes first, followed by counsel for the applicant, who has the last word.

The speeches and questions focus on each party's theory of the case with reference to the statutory checklist and the 'no order' principle. For example, in a residence dispute, you want to convince the court that it would be better for the child to reside with your client than the other party. Go through the checklist of factors and see what arguments you can develop in your favour. For example, when looking at the child's physical needs you want to look at the daily care and routine of the child. If your client is at home during the day then he or she will arguably be better able to satisfy this criteria than the other party who will be relying on a helper. On the other hand, the older the child the less important this criteria becomes. Or it may be that the working parent's helper is a loving grandmother or a reliable and much loved au pair. You must be able to see things from all sides, anticipate the submissions that will be made against you and put your own points persuasively. And, as always, use your common sense — the judge you are appearing in front of may have left her children home with the nanny!

7.19 Public Funding

Public funding (subject to means and merits tests) is available under the Community Legal Services scheme for proceedings under the Children Act 1989. For most *private* law cases, however, before funding is approved, the applicant will first be required to attend a meeting with a mediator to determine whether the case is suitable for mediation.

7.20 Decision with Reasons

After the final hearing, the court must make its decision 'as soon as practicable'. In so doing, it must set out any findings of fact and give reasons for the court's decision. Section 8 orders must be properly recorded and served on all affected parties (FPR 1991, r. 4.21 and Family Proceedings Courts (Children Act 1989) Rules 1991 (SI 1991 No. 1395), r. 21.

7.21 Appeals

Appeals against a decision of the Family Proceedings Court (i.e., the magistrates) will lie to the High Court and are generally heard in public. An appeal against a decision of the District Judge will usually be made to the judge; such will not, however, be by way of rehearing. Appeals against a decision of the County Court or High Court lie directly to the Court of Appeal. The procedure for conducting appeals is contained in FPR 1991, r. 4.22.

7.22 Costs

Costs are now governed by the Civil Procedure Rules 1998, as adjusted for family proceedings. However, given the inquisitorial element in Children Act cases, and the fact that the child is the focus of the proceedings, it is still the case that courts are reluctant to make costs orders in cases about children unless one of the parents has behaved unreasonably or there is a hugh disparity in the parties' means (*M* v *M* (*Costs in Children Proceedings*) [2000] Fam Law 877).

7.23 Public Law: An Example of a Care Case

The following is an example of a care case which commenced in the Family Proceedings Court (i.e., the magistrates' court) and was transferred to the county court because of the estimated length of the hearing. It contains examples of documents you might expect to see including the initial application of an interim care order, the first interim care order and directions, and an example of a standard form of directions. We have not included every interim care order and the different directions which would have been made in the proceedings prior to the final hearing itself. By way of illustration, we have included the initial and final statements of the social worker who has performed a comprehensive assessment of the child, the statement of the mother and the care plan. Typically, you might also see statements by some or all of the following:

- the father, grandparents or other relatives who have been involved in the care of the child,

- the foster carer,

- a party's boy/girlfriend/cohabitee.

In addition, in every case there will be the report of the children's guardian unless the court thinks (exceptionally) that it is unnecessary. There may also be expert evidence (usually from a child psychiatrist) filed on behalf of one or both of the parties. It is important, particularly if you are acting for a parent, to examine the children's guardian's report and other expert evidence critically. Although often difficult to challenge, do not feel you have to accept uncritically the conclusions of the experts. Look carefully at the factual basis for their conclusions (which you may wish to dispute) and see if the conclusions can be justified.

Welfare reports in public law cases tend to be provided by the local authority officer who has been dealing with the child's case, known for these purposes as a 'welfare officer', rather than the child and family report. However, it is often unnecessary, certainly when they agree, to have a report from both the children's guardian and a welfare officer/child and family reporter. Usually the latter's report will suffice.

Finally, we have included examples of skeleton arguments for the applicant and the respondent. There would also be one for the children's guardian but here they supported the local authority's application and repeated the same points. There is no prescribed way for drafting a skeleton argument, but it is important to identify the issues and your client's case in relation to each issue as precisely and persuasively as you can. Ideally, you should support each conclusion you draw with the evidence in the bundle (refer to the witness statement, page and paragraph). Read the papers and then go through the two skeletons. Find the facts which support the conclusions and note the references.

Please note, we have *not* included all reports referred to in the papers for the sake of brevity. The documents contained in the case are as follows:

1. Court forms

2. Statement of Emily Cromack dated 4 June 2001

3. Statement of Frances James dated 21 June 2001

4. Statement of Emily Cromack dated 28 September 2001

5. Psychology Report by Dr Ralph Peters dated 19 July 2001

6. Pyschiatric Report by Dr John Head dated 19 September 2001

7. Care Plan dated 22 October 2001

8. Report of the Children's Guardian dated 23 November 2001

9. Skeleton Argument on behalf of the Applicant

10. Skeleton Argument on behalf of the Respondent.

When preparing for a care hearing you are strongly recommended to refer to *The Guide for Social Workers Undertaking a Comprehensive Assessment* (known in practice as 'the Orange Book'). This will give you an insight into what steps the social worker should have taken. See also *Re E (Care Proceedings: Social Work Practice)* [2000] 2 FLR 254.

At the hearing itself, counsel for the local authority (the applicant) would open and call its witnesses. Counsel for the mother (the respondent) would cross-examine first (if there was another respondent, they would follow), with the children's guardian cross-examining last. Counsel for the mother then calls her witnesses and the local authority cross-examines first. Again, if there was another respondent they would cross-examine second and counsel for the children's guardian would cross-examine last. Finally, the children's guardian may call any expert evidence he or she wishes to adduce. Then, he or she gives evidence and is cross-examined in turn by the applicant and the respondent(s).

Application for an order

Form C1

Children Act 1989

The court	To be completed by the court

Aardvark Magistrates' Court

Date issued 4.6.01

Case number FPC/2001/99/111

The full name(s) of the child(ren)

Child(ren)'s number(s)

Mark James

1 About you (the applicant)

> *State* • *your title, full name, address, telephone number, date of birth and relationship to each child above*
> • *your solicitor's name, address, reference, telephone, FAX and DX numbers.*

Aardvarkshire County Council
Aardvark Social Services
Department
2 Howard Road
Aardvark
AA1 1AA
Tel: 01100 222 222

Ms Janet Grey
Legal Department
County Hall
Aardvark
Tel: 01100 333 444
Fax: 01100 444 333
DX: 0000 Aardvark

2 The child(ren) and the order(s) you are applying for

> *For each child state* • *the full name, date of birth and sex*
> • *the type of order(s) you are applying for (for example, residence order, contact order, supervision order).*

Mark James (d.o.b. 2.2.98)
Care order

3 Other cases which concern the child(ren)

If there have ever been, or there are pending, any court cases which concern
- *a child whose name you have put in paragraph 2*
- *a full, half or step brother or sister of a child whose name you have put in paragraph 2*
- *a person in this case who is or has been, involved in caring for a child whose name you have put in paragraph 2*

attach a copy of the relevant order and give
- *the name of the court*
- *the name and panel address (if known) of the guardian ad litem, if appointed*
- *the name and contact address (if known) of the court welfare officer, if appointed*
- *the name and contact address (if known) of the solicitor appointed for the child(ren).*

No

4 The respondent(s)

Appendix 3 Family Proceedings Rules 1991; Schedule 2 Family Proceedings Courts (Children Act 1989) Rules 1991

For each respondent state
- *the title, full name and address*
- *the date of birth (if known) or the age*
- *the relationship to each child.*

Ms Frances James   d.o.b. 1.4.71
(mother)
Amble House Hostel
Amble Rd
Aardvark

5 Others to whom notice is to be given

Appendix 3 Family Proceedings Rules 1991; Schedule 2 Family Proceedings Courts (Children Act 1989) Rules 1991

For each person state • *the title, full name and address*
 • *the date of birth (if known) or age*
 • *the relationship to each child*

Mrs Beatrice James (maternal grandmother)
8 Eaton Rd.
Aardvark

Mrs Jean Brady (paternal grandmother)
2 Aylsham Rd,
Aardvark

6 The care of the child(ren)

For each child in paragraph 2 state
 • *the child's current address and how long the child has lived there*
 • *whether it is the child's usual address and who cares for the child there*
 • *the child's relationship to the other children (if any).*

— currently residing with maternal grandmother (since 17.5.01)

— child's usual address is Amble House Hostel, Amble Rd, Aardvark, (mother's address).

7 Social Services

For each child in paragraph 2 state
 • *whether the child is known to the Social Services.*
   If so, give the name of the social worker and the address of the Social Services department.
 • *whether the child is, or has been, on the Child Protection Register. If so, give the date of registration.*

— Child's social worker is Emily Cromack, Aardvark Social Services

— 19.2.01 child's name placed on the Aardvark Child Protection Register — "likely physical injury" .

8 The education and health of the child(ren)

For each child state
- *the name of the school, college or place of training which the child attends*
- *whether the child is in good health. Give details of any serious disabilities or ill health.*
- *whether the child has any special needs.*

The child is too young for school.
His health is average with no special
needs.

9 The parents of the child(ren)

For each child state
- *the full name of the child's mother and father*
- *whether the parents are, or have been, married to each other*
- *whether the parents live together. If so, where.*
- *whether, to your knowledge, either of the parents have been involved in a court case concerning a child. If so, give the date and the name of the court.*

Mother — Frances James

Father — Richard Brady (deceased)

10 The family of the child(ren) (other children)

For any other child not already mentioned in the family (for example, a brother or a half sister) state
- *the full name and address*
- *the date of birth (if known) or age*
- *the relationship of the child to you.*

N/A

11 Other adults

State
- the full name of any other adults (for example, lodgers) who live at the same address as any child named in paragraph 2
- whether they live there all the time
- whether, to your knowledge, the adult has been involved in a court case concerning a child. If so, give the date and the name of the court.

None

12 Your reason(s) for applying and any plans for the child(ren)

State briefly your reasons for applying and what you want the court to order.
- **Do not** give a full statement if you are applying for an order under Section 8 of Children Act 1989. You may be asked to provide a full statement later.
- **Do not** complete this section if this form is accompanied by a prescribed supplement.

The department is seeking an Interim Care Order in respect of Mark. Please see Form 13 for further information.

13 At the court

State
- whether you will need an interpreter at court (parties are responsible for providing their own). If so, specify the language.
- whether disabled facilities will be needed at court.

Signed _Sarah Morgan_ Date 4. 6. 01
(Applicant) Practice Manager

Supplement for an application for
a Care or Supervision Order

Form C13

Section 31 Children Act 1989

The court

Aardvark
Magistrates' Court

To be completed by the court

Date issued 4.6.01

Case number FPC/2001/99111

The full name(s) of the child(ren)

Mark James

Child(ren)'s number(s)

1 The grounds for the application

and

The grounds are that the child[ren] [is] [are] suffering or [is] [are] likely to suffer, significant harm and the harm, or likelihood of harm, is attributable to

[✓] the care given to the child[ren], or likely to be given to the child[ren] if the order were not made, not being what it would be reasonable to expect a parent to give to the child[ren]

[ ] the child[ren] being beyond parental control

2 The reason(s) for the application

If you are relying on a report or other documentary evidence, state the date(s) and author(s) and enclose a copy.

Mark has suffered significant physical harm from his mother in the past, which led to his name being placed on the Child Protection Register on 19.2.01. A further Child Protection Investigation was carried out on 30.4.01 following mother's admission that she hit Mark over the head with a can of baked beans. The mother is unable to care for the child at present. Since February 2001 Mark has been subjected to at least 4 sudden changes of carers which has led to his suffering significant harm.

3 Your plans for the child(ren)

Include • *in the case of supervision orders only, any requirements which you will invite the court to impose pursuant to paragraph 1 Schedule 3 Children Act 1989*

• *in all cases, whether you will invite the court to make an interim order.*

i) Interim Care Order for 8 weeks to Aardvarkshire County Council.

ii) Interim Care Plan for Mark to remain with his maternal grandmother Mrs Beatrice James whilst a comprehensive assessment is undertaken of his short and long term needs.

iii) Supervised contact between Mark and his mother, either by Aardvarkshire County Council or a person nominated by Aardvarkshire County Council at least twice weekly.

4 The direction(s) sought

Family Proceedings Rules 1991 Rule 4.14

Family Proceedings Courts (Children Act 1989) Rules 1991 Rule 14

Signed (Applicant) Sarah Morgan Practice Manager

Date 4. 6. 01

In the

Aardvark
Magistrates' Court

Case Number:

Child(ren)'s Number(s):

FPC/2001/99/111

Order | Interim Care Order
Section 38 Children Act 1989

The full name(s) of the child(ren) | Date(s) of birth

Mark James | 2.2.98

The Court orders | that the child[ren] be placed in the care of

Aardvarkshire _____ local authority

The order expires on | 2 August 2001

[The Court directs | that a directions hearing take place on 2 July 2001 at 2.00 pm at Aardvark Magistrates' Court to discuss venue and timetable.

Warning | While a Care Order is in force no person may cause the child[ren] to be known by a new surname or remove the child[ren] from the United Kingdom without the written consent of every person with parental responsibility for the child[ren] or the leave of the court.

However, the local authority, in whose care a child is, may remove that child from the United Kingdom for a period of less than 1 month.

It may be a criminal offence under the Child Abduction Act 1984 to remove the child[ren] from the United Kingdom without the leave of the Court.

Ordered by | ~~[Mr] [Mrs] Justice~~
~~[His] [Her] Honour Judge~~
~~District Judge [of the Family Division]~~
Justice[s] of the Peace
~~Clerk of the Court~~ Mr Alpha - Mrs Beta - Mr Orange

on | 7 June 2001

In the

Aardvark Magistrates Court

Case Number:

FPC/2001/99/111

The full name(s) of the child(ren)	Date(s) of birth	Child(ren)'s Number(s)
Mark James	2.2.98	

[Order]   [Direction]

Children Act 1989

Leave be given for the papers to be disclosed to a psychologist for the purpose of assessing the mother's mental state and intellectual capacity; and a report be prepared for the Court.

Leave be given for the GAL to disclose the papers to Dr John Head for the purpose of preparing a report for the Court in respect of Mark.

Also leave for the GAL to instruct Dr John Head for the above purpose. (The GAL will agree a joint letter of referral to Dr John Head with all solicitors involved; in the event of a dispute as to the content of such a letter the GAL will be the final arbiter.

Ordered by   ~~[Mr] [Mrs] Justice~~
                  [His] [Her] Honour Judge
                  District Judge [of the Family Division]
                  Justice[s] of the Peace
                  Clerk of the Court
                  ~~[Assistant] Recorder~~

on   **7** June 2001

IN THE AARDVARK FAMILY PROCEEDINGS COURT

IN THE MATTER OF: .... AND ....
    AND .... CASE NUMBER ....
RE THE CHILDREN ....
BEFORE: ....
PRESENT: (APPLICANT) (APPLICANTS SOL/CNSL ....)
(Delete as (RESPONDENT)(RESPONDENTS SOL/CNSL..)
appropriate) (CHILDREN ....)
   (GUARDIAN AD LITEM)(G.A.L. SOL.CNSL ....)
   (WELFARE OFFICER ....)

IT IS DIRECTED THAT: (Tick as appropriate)

[ ] 1. .... be joined as a party to the proceedings
[ ] 2. Leave be given for the child/ren not to attend any further proceedings
[ ] 3. Leave be given to disclose the papers to ....
[ ] 4. A Guardian ad litem be appointed
[ ] 5. As the parties agreed to mediation the Court Welfare Service is requested to make an appointment
[ ] 6. The (Guardian ad litem) (Welfare Officer) file a report by ....
[ ] 7. The (Guardian ad litem) (Welfare Officer) attend the (next directions hearing)(court hearing)(final hearing)
[ ] 8. The time limit specified in the F.P. Rules is abridged (to ....) (to allow this application to proceed forthwith
[ ] 9. (i) .... do (file and) serve a statement in accordance with F.P. Rule 17 (1) on the parties and the (Guardian ad litem)(Welfare Officer) by ....
   (ii) .... do (file and) serve a statement in accordance with F.P. Rule 17 (1) on the parties and the (Guardian ad litem)(Welfare Officer) by ....
   (iii) The additional witnesses listed overleaf do (file and) serve a statement in accordance with F.P. Rule 17 (1) on the parties and the (Guardian ad litem)(Welfare Officer) by ....
   In the event of non compliance with the time limit above, further direction need only be sought if agreement cannot be reached between the parties, and any amendment would not affect direction 11
[ ] 10. The requirement to file statements under Rule17 be amended to the need to file in accordance with direction 11
[ ] 11. The (Applicant)(Respondent) to prepare, file and serve on the parties the following by 4.00 pm on ....
   [ ] a summary of the history of the case
   [ ] a summary of agreed facts and disputed facts
   [ ] a summary of the issues to be resolved between the parties
   [ ] a bundle, paginated and indexed, with as many copies as may be necessary including four for the court, of the statements and reports previously served
   [ ] a skeleton argument
   [ ] any references to case law sought to be relied upon
[ ] 12. The oral evidence upon which the parties intend to rely at the final hearing of this matter is to be limited to themselves and the witnesses whose statements have been filed
[ ] 13. Leave is given for the child to be examined by ....
   and the resulting report is to be filed by ....
   (Blood tests) (D.N.A.) be taken and the (Applicants)(Respondents) solicitors make the necessary arrangements
[ ] 15. The application be listed for (further directions)(a court hearing)(final hearing) on ....
[ ] 16. A draft consent order, including findings of facts and details of the order with supporting reasons be filed and served on the parties by ....
[ ] 17. For the purposes of the final hearing, the Applicant shall prepare, with as many copies as may be necessary, including four copies for the court, (A) a historical chronology of the main relevant events in the child's life and these proceedings and (B) a bundle, paginated and indexed, of copies of all written statements, documentary evidence and experts reports served by the parties. Both (A) and (B) to be agreed as far as possible and indicating on the first page those facts and documents which are agreed and those that are not agreed and to be filed by ....

NOTE THE "STATEMENTS" REFERRED TO ABOVE ARE THE WRITTEN STATEMENTS OF THE SUBSTANCE OF THE ORAL EVIDENCE WHICH A PARTY INTENDS TO GIVE AT A HEARING WETHER FROM HIM OR HERSELF OR FROM WITNESSES CALLED ON THAT PARTY'S BEHALF SUCH STATEMENTS MUST BE DATED, SIGNED BY THE PERSON MAKING THE STATEMENT AND CONTAIN A DECLARATION THAT SUCH PERSON BELIEVES IT TO BE TRUE AND UNDERSTANDS IT MAY BE PLACED BEFORE THE COURT THE STATEMENT SHOULD BE NUMBERED PARAGRAPHS, EACH OF REASONABLE LENGTH FOR EASE OF REFERENCE AND PREFERABLY TYPED. "FILE" MEANS TO SEND THE STATEMENT TO THE COURT AND "SERVE" MEANS TO SEND COPIES TO EACH OF THE PARTIES.

These directions were given on .... and were (not) made ex parte

(Justice of the Peace) (Clerk of the Court)

Statement by Emily Cromack (1)

Statement of E. R. Cromack
Dated: 4.6.01
Filed on behalf of Aardvarkshire County
Council

IN THE AARDVARK MAGISTRATES' COURT

IN THE MATTER OF MARK JAMES D.O.B. 2.2.98   Case No. FPC/2001/99/111

AND IN THE MATTER OF THE CHILDREN ACT

I, Emily Rosalind Cromack, make this statement believing the same to be true and knowing that it may be placed before the court in evidence.

Signed .... *Emily Cromack* ....

Dated .... *4/6/01* ....

STATEMENT OF EMILY ROSALIND CROMACK

I am Emily Rosalind Cromack. I hold the Certificate of Qualification in Social Work which was gained at the University of Leicester in 1983, and the Diploma in Social Studies. I am a social worker employed by the Applicant, the Aardvarkshire County Council.

In preparing this report I have consulted social services' files, visited and interviewed Miss Frances James, Mrs Beatrice James (maternal grandmother), Mrs Jean Brady (paternal grandmother) and I have seen Mark three times. I have consulted Dr Busby, general practitioner to Mark and Frances, Mrs Elsa Dredge, Aspen Family Centre worker and Miss Wendy Clerk, family assistant.

CHRONOLOGY — MARK JAMES

4.1.01   Referral to social services by Miss Frances James' solicitor asking for support for Frances in caring for Mark. Mark and Frances left family home and staying with friends in Hillside.

8.1.01   Assessment visit by social worker. Frances agreed to receiving support from Aspen Family Centre.

11.1.01   Request made to Aspen Family Centre for help for Frances in parenting skills.

28.1.01   Frances and Mark move from friends to Amble House Hostel, Aardvark.

11.2.01   Police called to Amble House Hostel because Frances had lost control and was slapping Mark around the head. Police removed Mark on a s. 46 and he was placed with foster parents.

12.2.01   Foster mother reports that Mark is very distressed.

16.2.01   Mark returns to the care of his mother.

19.2.01   Child Protection Case Conference; Mark's name placed on Child Protection Register. Comprehensive package of support offered to Frances to include attendance at Family Centre, and home visits by family centre worker and family assistant. Category of Child Protection Registration 'Likely Physical Injury'.

23.2.01   Frances and Mark did not attend the family centre.

8.3.01   Mrs Brady tells social worker that Frances has always hit Mark around the head and they could not stop her.

9.3.01   Frances tells Aspen Family Centre that she is hitting Mark around the head and is worried that she could kill him. Mark goes to stay with Mrs Beatrice James (maternal grandmother).

26.3.01   Mrs James unwell. Mark returns to mother at Amble House.

27.4.01   Frances tells family assistant that she is still hitting Mark.

29.4.01   Frances hits Mark with a can of beans.

30.4.01   Child Protection investigation by social worker. Mark stays with Frances. Frances wants to prove that she can look after him.

2.5.01   Frances and Mark move in with Mr David Farley at 3 Waterside, Aardvark.

10.5.01   Mr Farley telephones social services asking that Frances and Mark be placed in other accommodation. Frances tells social worker she slapped Mark on the head. Mark goes to stay with Mrs Jean Brady (paternal grandmother). Frances returns to Amble House.

11.5.01   Social worker visits Mrs Brady and Mark. Mark is very distressed and asking for his mother constantly and crying.

14.5.01   Mrs Brady finding it difficult to cope with Mark.

17.5.01   Planning Meeting at Social Services. Miss Frances James, Mrs Beatrice James and Mrs Jean Brady invited. Mrs Brady unable to cope looking after Mark. Frances has not had contact with Mark since he moved to Mrs Brady's. Mark moved to Mrs Beatrice James. Frances says she will recommence seeing Mark.

INTRODUCTION

1.   Frances James first came to the notice of social services on 4 January 2001 when her solicitor contacted the department asking for help in parenting skills for Mark following her departure from her mother's home with Mark. Frances first approached her solicitor regarding the administration of the estate of Mark's father, Mr Robert Brady (deceased).

2.   Frances was reluctant to access resources available to help her. Therefore it was agreed that Mrs Elsa Dredge from Aspen Family Centre would provide outreach services to her at her friends' home in Hillside and Amble House Hostel upon accommodation becoming vacant.

3.   On 11 February 2001 police were called to Amble House Hostel following a call stating that other residents had heard a child screaming. Mr David Farley, a friend of Frances, expressed his concerns on Frances' parenting. He had witnessed Frances hitting Mark about the head. Frances admitted hitting Mark. A police protection order was applied for and Mark was taken to foster carers.

4.   Later that day Frances presented herself to social services and told the social worker, that she hits Mark and she does this because she does not know how to cope with him. Frances agreed to accept help and support if Mark were returned to her.

5.   Mark was so distressed at the separation from his mother that he was returned to her on 16 February 2001.

6.   A 'Child Protection' Case Conference was held on 19 February 2001. Frances did not attend. It was further concluded that Mark's name be placed on the 'Child Protection' Register under the category 'Likely Physical Injury'. A protection plan was agreed to include the following:

(i)   Frances James should not be physically violent towards Mark. Work to be undertaken with her to explore alternative methods of discipline which do not involve physical chastisement.

(ii)   A family assistant would make a home visit once a week to offer support of a practical nature.

(iii)   Frances and Mark to attend Aspen Family Centre twice a week. The family centre worker to make one outreach visit per week to the family home.

THE FAMILY MEMBERS

7.   MISS FRANCES JAMES

I understand that Miss Frances James has had many difficulties in her life which have resulted in a certain level of depression. Social services, together with Dr Busby, her G.P., have obtained psychiatric help for her and an assessment is underway.

8.   MRS BEATRICE JAMES

Mrs Beatrice James has been very involved in Mark's upbringing since 3 February 2000, when Mark's father Robert Brady died and Frances together with Mark moved in to live with her mother. She has offered considerable encouragement and support.

9.   MRS JEAN BRADY

Mrs Brady is very keen to offer every assistance for Mark and has found it very distressing that Frances resists her involvement in Mark's care. She also finds Mark a very difficult boy to comfort and console. She says that when Mark stayed with her he was extremely distressed by not being with his mother and she feels that she will not be able to offer Mark the care he needs.

10.   MARK JAMES

Mark is a friendly and intelligent child. He has been disturbed by the events over the last year which is manifested by his showing aggression to other children on occasion. He has been found by both grandmothers to be very difficult to handle and he suffers enormous distress when he is parted from his mother. The Aspen Family Centre have noticed eating problems.

CURRENT SITUATION

11.   I was appointed to be the social worker for Mark James on 4 May 2001. I was asked to co-ordinate the care plan and prepare a thorough assessment of risk for the first Child Protection Review. Sadly I have been unable to carry out these tasks due to the difficulties Frances experiences both in remaining at the same address and in keeping Mark with her. It is true that both have been ill — Frances with food poisoning and Mark with 'flu but this does not explain the series of crises with which social services have been confronted.

12.   As will be seen from the Chronology, since 19 March 2001 Frances has asked for Mark to be placed with alternative carers three times. In the last year he has also moved many times with his mother.

13.   It is particularly sad that Frances has not been able to avail herself of the help which has been offered; in particular she has only attended the Aspen Family Centre twice. The visits of the family assistant have not been frequent because Mark has not remained in Amble House Hostel but has been moved around.

14.   Frances finds it very difficult to discipline Mark other than by physical chastisement and she has confessed on a number of occasions that she hits him on the head. She hit Mark on the head on one occasion with a can of baked beans on 29 April 2001.

15.   As a result of this chastisement a further 'Child Protection' Investigation was under-taken. The decision of the social worker undertaking the investigation was that Mark should remain with his mother, who expressed a strong desire to prove that she could cope with Mark.

16.   Social services have been keen to encourage Frances to learn to cope with Mark because he is very distressed when separated from her. However, this must be balanced against the risk of physical injury to Mark. In fact, Mark has been placed with his grandmothers on a number of occasions and when he was last placed with Mrs Brady, Frances did not contact him and resisted attempts of Aspen Family Centre to encourage her to do so.

CONCLUSION AND RECOMMENDATION

17.   The Social Services Department is extremely concerned both at the number of times mark has been separated from his mother and the abrupt way in which these separations have been organised. We also remain alarmed at Frances' difficulties in handling her son, and in particular at her frequent recourse to physical punishment.

18.   As a result of the above, the department is of the opinion that the child has suffered significant physical and emotional harm.

19.   In order to establish some stability and security for Frances we feel it is vital for the department to have a degree of control over the situation since it has been shown that at present she is unable to care for Mark.

20.   With this aim we would respectfully ask the Court to make Mark James the subject of an Interim Care Order for eight weeks. Most importantly this would provide the child with a much needed period of security and would also enable the social services department to undertake a comprehensive assessment of the child's needs.

CARE PLAN

21.   Were the Court to make such an order, the care plan would be as follows:

(i)   Mark to remain in the short-term care of Mrs Beatrice James at 8 Eaton Road, Aardvark.

(ii)   Supervised contact between Mark and his mother either at Aardvarkshire County Council or a person nominated by Aardvarkshire County Council, at least twice weekly.

(iii)   Aardvarkshire County Council Social Services Department to undertake a thorough assessment of the long-term needs of Mark in order to help the family to plan realistically for his future.

Emily Rosalind Cromack

Aardvark Social Services

Date: 4.6.01

Statement by Frances James

First statement of
Frances James
Dated 21 June 2001

IN THE AARDVARK FAMILY PROCEEDINGS COURT

IN THE MATTER OF THE CHILDREN ACT 1989   Case No. FPC/2001/99/111

IN THE MATTER OF MARK JAMES D.O.B. 2.2.98

BETWEEN   AARDVARKSHIRE COUNTY COUNCIL   <u>Applicant</u>

and

FRANCES JAMES   <u>Respondent</u>

STATEMENT OF FRANCES JAMES

I, FRANCES JAMES, of Amble House Hostel, Amble Road, Aardvark, Aardvarkshire make this statement believing it to be true and knowing that it may be used in Court proceedings.

1. I am aged 30 years and I was married to Mr Robert Brady on 2 February 1995. We lived with his mother at 2 Aylsham Road, Aardvark until Robert's death on 3 February 2000. Mark and I went to live with my mother at 8 Eaton Road, Aardvark until New Year's Day when Mark and I left to stay with some friends in Hillside.

2. I found it quite difficult looking after Mark on my own and mentioned this to my solicitor when I visited her concerning Robert's estate. It was at my request that the Social Services were contacted to help me look after Mark. Through Social Services I received support from the Aspen Family Centre. I also contacted the local authority and was provided with temporary half-way accommodation at my present address. It is a bedsit in a large house and bathroom and toilet facilities are shared with other residents. I had understood that as and when suitable Council accommodation became available this would be provided by the local authority for myself and Mark. Being on my own again I found it increasingly difficult to cope and this was why the Social Services became more involved again and led to the interim care order being made, to which I consented, and to which I refer to below.

3. I have been shown a copy of the initial report to this Court by Emily Rosalind Cromack dated 4 June 2001 and would, firstly, comment on the chronology as follows:

11.2.01 As stated above, I found it difficult on my own when I first moved into Amble House with Mark. On the afternoon/evening of the 11 February I returned to Amble House after doing some shopping and, for a reason that I cannot recall, I slapped Mark across the back of his head. It was only a light slap. I think that David Farley was in the bedsit with me when this happened. Understandably Mark cried and I understand that a neighbour or the warden called the police as I had also had an argument with a neighbour. Mark was placed with foster parents for a couple of days but returned to me soon because he was very distressed about not being with me.

23.2.01 I could not attend the Aspen Family Centre as I was unwell and could not get to a pay phone which is in the street outside.

9.3.01 I admit that I told Mrs Elsa Dredge of the Aspen Family Centre that I was having problems with Mark and had hit him around the head as a form of discipline. I did not say that I was worried that I could kill him. I accept that I asked for Mark to be looked after by someone else and was happy for my mother to look after him.

29.4.01   I admit that I hit Mark with a can of beans. I was cooking in the bedsit and Mark was crawling around my feet. I think that it is very dangerous to have Mark in the kitchen area when I am cooking and tried to encourage Mark to play on the bed. He refused and kept on twisting himself around my legs so that I nearly lost my balance. The can was in my hand and I did tap him on the head with it. I explained this to Wendy Clark and she seemed to understand my difficulties.

10.5.01   I did slap Mark twice on the head. They were only light slaps and I did admit this to the social worker.

4.   I accept that I have had personal difficulties in the past. This was made worse because of the unsatisfactory accommodation arrangements living with my husband's parents when my husband was alive. I always felt that the house was run by my mother-in-law and there were constant stresses and arguments within the family and between my husband and myself. Likewise, after Robert's death, upon moving in with my own mother I found it very difficult to feel in charge of my own baby and my life. Whilst I felt that I had to get out of the situation I was lonely and found it difficult to cope in the bedsit at Amble House.

5.   However, immediately upon explaining to my solicitor that I needed help and finding out that Social Services could help, I have kept in contact with them and freely told them about the problems and difficulties which I have had. The only exception is when I was ill.

6.   It is my long-term intention that Mark should live with me. There is a very strong bond of affection between us. My present plans are that David Farley and I intend to live together. Prior to the interim care order being made I was told by the local authority that I would be allocated a council flat but I am worried that these arrangements may be delayed or cancelled because Mark is not with me. I am sure that if I had proper accommodation I would be able to look after Mark on my own. My situation would be much easier as and when David Farley and I live together and I accept that there may be the necessity for some initial supervision by the Social Services Department.

DATED this twenty first day of June 2001

SIGNED ....*F. James*.........................

FRANCES JAMES

Statement by Emily Cromack (2)

Report of E. R. Cromack
Dated: 30/9/01
Filed on behalf of Aardvarkshire County
Council

TO THE AARDVARK COURT

IN THE MATTER OF THE CHILDREN ACT 1989

IN THE MARK JAMES D.O.B. 2.2.98   Case No. 01/CCO 222

Date of Hearing:

A REPORT TO THE COURT

Completed by: EMILY ROSALIND CROMACK
                              B.A.DIP.SOCIAL STUDIES C.Q.S.W

This Report has been prepared for the Court and should be treated as confidential.

Signed ....*Emily Cromack*...

Dated ....*30/9/01*..

1.   I am Emily Rosalind Cromack. I hold the Certificate of Qualification in Social Work which was gained at the University of Leicester in 1983, and the Diploma in Social Studies. I am a social worker employed by the Applicant, the Aardvarkshire County Council.

2.   In preparing this report I have consulted social services' files, visited and interviewed Miss Frances James, Mrs Beatrice James and Mrs Jean Brady. Whilst Mark was living with his maternal grandmother I saw him three times. I also saw him once when he was living with Mrs Jean Brady.

3.   I have also spoken to Dr. Alfred Moon, Consultant Paediatrician, Mrs Elsa Dredge, Aspen Family Centre worker and Miss Wendy Clark, family assistant.

INTRODUCTION

4.   Following the granting of an interim care order on 7 June 2001, Mark remained in the care of his maternal grandmother, Mrs Beatrice James. On 15 June 2001 Mrs James suffered a mild heart attack and as a result was unable to look after Mark. Since this time Mark has been staying with an experienced foster carer, Mrs Annette Falls.

5.   In early March Aardvarkshire County Council Social Services Department had started a thorough assessment of Mark's long-term needs in order to help the family to plan realistically for his future; this assessment was completed in August 2001.

6.   The following is a summary of the assessment:

Problems experienced by the child, areas of concern about him and his upbringing.

(i)   Repeated abuse resulting from lack of control

7.   Miss Frances James makes no secret of the fact that she has frequently resorted to hitting Mark about the head (on one occasion with a can of baked beans) in her attempts to discipline him. This information has been corroborated by Mr David Farley and Mrs Brady who said that when Frances and Mark were living with them Frances frequently hit her child.

Attempts by members of the family to alter this behaviour were allegedly met with the response 'he is my child and I will do what I like with him'. On occasion, however, Frances was sufficiently concerned by her own behaviour to report it to the health visitor who unfortunately took no action.

8. Miss James has given two main reasons for the way she has treated Mark; one is that she herself was under considerable mental stress and often heard voices telling her to hurt the child; the other is that she admits she is unable to discipline Mark in more acceptable ways.

(ii) Neglect

(a) Inappropriate food

9. Mark was a very poor eater whilst in his mother's care. On a visit to Miss James on 27 April 2001 Miss James described a typical day's meals as cereals for breakfast, no lunch except crisps, and a pizza or sausage for supper. Miss James says that she cannot cook. The diet given to Mark when he was living with Mrs Brady was marginally better but Mrs Brady told me on 14 May 2001 that often he had no breakfast, a snack for lunch, a pizza, baked beans, sausages and chips, or spaghetti for tea. The only vegetables he liked were cabbage and peas.

10. Whilst living with Mrs Beatrice James, Mark's appetite increased markedly. He began to eat a wide and varied diet and put on weight. There have been no further problems with appetite whilst he has been with the foster carer.

(b) Exposure to physical danger

11. When I saw Mrs Brady on 14 May 2001 she reported to me that when Miss James and Mark lived with them Frances used not to keep a proper watch on Mark; for example, the child would follow his mother upstairs and the latter would not be aware of what he was doing. Twice Mark fell downstairs, once down a whole flight.

(iii) Emotional Abuse

(a) *Inappropriate handling*

12. Frances James' attitude towards Mark was reminiscent of a four-year-old with a doll; she would sometimes give him a lot of attention, relating to him most affectionately and playing with him patiently and appropriately. However, she would then become tired of him and pass him to someone else to look after. This behaviour was reported to me by both grandmothers and Mrs Brady on 14 May 2001 also said that if Frances was watching television and Mark wanted cuddles she would push him away. Frances' explanation for this was 'he winds me up'.

(b) *Serious over protectiveness*

13. Prior to the making of the Interim Care Order, the relationship between Mark and his mother was unhealthily close during the times when Frances James was paying Mark attention. When I first met them on 4 May 2001 Mark was physically clinging to his mother throughout the interview. On that date also the family center worker told me that, far from trying to foster some independence, Frances James seemed to be encouraging dependency.

(c) *Lack of continuity of care*

14. Before leaving the family home of her husband and mother-in-law, Frances James once went away for a week taking Mark with her. Mark was also placed with both his grand-mothers since the incident of physical abuse on 9 March 2001. Since 4 January 2001 Mark was moved seven times and been cared for by three different carers.

(d)   *Inappropriate non-physical punishment*

15.   Mark has reported to Mrs Jean Brady that Mr David Farley used to lock him in his bedroom when he was naughty whilst he and his mother were staying with him, and one assumes that Frances James did nothing to prevent this.

(e)   *Family conflict*

There is a good deal of conflict between Frances James and Mrs Jean Brady. When Mark was staying with his paternal grandmother Frances refused to have any contact with him. In her dealings with social services Frances James has shown herself to be of a volatile disposition; Mrs Jean Brady told me on 14 May 2001 that she and Frances would argue frequently in front of Mark and Mark would cry on these occasions.

(iv)   Physical problems exhibited by the child

16.   Mark is in average health and there has been no concern on the part of doctors or health visitors.

(v)   Behavioural or emotional problems exhibited by the child

17.   Both Frances James and Mrs Jean Brady reported sleep disturbance; they said that Mark was very restless in his sleep and tugged at his hair; Frances James told me that he often cried in his sleep as though he were having a nightmare. This problem has also now been overcome.

18.   Frances James, both grandmothers and staff at the Aspen Family Centre have reported Mark to be aggressive, both to other children and to adults. He did not play well with other children and found it impossible to share.

19.   Mark was prone to temper tantrums if he did not get his own way and there was also a suggestion that he started tormenting Mrs Jean Brady's cat.

20.   Both the health visitor and I have noted that Mark is over-friendly to adults and seems extremely anxious to please.

21.   The most positive features to emerge from this assessment are:

(i)   the very real affection which each of the adults has for him, and the reasonably good understanding of ways to stimulate and play with him. He has always been kept clean and appropriately clothed.

(ii)   the progress which Mark made whilst in the care of Mrs Beatrice James, a progress which has continued in his present foster placement. Mark's temper tantrums have diminished and he is relating better to other children. As well as overcoming his eating problems, the child now sleeps in a bed, and a room, of his own and has a strict routine for bedtimes. His temper tantrums are diminishing and he has responded well to clear boundaries of behaviour. He has grown in confidence; he no longer has a fear of adults and no longer clings to his mother.

FAMILY COMPOSITION

FRANCES JAMES (d.o.b. 1.4.71)

22.   Miss Frances James has told me of continuing difficulties in her parents' relationship during her childhood. She recalls her parents frequently arguing and fighting. She has also told me of physical abuse in her childhood by her father who used to hit her around the head and sometimes throw crockery at her.

23. Frances James went to Hap School, Aardvark. This is a school for children with learning difficulties. She was never happy there and was bullied. As a result she used to truant. After leaving school she had a few jobs as a shop assistant but has not worked since her marriage.

24. Six years ago Mr and Mrs James moved to Cornwall to live for a year. Frances was so upset at being left and losing their support that she attempted suicide by taking an overdose. She was found by Mr Robert Brady who was living next door at the time. She remained in hospital for two weeks and then received psychiatric treatment as an outpatient.

25. Both grandmothers say that Frances James has always had difficulty in caring for herself and it appears that the stress of being expected to look after herself and Mark caused her to panic. Certainly she has become much more relaxed since this repsonsibility has been lifted from her.

26. The Social Services Department and Dr Busby, Frances James' general practitioner, had serious concerns regarding Frances' mental state, primarily caused by her assertions that she was hearing voices which had told her to harm herself. She was referred by Dr Busby to Dr Doogle, Psychiatrist at Aardvark General Hospital, who, in turn, referred her to Dr Farmer, a consultant psychiatrist for people with learning difficulties. It was Dr Farmer's opinion that Frances James was not suffering from a psychiatric illness.

27. I understand that there is a report before the Court in respect of Miss James, completed by Dr Peters, Community Clinical Psychologist. He detected no evidence of a psychiatric illness during the time of his assessment.

28. With regard to Miss James' parenting capacities I noted that he included the following: 'Miss James will need continuing support in parenting, home making skills, and organisation, setting boundaries for her child and emotional and physical support for her. Frances may find Mark's needs and behaviour very demanding and stressful and there should be some respite facility built in, even at short notice in order to give her a break before things reach a crisis situation.'

29. Miss James is currently living with her partner, Mr David Farley, and they have both told me that they intend to remain together, although I understand from Miss Wendy Clark, the family assistant, that the relationship is a volatile one and that Miss James has complained to her of the difficulties between them.

30. Mark does not like Mr Farley and has repeatedly expressed this dislike to the foster carer and to Wendy Clark. One example occurred on 10 August 2001 on a contact visit with his mother, Miss Clark noted that Mark refused to approach, or speak to, Mr Farley, and appeared quite uncomfortable throughout the visit and asked several times whether it was time to go home. Mark has not as yet been able to give any reason for this dislike.

MARK JAMES (d.o.b. 2.2.98)

31. Mark is an extremely attractive child, both in appearance and in personality. He is bright and lively and his behaviour is probably in advance of his age and stage of development. He concentrates well and is rewarding company. He responds well to affection and returns it happily.

32. Mark has been very upset by the lack of continuity of care, and in particular was quite devastated when first his mother and then his grandmothers appeared to abandon him. Despite this he settled in reasonably well in his current foster placement.

33. Mark is very attached to his mother. He is now friendly towards other children and plays well with them. He has started nursery school at Aardvark Nursery School three mornings a week.

34. Mark's capacity for adapting to changes in his circumstances is great, but I fear that, if major disruptions continue, this capacity will become superficial and may mask an inability to make and maintain close relationships.

CONCLUSION AND RECOMMENDATION

(i) OPTIONS AVAILABLE TO THE COURT

(a) *Making no order*

35. As will be seen from the chronology, between 4 January 2001, when Frances left her mother's home and 15 June 2001 when Mark was placed with his present foster carer, Mark has experienced 8 moves. It was with the prime intention of seeking some stability for Mark, pending the completion of the comprehensive assessment, that the local authority applied to the Court for an Interim Care Order. Sadly this stability was not achieved and not surprisingly Mark has now expressed the belief that 'nobody wants me'. The Court may now well take the view that making no order at all would return this child to the same chaotic situation from which we sought to protect him.

(b) *Making a residence order in favour of Miss Frances James*

36. There is genuine love between Miss James and her son but she is unable to care for him on a permanent basis as has been well demonstrated in this statement. The grounds for making the interim care order on 7 June 2001 were that it was reasonable to believe that the child would be at risk of significant harm were such an order not granted to the local authority.

37. Miss James maintains that she is now in a stable relationship and will receive assistance from her partner, Mr David Farley, in caring for Mark. However, this assertion in itself underlines her own doubts about her capacity to look after Mark without substantial assistance. Furthermore, Mark has no relationship with Mr Farley and indeed has taken a very strong dislike to him.

38. It remains the opinion of the local authority that the situation which obtained when the first interim care order was granted has not changed, and that Mark would still be at risk of significant physical and emotional harm in the care of his mother.

THE WELFARE CHECKLIST

39. Before taking a decision, the Court will wish to pay particular regard to the following factors:

(i) *The wishes and feelings of the child*

40. Mark is not yet four years old and is too young to take a long-term view of his situation. He has clearly demonstrated his affection for his family members and continued contact with them is a priority. However, he has also demonstrated feelings of anxiety and insecurity at his frequent moves and a fear that 'nobody wants him'.

(ii) *Physical, educational and emotional needs*

41. Mark has settled well in his present placement, has formed a good relationship with his foster carer, Mrs Annette Falls, and relates well to various relatives and friends of the foster mother, and to her grandchildren.

42. There is no doubt that Mark's physical and emotional needs are well met in his present foster placement. His educational needs will be met by local authority primary and secondary education.

(iii) *The likely effect on him of changes in circumstances*

43. Mark has experienced repeated moves in his short life and he must find it very difficult to understand why. Unfortunately, neither grandmother can look after Mark because Mrs Beatrice James is physically unable to look after him and Mrs Jean Brady cannot control him and Mark is very anxious and distressed from not seeing his mother.

44.   Mrs Annette Falls is committed to caring for Mark until a permanent home is found for Mark. A further move is unavoidable and it is hoped that Mark will not be too distressed by this. Certainly, the next move must be the final move for Mark.

(iv)   Ability of the parent to meet the child's immediate and long-term needs

(v)   Any harm which Mark has suffered or is at risk of suffering

45.   These are well documented in this Report.

GRANTING AN ORDER IN FAVOUR OF AARDVARKSHIRE COUNTY COUNCIL

46.   It is my professional opinion that, without the granting of an order to Aardvarkshire County Council, Mark would return to the situation from which the local authority originally sought to protect him, a situation which comprised repeated moves and different carers and which caused him both physical and emotional harm. It is, therefore, the considered view of the local authority that Mark would be at risk of further significant emotional and physical harm were the Court not to make an order today.

47.   It is of paramount importance that Mark is allowed to settle, as quickly as possible, with a famiy with whom he will remain throughout the rest of his childhood. This, in my opinion, would not be achieved through the means of a supervision order. Past experience has unfortunately shown that children under such an order do not experience the sense of security and permanency which are vital to their emotional development and well-being.

48.   In my view, the only option which will confer upon the local authority parental responsibility is a care order which will enable the local authority to make long-term plans for Mark. His over riding need at present is for a warm, secure, stable environment where he can grow and develop to his full potential. In the longer term the local authority would seek to secure his future within a permanent alternative family, preferably in an adoption placement. The local authority plan is detailed in the care plan.

49.   Mark has strong attachments to his family, particularly to his mother. However, the need for contact with her must be balanced against the need to find him a permanent alternative family. The latter need is a priority in Mark's life and cannot be allowed to be jeopardized by contact with his birth family which could undermine a permanent placement.

I therefore respectfully recommend to the Court that it grants to Aardvarkshire County Council a care order in respect of Mark James.

EMILY ROSALIND CROMACK

SOCIAL WORKER, AARDVARKSHIRE COUNTY COUNCIL   DATE: 28.9.01

Psychology report by Dr Ralph Peters

AARDVARK COMMUNITY HEALTH (NHS) TRUST
Psychology Department
Aardvark Hospital, Aspen Lane, Aardvark.
Tel: 01100 111111 ext. 2222 Fax: 01100 1111113

Private & Confidential

PSYCHOLOGY REPORT

Name: Ms Frances James

Address: Amble House Hostel
               Amble Road
               Aardvark

DOB: 1.4.71

GP: Dr Busby
               Aardvark

Background Information

Ms James talked about aspects of her past life including alcohol, drugs and also about the family situation quite candidly and accurately. She was reticent about her husband's recent death. She did not like living with his family. She said Mark was a 'handful' and would throw temper tantrums.

Ms James said that she had attended special school. Past occupation which was of short duration centred around cleaning work which she said she enjoyed. Ms James said that she would also enjoy working with animals.

I gained the impression that Ms James did not continually want her child with her. She said that her current boyfriend, David, was seeing another woman and might leave Ms James.

Presentation

Ms James presented as a slightly shy fairly well dressed person who was punctual for the assessment. She was quite articulate, friendly and polite. We got along well. Ms James reported accurately details of her life and was well aware of time and place. She spoke clearly in answer to questions. Most of the time she gave the impression of someone with a low average level of intelligence although occasionally there were signs of a borderline learning disability.

Ms James was co-operative and well motivated throughout, rarely losing concentration. This was for two one and a half hour sessions separated by one and a half hours.

Tests Given:

1.   The Weschsler Adult Intelligence Scale — Revised (WAIS–R)

2.   Ravens Coloured Progressive Matrices

3.   Schonnel Reading Test

Tests Results:

1.   WAIS–R

Verbal Sub Tests	Scaled Score (Average intelligence is approximately 10)
Information	3
Digit Span	5
Vocabulary	5
Arithmetic	3
Comprehension	5
Similarities	6

Performance Sub Tests	
Picture Completion	6
Picture Arrangement	4
Block Design	6
Object Assembly	2
Digit Symbol	4

Verbal IQ	= 70 (lower end of the borderline range of learning disability)
Performance IQ	= 67 (top end of the mild range of learning disability)
Full Scale IQ	= 67 (top end of the mild range of learning disability)

2.   Coloured Progressive Matrices

Mental Age	= 9.25 years

3.   Schonnel Reading Test

Reading Age	= 7.9 years

Discussion of Test Results:

Ms James presented as someone who is functioning intellectually within the mild/low borderline range of learning disability (IQ = approximately 70 World Health Organisation classification) in both the verbal and performance areas of IQ. Her verbal abilities were very slightly superior to her performance abilities.

Out of interest I compared the current sub test scaled scores with those obtained by a psychologist in 1994. The Verbal IQ was an improvement this time. IQ 70 compared with IQ 61. The Performance IQ was very slightly poorer this time, IQ 67 compared with IQ 71. However if one scores the best scaled scores from the two assessments the result still shows Ms James to be just into the borderline range of IQ.

The Ravens Progressive Matrices concurs with the intellectual level reached on the WAIS. This test sees if a person is capable of forming comparisons and reasoning by analogy. In this test, Ms James was capable of solving some of the more difficult problems. The Ravens Coloured Progressive Matrices showed Ms James had a reasonable grasp of non-verbal reasoning. Such a person often learns to read and write, acquires a moderate vocabulary and adjusts not unsuccessfully to a stable environment, but lacks originality and finds difficulty in meeting novel situations effectively.

From the information subtest, Ms James' verbal skills and general knowledge ability are very limited which has a bearing on her educational background as well as a low intelligence. It could reflect a lack of academic opportunity or interest.

Ms James' immediate auditory memory was well below average ability. She showed difficulty in reverse sequencing of a series of digits which shows some spatial deficit; it showed that Ms James could hold only a few data bits in her immediate memory briefly and at the same time juggle them around mentally. Lack of perseverance seemed to be a factor here.

The Vocabulary Subtest which is a measurement of both verbal and general mental ability (intelligence) was well below average and reflects poor early socialisation experiences and schooling. Ms James was able to describe the meaning of 'assemble', 'fabric' and 'repair' but not 'regulate', 'terminate' or 'domestic'.

Ms James was only able to cope with the most simple mental arithmetic problems in the form of adding and subtraction. She showed only very basic numerical reasoning. This reflects poor early schooling attitudes or experiences. The arithmetic results may predict Ms James' ability to work with arithmetic problems in logical and daily problems. Although Ms James seemed to 'build up a barrier' and seemed defeated quite early, I feel that if so motivated Ms James could improve on her mathematics skills.

Ms James' low comprehension score showed a low social knowledge ability, common sense judgment and practical reasoning. An inability for Ms James to describe proverbs suggests poor practical reasoning and abstract abilities. The verbal factors on this subtest is influential and to some extent long-term memory and experience.

The similarity subtest is a test of verbal concept formation. Ms James was asked to explain what each of a pair of words had in common. She showed difficulty with more advanced logical and abstract reasoning parts of the test. This test showed that Ms James has low verbal skills and she responded in a concrete fashion generally to the questions. This was her best verbal subtest result and was well below average.

The Performance subtests were well below average ability. They showed Ms James to have limited planning ability and foresight, a limited ability to assess non-verbal social interactions and in her sequential thinking, including the ability to see relationships between events, establish priorities and order activities chronologically. She also showed difficulty with forming and testing hypothesises (possible stories) and in sequencing material in a logical order (Picture Arrangement). Ms James could describe each scene in the picture arrangement subtest, but was unable to link things together in a story scenario except for the simplest one. This suggests an inability to think through the consequenes of an event, demonstrating somewhat a lack of ability to plan ahead.

Ms James' visual motor co-ordination was good on both the Block Design and the Object Assembly subtest. Her (non-verbal) reasoning and organisation ability on both tests however was well below average. Most of the simpler items on the Block Design test showed good basic planning, problem solving and pattern replication. The more difficult items gave more hit and miss responses with this test but Ms James persevered until the time was up on each design. Ms James followed instructions completely. There was evidence that she became defeated early on in the Object Assembly subtest.

The Digit Symbol subtest showed that Ms James quickly 'caught on' to what was required in that she was able to associate a particular symbol with a particular number. This test measures basic learning skills and visual memory. Her approach was accurate and very neat but very slow which penalised her. This test score can also be effected by anxiety, although none was detected by the examiner.

Conclusions and Recommendations:

Ms James presented on this occasion as a cooperative, quiet, cheerful, friendly lady with a mild/borderline learning disability. She was well motivated to attend the interviews, both lasting one hour and a half. She accepted the usefulness of such an assessment and responded to positive feedback. She was anxious to receive results. Ms James was well aware of time and place. She appeared to be well aware of her current situation and gave accurate descriptions.

Ms James from the assessment appears to be functioning at a concrete level and her short-term memory has some limitations.

I feel that Ms James in theory already has enough ability to act as a base for appropriate housekeeping and parenting. Her concentration seems to be good. A quiet and respectful approach would seem to be ideal in order to maintain her interests and maximise learning of which there were some evidence during the assessment. Ms James' reading ability is reasonable, although her comprehension level is lower than this. She would be able to read instructions given to her by experts regarding parenting skills, but I feel that the material would need to be presented in a very clear way and repeated a number of times. Any parenting intervention by care staff would, I feel, need to be tactfully and carefully implemented or else there could be a danger that it might be seen by Ms James as intrusive and hence possibly rejected. Her ability to change is possible but would be a slow process I feel. It would need careful planning with much repetition and consolidation. Mark needs consistency and a predictable and non-violent upbringing.

The arithmetic subtest results are such that Ms James, although being able to deal with basic arithmetic problems, would need help in some areas of budgeting for example.

It appeared to me that Ms James' feelings towards her child and her commitment to him is unclear. In any case, I feel that Ms James, would need continuing support in parenting, home making skills, and organisation, setting boundaries for her child and emotional physical support for her. I feel that Ms James' behaviour towards Mark and the consequences of this could be discussed with her in detail. I think that at times Ms James may find Mark's needs and behaviour very demanding and stressful and there should be some respite facility built in even at short notice in order to give her a break before things reach a crisis situation.

I am a bit concerned about the reliability, stability and commitment by Ms James' boyfriend from what she said. An earlier report talked of Ms James being beaten by her father in childhood. This early violent environment could have some impact on Ms James' parenting in times of stress. Any wish for Mark to live with Ms James in the future should be carefully planned, I feel, with a detailed risk assessment.

Assertiveness training could be useful for Ms James so that she may learn to communicate her needs and feelings more effectively and appropriately and would also presumably increase her self confidence. Counselling of Ms James could be offered to help her to come to terms with difficulties in her life and with her suicidal ideas of the recent past.

I detected no evidence of a psychiatric illness during the time of the assessment.

Further education classes (programmed) or sheltered employment/job training could be considered. A befriender could also be considered for Ms James.

RALPH JJ PETERS B.Sc., (Hons), C. Psychol., AFBPS
Principal Community Clinical Psychologist   19.7.01

Pyschiatric report by Dr John Head

PSYCHIATRIC REPORT on

FRANCES JAMES D.O.B. 1.4.71

REF: CASE No. 01/CCO 222

Applicant: Aardvark County Council

Respondent: Frances James

PREPARED BY DR JOHN HEAD
M.B., Ch.B., D.P.M.F.R.C.Psych.

TRAUMATIC STRESS CLINIC
AARDVARK COMMUNITY HEALTH SERVICES NHS TRUST

1. This report is by Dr John Head M.B., ChB., D.M.F.R.C.Psych. I have been a Consultant in Child and Adolescent Psychiatry for nineteen years and currently am Consultant to the Traumatic Stress Clinic, Aardvark. I have a special interest in the forensic psychiatry of my speciality and in particular concerning the effects upon children of psychological trauma.

2. The report is written in response to a letter of instruction from the solicitor to the Guardian *ad litem*, Helen Goulding, dated 8.6.01, and should be read in conjunction with that letter and the list of documents supplied to me which is attached as an appendix.

3. This is a very sad story outlined only in brief detail in the documentation supplied. Throughout I have had the benefit of regular discussions with Helen Goulding the Guardian *ad litem* and Ms Elsbeth Haps, Mark's solicitor, but regret that there has been no further written information from the Department of Social Services since Emily Cromack's statement of June 2001.

4. This report should be read in particular with that currently in preparation by Helen Goulding.

5. In brief summary, Mark was not known to the Department of Social Services until January 2001 when his mother's solicitor referred Miss James and her son to them to obtain support for Miss James in caring for Mark. Miss James and Mark had left the home where they had lived with Mark's father, Mr Brady, and paternal grandparents on the death of Mr Brady.

6. Ms Cromack's chronology describes subsequent events. It is puzzling to read this since on 9 March 2001 Miss James admitted to the local authority that she was 'hitting Mark round the head and is afraid she will kill him'. Mark stayed briefly with his maternal grandmother and then, even though the local authority had also heard from Mark's paternal grandmother that the child's mother was liable to hit the child on the head, he returned to live with his mother. Similarly, on 29 April 2001 Miss James hit the child on the head with a can of beans. Mark was taken to live with his mother at David Farley's flat on 2 May 2001 but Miss James was unable to look after Mark and Mr Farley telephoned Social Services asking for assistance.

7. The local authority commenced care proceedings on 4 June 2001.

8. There is common ground that Mark was a very disturbed little boy at the time he joined his maternal grandmother in May 2001, that he became able to eat and sleep better and to show less disturbed behaviour during his time with Mrs James and that he is in need of a permanent home.

176

9. My concern on reading the papers was that Mark already had had a number of moves, that little was known about the family history on either side and that the assessment by the local authority was as yet brief.

10. My original letter of instruction asked me to see Mark separately and with his mother and Mr David Farley. These interviews took place at the Aspen Family Centre in Aardvark. Helen Goulding arranged that Miss James and Mr Farley would arrive first and that Mark would be brought to the centre by his foster mother at a later part of the morning. In the event Mark arrived very soon after we had begun to talk to his mother, but was able, having briefly greeted his mother, to play within the family centre while we interviewed his mother and Mr Farley.

11. Miss James understandably was tearful and angry throughout our discussion though she remained in control of herself. She said that she was very, very upset and that she felt suicidal. Earlier that week she had been on her own while Mr Farley went to visit some of his family and she had just passed out and had not answered the phone. Mr Farley had been so worried he had thought of phoning the police and ambulance. Two months ago Miss James had attempted suicide and 'took a bottle full of tablets'. She only had outpatient treatment and would not consult doctors because she did not like them.

12. She spoke approvingly of Dr. Peters (clinical psychologist) who, she said, 'had given her a good report'.

13. I would like to have got a history of Mark's birth and development but understandably enough, Miss James was too distressed for this to be a possibility.

14. The picture I did get was a fragmentary one. She spoke of her own childhood. She said her parents 'dumped her'. She said 'I used to be an alcoholic before I had my kid'. She said she could not read. 'I was never at school — trying to sort myself out. My Mum reckons I shouldn't have kids'. Miss James said her own father used to hit her. I could not get her to say anything about her husband and his death and how it has affected her.

15. Mr Farley was very quiet during much of this except when he joined in to blame Social Services that Mark had been moved. I asked Miss James what could be said to a judge to show that things would be different and better for Mark if he were now to live with his mum again when things had gone so badly wrong this year. Miss James says that she has changed. Mr Farley said that she had 'stopped flying off the handle'.

16. Miss James said that Mark was different; Mark had held her hand crossing the road and she thought somebody must have been talking to Mark about this.

17. Mark then spent time with his mother, sitting on her knee and chattering. Miss James was very gentle and affectionate with Mark during this period.

18. Mark acknowledged Mr Farley with one brief, smiling look, otherwise his attention was entirely with his mother.

OPINION AND RECOMMENDATIONS

19. This is a very sad story, and one which is difficult to piece together. Miss James is reticent about her husband, and has struggled to look after Mark since his death. The grandmothers have tried to assist but the solutions are only piecemeal and Mark has been subjected to many moves this year.

20. The overreaching need now is for a coherent plan so that Mark has a stable and secure upbringing and that Mark's needs are also explored. He does not appear to have been affected by his father's death — see the report of his Child Psychologist, Dr Abby.

My recommendations are as follows:

20.1.   There is need for sight of the evaluation and care plan concerning Mark which is in the course of preparation by the Department of Social Services.

20.2.   It is a relief to read the report of Dr Abby but it is important that the little boy continues to receive detailed paediatric assessment and there may be need for psychological assessment to enable better planning of his early learning needs and emotional state.

20.3.   There is need for a detailed life history to be put together of Mark whatever the decision of the court.

20.4.   I was very concerned about Miss James and her high level of distress. There is as yet, I note, no psychiatric assessment available as was agreed by her solicitor and I hope that this will happen but the need also is for Miss James to receive some psychological help via her family practitioner and the National Health Service. If Miss James does agree to a psychiatric as well as a psychological assessment, I hope that agreement will be reached that this information is available to Miss James's general practitioner. I hope also that Miss James will seek help in her own right.

20.5.   There should be a claim in respect of Mark to the Criminal Injuries Compensation Board and permission should be given for relevant documentation from the court proceedings to be used in this claim.

20.6.   Whilst each grandmother has done her best to assist Mark in his upbringing, they are not able to have the daily care of him. It is very sad when a relative would like to but is unable to look after a child. It is saddest of all to talk to Miss James whose limited understanding, unhappiness and entirely unrealistic expectations of a new relationship indicate that she herself is very vulnerable and that a child in her care would be even more so.

20.7.   I agree with the view of the Guardian *ad litem* that this little boy needs a legally secure home and that adoption is the best way forward. Thought must be given to the nature of the adoption, with a least indirect contact between Mark and his mother. However, Mark's need for reliable, predictable adult attachment figures must in my view overreach any other consideration.

SUMMARY

21.   I support the making of a care order and that Mark James be placed for adoption.

22.   I write this report believing it to be true and knowing that it may be made available in a court of law.

                      John Head
....

Dr Head   19th September 2001

LIST OF DOCUMENTS

1.   Statement of Frances James dated 21.6.01

2.   Statement of Emily Cromack dated 4.6.01

3.   Psychology report of Dr Ralph Peters dated 19.7.01

4.   Application by the local authority for a care order dated 4.6.01

5.   Report of Dr Abby dated 1.7.01

Care plan

AARDVARK COUNTY COURT

CARE PLAN IN RESPECT OF MARK JAMES, DOB 2/2/98

This Care Plan is based upon the guidance contained in The Children Act 1999 Guidance and Regulations (Family Placements), Volume 3, Page 13, Paragraph 2.62.

1. MARK'S IDENTIFIED NEEDS

    (a) Mark is of white European origin, his parents do not practice any particular religious denomination and have not stipulated any particular religious preference for Mark.

    (b) Mark is a healthy child and has no particular health needs at present.

    (c) Mark is an intelligent child and is currently attending Aardvark Nursery School three mornings a week.

    (d) Mark may need specialist psychologist help in the future as a result of his experiences.

2. HOW THE ABOVE NEEDS MIGHT BE MET

    The above needs can be met in a warm, stable, secure environment within a permanent family placement. Given Mark's age it is the view of the Local Authority that an adoptive placement would most appropriately meet his needs.

3. AIM OF PLAN AND TIMESCALE

    (a) By the date of the final hearing the Local Authority plans for Mark will be well on the way. Whilst not wishing to pre-empt the Court's decision, such plans have been undertaken to avoid undue delay.

    (b) The E Forms will have been completed and these will be presented to a Permanency Planning Meeting on 29.10.01. If the Department plans are approved in the Permanency Planning Meeting, a date will then be sought to present Mark's needs to the Adoption Panel. Until a suitable adoptive placement is found, Mark can remain in his present placement.

4. PROPOSED PLACEMENT (TYPE AND DETAILS)

    This has already been dealt with in 2./3. above.

5. OTHER SERVICES TO BE PROVIDED TO MARK AND/OR FAMILY EITHER BY LOCAL AUTHORITY OR OTHER AGENCIES

    Life story work is currently being undertaken to help Mark unravel the emotions of his past experiences and hopefully to develop an understanding of his true circumstances.

6. ARRANGEMENTS FOR CONTACT AND REUNIFICATION

    (a) At the present time Mark has contact with his birth family as follows: weekly supervised contact with his mother which takes place at the Aspen Family Centre and fortnightly unsupervised contact with his grandparents at their homes.

    (b) If the Local Authority application for a care order is granted, its intention would be to reduce contact with his mother to fortnightly contact.

(c) Thereafter for the next four contacts, they will again be reduced to monthly contact. From this time onwards until an adoptive placement is identified, the Local Authority would seek to offer mother and the grandparents monthly face to face contact.

(d) The Local Authority will make the utmost effort to identify an adoptive family who will be able to tolerate face to face contact. However, in the view of all professionals involved, in the event that such a family could not be found, Mark's need for a permanent family must take precedence over contact.

For this reason the Local Authority will seek leave at the final hearing of his care proceedings to refuse face to face contact between Mark and his mother. This will ensure that if a placement which could tolerate face to face contact cannot be identified within a time scale consistent with Mark's need for permanency, he could be placed with an appropriate family without delay. Clearly this option would be the last resort.

(e) Alternative forms of contact, i.e., exchange of photographs and progress reports, are considered to be an appropriate method of meeting the majority of Mark's contact needs.

7. SUPPORTING THE PLACEMENT

(a) The present carers are being supported by the Family Placement Team.

(b) Mark continues to have regular input from social workers and an important focus of this work is compiling the life-story work.

8. LIKELY DURATION OF PLACEMENT IN THE ACCOMMODATION

Unable to comment at this present time.

9. CONTINGENCY PLAN — IF PLACEMENT BREAK DOWN

The Local Authority will seek to find an alternative placement.

10. WHO IS RESPONSIBLE FOR IMPLEMENTING THE PLAN (SPECIFIC TASKS AND OVERALL PLAN)

(a) Life-story work — Emily Cromack, Social Worker

(b) Contact arrangements — Jane Fowler, Social Worker and Wendy Clark, Family Assistant.

(c) Jane Fowler is now the allocated Social Worker.

11. SPECIFIC DETAIL OF THE MOTHER'S ROLE IN THE DAY TO DAY ARRANGEMENTS

The mother would be consulted, where appropriate, for example major decision making and the Local Authority will continue to work in partnership. However, as the mother is not the primary carer, it is envisaged that she would have only limited roles in Mark's day to day care.

12. THE EXTENT TO WHICH THE WISHES AND VIEWS OF MARK, HIS MOTHER AND ANYONE ELSE WITH A SUFFICIENT INTEREST IN THE CHILD HAVE BEEN OBTAINED AND ACTED UPON AND THE REASONS SUPPORTING THIS

(a) Mark is too young to express a realistic view about his immediate and long-term needs. As far as Miss James is concerned she has been made aware of the Local Authority's plan and has indicated through statements to the Courts she will oppose the plan.

(b) The view of the Children's Guardian (Guardian *ad litem*) has been sought and it is understood that she supports the Local Authority proposal to seek an alternative family for Mark.

13. ARRANGEMENT FOR INPUT BY MOTHER, MARK AND OTHERS INTO THE ONGOING DECISION MAKING PROCESS

Miss James would be consulted as described in Paragraph 11 and in addition would be invited to attend statutory reviews and planning meetings. The allocated Social Worker would be the first point of contact in the intervening periods in between these meetings.

14. ARRANGEMENTS FOR NOTIFYING THE RESPONSIBLE AUTHORITY OF DISAGREEMENTS OR MAKING REPRESENTATION

The mother would be given a copy of the complaints procedure and would be advised of the Local Authority policies.

15. ARRANGEMENTS FOR HEALTH CARE (INCLUDING CONSENT TO EXAMINATION AND TREATMENTS)

Currently Miss James has refused to sign medical consent for emergency treatment. The mother would be notified wherever possible of any planned medical appointments and, except in an emergency, her view would be sought.

16. ARRANGEMENTS FOR EDUCATION

Mark's educational needs will be met by the Local Authority primary and secondary education. Mother can approach the school direct for progress report.

17. DATES OF REVIEWS

The next Statutory Review is arranged to take place on 12 November 2001. At 12 midday.

Emily Rosalind Cromack
Social Worker
Children and Families

Aardvarkshire Social Services

Report of the children's guardian

REPORT OF THE CHILDREN'S GUARDIAN FOR

AARDVARK FAMILY COURT

REGARDING

MARK JAMES (D.O.B. 2.2.98)   Case No. 01/CCO 222

DATE OF HEARING 3.12.01

REPORT PREPARED BY   HELEN GOULDING
                                 AARDVARK PANEL OF GUARDIAN
                                 AD LITEM REPORTING OFFICERS
                                 AARDVARK

CONFIDENTIAL

It is an offence punishable by fine and/or imprisonment to reveal the contents of this report to any person who are not either a party to these proceedings or the legal advisor to such a party. In addition you may be liable for damages for the libel or slander on the publication of its contents.

INTRODUCTION

1. This is my consolidating report for the Final Hearing.

NATURE OF THE PROCEEDINGS

2. This is an application by Aardvarkshire County Council under s. 31 of the Children Act 1989 for a Care or Supervision Order in respect of Mark James d.o.b. 2.2.98. The first hearing took place in the Aardvark Family Proceedings Court on 7 June 2001 and Mark was made the subject of an Interim Care Order. This was subsequently renewed on 2 August 2001, 30 August 2001 and 27 September 2001. The proceedings were transferred to the County Court on 27 September 2001 given the increasing complexity of the case and estimated length of a final hearing in excess of 5 days.

THE GUARDIAN'S INVESTIGATION

3. I was appointed to this case on 4 June 2001

4. I have interviewed or discussed the case with the following people:

Emily Cromack	Social Worker	4.6.01; 27.9.01
Sarah Morgan	Manager	4.6.01; 27.9.01
Frances James	Mother	21.6.01; 23.7.01; 30.7.01; 10.9.01; 19.9.01
Beatrice James	Maternal Grandmother	7.6.01; 10.7.01; 21.9.01
Jean Brady	Paternal Grandmother	11.6.01; 9.7.01; 27.9.01
Dr John Head	Consultant Child and Adolescent Psychiatrist	12.7.01; 9.8.01; 26.9.01
Annette Falls	Foster Carer	18.6.01; 19.7.01; 16.8.01

5.   I have seen the following documents:

- a copy of the Local Authority's application for a Care or Supervision Order dated 4.6.01

- statement of Emily Cromack, social worker, dated 4.6.01

- statement of Frances James, mother, dated 21.6.01

- statement of Emily Cromack, social worker, dated 28.8.01

- Psychological Report by Ralph Peters dated 19.7.01

- Medical Report by Dr Abby dated 1.7.01

- Psychiatric Report of Dr John Head, Consultant Child and Adolescent Psychiatrist dated 19.9.01

- Statement of Wendy Clark, family assistant

6.   I have attended two Professionals meetings on 17.7.01 and 16.8.01 where issues were clarified.

7.   I have had access to Aardvarkshire's records relating to Mark James on 17.6.01. It was helpful to see this material. I have received minutes of reviews and planning meetings I was unable to attend. This has also been informative.

8.   At the time of writing this report I am not aware of additional evidence being relied on in this case.

EVENTS LEADING TO THESE PROCEEDINGS

9.   Social Services contact with the James' family in the period preceding these proceedings is outlined in the chronology at the front of Emily Cromack's statement dated 4.6.01. The main events leading to the Local Authority's application are outlined in this statement. They may be summarised as:

- Mark James being placed by his mother with other carers on a number of occasions and has been unsettled by these temporary arrangements.

- Frances James' physical and emotional abuse of Mark.

- The concerns were emphasised by Mark's name being placed on the Child Protection Register on 19.2.01.

- Frances James' lack of co-operation with the help and services she was offered.

FAMILY HISTORY

10.   I do not believe it is necessary for me to duplicate the basic information contained in Emily Cromack's statement or chronology.

THE CHILD

11.   Mark James will be 4 next February. He is a white male child of British origin. He has short straight hair and blue eyes. He has an assertive personality, can be quite a chatter box and is not shy in asking questions about his circumstances and family.

12.   Mark enjoys attending Nursery School three mornings a week. He gets on well with his peers. He can be stubborn and independent but is learning to co-operate and join in. He is interested in books and puzzles. He loves stories being read to him and is at his happiest at

bath times — the quiet time of the day when he is particularly responsive. He has a good routine and frequently tests the boundaries. He can be very demanding and quite fixed in his stance sometimes but responds to individual encouragement. He needs a great deal of consistent and firm encouragement. It is clear that Mark's behaviour can at times be very challenging and may require additional input. Also, that urgent action as per the Care Plan is indicated.

THE WISHES AND FEELINGS OF THE CHILD

13.   Mark is not old enough to express an informed view of his own. He had hoped to live long-term with Mrs Beatrice James, his maternal grandmother. In part, he feels let down by her. He enjoys contact with his mother but is not distressed on concluding these sessions and returning to his foster carer. Mark understands the plan is for his Social Worker to look for a family where he will be special and be able to stay there while he grows up. He likes the idea of being somewhere special but he does not fully understand what this means.

ASSESSMENT OF FRANCES JAMES AS A CARER

14.   Frances James is 30 years old. She lives with her partner David Farley at 3 Waterside, Aardvark. This is a two bedroom flat. She has lived in this accommodation with Mark on a previous occasion and intends to look after Mark at this address.

15.   At a general level I believe Miss James is fond of Mark. She has co-operated with Social Services and my own enquiries. She has also attended contact and planning meetings regularly. However, in the period between February and May 2001 Miss James' parenting of Mark fell below an acceptable level. This is the main thrust behind the Care Proceedings. Mark was subjected to physical abuse on a number of occasions. This resulted in Mark being temporarily separated from his mother. The physical assaults on Mark were the subject of Child Protection investigations. The serious view taken of the initial incident is reflected in Mark's name being placed on the Child Protection Register for likely physical abuse on 19.2.01. It is evident that Miss James felt Mark was beyond her control. Also that she was not able to make effective use of the help and support she was offered at the time.

16.   When the Care Proceedings commenced Mark's behaviour was unsettled and disturbing. He appeared to lack sound boundaries in his daily life. He needed a basic routine, careful reassuring about sleeping in a bed by himself in a separate room, was prone to tantrums as a means of stubbornly obtaining his own way and had an unsettled sleep pattern. He frequently experienced nightmares. There is also an impression that his diet was inadequate and lacked quality and reasonable variety. This is not a positive reflection on his mother's parenting.

17.   In her statement Miss James describes her early married life as being stressful living in the Brady household. It is clear that the marriage ran into difficulties and the couple were in frequent dispute. Also, that a number of their conflicts were unfortunately played out in front of Mark.

18.   A separate tension is apparent — Miss James' commitment to developing her relationship with Mr Farley. In this respect Mark's needs did not come first. In discussions Miss James said her relationship with Mr Farley is of several months standing. It has already been through a number of crises as Mr Farley prevaricated over whether he would live with Miss James. The relationship is a relatively new one. I note Emily Cromack describes Mark's reticence toward Mr Farley and the allegations that he is said to have locked Mark in his room.

SUMMARY

19.   Miss James has experienced a stressful life which has contained significant rejections and losses (parent, husband, daughters and sister). While she is fond of Mark she has not always been able to put his needs first. Her standard of parenting has been less than adequate and Mark's development has been harmed. At times Miss James subjected Mark to

physical and emotional abuse. She is in the early stage of developing a relationship with Mr Farley. At present I have reservations about its stability. I do not believe it is in Mark's interests for him to be placed in this environment. Using the past as a guide to the future, there is a likelihood of harm to Mark.

THE LOCAL AUTHORITY PLAN

20.   The Guardian is expected to comment on the Local Authority's activities and plans.

ACTIVITIES

21.   This is an appropriate application by the Local Authority as the threshold criteria was met.

22.   With hindsight it is clear that the focus on Mark's needs could have been sharper. In the February to May period there are a number of occasions on which Mark was hit by his mother. This is linked with Miss James' allegedly hearing voices telling her to do this and on 9 March 2001 she said she was afraid she would kill him. I do not understand why he was returned to his mother's care after the Police Protection Order lapsed in March. I am surprised the Local Authority did not adopt a more assertive approach given the background context of the Child Protection Registration on 19 February 2001.

23.   Statutory Reviews took place satisfactorily and the case records were in good order.

PLANS

24.   The Local Authority has provided a detailed Care Plan in relation to Mark.

25.   The central thrust of the plan is to seek a permanent family placement for Mark outside his natural family, preferably through adoption. If a Care Order is granted the Local Authority intends to reduce current parental contact. Having attended the professionals meeting on 16.8.01 I understand the contradiction in paragraph 6(d) of the Care Plan has been clarified. When the right family has been identified the Department will return to Court to ask for permission to refuse contact and will plan goodbye meetings between Mark and his mother. It is not anticipated that face to face contact will take place beyond the permanent placement. However, an annual indirect post box contact will be offered.

26.   There is nothing in the account of Miss James to indicate that Mark safely could be returned to her. Miss James appears to have limited understanding and has entirely unrealistic expectations of her new relationship. Miss James is herself of a vulnerable disposition and a child in her care would even more so.

27.   I endorse the need for detailed life story work.

SUMMARY OF THE GUARDIAN'S ASSESSMENT

28.   In reaching a decision about which course of action will best safeguard the child's welfare the Court must have regard to s. 1(3) of the Children Act 2001.

s. 1(3)(a)   The ascertainable wishes and feelings of the child concerned considered in the light of his age and understanding

29.   I have commented on this in paragraph 14.

s. 1(3)(b)   The physical, emotional and educational needs

30.   *Physical* — Mark is making satisfactory developmental progress.
      Educational—Mark has been harmed by his family's inability to offer him enduring security and affection. He is puzzled about his future and firming up the Care Plan is a matter of the extreme urgency. The provision of future psychological and health inputs needs to be borne in mind.

Intellectual — The early indications are that Mark has reasonable abilities and needs encouragement to use them to the full.

s. 1(3)(c)   The likely effect of any change in his circumstances

31.   The plan is for Mark to remain in the beneficial foster placement until he has been prepared and is ready to move to the family (preferably adoptive) that will be special for him and is matched to meet his needs. This will need to be planned and carried out with suitable sensitivity.

s. 1(3)(d)   His age, sex background and any characteristics which the Court considers relevant

32.   I have commented on this in paragraphs 12 and 13.

s. 1(3)(e)   Any harm which he has suffered or is at risk of suffering

33.   Mark has been physically abused by his mother. It is also clear that Mark has been harmed by the many temporary moves he has already unfortunately experienced. His grandmothers are not able to look after him.

s. 1(3)(f)   How capable is the mother in meeting Mark's needs?

34.   I have commented on this in paragraphs 16 to 20. Mark's long-term needs are most likely and effectively to be met outside his natural family.

OPTIONS AVAILABLE TO THE COURT

s. 1(3)(g)   The range of powers available to the Court
Is the making of an Order better than making no Order?

35.   I believe the threshold criteria of significant harm is established in this case. Mark has been subject to physical and emotional abuse and there is a likelihood of future harm. I believe an Order is indicated so that he is protected by a statutory monitoring of his welfare. Also that the Care Plan is implemented with a sense of urgency to meet his future needs. Sadly his natural family is not able to meet them.

Section 8 Orders

36.   I do not think the use of s. 8 Orders (Residence, Contact, Prohibitive Steps or Specific Issue orders) are appropriate in this case.

Supervision Order

37.   A Supervision Order would place the Local Authority under a duty to offer advice, assistance and befriending which would benefit Mark. The Order would last for one year in the first instance but could be renewed for a further period — up to three years in total — if appropriate. Social Services would have a statutory monitoring role in relation to Mark's welfare.

Care Order

38.   Would share parental responsibility between the Local Authority and Frances James.

SUMMARY AND RECOMMENDATIONS

SUMMARY

39.   This is an application by the Local Authoirty for a Care Order in respect of Mark James. The application is based on the harm he experienced in his mother's care (physical and

emotional). It is likely Mark would be harmed by returning to his mother's care. Mark has been very unsettled by the rejections he has experienced. In key respects he is a rather anxious, insecure little boy whose *urgent* need is for a secure settled family that he can invest in, form attachments that will endure and where he will benefit from being offered structure, control and encouragement. Dr John Head supports this approach. The preferred course is with a carefully selected adoptive family. If the Court accepts the recommendation below the search for a special family can begin. Contact with his natural family will be gradually reduced and life history work will be undertaken.

RECOMMENDATION

40.   I recommend that:

(i)   Mark James is made the subject of a Care Order. I understand the Local Authority will look for a suitable permanent family for Mark.

(ii)   No Order is made regarding Contact. Reasonable contact is assumed under the Children Act and the intention to offer diminishing contact is outlined in the Care Plan. In the circumstances I do not think it is necessary or beneficial for Mark to ask that contact be defined.

41.   I believe these recommendations are the most effective way of ensuring that Mark's long-term needs are met.

   H. Goulding

HELEN GOULDING
Children's Guardian   23.11.01

Skeleton argument on behalf of the applicant

IN THE AARDVARK COUNTY COURT   Case No. 01/CCO222

IN THE MATTER OF SECTION 31 CHILDREN ACT 1989

AND IN THE MATTER OF MARK JAMES (D.O.B. 2.2.98)

SKELETON ARGUMENT ON BEHALF OF THE APPLICANT
AARDVARKSHIRE COUNTY COUNCIL

The Local Authority seek a Care Order combined with no order as to contact.

I   THE THRESHOLD CRITERIA

It is submitted that Mark James has suffered significant harm attributable to the care given to him by Frances James. This harm has been of both a physical and emotional nature. The threshold criteria are met.

(i)   Physical harm

It is submitted that Frances James has failed to control her own behaviour and has excessively physically chastised Mark.

(ii)   Emotional harm

It is submitted that:

- Frances James has failed to provide any continuity of care. Between 4.1.01 and 17.5.01 Mark moved 7 times.

- Whilst Mark was in the care of his mother, he was emotionally over-protected to an excessive extent and Frances James' handling of him was inconsistent.

- Mark was not fed appropriately by Frances James whilst in her care.

II   DISPOSAL

(i)   Care Order

It is submitted that a Care Order should be made in this matter. Social Services, Dr John Head and the GAL believe that Mark needs a secure and dependable home environment, free from the chaotic, itinerant lifestyle which has characterised this year. It is submitted that a Care Order is the only way to safeguard this and that it is in Mark's best interest that he be permanently placed for adoption.

It is submitted that if the Court were minded to make either No Order or a Residence Order in favour of Frances James then Mark would be likely to suffer significant harm similar to that outlined in I above.

(ii)   Parental contact

It is submitted that the overriding consideration for Mark's future is a suitable, permanent, adoptive family. It is proposed that contact between Mark and Frances James be gradually reduced to one monthly visit in preparation for this. It is submitted that it would not be in Mark's interest to have post adoptive parental contact because it may undermine future placement.

It is submitted that the Court should endorse the proposals for contact set out in the Care Plan and that the Court should make no order as to contact. It is argued that the Care Plan sets out reasonable provision for contact and a defined contact order would limit and prejudice Mark's prospects of a suitable and adoptive placement.

As regards Article 8(1) of the European Convention on Human Rights, it is submitted that the orders sought are 'necessary and proportionate' (*Re C and B (Care Order: Future Harm)* [2001] 1 FLR 611).

A BARRISTER
ADDRESS

Skeleton argument on behalf of the respondent

IN THE AARDVARK COUNTY COURT   Case No. 01/CCO222

IN THE MATTER OF SECTION 31 CHILDREN ACT 1989

AND IN THE MATTER OF MARK JAMES

SKELETON ARGUMENT ON BEHALF OF FRANCES JAMES

I   HAVE THE THRESHOLD CRITERIA BEEN SATISFIED?

(i)   Section 31(2) empowers the court to make a care order only if its satisfied:

'(a)   that the child concerned is suffering, or is likely to suffer, significant harm; and
(b)   that the harm, or likelihood of harm, is attributable to:
  (i)   the care given to the child, or likely to be given to him if the order were not made, not being what it would be reasonable to expect a parent to give to him . . .'

<u>Physical harm</u>

It is conceded that Mark has suffered significant physical harm.

<u>Emotional harm</u>

It is denied that Mark has suffered significant emotional harm that is attributable to the care given to him by mother:

The Local Authority case is that from between 4.1.01 and 17.5.01 Mark moved 7 times. This is not a fair representation of the position:

  11.2.01 — Mark stayed at foster parents for five nights.
  9.3.01 — respite care with Mrs Beatrice James.
  2.5.01 — mother and child moved in with Mr David Farley.
  10.5.01 — respite care with Mrs Jean Brady.
  17.5.01 — respite care with Mrs Beatrice James.

Likelihood of future harm — physical or emotional

Although mother accepts that she had difficulty coping with Mark between 4.1.01 and 11.2.01 (first period); 16.2.01 and 9.3.01 (second period) and 25.3.01 and 10.5.01 (third period), it is important to consider the risk of future harm in the context of the following factors:

- recently widowed

- unsuitable accommodation (newly moved into bedsit in hostel in first period)

- mother's illness (she had food poisoning in the second period)

- mother's new relationship in the third period.

c.f. mother's improved stability: permanent accommodation and permanent relationship with Mr David Farley.

Mother acknowledges the inappropriateness of her behaviour.

Mother accepts the need for future work.

II THE LOCAL AUTHORITY'S CARE PLAN

The Court must consider whether to make a Care Order, notwithstanding the concession by the mother that the threshold criteria have been satisfied.

The welfare of the child must be the paramount consideration and the welfare checklist applies (CA 1989, s. 1(3)).

It is submitted that Mark should be returned to the care of his mother.

The proposed care plan for Mark, namely closed adoption, is not in Mark's best interests, for the following reasons:

(i)   The LA has a duty to attempt to make arrangements for Mark to live with his parents or a relative, friend or other person connected with him, unless that would not be reasonably practicable or consistent with his welfare:

see CA 1989, s. 23(6)
CA 1989 Guidance (Vol 3), para. 2.6

There has been no attempt to rehabilitate Mark with his mother.

(ii)   The Care Plan fails to take account of Mark's very close relationship with his mother.

(iii)   The Care Plan advocates a further major change for Mark and will uproot him from all that is familiar to him.

It is the duty of the Court to scrutinise the LA's Care Plan. If the Court is not satisfied that the Care Plan is in the best interests of the child, the Court should refuse to make a care order.

Rehabilitation with mother

- Mother and Mark have a good relationship.

- Mother acknowledges that her behaviour was inappropriate. She should be given credit for reporting her problems with Mark to the LA.

- Mother has co-operated with Social Services and the GAL. She has demonstrated her commitment by attending contact and planning meetings regularly.

- Mother has enough ability to act as a base for appropriate housekeeping and parenting. Her ability to change is possible although a slow process.

- Mother accepts the need for support in parenting, and will co-operate with the LA in order to work for changes in her parenting skills. Mother also accepts the need for Mark to be introduced to Mr David Farley gradually.

- Article 8(1) of the European Convention on Human Rights guarantees the right to respect for family life.

Contact

- Mother seeks ongoing contact, including direct contact, in the event that a care order is made. Submissions as to the level of such contact will be made at the hearing.

- Family life, as protected by Article 8(1), involves regular contact.

IV CONCLUSION

1. There should be a residence order in favour of mother

2. There should be a family assistance order

O. COUNSEL, QC
ADDRESS

7.24   The Position Prior to the Children Act 1989

Because orders made prior to this Act remain in force, and old terminology such as 'custody' may still be used, it is important to have some familiarity with the former law if you practise in this area.

7.24.1   PRIVATE LAW

On divorce or separation a parent could apply for an order for 'custody' of a child, which if awarded would give the person with custody the right to take most major decisions with regard to the child. Custody was normally awarded to one parent alone, and might therefore be strongly contested, though a joint order could be made if it was thought there would be co-operation.

A separate order for 'care and control' could be made for the day-to-day care of the child as distinct from the power to take decisions about the child. There might therefore be an order for joint custody of a child with care and control to one parent.

Orders could also be made for 'access', which was roughly equivalent to the current contact order.

Orders could be made by the High Court, or by a county court or magistrates' court under a range of statutory provisions. Although the need to make the welfare of the child paramount was enshrined in statute, relevant factors were a matter of case law alone. The factors were broadly similar, but not identical, to the current statutory provisions.

7.24.2   PUBLIC LAW

A child could be received into care on a voluntary basis under s. 2 of the Child Care Act 1980.

Parental rights could be taken over by a resolution of the local authority under s. 3 of the Child Care Act 1980. Other circumstances in which a child could be ordered to be taken into care existed under the Children and Young Persons Act 1969, s. 1, if, for example, the child had committed an offence. Emergency action could be taken under the place of safety order.

EIGHT

MEDIATION IN THE CONTEXT OF THE FAMILY

8.1   Mediation and ADR

Mediation is one of a number of settlement-seeking processes which include negotiation and arbitration. These processes are loosely grouped together under the collective heading of *Alternative Dispute Resolution* and its acronym, ADR. *Alternative* in this context is generally understood to mean alternative to court proceedings. **Appropriate Dispute Resolution** would be a more accurate term, for two reasons. The first is that some countries, such as Australia, use negotiation and mediation as the standard means of settling disputes. Adjudication is rarely needed. When negotiation and mediation fail to settle the dispute, judicial determination provides an alternative, rather than the other way round. Secondly, negotiation and mediation are often used in conjunction with court proceedings, rather than as a substitute for them. Mediation needs to be used selectively, according to the nature of the dispute and the willingness of potential participants.

8.2   Research Findings have Underlined the Need for Family Mediation

A study carried out at the Department of Child Health at the University of Exeter (Cockett and Tripp, 1994) found that:

- Most adults suffer distress and turmoil when a marital or close relationship breaks down. Many couples need help to communicate with each other at this time, because communication between them often breaks down as well. If children are involved, parents need to be able to discuss arrangements and co-operate over their children.

- Fewer than half the children whose parents had separated had regular contact with the parent they no longer lived with. Half these children did not even know where the other parent was living.

- Only 6% of chldlren had been given a joint explanation from both parents of the impending separation or divorce. In over 70% of families, it was left to the mother to tell the children. In some cases the mother told the children only that their father had left, without giving them any explanation or reassurance.

- Most of the children had been very aware of the conflict between their parents. When the children were asked what they thought would have helped them, most said that they needed much more information, explanation and reassurance from their parents than they actually received.

193

- Many children felt they should have been involved in decisions about contact. This does not mean that they wanted to be given responsibility for decisions. A significant minority, however, had made their own arrangements to keep in contact with the non-resident parent, because their parents were unable to agree or because their parents were no longer speaking to each other.

- Children were also likely to lose touch with grandparents and other relatives who played an important part in the children's lives, prior to the parents' separation.

8.3　Council of Europe Recommendations on Family Mediation

The Third European Conference on Family Law, held in Cadiz, Spain, in April 1995 on 'Family Law in the Future', considered research findings and experience of mediation and concluded that the Council of Europe should promote the use of mediation to resolve family disputes. The Council of Europe's Committee of experts on family law made recommendations which were formally adopted by the Committee of Ministers of the Council of Europe in a Recommendation published on 21 January 1998:

> Research in Europe, North America, Australia and New Zealand suggests that family mediation is better suited than more formal legal mechanisms to the settlement of sensitive, emotional issues surrounding family matters. Reaching agreements in mediation has been shown to be a vital component in making and maintaining co-operative relationships between divorcing parents: it reduces conflict and encourages continuing contact between children and both their parents.

The Council of Europe's Ministers, 'convinced of the need to make greater use of family mediation', recommended the governments of member States 'to introduce or promote family mediation, or, where necessary, strengthen existing family mediation'. Mediation is defined as:

> a means of settling family disputes, particularly those arising during the process of separation and divorce, with the following objectives:
> i.　to promote consensual approaches, thereby reducing conflict in the interest of all family members;
> ii.　to protect the best interests and welfare of children in particular, by reaching appropriate arrangements concerning custody and access;
> iii.　to minimise the detrimental consequences of family disruption and marital dissolution;
> iv.　to support continuing relationships between family members, especially those between parents and their children;
> v.　to reduce the economic and social costs of separation and divorce, both to families and to States.

(Recommendation No. R (98) 1, 21January 1998, para. 7).

8.4　Special Characteristics of Family Disputes

The Council of Europe Memorandum pointed out that family disputes have special characteristics which need to be taken into account in mediation:

(a)　There are usually continuing and interdependent relationships. The dispute settlement process should facilitate constructive relationships for the future in addition to enabling the resolution of current disputes.

(b)　Family disputes usually involve emotional and personal relationships in which feelings can exacerbate the difficulties, or disguise the true nature of the conflicts and disagreements. It is usually considered appropriate for these feelings to be acknowledged and understood by parties and by the mediator.

(c)   Disputes which arise in the process of separation and divorce have an impact on other family members, notably children who may not be included directly in the mediation process, but whose interests may be considered paramount and therefore relevant to the process.

8.5   Basic Principles and Requirements of Family Mediation

The basic principles and requirements of family mediation establish it as a professional discipline in its own right, to be distinguished from advising, arbitrating, counselling and informal kinds of mediation undertaken by friends or relatives. Essential principles are:

- Voluntary participation. There is no compulsion to take part and the willingness of all parties to the mediation must be ascertained before it begins. Any party to the mediation may also choose to withdraw at any time.

- Impartiality of the mediator(s). No prior involvement as one party's legal advisor or in some other role. A conflict of interest check is carried out prior to mediation.

- Neutral ground providing suitable facilities for mediation meetings.

- Privacy and informality. Discussions are confidential and legally privileged (except where an adult or child is said or believed to be at risk of serious harm). Financial and other material information is, however, provided on an 'open' basis and may be referred to in court.

- Screening procedures are used to check whether mediation is suitable in the circumstances. Ground-rules during the process are designed to manage power imbalances and control abusive behaviour. Neither party is permitted to bully the other to accept a settlement.

- A clear structure in which participants are helped to define the issues they need to settle and to identify immediate priorities, while also considering longer-term needs.

- Full financial disclosure. Both parties undertake to provide full information with supporting documents. Mediators assist parties to gather all the relevant information and to consider it together. Financial disclosure is also checked by legal advisors.

- Parents are helped by mediators to consider their children's needs, feelings and views and to co-operate over arrangements for children and parental responsibility.

- Non-binding outcomes. Proposals for settlement that are worked out in mediation are subject to independent legal advice to each party.

- Professional standards regulate family mediators' training and competence.

8.6   Potential Benefits of Family Mediation

Although some lawyers remain sceptical of mediation or opposed to it altogether, others have been impressed by its positive outcomes and recognise its benefits:

- participants are helped to reach their own decisions and to retain control over their own lives, instead of having decisions imposed on them by the court;

- disputes can be settled at an early stage, before parties become entrenched;

- participants are encouraged to look towards the future, rather than focusing on grievances about the past;

- separated parents are helped to take part in direct discussions about their children, so that communication is eased regarding continuing contact with the children;

- children's needs are kept in the forefront of discussions — parents are helped to take full account of their children's needs and feelings, as well as their own;

- misunderstandings can be cleared up or avoided;

- stress, animosity and bitterness can be reduced;

- all available options can be explored in joint discussions, before decisions are taken;

- possibilities of reconciliation are not ruled out and may emerge through discussion;

- arrangements can be tailored to particular family circumstances and needs;

- meetings are informal and can be arranged quickly, compared with the formality and delays of court proceedings;

- face-to-face discussions reduce the costs and delays of lengthy correspondence;

- legal costs may be reduced and the costs of litigation may be avoided altogether;

- mediation can address the links that couples see between different issues, in practical and emotional terms, whereas the Code of Practice of the Solicitors Family Law Association states that arrangements for children on the one hand and finance on the other must be kept separate and referred to in separate letters (SFLA, 1996).

8.7   Potential Disadvantages of Mediation

There could be disadvantages for one or more parties if:

- mediation is used inappropriately and without adequate safeguards;

- the mediator is not competent to deal with the issues;

- the mediator is biased and/or directive;

- the mediation service lacks adequate facilities;

- mediation continues without financial disclosure by one party;

- power imbalances are not recognised or managed adequately;

- discussions are allowed to get out of hand, intensifying conflict and distress;

- delays prolong the status quo and defer settlement;

- mediation continues despite evident mistrust of one party's good faith;

- the process is rushed and too little time is allowed for careful consideration;

- participants are pushed into agreements without independent legal advice.

Concerns about possible disadvantages need to be weighed against potential benefits. Clients who are doubtful or afraid of taking part need to know that consumer experience is generally positive. On the general principle of 'nothing ventured, nothing gained', there should be encouragement to give mediation a try, since either party or the mediator may end the mediation at any stage. The mediator should do so, if he or she finds that mediation is not appropriate or that no progress can be made.

8.8 Provision of Family Mediation under the Family Law Act 1996

Part II of the Family Law Act 1996 provided the framework for a fundamental reform of divorce law, removing the concept of fault and introducing a new process of divorce over time. Although the principle of no-fault divorce was strongly supported, the procedures designed to accompany it were rejected as cumbersome and ultimately unworkable. The government's subsequent announcement that Part II of the Family Law Act 1996 was being abandoned altogether was widely taken to mean that family mediation was off the agenda as well. This was not the case. Publicly-funded mediation continued to be developed under Part III of the Act, with block funding available through contracts awarded to 'suppliers' who met the Legal Aid Board's requirements and standards. These requirements covered family mediators' training and supervision, Code of Practice, procedures, recording systems, premises and facilities.

Although the voluntary nature of mediation was stressed, s. 29 of the Family Law Act 1996 provided that:

> a person shall not be granted representation for the purpose of proceedings relating to family matters, unless he has attended a meeting with a mediator—
> (a) to determine:
> (i) whether mediation appears to be suitable to the dispute and the parties and all the circumstances, and
> (ii) in particular, whether mediation could take place without either party being influenced by fear of violence or other harm; and
> (b) if mediation does appear suitable, to help the person applying for representation to decide whether instead to apply for mediation.

Section 29 was piloted and the results monitored by a team of researchers (Davis G. et al., 'Monitoring Publicly Funded Family Mediation — Report to the Legal Services Commission', Legal Services Commission, 2000). In the light of the research findings, the requirement in certain circumstances to attend an assessment meeting with a recognised family mediator has been re-enacted, with modifications, under section 7 of Part C of the Community Legal Service Funding Code (Legal Aid Board, 1999). Revisions to this Code continue to be made.

8.9 Community Legal Service Funding Code on Family Mediation

Family mediation is a separate level of service under the Funding Code, which authorises mediation of a family dispute and assessment of whether mediation appears suitable to the dispute and the parties and all the circumstances (Procedures C27–29). Unless exempt (see **8.11** below), a person must attend an assessment meeting with a recognised mediator before he or she may make an application for General Family Help or Legal Representation in Family Proceedings. General Family Help may be refused if mediation, supported if necessary by Help with Mediation, is considered more appropriate than General Family Help. A recognised family mediator is one who has taken a recognised course of training, works in a franchised service and has successfully passed an Assessment of Competence. The requirement to attend an assessment meeting with a recognised mediator applies to applications for General Family Help or for Legal Representation in Family Proceedings, whether by way of an amendment to cover additional proceedings (for example, contact where there is an existing certificate covering ancillary relief) or a separate application for funding, other than proceedings under:

(a)   s. 37 of the Matrimonial Causes Act 1973 (injunctions to prevent and orders to set aside disposal of property);

(b)   the Inheritance (Provision for Family and Dependants) Act 1975.

Although proceedings under the 1975 Act are exempt from the requirement to attend an assessment meeting, there is nothing to prevent mediation taking place voluntarily in such cases or in any family proceedings where the mediator deems the case, the parties and all the circumstances suitable.

8.10   Family Relationships

The scope of the mediation assessment requirement therefore covers the great majority of private law cases coming within the definition of family proceedings under the Funding Code. Disputes or proceedings come within the family category if they 'arise out of' family relationships. These include:

- marriage;

- heterosexual or homosexual relationships between partners, whether cohabiting or not;

- blood relations;

- step relations

- adoption or long-term care of children such that they can reasonably be regarded as part of a family.

A wide definition of family proceedings and family relationships is in line with the wide meaning of 'family life' under Article 8 of the European Convention on Human Rights.

8.11   Exemptions (Funding Code Procedures C29)

Exemptions from the requirement to attend an assessment meeting with a recognised mediator include the following circumstances:

- emergency applications;

- where there is no recognised mediator able to offer an appointment within 15 working days of the mediation service being contacted by the client or their solicitor;

- where a recognised mediator is satisfied that mediation is not suitable to the dispute because another party to the dispute is unwilling to attempt mediation — a recognised mediator assesses the willingness of the other party by contacting them to ascertain whether they would be prepared to attend an assessment meeting;

- where family proceedings are already in existence and the client is a respondent who has been notified of a court date within eight weeks of the notification;

- where the client has a fear of domestic abuse from a potential party to the mediation and is therefore unwilling to participate in mediation;

- where the client, the client's (ex) partner or the other party lives abroad or further away from the mediation service than a 1. 5 hour journey time;

- where, due to any disability, inability or restriction on the client, (ex) partner or other party, he or she is unable to travel to see a mediator (e.g., in hospital or prison);

- where, due to a disability or inability of the client, (ex) partner or other party, mediation is unavailable, e.g., where one of the parties' hearing is impaired and there are no mediators available with appropriate facilities.

8.12 Assessment Meetings with a Recognised Family Mediator

Clients may contact a mediation service directly and many do so. The Legal Services Commission recommends that solicitors should make the referral and provide the mediation service with contact details for both parties. It is for the clients (the applicant and the other party) to decide which type of meeting (together or separate) would be more appropriate for them. Where either party requests a separate meeting, the service should offer separate meetings to both parties. If they both choose a joint meeting, the mediator should carry out domestic abuse screening with each party separately, before the joint meeting.

It is extremely important to distinguish cases suitable for mediation from those which are not. The Funding Code makes it clear that it is the responsibility of solicitors to screen for domestic abuse. Mediators are also required to identify as soon as possible cases where either party may be influenced by fear of abuse. The Code goes on to say that research has shown that violence in the past is not necessarily a bar to mediation. Some clients want to take part in mediation, despite having experienced violence, usually because mediation enables them to have some necessary discussion with their ex-partner, often concerning the children, with a third party present and with other safeguards. Mediators are required to have training in screening for domestic abuse and child protection issues and to carry out this screening not only at the initial assessment meeting but also throughout the mediation process.

Mediators should consider whether referral for legal advice, counselling, welfare benefits advice or other help is needed and, if mediation is to take place, whether any special arrangements are needed. The level of conflict, any language difficulties and the existence of different kinds of power imbalance need to be taken into account. Body language needs to be observed and any indications of fear or intimidation should be picked up and asked about — although not in a way that may inflame a high conflict situation and increase risks.

At the assessment meeting, the mediator explains the mediation process and the ways in which mediation may help to settle the issues. There are three main categories:

- children;

- property and fmance issues;

- all issues.

The mediator completes an Eligibility Certificate showing the category of mediation and the main issues, whether each party qualifies for publicly-funded mediation and whether mediation is suitable. If it is suitable and one party qualifies for public funding and the other does not, Client A receives mediation free of charge while Client B is charged at the mediator's private hourly rate. This is usually acceptable, as Client B would otherwise be paying his solicitor's costs and realises that direct discussions with Client A may be cheaper and quicker. The statutory charge does not apply to publicly-funded mediation (at the time of writing). The mediator also has to give a cost comparison between the costs of mediation, irrespective of whether the client is paying, and the estimated costs of litigation.

8.13   Is Mediation Desirable at an Early Stage in Proceedings?

There are different views about mediation taking place at an early stage of separation. The Chinese characters for 'crisis' combine two characters, one meaning 'danger' and the other 'opportunity'. The period leading up to and immediately following separation is often one of acute crisis, for one partner or both. Sometimes there is too much shock or distress for mediation to be possible or appropriate. On the other hand, there may be urgent questions concerning a parent's contact with the children. The situation may be very confused and volatile. When things are in a state of flux there is more scope for change, including the possibility of reconciliation in some cases. As time goes by, the range of options usually narrows and positions may become entrenched. Attitudes are liable to harden in prolonged disputes over children's residence or contact. The more children lose touch with the parent they no longer live with, the harder it becomes to resume contact and rebuild a damaged relationship (Wallerstein and Kelly, 1980).

When there are concerns about mediation taking place too early, before one or both partners are emotionally ready to deal with the issues, the concerns are usually about pressure to take decisions and risks of premature agreement. Skilled mediators should be aware of these concerns and able to help couples work out interim or holding arrangements, without pressure to take long-term decisions. Interim arrangements, provided there are sufficient safeguards, can reduce stress greatly and help separating couples to work out long-term arrangements at a pace they can both cope with. Entrenched positions may also relax, when couples find they can work out limited arrangements without having to deal with everything at once.

Mediators should be careful not to push people into quick agreements and should explain the need for independent legal advice, often during the process and certainly at the end. The pace of mediation and the interval between mediation sessions can be adjusted to meet the needs of both partners, as far as possible. Sessions can be arranged close together where there is urgency, or spaced at longer intervals when more time is needed. Some couples come back for several phases of mediation spread out over a year or more. Mediators need to be alive to the risks of rushed agreements and to the possible disadvantages to either or both participants of establishing a status quo or losing bargaining power.

8.14   Confidentiality and the Protection of Legal Privilege

There is no statutory privilege in England and Wales protecting the confidentiality of mediation. The privilege attaching to statements and communications made for reconciliation, conciliation or mediation has been established through case-law (*McTaggart v McTaggart* [1948] 2 All ER 754; *Mole v Mole* [1950] 2 All ER 328; *Theodoropoulos v Theodoropoulos* [1963] 3 WLR 354; *Pais v Pais* [1970] 3 WLR 830; *D v NSPCC* [1977] 2 WLR 201; *Re D (Minors)* 11 February 1993, unreported (CA). The privilege attaching to mediation belongs to both parties jointly and may be waived with their joint consent. This has occasionally happened, but only rarely.

The privilege may be overridden where a child is said or believed to be at risk. The Court of Appeal's ruling in *Re D* (above) stated that 'the only exception would be in rare cases where a statement made during conciliation indicates that the maker has caused or is likely to cause serious harm to a child'. Where necessary in order to protect a child from significant harm, the mediator must advise the parties that they should seek help from an appropriate agency and the mediator must in any event contact the appropriate agency or take such steps outside the mediation as may be necessary.

8.15   Managing Power Imbalances in Mediation

One of the greatest challenges for family mediators is to manage the complex inequalities of power which couples bring to mediation, while at the same time maintaining balance and impartiality. Concerns tend to centre on the question of whether women are disadvantaged in mediation, although men could be disadvantaged too. Irving and Benjamin (1995) discuss feminists' concerns and conclude from their research that mediation does not disadvantage women, most of whom report the process as more sensitive and helpful than they believe litigation would have been.

However, when there are difficult financial issues and high levels of conflict or distress, the choice of mediation model and the mediator's skills are very important. Co-mediators may offer more expertise and greater support for both parties, who may then find the process less daunting or intimidating. The Legal Services Commission allows payment to be made to two mediators in franchised services using this model.

Power relationships tend to shift during marriage breakdown and divorce. Although some patterns remain the same, during separation and divorce previous power imbalances between a couple may change in critical ways. One partner's decision to leave the other may alter the previous balance of power. Women are often more strongly placed than men in disputes over children, whereas men often have greater control over financial assets. In mediation, some balancing of these different areas of responsibility and control may become possible in considering mutual interests and common concerns.

Mediators should not be partisan, but they cannot be entirely neutral. They often need to make temporary shifts between participants to enable a less articulate party to speak or to encourage a person who feels emotionally overwhelmed. They also need to restrain individuals who try to dominate and take over the mediation. These shifts around a midway position need not be perceived as bias, provided there is rapport with both parties and an overall balance.

8.16 Ethnic Minority Groups and Cross-cultural Family Mediation

Family mediators need to consider the particular needs of couples from ethnic minorities, including the need to translate information and provide access to interpreters. To be fully acceptable to the couple concerned, mediators may need to be from the same ethnic background and able to speak their language. If language is not a problem, the mediator should be acceptable to the couple in having enough knowledge and understanding of their cultural traditions and religious values. Gender is likely to be an issue, because of the low status of women in some cultures where they are brought up to be subservient to men.

The use of mediation by couples from ethnic minorities is so far largely untested in the UK. Even if the mediator comes from the same background as the couple, he or she cannot make assumptions about their family traditions and values. In any family, but more often in families from ethnic minorities, other family members may be closely involved in looking after the children while both parents study or work. These family members may need to be included in the mediation. The extended family may have direct financial involvement, as well as strong moral influence.

8.17 The Main Stages of Mediation on all Issues

Family mediators work very differently from civil and commercial mediators. It may be helpful to set out the typical stages of a mediation on all issues.

8.17.1 STAGE 1: EXPLAINING MEDIATION AND ASCERTAINING SUITABILITY AND WILLINGNESS

The assessment of suitability has already been considered in some detail. Explaining mediation is very important, because many people confuse it with reconciliation or expect the mediator to act as an arbitrator. Family mediation is a process in which the couple, and in some cases other family members, are helped by an impartial third party or parties (mediators) to identify the issues that need to be settled between them, to consider the options available and to work out mutually acceptable arrangements which take account of the needs of all those involved, including children. Participants retain control over their decisions and are encouraged to seek independent legal advice before entering into any agreement that may have legal or financial consequences.

8.17.2 STAGE 2: SIGNING THE CONSENT TO MEDIATION OR AGREEMENT TO MEDIATE

The Consent to Mediation or Agreement to Mediate is a written document which explains the objectives and principles of mediation and the role of the mediator. Confidentiality and the limits of the process need to be explained carefully, also procedures and costs as applicable. Participants are encouraged to ask questions and then invited to sign the document, if they accept mediation on these terms.

In signing, they undertake to make full disclosure of all financial and other material information, with supporting documents as necessary. The consent to mediation makes it clear, however, that the mediator does not undertake to investigate the information provided. Mediators may terminate the mediation if a participant refuses to provide information or provides information which the other party considers incomplete or inaccurate.

8.17.3 STAGE 3: IDENTIFYING THE ISSUES FOR MEDIATION AND AGREEING THE AGENDA

Each participant is invited to explain his or her issues and priorities. Concerns and feelings — anger, anxiety, distress — need to be expressed and acknowledged. Mediators seek to ensure that all participants are treated with respect and that they understand and accept that certain ground-rules are necessary. For example, participants are assured that each of them will be given a chance to speak and requested not to interrupt each other. Mediators may suspend or terminate the mediation if participants disregard the ground-rules. However, the presence of a third party normally has a restraining effect. Many couples comment that the only place where they can talk together sensibly is in the mediation room. The mediator seeks to create a friendly atmosphere, provides a positive focus and helps to keep the discussions on track.

The agenda for mediation needs to be clear and agreed. Urgent issues need to be prioritised. When there is an agreed agenda which lists the issues raised according to participants' priorities and the urgency of the issue, the next stages of the mediation can be planned.

8.17.4 STAGE 4: GATHERING AND SHARING INFORMATION

Gathering and considering information is a central part of mediation. Many participants are anxious to know the overall financial position and to discuss housing options, before they discuss arrangements for the children. This is especially so where residence is already agreed and/or where parents expect the children to divide their time roughly equally between two homes. Financial information needs to be shared and fully understood. The information often needs to be amplified and clarified to give a clear picture of the assets available, now and in the future, and any liabilities. Very often, one party knows about the finances and the other is disadvantaged by lack of information. Mediation helps to overcome this major imbalance. The information is usually put on a flip-chart to provide a clear overview. Mediators request supporting documents, enquire about gaps, clarify discrepancies and provide neutral and verifiable information, but they do not advise. Further information, valuations and more supporting documents may be asked for, until participants and mediators are satisfied that complete disclosure has been made. If either party refuses to disclose information or provide supporting documents, the mediation would be terminated.

After obtaining full disclosure from both parties and agreeing the accuracy of the figures, there is a basis for exploring the options available to them both.

8.17.5   STAGE 5: CONSIDERATION OF CHILDREN'S NEEDS, WISHES AND FEELINGS

Wherever there are urgent issues concerning the children, these are given priority and not left until this stage. Discussions may be about the children from the outset. In other cases, disputes over contact melt away once progress is made on financial issues. Parents are helped to co-operate with each other, as parents, and to separate as far as possible their marital conflicts from shared concerns over the children. They are encouraged to accept each other's continuing involvement in the children's care and upbringing, to maintain the children's relationships with other important people in their lives and to agree arrangements that will work in practice. This may entail detailed discussions over contact visits, who else will be present, the amount of time the children will spend with each parent during term-time and school holidays, health and special needs, leisure activities and so on. When conflict between the parents is high, short-term or interim arrangements may be worked out. These help to ease a fraught situation, on a step-by-step basis.

Parents — and any other family members who may be involved — are helped to consider the welfare, wishes and feelings of each child, and whether and to what extent each child should be given the opportunity to express his or her feelings in the mediation (Family Law Act 1996, s. 27(8)).

The direct involvement of children in mediation needs very careful consideration. There must be agreement between both parents and the mediator that it is appropriate for children or teenagers to be involved, clarity about the reasons for doing so and agreement about the way in which the child or children are to be involved. The extent of the confidentiality of discussions involving a child in the mediation process and of any feedback given to parents by a mediator who has seen a child alone, should be clarified very carefully beforehand and included in a written contract agreed with the parents and with older children.

Generally, mediators help parents to discuss with each other what they have explained to the children so far and what may need to be explained to them now. Most parents prefer to do this at home, without involving the children directly in the mediation. However, parents may welcome an adolescent who may have become very reticent being offered an opportunity to talk with the mediator on his or her own, to express his or her views and feelings and to suggest what would help. This is usually done on the basis that the adolescent decides what, if anything, will be said to the parents afterwards, and by whom. For example, Rachel's parents were in dispute over which school Rachel should go to for her 'A' levels. They agreed that Rachel should be offered the opportunity to meet with the mediator. After two meetings on her own, Rachel felt clear about her preferred option and she and her parents reached an agreed decision.

Where parents make or propose arrangements which could cause difficulties for a child, without being actually harmful, mediators ask questions to encourage further reflection and discussion. Where mediation ends without these issues having been resolved, they may be identified in the Memorandum of Understanding as matters on which legal advice or other help may be needed.

8.17.6   STAGE 6: EXPLORING OPTIONS

This stage involves consideration of all the available options and how they would work in practice (reality-testing). 'What would happen if …?' Pros and cons need to be explored from different perspectives. Participants may need the mediator's help to identify questions to take to their legal and/or financial advisers. For example, George and Rosemary, a couple in their fifties without dependent children, needed financial advice on endowment policies and pensions, before they could decide whether the family home should be sold, and if so, how the net proceeds of sale should be split between them. Likewise, Dave and Jess, a couple in their thirties with three young children, needed to work out their monthly incomes and expenditure in detail, before negotiating about the family home and child support payments. Many parents in part-time work are unaware of their eligibility for Working Families Tax Credit. If they qualify for this benefit, it can bridge the gap in their financial needs.

8.17.7 STAGE 7: NEGOTIATING TOWARDS SETTLEMENT

Developing proposals for settlement can involve working out interim and/or longer-term arrangements. To return to the examples, Dave and Jess found that Jess could manage on a combination of monthly payments from Dave for Jess and the children, supplemented by Working Families Tax Credit. This left Dave just enough for his own needs. Parenting of the children continued to be shared between them. Rosemary and George worked out a provisional agreement, subject to legal advice, on a 60/40 split in the equity of the family home, in Rosemary's favour and in the context of other detailed proposals on related financial issues.

8.17.8 STAGE 8: GAINING THE CO-OPERATION OF CHILDREN AND OTHERS INVOLVED

Where children and new partners are involved, they need to understand and accept decisions and arrangements, if they are to work in practice. Parents need to consider how to explain new arrangements to their children and new partners, how to take account of their reactions and views and how to give children the reassurances they are looking for. For example, Jess and Dave were able to explain their agreements to their children, although the involvement of Dave's new partner, Samantha, was still a sensitive issue.

8.17.9 STAGE 9: DRAFTING THE MEMORANDUM OF UNDERSTANDING

At the end of the mediation, mediators prepare a final Memorandum of Understanding setting out the proposals for settlement or, if issues are unresolved, the options considered and a brief statement of each party's position, in terms each accepts. The financial information is set out in an 'open' Statement of Financial Information, with supporting documents attached. Participants are encouraged to seek independent legal advice on their proposals, financial disclosure and outstanding issues. Further negotiation often takes place between legal advisors to fine-tune the proposals and tie up any loose ends, prior to formal agreements or consent orders being drafted. The final stage of reaching agreement is greatly eased when antagonism has given way to co-operation and mistrust replaced by mutual concern to work together for the children's benefit. Where this has not happened and dispute continues, the issues may at least have been clarified and both parties should be clearer about their options, including the likely costs and time-scale of court proceedings. Settlement through mediation is an option. Referring a dispute to the court is another option which may be preferred or, in some circumstances, unavoidable.

8.17.10 STAGE 10: ENDING MEDIATION

Parties and/or mediators may withdraw from mediation at any stage. Mediation often ends before it has run its full course, but this need not mean that no progress has been made. Mediation may have narrowed the issues and paved the way for a negotiated or court-ordered settlement. Sometimes mediation takes place in several phases spread over a year or even several years. Interim arrangements for a separation agreement may be worked out in the first phase and a full and final settlement may be worked out some time later, when both partners are ready to divorce.

Family circumstances are likely to change in any event and further mediation may be sought to deal with fresh issues or to modify arrangements for children whose needs inevitably change, as they grow up.

8.17.11   CASE RECORDS AND FILE REVIEWS

Detailed records have to be kept. Auditing of mediation records and file reviews are requirements for franchised services and recognised mediators. Mediators must have a recognised Professional Practice Consultant with whom they meet at regular intervals to discuss and review their practice.

8.18   Different Approaches to Family Mediation in the UK

Family mediation services have been developing in this country since the opening of the pioneer service in Bristol in 1978. Initially, these services concentrated on helping separating or divorcing parents to reach agreements concerning their children. In the mid-1980s, a pilot scheme in London called 'Solicitors in Mediation' extended mediation to all issues in separation and divorce, including financial and property matters. For the first time, family lawyers with further training in mediation took on the different role of mediator, initially in a co-mediation model in which a lawyer mediator was teamed with an experienced family mediator who had co-ordinated the Bristol service. Great interest in this pilot scheme led to its members setting up the Family Mediators Association in December 1988, to provide training in interdisciplinary mediation on all issues and to develop practice.

The network of family mediation services is growing. Yet despite considerable efforts to publicise mediation and encourage take-up, public awareness is still low and misconceptions are still common. Many family lawyers support mediation and have trained as mediators. It is essential for legal advisors and other helping agencies to understand the mediation process and the services available in their area. Many mediators work part-time in services affiliated to National Family Mediation (NFM) and come from a social work or counselling background. Although most trained originally to mediate on children issues, an increasing number have now had some further training to mediate on all issues, including finance and property. Mediation is also offered by some firms of solicitors as a separate professional service. Mediation training for family lawyers generally requires them to be qualified solicitors, barristers or Fellows of the Institute of Legal Executives, holding a current unconditional practising certificate or equivalent and practising in the field of family law, with at least three years' post-qualification experience (preferably five) including substantial experience in matrimonial and family law. Many couples and mediators prefer the co-mediation model in which a lawyer mediator works with a family mediator from a counselling, family therapy or social work background.

Co-mediation offers a number of advantages:

- Complementary knowledge, expertise and skills in dealing with emotional, child-related, legal and financial issues. The family mediator's expertise in handling emotional and family issues complements the lawyer mediator's expertise on legal and financial aspects.

- Balanced negotiations and conflict management. Power imbalances can be managed more easily in co-mediation and more options can be generated. The stresses of the process can be shared as well as its challenges and satisfactions.

- Gender issues underlie many disputes in divorce. With one mediator, there is inevitably a gender imbalance in the room. A male-female team is the model of choice, but not always available as most non-lawyer mediators and many family law mediators are female. A man facing his (ex) partner and two female mediators is liable to feel outnumbered, just as a woman is likely to feel very uncomfortable in a room with her (ex) partner and two male mediators. The latter scenario is however extremely uncommon. Co-mediation with a male-female team is appreciated by couples because it provides a gender balance in the room and opportunities to combine and integrate different perspectives. However, this is not to say that this model always works well or that same-sex mediators cannot work together effectively. A number of conditions, including adequate training and preparation, mutual trust and good communication, are necessary for co-mediation to work well.

8.19 Caucusing or Shuttle Mediation

Following separate assessment meetings, mediation meetings may occasionally take place with each participant separately, instead of the usual practice of meeting with both together. This model, known as 'caucusing' or 'shuttle mediation', is used to a large extent in civil and commercial mediations. It is not widely favoured in family mediation because it does not fulfil the main aim of helping participants — often parents — communicate more easily with each other.

Caucusing in family mediation should be used with great care. The first issue to address is that of confidentiality. A common practice in civil and commercial mediation is for the mediator to hold what each party says in confidence, disclosing to the other only what has been authorised. The mediator in a commercial or industrial dispute may hold in confidence the terms on which one party would be willing to settle, without revealing them to the other. In family mediation, separate sessions may be held in certain circumstances on the basis that the family mediator will not hold anything in confidence except possibly a private address or telephone number. Participants are asked to accept that the mediator may share the content of separate discussions with both of them, without necessarily reporting everything that has been said. Caucusing in family mediation risks drawing mediators into a counselling role. The more discretion they have over what is reported back, the more influence they have on the process and its outcome.

8.20 Regulation of Family Mediation in the UK

The Legal Services Commission regulates the provision of publicly-funded family mediation in England and Wales. Scotland has a different system. The other main regulatory body is the UK College of Family Mediators, an independent, non-government association which provides an umbrella body for training providers and associations of family mediators which meet the College's standards. Individual members must adhere to the College's Code of Practice for family mediation and its standards for training and practice, professional practice consultancy, competence assessment and continuing training. The Legal Services Commission has delegated to the UK College responsibility for managing the competence assessment procedure for mediators wishing to be recognised to undertake assessment meetings and publicly-funded mediation. The College carries out audits of national associations and training providers to check compliance with standards and procedures.

The Law Society of England and Wales is also establishing a Family Mediation Panel composed of solicitors and legal executives who have completed recognised training in family mediation and who satisfy the Law Society's other requirements. Scotland has a different system in which the courts may refer disputed cases to either of two recognised associations:

- CALM, an association of family lawyer mediators accredited by the Law Society of Scotland; and

- Family Mediation Scotland, a constituent body within the UK College, whose mediators are mainly non-lawyers.

8.21 Evaluating Family Mediation — Does it Work?

Research on the Family Mediation Pilot Project co-ordinated by the University of Bristol (Davis et al., 2000) was based on a sample of 4,593 cases in which couples were offered mediation as an alternative to litigation. 70% were referred by lawyers, 12% by the court and the remainder were self-referred. The researchers found that 60–65% of lawyer or court referrals and 52% of self-referrals (often from one party alone) led to mediation taking place, whereas only 30% of referrals for an assessment meeting 'converted' into mediations. The latter involved cases in which one or both parties were already heading towards the court. Experience of mediation was generally positive, with 71% of parents saying that they would recommend mediation to other parents in dispute over their children. There was evidence from the research that mediators are now more skilled in negotiating settlements. Nonetheless, the proportion of financial settlements reached (34%) was lower than agreements relating to children (50%). Of those who reached some level of agreement, 59% said they thought they would be able to negotiate modifications between themselves if necessary. The researchers concluded that mediation as a process has its own distinctive and positive features and that mediation should be supported as a separate system running in parallel to the court system, without replacing it.

8.22 Why Did People Go to Mediation?

What brings people to mediation, despite their distress and anger and anxieties about face-to-face discussions? Mediation clients were asked by researchers at the University of Newcastle (Walker, McCarthy and Timms, 1994) why they had decided to go to mediation. Clients gave the following reasons (not listed in order of priority):

- needing to sort out issues they were unable to deal with by themselves;

- wanting to work out agreements together, instead of going to separate solicitors;

- wanting to do their best for the children;

- wanting an amicable divorce and to stay on good terms with each other;

- needing someone impartial to help them manage discussions on specific issues;

- wanting to avoid legal costs as far as possible;

- wanting an out-of-court settlement;

- wanting someone who would be unbiased, objective and knowledgeable;

- wanting practical and emotional help at the same time;

- wanting reconciliation — 'hoping for a miracle';

- wanting to be told 'what's fair' (although this is not the mediator's role).

One husband said he went to mediation hoping for a miracle. Although he and his wife did not get back together, he found it a great help 'to get things resolved' (*op. cit.*, at p. 38). Another husband saw mediation as 'somewhere we could have a more structured discussion where the focus would be brought back to what were really the major issues by someone who might command the respect of both of us' (*ibid.* at p. 37). A wife said she wanted 'to be able to do it together ... to have a referee; somebody there to make us talk, if you like' (*ibid.*, at p. 37).

8.23 Family Mediation in Europe

Family mediation in Europe at the beginning of the 21st century is developing rapidly. Countries are at different stages in developing family mediation and introducing legislation on mediation. In Holland, family mediation is undertaken exclusively by lawyers, whereas in Norway, child-related mediation is mandatory and family mediators are mainly counsellors or social workers. The Council of Europe's Recommendation on Family Mediation recognised the increasing number of disputes involving children in international cases. Mediation is recommended to help parents resolve disputes and reach agreements concerning their children's residence and relationships with both parents and other family members. Mediation is difficult because of the different countries and distances involved and where there is more than one judicial or competent authority. International mediators need to work flexibly, using a variety of models, for example shuttle mediation and teleconferencing, and they need the ability to work in several languages.

Mediation in international cases can help divided families. It encourages co-operation between mediators in different countries, some of whom are already working together in the European Forum on Family Mediation Training and Research to promote the culture of mediation and high standards of practice in helping to resolve family disputes.

8.24 Further reading

Ahrons, C., *The Good Divorce*, Bloomsbury (1995).
Brown, H. and Marriott, A. *ADR Principles and Practice*, Sweet & Maxwell (1993).
Cockett, M. and Tripp, J., *The Exeter Family Study: Family Breakdown and its impact on children*, University of Exeter Press (1994).
Davis, G., et al., *Monitoring Publicly Funded Family Mediation — Report to the Legal Services Commission*, Legal Services Commission (2000).
Parkinson, L., *Family Mediation*, Sweet & Maxwell (1997).
Walker, J., McCarthy, P., Timms, N., *Mediation: the Making and Remaking of Co-operative Relationships*, Relate Centre for Family Studies, University of Newcastle (1994).
Wallerstein, J. and Kelly, J. *Surviving the Break-up — how children and parents cope with divorce*, Grant McIntyre (1980).

NINE

RELEVANT PRINCIPLES OF TAXATION

9.1 Principles

It is very important to be familiar with the way that maintenance is taxed, as many barristers early in practice may be asked to deal with such cases. Those who are going to specialise in family law must be fully conversant with the tax provisions relevant to divorce.

There has been no very coherent policy on the taxation of husband and wife. The historical concept of the husband and wife as one person was used for income tax and capital gains tax, taxing the married couple as one unit, but inheritance tax from the time of its introduction as capital transfer tax taxed spouses independently. Increasingly the approach is to limit special reliefs and allowances available to spouses. There are also some provisions to prevent tax avoidance within the family.

Generally, a child is taxed separately from his or her parents, the child being separately taxable on any income it receives and having a personal tax allowance from the time of birth, but again there are provisions to stop tax avoidance.

For more information, see the Inland Revenue website (www.inlandrevenue.gov.uk) and Inland Revenue leaflets such as IR171, 'Income Tax, A guide for people with children'.

9.2 Income Tax

9.2.1 SPOUSES MARRIED AND LIVING TOGETHER

Historically a husband and wife were treated as a single unit for tax purposes and automatically assessed jointly. This system was replaced with separate taxation from the 1990–91 tax year, and now married people are independently liable for tax on their own income with an individual personal allowance, currently £4,535. An additional tax allowance for married men was available, but this was abolished from April 1999 save in the case if those of pensionable age. A married person is therefore in almost the same tax position as an unmarried person.

The situation as regards tax allowances for children has changed over the years. The current position is that a child is liable for tax on any personal income with an individual tax allowance. From April 2001 a child tax credit has been introduced for parents, and this is available to any parent who is single, married or living with someone and has at least one child under the age of 16 living with them. The maximum allowance can provide a tax saving of £520, and if parents are not liable to higher rate tax, this allowance can go to either of them or be shared. If either of the parents is liable to higher rate tax, the allowance goes to that parent, and the allowance tapers off so as to provide no benefit if income exceeds the higher rate tax threshold by £7,800 or more. The higher rate tax threshold is currently £29,400. A Working Families Tax Credit is available for families with very low income, and should be researched if appropriate.

9.2.2 SEPARATION AND DIVORCE

Provisions for the taxation of maintenance payments are set out in FA 1988, ss. 36–40, see **9.6**.

9.3 Capital Gains Tax

9.3.1 SPOUSES MARRIED AND LIVING TOGETHER

As with income tax, the principle of joint assessment of husband and wife survived for many decades, but as with income tax this was abandoned for the 1990–91 and following tax years. Each spouse is now separately liable for tax on their own gains, and each has a separate annual allowance of £7,500.

Married couples have a substantial advantage in that disposals between spouses are treated as being at no gain, no loss, so that no capital gains tax will be payable on such a disposal (TCGA 1992, s. 58). Note, however, that the original acquisition price of the asset will be retained for calculating gains on a later disposal by the recipient spouse. On the operation of this section, see *Gubay* v *Kington* [1984] 1 WLR 163.

9.3.2 SEPARATION AND DIVORCE

It is important to note that disposals made as part of financial provision on divorce are not necessarily exempt from CGT, and the divorce settlement should be considered carefully to avoid CGT. See *M* v *M (Sale of Property)* [1988] 1 FLR 389. In *Aspden* v *Hildesley* [1982] 1 WLR 264 a husband agreed to transfer his share in a second home to the wife but it was held that this transaction was not exempt so he would have to pay CGT on the value of his share.

As suggestions for avoiding CGT:

(a) Make disposal or agreement before separation and divorce, so it will be at no gain/no loss (but remember you keep the original acquisition cost).

(b) Use exempt assets for provision, e.g., car.

(c) Remember a sterling lump sum will not be liable to CGT (but consider how such a sum could be raised).

(d) Remember that a main private residence is not liable to tax.

(e) After separation and divorce the spouses will not be 'connected', so it may be possible to argue market value should not be taken.

9.4 Inheritance Tax

9.4.1 SPOUSES MARRIED AND LIVING TOGETHER

Spouses are separately liable for inheritance tax on their own estates with their own allowances and own cumulative totals. This can be important in tax planning: assets can be divided between the spouses to use the full nil rate band of £242,000 each.

Transfers between spouses are exempt (ITA 1984, s. 18); and they can benefit from other exemptions and reliefs, such as provision for maintenance (ITA 1984, s. 11) and gifts in consideration of marriage (ITA 1984, s. 22).

9.4.2   SEPARATION AND DIVORCE

While there is no complete exemption for provision on divorce, it is unlikely inheritance tax will be payable on divorce. The provision that dispositions for maintenance of the family are not transfers of value applies to maintenance on divorce (ITA 1984, s. 11), and if there is provision under a court order it can be argued that there is no intention to confer a gratuitous benefit (ITA 1984, s. 10).

9.4.3   DEATH OF ONE SPOUSE

Tax will be chargeable on the estate of the deceased, including their share of jointly owned property, subject to their cumulative total. Property passing to the surviving spouse will be exempt, but will be chargeable to tax when the survivor dies, so exemptions should be used carefully.

9.5   Couples Living Together

Formerly the couple living together could be better off from the tax point of view if they were reasonably well off. This is no longer the case.

9.5.1   INCOME TAX

Couples living together will each be taxed as a single individual, paying tax on their own income with a single person's allowance each. Each will have their own 10% band before paying tax at the basic rate.

9.5.2   CAPITAL GAINS TAX

Each cohabitee will be separately taxed and will have their own allowances. Disposals between them will not be at no gain/no loss, which may be a problem if they split up and need to divide assets, especially as the possibility of claiming hold over relief has gone.

9.5.3   INHERITANCE TAX

Each cohabitee will be separately taxed and will have their own allowances and cumulative total. Transfers between cohabitees will not be exempt, but they may be PETs if they are gifts. A problem can arise if one cohabitee dies as assets left to the other will not be exempt.

9.6   Taxation of Maintenance Payments

9.6.1   GENERALLY

The approach of the tax system to maintenance payments has varied over the years. The current system is relatively straightforward, but confusion may be caused in dealing with a variation in a case where an original order was made some years ago. Payments made under obligations entered into before 15 March 1988 were taxed under a complex process by which tax was paid in advance by the payer, but then became a tax credit of which the payee might be able to reclaim all or part depending on her or his own tax position. This system was greatly simplified from 15 March 1988, though some aspects of the former system were retained. For example, the possibility that the payer of maintenance could deduct maintenance payments for tax purposes (which could be a significant benefit for higher rate tax payers) was retained until abolished by the Finance Act 1999. The current approach is that maintenance payments should have limited and simple tax consequences. The Inland Revenue website and section 20 of 'At a Glance' provide useful detail.

9.6.2   TAX EFFECTS FOR THE PERSON PAYING MAINTENANCE

Maintenance payments are not deductible for tax purposes and must be paid in full from taxed income. This applies to payments to or for a former spouse or a child, including assessments under the Child Support Act.

Until 2000–01 an additional personal allowance (the equivalent of a married man's allowance or the actual amount of the maintenance if lower) was available to someone paying maintenance to a former spouse. From 2001–02 such relief will only be available where the payer or the former spouse is of pensionable age, and relief is only available at the 10% tax rate and not higher rates.

9.6.3   TAX EFFECTS FOR THE PERSON RECEIVING MAINTENANCE

Whether the recipient of the payments is a former spouse or a child, the payments will not be taxable in his or her hands, though he or she will be fully liable to tax on any other income he or she has. The recipient will not be able to set any tax allowance against the maintenance payment, or be able to reclaim any tax paid by the payer in respect of the payment.

9.7   Illustration of Tax Issues Relevant to Divorce

Jasper and Fiona married in 1990 and separated in 1995, since when they have not lived together. They have one child, Gemma, currently aged seven.

Fiona has petitioned for divorce and has been granted a decree nisi. Financial provision is currently being negotiated, and Fiona has proposed the following terms. Advise Jasper on any potential tax implications of each term to help him to decide how he should respond.

(a) Jasper should transfer to Fiona his share in the former matrimonial home, which is registered in their joint names and which is currently valued at £150,000. The house was purchased in 1990 for £80,000.

(b) Alternatively, the former matrimonial home should be settled, to be sold when Gemma becomes 18, the proceeds then to be divided with 75% to Fiona and 25% to Jasper.

(c) Fiona should transfer to Jasper a yacht that was purchased in 1992 for £20,000. Although the purchase price was provided by Jasper, the yacht was put into Fiona's name as Jasper at the time had a slight fear that he might go bankrupt. The yacht is now worth £50,000.

(d) Fiona should keep a Volvo car bought for her by Jasper which is currently worth £10,000.

(e) Jasper should pay to Fiona a lump sum of £20,000. To raise this sum he would have to sell shares that he purchased in 1987 for £2,000, and they are now worth £30,000.

Advice to Jasper

There will be no inheritance tax consequences as all the transfers would apparently be to meet reasonable claims on divorce and would therefore be 'non-gratuitous' (ITA 1984, s. 10).

(a) There is an apparent capital gain of £70,000 on the matrimonial home; however, the gain will be exempt from capital gains tax as it relates to a main private residence (TCGA 1992, s. 222 and see also Extra-Statutory Concession D6 as the couple are already living separately).

(b) If the house is settled, it will become the main private residence of Fiona alone. Therefore when the home is eventually sold (or if Fiona later buys out Jasper's interest) then the gain that Jasper makes will be subject to capital gains tax (calculated as the gain his 25% has made since the settlement). This must be considered in deciding how attractive this option is.

(c) The yacht has apparently gained £30,000 in value. If Fiona transfers ownership to Jasper this gain will *prima facie* be liable to tax at Fiona's marginal rate of income tax, and reduced by Fiona's annual allowance of £6,300 if this has not yet been used for another transaction.

(d) There is no disposal if a spouse keeps an asset, and in any event motor cars are not subject to capital gains tax.

(e) The transfer of money will not in itself attract capital gains tax as sterling is not liable to the tax. However the gain of £28,000 that will accrue on the sale of the shares will attract capital gains tax at Jasper's marginal rate of tax, reduced by his annual allowance of £7,500 if this has not yet been used on another transaction, and also reduced by the costs of sale. If a capital sum is to be paid it is always important to consider how it will be raised.

APPENDIX A

FAMILY LAW ACT 1996

Rights to occupy matrimonial home

30. Rights concerning matrimonial home where one spouse has no estate, etc.

(1) This section applies if—

(a) one spouse is entitled to occupy a dwelling-house by virtue of—

(i) a beneficial estate or interest or contract; or

(ii) any enactment giving that spouse the right to remain in occupation; and

(b) the other spouse is not so entitled.

(2) Subject to the provisions of this Part, the spouse not so entitled has the following rights ('matrimonial home rights')—

(a) if in occupation, a right not to be evicted or excluded from the dwelling-house or any part of it by the other spouse except with the leave of the court given by an order under section 33;

(b) if not in occupation, a right with the leave of the court so given to enter into and occupy the dwelling-house.

(3) If a spouse is entitled under this section to occupy a dwelling-house or any part of a dwelling-house, any payment or tender made or other thing done by that spouse in or towards satisfaction of any liability of the other spouse in respect of rent, mortgage payments or other outgoings affecting the dwelling-house is, whether or not it is made or done in pursuance of an order under section 40, as good as if made or done by the other spouse.

(4) A spouse's occupation by virtue of this section—

(a) is to be treated, for the purposes of the Rent (Agriculture) Act 1976 and the Rent Act 1977 (other than Part V and sections 103 to 106 of that Act), as occupation by the other spouse as the other spouse's residence, and

(b) if the spouse occupies the dwelling-house as that spouse's only or principal home, is to be treated, for the purposes of the Housing Act 1985, Part I of the Housing Act 1988 and Chapter I of Part V of the Housing Act 1996, as occupation by the other spouse as the other spouse's only or principal home.

(5) If a spouse ('the first spouse')—

(a) is entitled under this section to occupy a dwelling-house or any part of a dwelling-house, and

(b) makes any payment in or towards satisfaction of any liability of the other spouse ('the second spouse') in respect of mortgage payments affecting the dwelling-house,

the person to whom the payment is made may treat it as having been made by the second spouse, but the fact that that person has treated any such payment as having been so made does not affect any claim of the first spouse against the second spouse to an interest in the dwelling-house by virtue of the payment.

(6) If a spouse is entitled under this section to occupy a dwelling-house or part of a dwelling-house by reason of an interest of the other spouse under a trust, all the provisions of subsections (3) to (5) apply in relation to the trustees as they apply in relation to the other spouse.

(7) This section does not apply to a dwelling-house which has at no time been, and which was at no time intended by the spouses to be, a matrimonial home of theirs.

(8) A spouse's matrimonial home rights continue—

(a) only so long as the marriage subsists, except to the extent that an order under section 33(5) otherwise provides; and

(b) only so long as the other spouse is entitled as mentioned in subsection (1) to occupy the dwelling-house, except where provision is made by section 31 for those rights to be a charge on an estate or interest in the dwelling-house.

(9) It is hereby declared that a spouse—

(a) who has an equitable interest in a dwelling-house or in its proceeds of sale, but

(b) is not a spouse in whom there is vested (whether solely or as joint tenant) a legal estate in fee simple or a legal term of years absolute in the dwelling-house,

is to be treated, only for the purpose of determining whether he has matrimonial home rights, as not being entitled to occupy the dwelling-house by virtue of that interest.

Occupation orders

33. Occupation orders where applicant has estate or interest etc. or has matrimonial home rights

(1) If—

(a) a person ('the person entitled')—

(i) is entitled to occupy a dwelling-house by virtue of a beneficial estate or interest or contract or by virtue of any enactment giving him the right to remain in occupation, or

(ii) has matrimonial home rights in relation to a dwelling-house, and

(b) the dwelling-house—

(i) is or at any time has been the home of the person entitled and of another person with whom he is associated, or

(ii) was at any time intended by the person entitled and any such other person to be their home,

the person entitled may apply to the court for an order containing any of the provisions specified in subsections (3), (4) and (5).

(2) If an agreement to marry is terminated, no application under this section may be made by virtue of section 62(3)(e) by reference to that agreement after the end of the period of three years beginning with the day on which it is terminated.

(3) An order under this section may—

(a) enforce the applicant's entitlement to remain in occupation as against the other person ('the respondent');

(b) require the respondent to permit the applicant to enter and remain in the dwelling-house or part of the dwelling-house;

(c) regulate the occupation of the dwelling-house by either or both parties;

(d) if the respondent is entitled as mentioned in subsection (1)(a)(i), prohibit, suspend or restrict the exercise by him of his right to occupy the dwelling-house;

(e) if the respondent has matrimonial home rights in relation to the dwelling-house and the applicant is the other spouse, restrict or terminate those rights;

(f) require the respondent to leave the dwelling-house or part of the dwelling-house; or

(g) exclude the respondent from a defined area in which the dwelling-house is included.

(4) An order under this section may declare that the applicant is entitled as mentioned in subsection (1)(a)(i) or has matrimonial home rights.

(5) If the applicant has matrimonial home rights and the respondent is the other spouse, an order under this section made during the marriage may provide that those rights are not brought to an end by—

(a) the death of the other spouse; or

(b) the termination (otherwise than by death) of the marriage.

(6) In deciding whether to exercise its powers under subsection (3) and (if so) in what manner, the court shall have regard to all the circumstances including—

(a) the housing needs and housing resources of each of the parties and of any relevant child;

(b) the financial resources of each of the parties;

(c) the likely effect of any order, or of any decision by the court not to exercise its powers under subsection (3), on the health, safety or well-being of the parties and of any relevant child; and

(d) the conduct of the parties in relation to each other and otherwise.

(7) If it appears to the court that the applicant or any relevant child is likely to suffer significant harm attributable to conduct of the respondent if an order under this section containing one or more of the provisions mentioned in subsection (3) is not made, the court shall make the order unless it appears to it that—

(a) the respondent or any relevant child is likely to suffer significant harm if the order is made; and

(b) the harm likely to be suffered by the respondent or child in that event is as great as, or greater than, the harm attributable to conduct of the respondent which is likely to be suffered by the applicant or child if the order is not made.

(8) The court may exercise its powers under subsection (5) in any case where it considers that in all the circumstances it is just and reasonable to do so.

(9) An order under this section—

(a) may not be made after the death of either of the parties mentioned in subsection (1); and

(b) except in the case of an order made by virtue of subsection (5)(a), ceases to have effect on the death of either party.

(10) An order under this section may, in so far as it has continuing effect, be made for a specified period, until the occurrence of a specified event or until further order.

35. One former spouse with no existing right to occupy

(1) This section applies if—

(a) one former spouse is entitled to occupy a dwelling-house by virtue of a beneficial estate or interest or contract, or by virtue of any enactment giving him the right to remain in occupation;

(b) the other former spouse is not so entitled; and

(c) the dwelling-house was at any time their matrimonial home or was at any time intended by them to be their matrimonial home.

(2) The former spouse not so entitled may apply to the court for an order under this section against the other former spouse ('the respondent').

(3) If the applicant is in occupation, an order under this section must contain provision—

(a) giving the applicant the right not to be evicted or excluded from the dwelling-house or any part of it by the respondent for the period specified in the order; and

(b) prohibiting the respondent from evicting or excluding the applicant during that period.

(4) If the applicant is not in occupation, an order under this section must contain provision—

(a) giving the applicant the right to enter into and occupy the dwelling-house for the period specified in the order; and

(b) requiring the respondent to permit the exercise of that right.

(5) An order under this section may also—

(a) regulate the occupation of the dwelling-house by either or both of the parties;

(b) prohibit, suspend or restrict the exercise by the respondent of his right to occupy the dwelling-house;

(c) require the respondent to leave the dwelling-house or part of the dwelling-house; or

(d) exclude the respondent from a defined area in which the dwelling-house is included.

(6) In deciding whether to make an order under this section containing provision of the kind mentioned in subsection (3) or (4) and (if so) in what manner, the court shall have regard to all the circumstances including—

(a) the housing needs and housing resources of each of the parties and of any relevant child;

(b) the financial resources of each of the parties;

(c) the likely effect of any order, or of any decision by the court not to exercise its powers under subsection (3) or (4), on the health, safety or well-being of the parties and of any relevant child;

(d) the conduct of the parties in relation to each other and otherwise;

(e) the length of time that has elapsed since the parties ceased to live together;

(f) the length of time that has elapsed since the marriage was dissolved or annulled; and

(g)   the existence of any pending proceedings between the parties—
(i)   for an order under section 23A or 24 of the Matrimonial Causes Act 1973 (property adjustment orders in connection with divorce proceedings etc.);
(ii)   for an order under paragraph 1(2)(d) or (e) of Schedule 1 to the Children Act 1989 (orders for financial relief against parents); or
(iii)   relating to the legal or beneficial ownership of the dwelling-house.

(7)   In deciding whether to exercise its power to include one or more of the provisions referred to in subsection (5) ('a subsection (5) provision') and (if so) in what manner, the court shall have regard to all the circumstances including the matters mentioned in subsection (6)(a) to (e).

(8)   If the court decides to make an order under this section and it appears to it that, if the order does not include a subsection (5) provision, the applicant or any relevant child is likely to suffer significant harm attributable to conduct of the respondent, the court shall include the subsection (5) provision in the order unless it appears to the court that—
(a)   the respondent or any relevant child is likely to suffer significant harm if the provision is included in the order; and
(b)   the harm likely to be suffered by the respondent or child in that event is as great as or greater than the harm attributable to conduct of the respondent which is likely to be suffered by the applicant or child if the provision is not included.

(9)   An order under this section—
(a)   may not be made after the death of either of the former spouses; and
(b)   ceases to have effect on the death of either of them.

(10)   An order under this section must be limited so as to have effect for a specified period not exceeding six months, but may be extended on one or more occasions for a further specified period not exceeding six months.

(11)   A former spouse who has an equitable interest in the dwelling-house or in the proceeds of sale of the dwelling-house but in whom there is not vested (whether solely or as joint tenant) a legal estate in fee simple or a legal term of years absolute in the dwelling-house is to be treated (but only for the purpose of determining whether he is eligible to apply under this section) as not being entitled to occupy the dwelling-house by virtue of that interest.

(12)   Subsection (11) does not prejudice any right of such a former spouse to apply for an order under section 33.

(13)   So long as an order under this section remains in force, subsections (3) to (6) of section 30 apply in relation to the applicant—
(a)   as if he were the spouse entitled to occupy the dwelling-house by virtue of that section; and
(b)   as if the respondent were the other spouse.

36.   One cohabitant or former cohabitant with no existing right to occupy

(1)   This section applies if—
(a)   one cohabitant or former cohabitant is entitled to occupy a dwelling-house by virtue of a beneficial estate or interest or contract or by virtue of any enactment giving him the right to remain in occupation;
(b)   the other cohabitant or former cohabitant is not so entitled; and
(c)   that dwelling-house is the home in which they live together as husband and wife or a home in which they at any time so lived together or intended so to live together.

(2)   The cohabitant or former cohabitant not so entitled may apply to the court for an order under this section against the other cohabitant or former cohabitant ('the respondent').

(3)   If the applicant is in occupation, an order under this section must contain provision—
(a)   giving the applicant the right not to be evicted or excluded from the dwelling-house or any part of it by the respondent for the period specified in the order; and
(b)   prohibiting the respondent from evicting or excluding the applicant during that period.

(4)   If the applicant is not in occupation, an order under this section must contain provision—
(a)   giving the applicant the right to enter into and occupy the dwelling-house for the period specified in the order; and

(b) requiring the respondent to permit the exercise of that right.

(5) An order under this section may also—

(a) regulate the occupation of the dwelling-house by either or both of the parties;

(b) prohibit, suspend or restrict the exercise by the respondent of his right to occupy the dwelling-house;

(c) require the respondent to leave the dwelling-house or part of the dwelling-house; or

(d) exclude the respondent from a defined area in which the dwelling-house is included.

(6) In deciding whether to make an order under this section containing provision of the kind mentioned in subsection (3) or (4) and (if so) in what manner, the court shall have regard to all the circumstances including—

(a) the housing needs and housing resources of each of the parties and of any relevant child;

(b) the financial resources of each of the parties;

(c) the likely effect of any order, or of any decision by the court not to exercise its powers under subsection (3) or (4), on the health, safety or well-being of the parties and of any relevant child;

(d) the conduct of the parties in relation to each other and otherwise;

(e) the nature of the parties' relationship;

(f) the length of time during which they have lived together as husband and wife;

(g) whether there are or have been any children who are children of both parties or for whom both parties have or have had parental responsibility;

(h) the length of time that has elapsed since the parties ceased to live together; and

(i) the existence of any pending proceedings between the parties—

(i) for an order under paragraph 1(2)(d) or (e) of Schedule 1 to the Children Act 1989 (orders for financial relief against parents); or

(ii) relating to the legal or beneficial ownership of the dwelling-house.

(7) In deciding whether to exercise its powers to include one or more of the provisions referred to in subsection (5) ('a subsection (5) provision') and (if so) in what manner, the court shall have regard to all the circumstances including—

(a) the matters mentioned in subsection (6)(a) to (d); and

(b) the questions mentioned in subsection (8).

(8) The questions are—

(a) whether the applicant or any relevant child is likely to suffer significant harm attributable to conduct of the respondent if the subsection (5) provision is not included in the order; and

(b) whether the harm likely to be suffered by the respondent or child if the provision is included is as great as or greater than the harm attributable to conduct of the respondent which is likely to be suffered by the applicant or child if the provision is not included.

(9) An order under this section—

(a) may not be made after the death of either of the parties; and

(b) ceases to have effect on the death of either of them.

(10) An order under this section must be limited so as to have effect for a specified period not exceeding six months, but may be extended on one occasion for a further specified period not exceeding six months.

(11) A person who has an equitable interest in the dwelling-house or in the proceeds of sale of the dwelling-house but in whom there is not vested (whether solely or as joint tenant) a legal estate in fee simple or a legal term of years absolute in the dwelling-house is to be treated (but only for the purpose of determining whether he is eligible to apply under this section) as not being entitled to occupy the dwelling-house by virtue of that interest.

(12) Subsection (11) does not prejudice any right of such a person to apply for an order under section 33.

(13) So long as the order remains in force, subsections (3) to (6) of section 30 apply in relation to the applicant—

(a) as if he were a spouse entitled to occupy the dwelling-house by virtue of that section; and

(b) as if the respondent were the other spouse.

37. Neither spouse entitled to occupy

(1) This section applies if—

(a) one spouse or former spouse and the other spouse or former spouse occupy a dwelling-house which is or was the matrimonial home; but

(b) neither of them is entitled to remain in occupation—

(i) by virtue of a beneficial estate or interest or contract; or

(ii) by virtue of any enactment giving him the right to remain in occupation.

(2) Either of the parties may apply to the court for an order against the other under this section.

(3) An order under this section may—

(a) require the respondent to permit the applicant to enter and remain in the dwelling-house or part of the dwelling-house;

(b) regulate the occupation of the dwelling-house by either or both of the spouses;

(c) require the respondent to leave the dwelling-house or part of the dwelling-house; or

(d) exclude the respondent from a defined area in which the dwelling-house is included.

(4) Subsections (6) and (7) of section 33 apply to the exercise by the court of its powers under this section as they apply to the exercise by the court of its powers under subsection (3) of that section.

(5) An order under this section must be limited so as to have effect for a specified period not exceeding six months, but may be extended on one or more occasions for a further specified period not exceeding six months.

38. Neither cohabitant or former cohabitant entitled to occupy

(1) This section applies if—

(a) one cohabitant or former cohabitant and the other cohabitant or former cohabitant occupy a dwelling-house which is the home in which they live or lived together as husband and wife; but

(b) neither of them is entitled to remain in occupation—

(i) by virtue of a beneficial estate or interest or contract; or

(ii) by virtue of any enactment giving him the right to remain in occupation.

(2) Either of the parties may apply to the court for an order against the other under this section.

(3) An order under this section may—

(a) require the respondent to permit the applicant to enter and remain in the dwelling-house or part of the dwelling-house;

(b) regulate the occupation of the dwelling-house by either or both of the parties;

(c) require the respondent to leave the dwelling-house or part of the dwelling-house; or

(d) exclude the respondent from a defined area in which the dwelling-house is included.

(4) In deciding whether to exercise its powers to include one or more of the provisions referred to in subsection (3) ('a subsection (3) provision') and (if so) in what manner, the court shall have regard to all the circumstances including—

(a) the housing needs and housing resources of each of the parties and of any relevant child;

(b) the financial resources of each of the parties;

(c) the likely effect of any order, or of any decision by the court not to exercise its powers under subsection (3), on the health, safety or well-being of the parties and of any relevant child;

(d) the conduct of the parties in relation to each other and otherwise; and

(e) the questions mentioned in subsection (5).

(5) The questions are—

(a) whether the applicant or any relevant child is likely to suffer significant harm attributable to conduct of the respondent if the subsection (3) provision is not included in the order; and

(b) whether the harm likely to be suffered by the respondent or child if the provision is included is as great as or greater than the harm attributable to conduct of the respondent which is likely to be suffered by the applicant or child if the provision is not included.

(6)   An order under this section shall be limited so as to have effect for a specified period not exceeding six months, but may be extended on one occasion for a further specified period not exceeding six months.

41.   Additional considerations if parties are cohabitants or former cohabitants
(1)   This section applies if the parties are cohabitants or former cohabitants.
(2)   Where the court is required to consider the nature of the parties' relationship, it is to have regard to the fact that they have not given each other the commitment involved in marriage.

Non-molestation orders

42.   Non-molestation orders
(1)   In this Part a 'non-molestation order' means an order containing either or both of the following provisions—
(a)   provision prohibiting a person ('the respondent') from molesting another person who is associated with the respondent;
(b)   provision prohibiting the respondent from molesting a relevant child.
(2)   The court may make a non-molestation order—
(a)   if an application for the order has been made (whether in other family proceedings or without any other family proceedings being instituted) by a person who is associated with the respondent; or
(b)   if in any family proceedings to which the respondent is a party the court considers that the order should be made for the benefit of any other party to the proceedings or any relevant child even though no such application has been made.
(3)   In subsection (2) 'family proceedings' includes proceedings in which the court has made an emergency protection order under section 44 of the Children Act 1989 which includes an exclusion requirement (as defined in section 44A(3) of that Act).
(4)   Where an agreement to marry is terminated, no application under subsection (2)(a) may be made by virtue of section 62(3)(e) by reference to that agreement after the end of the period of three years beginning with the day on which it is terminated.
(5)   In deciding whether to exercise its powers under this section and, if so, in what manner, the court shall have regard to all the circumstances including the need to secure the health, safety and well-being—
(a)   of the applicant or, in a case falling within subsection (2)(b), the person for whose benefit the order would be made; and
(b)   of any relevant child.
(6)   A non-molestation order may be expressed so as to refer to molestation in general, to particular acts of molestation, or to both.
(7)   A non-molestation order may be made for a specified period or until further order.
(8)   A non-molestation order which is made in other family proceedings ceases to have effect if those proceedings are withdrawn or dismissed.

Further provisions relating to occupation and non-molestation orders

43.   Leave of court required for applications by children under sixteen
(1)   A child under the age of sixteen may not apply for an occupation order or a non-molestation order except with the leave of the court.
(2)   The court may grant leave for the purposes of subsection (1) only if it is satisfied that the child has sufficient understanding to make the proposed application for the occupation order or non-molestation order.

44.   Evidence of agreement to marry
(1)   Subject to subsection (2), the court shall not make an order under section 33 or 42 by virtue of section 62(3)(e) unless there is produced to it evidence in writing of the existence of the agreement to marry.
(2)   Subsection (1) does not apply if the court is satisfied that the agreement to marry was evidenced by—
(a)   the gift of an engagement ring by one party to the agreement to the other in contemplation of their marriage, or
(b)   a ceremony entered into by the parties in the presence of one or more other persons assembled for the purpose of witnessing the ceremony.

45. Ex parte orders

(1) The court may, in any case where it considers that it is just and convenient to do so, make an occupation order or a non-molestation order even though the respondent has not been given such notice of the proceedings as would otherwise be required by rules of court.

(2) In determining whether to exercise its powers under subsection (1), the court shall have regard to all the circumstances including—

(a) any risk of significant harm to the applicant or a relevant child, attributable to conduct of the respondent, if the order is not made immediately;

(b) whether it is likely that the applicant will be deterred or prevented from pursuing the application if an order is not made immediately; and

(c) whether there is reason to believe that the respondent is aware of the proceedings but is deliberately evading service and that the applicant or a relevant child will be seriously prejudiced by the delay involved—

(i) where the court is a magistrates' court, in effecting service of proceedings; or

(ii) in any other case, in effecting substituted service.

(3) If the court makes an order by virtue of subsection (1) it must afford the respondent an opportunity to make representations relating to the order as soon as just and convenient at a full hearing.

(4) If, at a full hearing, the court makes an occupation order ('the full order'), then—

(a) for the purposes of calculating the maximum period for which the full order may be made to have effect, the relevant section is to apply as if the period for which the full order will have effect began on the date on which the initial order first had effect; and

(b) the provisions of section 36(10) or 38(6) as to the extension of orders are to apply as if the full order and the initial order were a single order.

(5) In this section—

'full hearing' means a hearing of which notice has been given to all the parties in accordance with rules of court;

'initial order' means an occupation order made by virtue of subsection (1); and

'relevant section' means section 33(10), 35(10), 36(10), 37(5) or 38(6).

46. Undertakings

(1) In any case where the court has power to make an occupation order or non-molestation order, the court may accept an undertaking from any party to the proceedings.

(2) No power of arrest may be attached to any undertaking given under subsection (1).

(3) The court shall not accept an undertaking under subsection (1) in any case where apart from this section a power of arrest would be attached to the order.

(4) An undertaking given to a court under subsection (1) is enforceable as if it were an order of the court.

(5) This section has effect without prejudice to the powers of the High Court and the county court apart from this section.

APPENDIX B

APPLICATIONS FOR COMMITTAL ORDERS: CHECKLISTS

B.1 Introduction

B.1.1 THE IMPORTANCE OF ABIDING BY CORRECT PROCEDURE

The Court of Appeal has stressed in several cases that, because committal for contempt of court is concerned with offences of a quasi-criminal nature and the liberty of the subject is at stake, the relevant rules of court must be complied with and the prescribed forms must be used. However, 'any procedural defect in the commencement or conduct by the applicant of a committal application may be waived by the court if satisfied that no injustice has been caused to the respondent by the defect' (Practice Direction — Committal Applications, para. 10, supplemental to RSC O. 52 and CCR O. 29).

In *Nicholls* v *Nicholls* [1997] 1 FLR 649, Lord Woolf MR, giving the judgment of the Court of Appeal, stated (at p. 655D) that:

> While the ... requirements of O. 29, r. 1 (County Court Rules) are there to be observed, in the absence of authority to the contrary, even though the liberty of the subject is involved, we would not expect the requirements to be mandatory, in the sense that any non-compliance with the rule means that a committal for contempt is irredeemably invalid.

Lord Woolf gave the following guidance (p. 661E):

> (1) As committal orders involve the liberty of the subject it is particularly important that the relevant rules are duly complied with. It remains the responsibility of the judge when signing the committal order to ensure that it is properly drawn and that it adequately particularises the breaches which have been proved and for which the sentence has been imposed.

> (2) As long as the contemnor has had a fair trial and the order has been made on valid grounds the existence of a defect either in the application to commit or in the committal order served will not result in the order being set aside except insofar as the interests of justice require this to be done.

> (3) Interests of justice will not require an order to be set aside where there is no prejudice caused as the result of errors in the application to commit or in the order to commit. When necessary the order can be amended.

> (4) When considering whether to set aside the order, the court should have regard to the interests of any other party and the need to uphold the reputation of the justice system.

(5)   If there has been a procedural irregularity or some other defect in the conduct of the proceedings which has occasioned injustice, the court will consider exercising its power to order a new trial unless there are circumstances which indicate that it would not be just to do so.

The checklists which follow are designed to cover the practical points which most often arise, and need to be considered, in preparation for, and in the course of, committal hearings. They are not comprehensive of every point which has reached the Court of Appeal.

B.1.2   COMMITTAL PROCEDURE: FORMS, RULES AND *PRACTICE DIRECTION*

Whichever prescribed form of committal application is required, the form 'must set out in full the grounds on which the committal application is made and should identify, separately and numerically, each act of contempt' (Practice Direction — Committal Applications, paras 2.5 and 2.6, and *Harmsworth* v *Harmsworth* [1998] 1 FLR 349). This requirement and the need to support the application with suitable evidence and give due notice to the respondent are the most important steps to ensure that an application for committal can achieve an effective hearing.

The Civil Procedure Rules 1998 and the Practice Direction — Committal Applications, supplemental to RSC O. 52 and CCR O. 29, have incorporated some of the previous case law and practice, but have made the selection of appropriate forms and rules more complicated. This affects family practitioners as orders and committals under the Protection from Harassment Act 1997 are governed by the CPR 1998.

Committal procedure is governed in the High Court by RSC O. 52 (preserved in sch. 1 to the CPR 1998) and, in civil proceedings, by Practice Direction — Committal Applications and, in the Family Division by FPR 1991, r. 7.2. In county courts CCR O. 29 (preserved in sch. 2 to the CPR) and, in non-family proceedings the same *Practice Direction*, apply. In family proceedings courts by FPC(MP)R 1991, r. 20 applies.

The prescribed form for initiating a committal application in family proceedings in county courts is Form N78. In family proceedings in the High Court the application is made by summons (FPR 1991, r. 7.2(1)). In civil proceedings in the High Court and county courts, under CPR, r. 8.6 and Practice Direction — Committal Applications. Under CPR, Part 8, if 'a final judgment has not yet been given' in civil proceedings, Practice Direction — Committal Proceedings, para. 2.6 applies and a committal application is made in the 'existing proceedings' by application notice in those proceedings, in Form N244. Where a 'final judgment' has been given in civil proceedings, CPR, r. 8.1(6) and Practice Direction — Committal Proceedings, paras 2.1 and 2.5 require an application for committal to be made by a claim form under Part 8 of the CPR, Form N208: this apparently applies where a free standing injunction has been granted under the Protection from Harassment Act 1997.

County court Forms N78 and N79 were designed to ensure that the procedural requirements of the rules were met, and the requirements for common disposals would be complied with. The Forms can be used as checklists as they incorporate the essential requirements in all committal applications and, in the case of Form N79, the menu of common disposal orders. In family proceedings courts similar Forms FL418 and FL419 apply. Practitioners are strongly recommended to use these Forms as simple checklists for ensuring that the essential procedural requirements are followed. Form N78 remains a convenient guide as to the contents required for a committal application by summons in the Family Division or committal application under CPR, Part 8, which must be issued in application notice in Form N244 or in claim form in Form N208. The checklists appearing after this introduction provide a sequential and extended framework for following good practice.

Form N79, the prescribed form for a committal order in county courts, and Form FL419 for family proceedings courts, contain most of the usual orders made on proof of disobedience of an injunctive order or breach of an undertaking. The court — judge or justices and clerk — can delete the orders not required, and enter the precise details of the orders made. Forms N79 and FL419 are supplied to courts with explanatory guidance notes attached and they can be used as a checklist at the time of making an order.

B.1.3 COMMITTAL HEARINGS

In general terms, hearings of committal proceedings are in many respects similar to hearings of criminal charges. Thus the burden of proof rests on the person making the allegation of contempt; the standard of proof is the criminal standard; the respondent must be allowed to cross-examine witnesses and to call evidence; the respondent is entitled to submit that there is no case to answer; if a contempt is found proved the contemnor must be allowed to address the court by way of mitigation or seeking to purge his contempt; and autrefois acquit and autrefois convict apply.

B.1.4 SENTENCING POWERS

Upon finding a contempt has been proved, whether by evidence or admission, the court has a range of powers. For a brief summary, see *Hale* v *Tanner* [2000] 2 FLR 879 (CA). The disposal must be proportionate to the seriousness of the contempt, reflect the courts' disapproval and designed to secure compliance in future. The court should briefly explain its reasons for the choice of disposal.

Where a first breach of an injunction is serious, an immediate committal to prison may be imposed and there is no principle that a first breach cannot result in a sentence of imprisonment: *Jordan* v *Jordan* [1993] 1 FLR 533, *Thorpe* v *Thorpe* [1998] 2 FLR 127. In an extreme case a mother who prevents contact which is the interests of a child may be sent to prison: *A* v *N (Committal: Refusal of Contact)* [1997] 1 FLR 533. However, all other remedies should be tried first: *Re M (Contact Order: Committal)* [1999] 1 FLR 810.

Where there has been a really substantial error leading to a demonstrable injustice to the victim of a contempt the Court of Appeal can allow an appeal by the claimant and increase the sentence: *Manchester County Council* v *Worthington* [2000] 1 FLR 411; *Wilson* v *Webster* [1998] 1 FLR 1097 (CA). A contemnor contemplating an appeal should be warned that the sentence can be increased.

B.2 Checklist 1: Preparing an Application for Committal for Disobedience of an Injunctive Order or Breach of an Undertaking

B.2.1 FORM OF INJUNCTIVE ORDER OR DOCUMENT RECORDING AN UNDERTAKING

(1) Was the order one which the court had jurisdiction to make?

If made in proceedings other than family proceedings, does the order support a legal right, e.g., forbid a recognised tort or harassment within the Protection from Harassment Act 1997, s. 1, or protect a legal or equitable interest?

If made in family proceedings (under the Family Law Act 1996, Part IV, the Children Act 1989, matrimonial proceedings begun by petition, or under the inherent jurisdiction of the High Court), was the order available as a non-molestation or occupation order? Or was the order available for the protection of family property? The High Court has further injunctive powers under the inherent jurisdiction.

An injunctive order or an undertaking must be obeyed, even if it is irregular, until it is discharged, but want of jurisdiction may affect the conduct of an application to commit and/or the approach to sentence for a contempt.

(2) Was the instruction to the other party, or the undertaking, precise and explicit as to what the person was required to do or abstain from doing? (See CPR, PD 25 (Interim Injunctions), para. 5.3.)

And, if the doing of an act was required, did the injunctive order specify when or by when the act was to be done, as required by RSC O. 42, r. 2(1), CCR O. 22, r. 3 or FPC(MP)R 1991, r. 20(6)(b); or did the undertaking specify when or by when the act was to be done?

(3)(a)   In the case of an injunctive order:

- In the High Court, was there 'prominently displayed on the front', of the copy of the order for service, a warning (penal) notice, as required by RSC O. 45, r. 7(4) and CPR, PD 40B, para. 9.1?

- In a county court, was the injunctive order issued with a penal notice indorsed or incorporated, as required by O. 29, r. 1(3) or FPR 1991, r. 3.9A(5) and CPR, PD 40B, para. 9.1; was it issued in prescribed Form FL404 or N16 or N138 or with Form N77 indorsed or incorporated?

  Note: a warning (penal) notice cannot be indorsed on or incorporated in an order under s. 8 of the Children Act 1989 unless a judge has so directed: FPR 1991, r. 4.21A.

- In a family proceedings court, was the injunctive order issued in Form FL404 or was it issued with a penal notice indorsed or incorporated, as required by FPC(MP)R 1991, r. 20(7)?

(b)   In the case of an undertaking:

- In the High Court or a county court, was the undertaking recorded in an order or form of undertaking in which a penal notice was incorporated or endorsed in accordance with CPR, PD 40B, paras 9.2 and 9.3, and in a county court as required by O. 29, r. 1A? Also, was it acknowledged by signature of the giver upon the direction of the court under CPR, PD 40B, paras 9.3 and 9.4? In a county court Form N117 should be used and in the Family Division practice form D787.

- In a family proceedings court, was the undertaking recorded in Form FL422, as required by FPC(MP)R 1991, r. 20(14)?

B.2.2   SERVICE OF INJUNCTIVE ORDER OR RECORD OF UNDERTAKING

(a)   In the case of an injunctive order:

(i)   Was personal service of the order, with a warning or penal notice prominently displayed on the front (High Court) **or indorsed on it or incorporated in it** (county or family proceedings court), **effected?**

Personal service is required by RSC O. 45, r. 7(2), CCR O. 29, r. 1(2) or FPC(MP)R 1991, r. 20(11) unless (i) the order recites that personal service was dispensed with, or (ii) the terms of the order are only prohibitory, and do not require an act to be done and, pending service, have been communicated to the other party.

(ii)   If the injunctive order required the other party to do an act, was the injunctive order served personally before the expiration of the time within which he was to do the act, as required by RSC O. 45, r. 7(2)(b), CCR O. 29, r. 1(2)(b) or FPC(MP)R 1991, r. 20(6)(b)?

Note *Davy International Ltd* v *Tazzyman* [1997] 3 All ER 183 and *Jolly* v *Hull; Jolly* v *Jolly* [2000] 2 FLR 69, as to the powers to dispense with service of the order at the hearing of a committal application, under RSC O. 45, r. 7(7) and CCR O. 29, r. 1(7).

(iii)   If served, is personal service proved?

Proof is usually by affidavit of service in judge courts and by Form FL415 in family proceedings courts.

(b)   In the case of an undertaking:

Was the Form FL422, D787 or N117 or the order recording the undertaking delivered to or served on the giver of the undertaking?

Personal service of a document recording an undertaking is not necessary to render the undertaking enforceable because it is the giving of the undertaking which makes it effective (see *Hussain* v *Hussain* [1986] Fam 134). However, unless either the giver of the undertaking signed the Form FL422, D787 or N117 or the court papers, or a document recording the undertaking was delivered to or served upon the giver, difficulties may arise on an application to commit (see *Hussain* v *Hussain* (above) at pp. 140 and 142).

In a county court CCR O. 29, r. 1A requires delivery by the court, to be recorded on the back of Form N117, alternatively personal service is required. FPC(MP)R 1991, r. 20(14) is to like effect.

B.2.3   FORM OF THE APPLICATION TO COMMIT AND THE REQUIREMENT OF AN AFFIDAVIT OR STATEMENT IN SUPPORT

(1)(a)   In civil proceedings in the High Court and county courts, does the Claim Form N208 or Application Notice N244 give the essential information to the respondent and to the court?

There is no separate prescribed form specific to committal applications. The prescribed requirements are in Practice Direction — Committal Applications, paras 2.2, 2.5 and 2.6. County court Form N78 is a useful guide.

(b)   In family proceedings, does the summons in the Family Division (FPR 1991, r. 7.2(1), or the Form N78 in a county court, or the form FL244 in a family proceedings court, give the essential information to the respondent and the court?

In particular (all courts: Practice Direction — Committal Applications, paras 2.5 to 2.6, CCR O. 29, r. 1(4A), FPC(MP)R 1991, r. 20(9).

> (i)   *Does the application accurately identify the terms of the injunctive order or undertaking of which breach is alleged (CCR O. 29, r. 1(4A))? And*

> (ii)   *Does the application 'list' (CCR O. 29, r. 1(4A)) or 'identify', separately and numerically, each alleged act of contempt (Practice Direction — Committal Applications, paras 2.5 to 2.6)?*

> (iii) *Does the application clearly inform the respondent when and where he must attend to show reason why he should not be sent to prison?*

The ways in which the party alleged to be in contempt is alleged to have committed the contempt(s) *must* be sufficiently clear to inform him what case he has to meet.

(2)   Is the application supported by an affidavit as required by RSC O. 52, r. 4(1) and Practice Direction — Committal Applications, paras 2.5 to 2.6 and 3.1 or CCR O. 29, r. 1(4A) or a statement signed and declared to be true as required by FPC(MP)R 1991, r. 20(9)(c)?

B.2.4   **SERVICE OF THE APPLICATION TO COMMIT AND THE AFFIDAVIT OR STATEMENT IN SUPPORT**

(1)   **Is personal service of the application and the affidavit or statement proved** (in judge courts usually by an affidavit of service, in family proceedings courts by Form FL415) **as required by RSC O. 52, r. 4(2), Practice Direction — Committal Applications, paras 2.5 to 2.6, CCR O. 29, r. 1(4) or FPC(MP)R 1991, r. 20(8), (9) unless the court has dispensed with service under RSC O. 52, r. 4(3), CCR O. 29, r. 1(7) or FPC(MP)R 1991, r. 20(12)? Or has provided for substituted service under RSC O. 65, r. 4(2), CCR O. 13, r. 4(1) (substituted service is not available in magistrates' courts).**

(2A)   **In family proceedings was personal service achieved at least two days, not counting Saturdays, Sundays or bank holidays, before the hearing, as required by RSC O. 8, r. 2(2), or at least two court office business days as required by CCR O. 13, r. 1(2) and O. 1, r. 9(4), FPC(MP)R 1991, r. 3A(5) unless the court has abridged time under RSC O. 3, r. 5(1), CCR O. 13, r. 4(1) or FPC(MP)R 1991, r. 3A(6)?**

(2B)   **In civil proceedings was personal service achieved at least 14 days before the hearing unless the court has directed otherwise (Practice Direction — Committal Applications, para. 4.2)?**

B.2.5   **EVIDENCE**

(1)   **Is there sufficient evidence to prove, to the criminal standard of proof, the alleged contempt(s)?**

(2)   **Is/are the witness(es) relied on available for cross-examination?**

B.3   Checklist 2: Preparing for Hearing following an Arrest under a Power or a Warrant of Arrest granted under section 47 of the Family Law Act 1996 or Arrest under a Warrant of Arrest granted under section 3 of the Protection from Harassment Act 1997

B.3.1   **INTRODUCTION: SUMMARY COMMITTAL FOLLOWING ARREST**

Some practitioners and judges consider that upon production in court of an arrested alleged contemnor it is good practice to adjourn, to remand the respondent if the arrest was under FLA 1996, s. 47, and to expect the applicant to issue an application for committal. However, FPR 1991, r. 3.9A(4) specifically authorises the established practice that when a person is brought before the court following an arrest under FLA 1996, s. 47, the court 'may (a) determine whether the facts, and the circumstances which led to the arrest, amounted to disobedience of the order, or (b) adjourn the proceedings . . . .'. RSC O. 94, r. 16(5)(a) specifically authorises summary trial in the case of an arrest under the Protection from Harassment Act 1997, s. 3. Form N79, for recording a finding of contempt, specifically provides for proceeding on the basis of the respondent being before the court upon an arrest without there having been served an application for committal in Form N78, in the case of an arrest under FLA 1996, s. 47, or in a claim form, in the case of an arrest on a warrant under the Protection from Harassment Act 1997, s. 3(5).

Where a person is arrested under either FLA 1996, s. 47 or the Protection from Harassment Act 1997, s. 3, and is brought before the court within the powers under the Acts, and there is sufficient evidence to proceed with a summary trial, and the arrested person is able to put his case adequately before the court, there clearly is power to proceed forthwith, without requiring preparation or service of a form of committal application. Further, there is no power to remand under the 1997 Act. Where the court does proceed forthwith without a form of committal application being prepared, the arrested person is before the court only for the matter upon which he has been arrested, previous alleged contempts are not before the court, and the court must be clear about what the circumstances of the arrest and alleged contempt are. Summary disposal in this way is convenient particularly where the respondent admits the contempt. Where he denies the alleged contempt, and he may need witnesses to support his denial, an adjournment will be appropriate.

B.3.2 FORM OF INJUNCTIVE ORDER

Was the order one to which the court had power to attach a power of arrest under FLA 1996, s. 47? (There is no power under the Protection from Harassment Act 1997 to attach a power of arrest.)

In other words, was there evidence on which the court which granted the power could have concluded that the respondent had used or threatened violence against the applicant or a relevant child? If not, the arrest was unlawful and the respondent must be released.

In the case of arrest under a power of arrest, the 'relevant provisions', i.e. the arrestable provisions and no other clauses of the injunctive order, should have been delivered to the appropriate police station in prescribed Form FL406: FPR 1991, r. 3.9A(1), FPC(MP)R 1991, r. 20(1).

A power of arrest cannot be attached to an undertaking: FLA 1996, s. 46(2); it must be an order, non-molestation or occupation.

If the arrest was under a warrant of arrest, were there injunctive non-molestation or occupation provisions available as the foundation for a warrant, i.e. provisions to which no power of arrest had been attached?

B.3.3 SERVICE OF THE INJUNCTIVE ORDER

(a) **Is personal service proved, as required by RSC O. 45, r. 7(2)(a), CCR O. 29, r. 1(2)(a) or FPC(MP)R 1991, r. 20(6)?**

Proof is usually by affidavit of service in judge courts and by Form FL415 in family proceedings courts. Note powers to dispense with service under RSC O. 45, r. 7(7) and CCR O. 29, r. 1(7) and see *Davy International Ltd* v *Tazzyman* [1997] 3 All ER 183 and *Jolly* v *Hull; Jolly* v *Jolly* [2000] 2 FLR 69.

OR

(b) **Was the arrested person aware of the terms of the injunctive order either by being present when it was granted or by being notified of its terms?** If so, under RSC O. 45, r. 7(6), CCR O. 29, r. 1(6) or FPC(MP)R 1991, r. 20(11) he may be dealt with for the matter for which he was arrested if it was something he was forbidden to do. The arrested person cannot be dealt with unless he was aware of the terms, because contempt involves disobedience and unless the respondent was aware of the terms he cannot be guilty of contempt.

B.3.4 THE ARREST

In the case of arrest under a power of arrest under FLA 1996, s. 47(6):

(1) Was the operative period of the power of arrest, as recited in the injunction and prescribed Form FL406, still running at the time of the arrest?

(2) Was the arrest by a constable who had 'reasonable cause for suspecting' the arrested person of being in breach of a provision of injunctive order to which the

power of arrest was attached (FLA 1996, s. 47(6))? If not, the arrest was unlawful and the arrested person must be released.

In the case of arrest under a warrant of arrest under FLA 1996, s. 47(8), (9):

(1) Were there injunctive non-molestation or occupation provisions available as the foundation for a warrant, i.e., provisions to which a power of arrest had not been attached? and

(2) Was there evidence on oath before the court which granted the warrant on which it could have had reasonable grounds for believing that the respondent had failed to comply with the injunctive order or the undertaking? Note that there is doubt as to whether a warrant can be granted for breach of an undertaking given in proceedings under FLA 1996, Part IV.

In the case of a warrant of arrest under the Protection from Harassment Act 1997, s. 3(3), (5), was there evidence on oath before the court which granted the warrant on which it could have had reasonable grounds for believing that the defendant had failed to comply with the injunction? Note that a warrant cannot be granted for breach of an undertaking in proceedings under the Protection from Harassment Act 1997.

B.3.5 THE HEARING

In the case of arrest under a power of arrest under FLA 1996, s. 47(6), will the hearing before the judge begin within the period of 24 hours beginning at the time of the arrest (no account being taken of Christmas Day, Good Friday or any Sunday) as required by FLA 1996, s. 47(7)(a)? If not, the proceedings are *ultra vires*, there being no power to detain the arrested person beyond the statutory period, and the arrested person must be released.

However, the court may remand the arrested person (FLA 1996, s. 47(7)(b) and adjourn the hearing to be resumed within 14 days of the arrest: FPR 1991, r. 3.9A(4)(b)(i), FPC(MP)R 1991, r. 20(4)(b)(i). If the court does adjourn the hearing, the arrested person may be remanded (s. 47(7)(b)) or released (FPR 1991, r. 3.9A(4)(b), FPC(MP)R 1991, r. 20(4)(b)); where the court does adjourn, the arrested person must be dealt with within 14 days of the day on which he was arrested, whether by the same or another judge, and the person must be given not less than two days' notice of the adjourned hearing (FPR 1991, r. 3.9A(4)(b)(ii), FPC(MP)R 1991, r. 20(4)(b)(ii)). Personal service of the notice of the adjourned hearing should be effected, unless the arrested person was given notice before being released (see *Chiltern DC* v *Keane* [1985] 1 WLR 619 at p. 622A).

If the arrested person is not dealt with within 14 days, FPR 1991, r. 3.9A(4), FPC(MP)R 1991, r. 20(4) permit the other party to request the issue of Notice to Show Good Reason under CCR O. 29, r. 1(4) or FPC(MP)R 1991, r. 20(8).

Following any arrest, is there sufficient evidence to prove, to the criminal standard of proof, the alleged contempt?

B.4 Checklist 3: Conduct of Hearing of Application for Committal or following Arrest under a Power or Warrant of Arrest

B.4.1 PRELIMINARY REQUIREMENTS

(1) If the application is made (civil proceedings) **by Claim Form N208 or Application Notice N244 or** (High Court Family Division) **by summons or issued** (county court) **in Form N78 or** (family proceedings court) **in Form FL418, is breach of a**

specific, explicit (not implied) direction in an injunctive order or a promise in an undertaking alleged? And has the notice of application been served personally on the alleged comtemnor (RSC O. 52, r. 4(2), CCR O. 29, r. 1(4), PD Committal Applications, paras 2.5 and 2.6, FPC(MP)R 1991, r. 20(8), (9)) 2 clear or office days before the hearing in family proceedings (RSC O. 8, r. 2(2), CCR O. 13, r. 2(2), CCR O. 13, r. 1(2) and O. 1, r. 9(4), FPC(MP)R 1991, r. 3A(5), or 14 days before the hearing in proceedings under CPR (PD Committal Applications, para. 4.2)?

Or, if the respondent has been arrested upon a power of arrest or warrant of arrest and brought before the court, was he arrested for an arrestable disobedience and, where arrested under a power of arrest, has the hearing begun within 24 hours of the arrest? And, *should the hearing proceed or should an adjournment be allowed to enable the case and evidence to be prepared?* FPR 1991, r. 3.9A(4) and FPC(MP)R 1991, r. 20(4) (and, under the Protection from Harassment Act 1997, CCR O. 49, r. 15A(7)) allow the court to deal forthwith with the matter upon which the respondent was arrested without service on him of a Notice to Show Good Reason or dispensation with this under CCR O. 29, r. 1(7) or FPC(MP)R 1991, r.20(12). Alternatively, the court may adjourn proceedings for not more than 14 days. In proceedings under the Family Law Act 1996 there is a general power to remand in s. 47(7)(b) and (10) and power to remand for a medical report under s. 48. There is no power to remand under the Protection from Harassment Act 1997.

(2) Was the respondent a party in the proceedings to whom the injunctive direction was ordered? With few exceptions, an injunctive order cannot be made against someone who is not a party. *Quaere* whether a non-party can give an undertaking without becoming a party.

(3) Was the injunctive order (with a warning notice prominently displayed on the front (High Court) **or penal notice indorsed or incorporated** (county or family proceedings court)**) personally served or, if it was prohibitory (not mandatory), was the respondent present when the order was made, or has he been notified of it?** (RSC O. 45, r. 7(6), CCR O. 29, r. 1(6), FPC(MP)R 1991, r. 20(11).)

Or, was the undertaking recorded in county court Form N117, Principal Registry Form D787 or family proceedings court Form FL422 or, in the Chancery or Queen's Bench Divisions of the High Court, in a document in which the giver signed a statement to the effect that he understood the terms of his undertaking and the consequences of failure to comply with it in accordance with CPR, PD 40B, paras 9.3 and 9.4? *Was that document delivered to or served on or acknowledged by signature of the respondent?*

(4) Was the direction or promise either:

(a) **To do a specified act or specified acts at or before a specified time?** *If so, is the act one which the court has power to enforce by committal proceedings?* Committal for contempt is not available, for example, to enforce payment of a money judgment (except where judgment summons is still available; see *Nwogbe v Nwogbe* [2000] 2 FLR 744 (CA)), or a declaratory order such as a defined pattern of contact with a child. *Also, was the order served before the time specified in the order for the act to be done, as required by RSC O. 42, r. 2(1), CCR O. 22, r. 3 or FPC(MP)R 1991, r. 20(5)(b)?* Or

(b) **To abstain from doing a specified act or acts?** Note the powers to dispense with service under RSC O. 45, r. 7(6), (7) and CCR O. 29, r. 1(6), (7) and see *Davy International Ltd v Tazzyman* [1997] 3 All ER 183 and *Jolly v Hull; Jolly v Jolly* [2000] 2 FLR 69.

(5) In the case of arrest under a warrant of arrest granted under the Protection from Harassment Act 1997, s. 3(5), has the person arrested already been convicted of an offence in respect of the alleged contempt? If so, he cannot be punished in contempt proceedings: s. 3(7).

B.4.2   TRIAL PROCEDURE

PRELIMINARY PROCEDURAL POINTS

A. Is the court following normal criminal procedure?

If the court is embarking on a re-hearing after a previous hearing in the absence of the respondent, either because the court dispensed with service of notice on him or the court accepts that his absence was not his fault, the entire procedure must be followed. No short cuts. Note that on a review on notice of a committal ordered in the absence of the respondent, the sentence cannot be increased.

B. In the case of proceedings under the Family Law Act 1996, should the court remand, before or after deciding whether the contempt(s) is (are) proved, for a medical report under FLA 1996, s. 48?

C. If the respondent is not legally represented, should a solicitor within the precincts of the court be invited to represent the respondent under the Assistance By Way Of Representation scheme? (Regulation 8 of the Legal Advice and Assistance (Scope) Regulations 1989 (SI 1989/550); reg. 7 ABWOR representation might, by amendment to the sch., art. 2(b), become available in family proceedings courts.) (Legal aid under s. 29 of the Legal Aid Act 1988 is NOT available for a person answering an allegation or breach of an injunction or undertaking.)

CONDUCT OF HEARING

(1)   In civil proceedings under CPR, Part 8 and Practice Direction — Committal Applications, has the respondent filed affidavits giving any evidence in opposition to the committal application (Practice Direction — Committal Applications, paras 3.1 and 3.2)? But the respondent does not need permission to adduce oral evidence if he has not filed affidavits (Practice Direction — Committal Applications, paras 3.3 and 3.4). In family proceedings also it is good practice to file affidavits in opposition to a committal application.

(2)   Amendment of the committal application can be permitted by the court (PD Committal Applications, para. 2.6(3)).

(3)   Does the respondent admit the allegation(s) and, if so, precisely what does he admit? The exact finding(s) of contempt will have to be recorded in the committal order (Form A85, High Court; Form N79, county court; Form FL419, family proceedings court). *Are the admissions adequate to enable the court to proceed to consideration of penalty without hearing evidence?*

(4)   Burden of proof on applicant.

(5)   Normal sequence of evidence. Chief, affidavit or statement and/or oral; cross-examination; re-examination. Applicant and his witnesses first; respondent and his witnesses after. The alleged contemnor is not compellable as a witness at the instance of the applicant or the judge (*Comet Productions UK* v *Hawkex Plastics Ltd* [1971] 2 QB 67) and cannot be directed to give information (PD Committal Applications, paras 6 and 7).

The privilege against self-incrimination applies in civil contempt proceedings: *Memory Corp. plc and another* v *Sidhu and another* [2000] 1 All ER 434.

(6)   Respondent entitled to submit 'no case'.

(7)   *Actus reus* and *mens rea* must be proved. *Mens rea* is knowledge of the injunctive direction plus deliberate conduct which in fact is a breach. Not necessary to prove that the respondent understood the nature of the court's procedures provided he knew what was forbidden (*P* v *P (Contempt of Court: Mental Incapacity)* [1999] 2 FLR 897 (CA)).

(8)   **Criminal standard of proof.**

(9)   **Contempt(s) found proved must be specified and recorded in committal order.** (Form A85, High Court; Form N79, county court; Form FL419, family proceedings court.)

B.4.3   **CONSIDERATION OF PENALTY**

RANGE OF POWERS AND APPROPRIATE APPROACH TO CHOICE OF DISPOSAL

The disposal must be proportionate to the seriousness of the contempt, reflect the disapproval of the court and be designed to secure compliance in the future (*Hale* v *Tanner* [2000] 2 FLR 879 (CA), where the range of powers is summarised).

(1)   **Does the contemnor wish to mitigate or attempt to purge his contempt?**

(2)   **In family cases, does the applicant wish to give her views?**

(3)   **Is the contemnor eligible for imprisonment being aged 21 or more, or eligible for detention being aged 18 or over and less than 21, or is no custodial sentence available the contemnor being aged less than 18?**

(4)   **If available, is an immediate custodial sentence the only appropriate disposal? What alternatives are available?** Note that there is no principle that 'a first breach [of an injunction] cannot result in a sentene of imprisonment'. Where the disobedience of an injunction or undertaking is serious an immediate custodial sentence may be imposed (*Jordan* v *Jordan* [1993] 1 FLR 169, *Thorpe* v *Thorpe* [1998] 2 FLR 127).

(5)   **What penalty should be imposed for each separate contempt found proved?** *If more than one contempt, should penalties be consecutive or concurrent? Is the total appropriate?* The maximum total imprisonment that can be imposed on one occasion is two years in a judge court, two months in a family proceedings court. Sentences can be consecutive, including an implemented suspended sentence, but the total cannot exceed the maximum of two years or two months.

(6)   **Should imprisonment** *(of contemnor aged 21 or more)* **be suspended or should consideration of penalty be adjourned with liberty to restore?** *If so,*

(a)   *For how long? and*

(b)   *What conditions should be ordered to define the event(s) which would render the contemnor liable to implementation or imposition of a penalty?*

The period of suspension or adjournment should be fixed, but an indefinite suspension can be valid: *Griffin* v *Griffin* [2000] 2 FLR 44 (CA). The power to remand an arrested person under FLA 1996, s. 47(7), (10) is not available where the contemnor appeared in answer to a Notice to Show Good Reason, therefore the case law which established that sentence could not be deferred by remand in custody, after finding contempt proved, should still apply.

B.4.4   **PREPARATION OF THE ORDER OF COMMITTAL OR OTHER DISPOSAL**

(1)   **What should be recorded in the order of committal (Form A85, High Court; Form N79, county court; Form FL419, family proceedings court)? In particular:**

(a)   **What precise findings of contempt? and**

(b)   **What precise terms of disposal have been ordered?**

Form N79 or Form FL419 should be checked and initialled by the judge or the chairman or bench of justices.

(2) If an immediate custodial sentence is ordered, can the committal order be issued in time to be served when the respondent is detained upon the warrant of committal? In a county court, O. 29, r. 1(5)(a) requires that the committal order be served when the warrant is executed, unless the warrant is signed by the judge; if the judge signs the warrant, 36 hours is permitted for preparation and service of the committal order (O. 29, r. 1(5)(b)). FPC(MP)R 1991, r. 20(10) permits the committal order to be served within 36 hours after execution of the warrant.

B.4.5 APPEAL

Where there has been a really substantial error leading to a demonstrable injustice to the victim of a contempt the Court of Appeal can allow an appeal by the claimant and increase the sentence: *Manchester County Council* v *Worthington* [2000] 1 FLR 411 (CA); *Wilson* v *Webster* [1998] 1 FLR 1097 (CA). A contemnor contemplating an appeal should be warned that a sentence imposed for contempt can be increased.

APPENDIX C

MATRIMONIAL CAUSES ACT 1973 AND DOMESTIC PROCEEDINGS AND MAGISTRATES' COURTS ACT 1978

Matrimonial Causes Act 1973

23.—*(1)   On granting a decree of divorce, a decree of nullity of marriage or a decree of judicial separation or at any time thereafter (whether, in the case of a decree of divorce or of nullity of marriage, before or after the decree is made absolute), the court may make any one or more of the following orders, that is to say—*

(a)   an order that either party to the marriage shall make to the other such periodical payments, for such term, as may be specified in the order;

(b)   an order that either party to the marriage shall secure to the other to the satisfaction of the court such periodical payments, for such term, as may be so specified;

(c)   an order that either party to the marriage shall pay to the other such lump sum or sums as may be so specified,

(d)   an order that a party to the marriage shall make to such person as may be specified in the order for the benefit of a child of the family, or to such a child, such periodical payments, for such term, as may be so specified,

(e)   an order that a party to the marriage shall secure to such person as may be so specified for the benefit of such a child, or to such a child, to the satisfaction of the court, such periodical payments, for such term, as may be so specified;

(f)   an order that a party to the marriage shall pay to such person as may be so specified for the benefit of such a child, or to such a child, such lump sum as may be so specified; subject, however, in the case of an order under paragraph (d). (e) or (f) above, to the restrictions imposed by section 29(1) and (3) below on the making of financial provision orders in favour of children who have attained the age of 18.

(2)   The court may also, subject to those restrictions, make any one or more of the orders mentioned in subsection (1)(d), (e) and (f) above—

(a)   in any proceedings for divorce nullity of marriage or judicial separation before granting a decree, and

(b)   where any such proceedigs are dismissed after the beginning of the trial, either forthwith or within a reasonable period after the dismissal.

(3)   Without prejudice to the generality of subsection (1)(c) or (f) above—

(a)   an order under this section that a party to a marriage shall pay a lump sum to the other party may be made for the purpose of enabling that other party to meet any liabilities or expenses reasonably incurred by him or her in maintaining himself or herself or any child of the family before making an application for an order under this section in his or her favour;

(b)   an order under this section for the payment of a lump sum to or for the benefit of a child of the family may be made for the purpose of enabling any liabilities or expenses reasonably incurred by or for the benefit of that child before the making of an application for an order under this section in his favour to be met; and

(c) an order under this section for the payment of a lump sum may provide for the payment of that sum by instalments of such amount as may be specified in the order and may require the payment of the instalments to be secured to the satisfaction of the court.

(4) The power of the court under subsection (1) or (2)(a) above to make an order in favour of a child of the family shall be exercisable from time to time; and where the court makes an order in favour of a child under subsection (2)(b) above, it may from time to time, subject to the restrictions mentioned in subsection (1) above, make a further order in his favour of any of the kinds mentioned in subsection (1)(d), (e) or (f) above.

(5) Without prejudice to the power to give a direction under section 30 ... for the settlement of an instrument by conveyancing counsel, where an order is made under subsection (1)(a), (b) or (c) above on or after granting a decree of divorce or nullity of marriage, neither the order nor any settlement made in pursuance of the order shall take effect unless the decree has been made absolute.

(6) Where the court—

(a) makes an order under this section for the payment of a lump sum; and

(b) directs—

(i) that payment of that sum or any part of it shall be deferred, or

(ii) that the sum or any part of it shall be paid by instalments,

the court may order that the amount deferred or the instalments shall carry interest at such rate as may be specified by the order from such date, not earlier than the date of the order, as may be so specified, until the date when payment of it is due.

24.—(1) On granting a decree of divorce, a decree of nullity of marriage or a decree of judicial separation or at any time thereafter (whether, in the case of a decree of divorce or of nullity of marriage, before or after the decree is made absolute), the court may make any one or more of the following orders, that is to say-

(a) an order that a party to the marriage shall transfer to the other party, to any child of the family or to such person as may be specified in the order for the benefit of such a child such property as may be so specified, being property to which the first-mentioned party is entitled, either in possession or reversion;

(b) an order that a settlement of such property as may be so specified, being property to which a party to the marriage is so entitled, be made to the satisfaction of the court for the benefit of the other party to the marriage and of the children of the family or either or any of them;

(c) an order varying for the benefit of the parties to the marriage and of the children of the family or either or any of them any antenuptial or post-nuptial settlement (including such a settlement made by will or codicil) made on the parties to the marriage;

(d) an order extinguishing or reducing the interest of either of the parties to the marriage under any such settlement;

subject, however, in the case of an order under paragraph (a) above, to the restrictions imposed by section 29(1) and (3) below on the making of orders for a transfer of property in favour of children who have attained the age of 18.

(2) The court may make an order under subsection (1)(c) above notwithstanding that there are no children of the family.

(3) Without prejudice to the power to give a direction under section 30 . . . for the settlement of an instrument by conveyancing counsel, where an order is made under this section on or after granting a decree of divorce or nullity of marriage, neither the order nor any settlement made in pursuance of the order shall take effect unless the decree has been made absolute.

24A.—(1) Where the court makes under any of sections 23 to 24 above a secured periodical payments order, an order for the payment of a lump sum or a property adjustment order, then, on making that order or at any time thereafter, the court may make a further order for the sale of such property as may be specified in the order, being property in which or in the proceeds of sale of which either or both of the parties to the marriage has or have a beneficial interest, either in possession or reversion.

(2)   Any order made under subsection (1) above may contain such consequential or supplementary provisions as the court thinks fit and, without prejudice to the generality of the foregoing provision, may include—

(a)   provision requiring the making of a payment out of the proceeds of sale of the property to which the order relates, and

(b)   provision requiring any such property to be offered for sale to a person, or class of persons, specified in the order.

(3)   Where an order is made under subsection (1) above on or after the grant of a decree of divorce or nullity of marriage, the order shall not take effect unless the decree has been made absolute.

(4)   Where an order is made under subsection (1) above, the court may direct that the order, or such provision thereof as the court may specify, shall not take effect until the occurrence of an event specified by the court or the expiration of a period so specified.

(5)   Where an order under subsection (1) above contains a provision requiring the proceeds of sale of the property to which the order relates to be used to secure periodical payments to a party to the marriage, the order shall cease to have effect on the death or remarriage of that person.

(6)   Where a party to a marriage has a beneficial interest in any property, or in the proceeds of sale thereof and some other person who is not a party to the marriage also has a beneficial interest in that property or in the proceeds of sale thereof then, before deciding whether to make an order under this section in relation to that property, it shall be the duty of the court to give that other person an opportunity to make representations with respect to the order; and any representations made by that other person shall be included among the circumstances to which the court is required to have regard under section 25(1) . . . .

25B.—*(1)   The matters to which the court is to have regard under section 25(2) above include—*

(a)   in the case of paragraph (a), any benefits under a pension scheme which a party to the marriage has or is likely to have, and

(b)   in the case of paragraph (h), any benefits under a pension scheme which, by reason of the dissolution or annulment of the marriage, a party to the marriage will lose the chance of acquiring,

and, accordingly, in relation to benefits under a pension scheme, section 25(2)(a) above shall have effect as if 'in the foreseeable future' were omitted.

(2)   In any proceedings for a financial provision order under [section 22A or 23] above in a case where a party to the marriage has, or is likely to have, any benefit under a pension scheme, the court shall, in addition to considering any other matter which it is required to consider apart from this subsection, consider—

(a)   whether, having regard to any matter to which it is required to have regard in the proceedings by virtue of subsection (1) above, such an order (whether deferred or not) should be made, and

(b)   where the court determines to make such an order, how the terms of the order should be affected, having regard to any such matter.

(c)   in particular, where the court determines to make such an order, whether the order should provide for the accrued rights of the party with pension rights ('the pension rights') to be divided between that party and the other party in such a way as to reduce the pension rights of the party with those rights and to create pension rights for the other party.

(3)   The following provisions apply where, having regard to any benefits under a pension scheme, the court determines to make an order under section 22A or 23 above.

(4)   To the extent to which the order is made having regard to any benefits under a pension scheme, the order may require the trustees or managers of the pension scheme in question, if at any time any payment in respect of any benefits under the scheme becomes due to the party with pension rights, to make a payment for the benefit of the other party.

(5)   The amount of any payment which, by virtue of subsection (4) above, the trustees or managers are required to make under the order at any time shall not exceed the amount of the payment which is due at that time to the party with pension rights.

(6) Any such payment by the trustees or managers—

(a) shall discharge so much of the trustees or managers liability to the party with pension rights as corresponds to the amount of the payment, and

(b) shall be treated for all purposes as a payment made by the party with pension rights in or towards the discharge of his liability under the order.

(7) Where the party with pension rights may require any benefits which he has or is likely to have under the scheme to be commuted, the order may require him to commute the whole or part of those benefits; and this section applies to the payment of any amount commuted in pursuance of the order as it applies to other payments in respect of benefits under the scheme.

(8) If a pension adjustment order under subsection (2)(c) above is made, the pension rights shall be reduced and pension rights of the other party shall be created in the prescribed manner with benefits payable on prescribed conditions, except that the court shall not have the power—

(a) to require the trustees or managers of the scheme to provide benefits under their own scheme if they are able and willing to create the rights for the other party by making a transfer payment to another scheme and the trustees and managers of that other scheme are able and willing to accept such a payment and to create those rights; or

(b) to require the trustees or managers of the scheme to make a transfer to another scheme—

(i) if the scheme is an unfounded scheme (unless the trustees or managers are able and willing to make such a transfer payment); or

(ii) in prescribed circumstances.

(9) No pensions adjustment order may be made under subsection (2)(c) above—

(a) if the scheme is a scheme of a prescribed type, or

(b) in prescribed circumstances, or

(c) insofar as it would effect benefits of a prescribed type.

25C.—(1) The power of the court under section 22A or 23 above to order a party to a marriage to pay a lump sum to the other party includes, where the benefits which the party with pension rights has or is likely to have under a pension scheme include any lump sum payable in respect of his death, power to make any of the following provision by the order.

(2) The court may—

(a) if the trustees or managers of the pension scheme in question have power to determine the person to whom the sum, or any part of it, is to be paid, require them to pay the whole or part of that sum, when it becomes due, to the other party,

(b) if the party with pension rights has power to nominate the person to whom the sum, or any part of it, is to be paid, require the party with pension rights to nominate the other party in respect of the whole or part of that sum,

(c) in any other case, require the trustees or managers of the pension scheme in question to pay the whole or part of that sum, when it becomes due, for the benefit of the other party instead of to the person to whom, apart from the order, it would be paid.

(3) Any payment by the trustees or managers under an order made under section 22A or 23 above by virtue of this section shall discharge so much of the trustees, or managers, liability in respect of the party with pension rights as corresponds to the amount of the payment.

25D.—(1) Where—

(a) an order made under section 22A or 23 above by virtue of section 25B or 25C above imposes any requirement on the trustees or managers of a pension scheme ('the first scheme') and the party with pension rights acquires transfer credits under another pension scheme ('the new scheme') which are derived (directly or indirectly) from a transfer from the first scheme of all his accrued rights under that scheme (including transfer credits allowed by that scheme), and

(b) the trustees or managers of the new scheme have been given notice in accordance with regulations,

the order shall have effect as if it has been made instead in respect of the trustees or managers of the new scheme; and in this subsection 'transfer credits' has the same meaning as in the Pension Schemes Act 1993.

(2) Regulations may—

(a) in relation to any provision of sections 25B or 25C above which authorises the court making an order under section 22A or 23 above to require the trustees or managers of a pension scheme to make a payment for the benefit of the other party, make provision as to the person to whom, and the terms on which, the payment is to be made, or prescribe the rights of the other party under the pension scheme,

(aa) make such consequential modifications of any enactment or subordinate legislation as appear to the Lord Chancellor necessary or expedient to give effect to the provisions of section 25B; and an order under this paragraph may make provision applying generally in relation to enactments and subordinate legislation of a description specified in the order,

(b) require notices to be given in respect of changes of circumstances relevant to such orders which include provision made by virtue of sections 25B and 25C above,

(c) make provision for the trustees or managers of any pension scheme to provide, for the purposes of orders under section 22A or 23 above, information as to the value of any benefits under the scheme,

(d) make provision for the recovery of the administrative expenses of—

(i) complying with such orders, so far as they include provision made by virtue of sections 25B and 25C above, and

(ii) providing such information,

from the party with pension rights or the other party,

(e) make provision for the value of any benefits under a pension scheme to be calculated and verified, for the purposes of orders under section 22A or 23 above, in a prescribed manner,

and regulations made by virtue of paragraph (e) above may provide for that value to be calculated and verified in accordance with guidance which is prepared and from time to time revised by a prescribed person and approved by the Secretary of State.

(3) In this section and sections 25B and 25C above—

(a) references to a pension scheme include—

(i) a retirement annuity contract, or

(ii) an annuity, or insurance policy, purchased or transferred for the purpose of giving effect to rights under a pension scheme,

(b) in relation to such a contract or annuity, references to the trustees or managers shall be read as references to the provider of the annuity,

(c) in relation to such a policy, references to the trustees or managers shall be read as references to the insurer, and in section 25B(1) and (2) above, references to benefits under a pension scheme include any benefits by way of pension, whether under a pension scheme or not.

(4) In this section and sections 25B and 25C above—

'the party with pension rights' means the party to the marriage who has or is likely to have benefits under a pension scheme and 'the other party' means the other party to the marriage,

'funded scheme' means a scheme under which the benefits are provided for by setting aside resources related to the value of the members' rights as they accrue (and 'unfunded scheme' shall be construed accordingly),

'subordinate legislation' has the same meaning as in the Interpretation Act 1978,

'pension scheme' means an occupational pension scheme or a personal pension scheme (applying the definitions in section 1 of the Pension Schemes Act 1993, but as if the reference, to employed earners in the definition of 'personal pension scheme' were to any earners),

'prescribed' means prescribed by regulations, and

'regulations' means regulations made by the Lord Chancellor;

and the power to make regulations under this section shall be exercisable by statutory instrument, which shall be subject to annulment in pursuance of a resolution of either House of Parliament.

(4A) Other expressions used in section 25B above shall be construed in accordance with section 124 (interpretation of Part I) of the Pensions Act 1995

27.—*(1) Either party to a marriage may apply to the court for an order under this section on the ground that the other party to the marriage (in this section referred to as the respondent)—*

(a)   has failed to provide reasonable maintenance for the applicant, or

(b)   has failed to provide, or to make a proper contribution towards, reasonable maintenance for any child of the family.

(2)   [Jurisdiction to grant orders.]

(3)   Where an application under this section is made on the ground mentioned in subsection (1)(a) above, then, in deciding—

(a)   whether the respondent has failed to provide reasonable maintenance for the applicant, and

(b)   what order, if any, to make under this section in favour of the applicant, the court shall have regard to all the circumstances of the case including the matters mentioned in section 25(2) ..., and where an application is also made under this section in respect of a child of the family who has not attained the age of eighteen, first consideration shall be given to the welfare of the child while a minor.

(3A)   Where an application under this section is made on the ground mentioned in subsection (1)(b) above then, in deciding—

(a)   whether the respondent has failed to provide, or to make a proper contribution towards, reasonable maintenance for the child of the family to whom the application relates, and

(b)   what order, if any, to make under this section in favour of the child, the court shall have regard to all the circumstances of the case including the matters mentioned in section 25(3)(a) to (e) ..., and where the child of the family to whom the application relates is not the child of the respondent, including also the matters mentioned in section 25(4) ...

(3B)   In relation to an application under this section on the ground mentioned in subsection (1)(a) above, section 25(2)(c) ... shall have effect as if for the reference therein to the breakdown of the marriage there were substituted a reference to the failure to provide reasonable maintenance for the applicant, and in relation to an application under this section on the ground mentioned in subsection (1)(b) above, section 25(2)(c) ... (as it applies by virtue of section 25(3)(e) ...) shall have effect as if for the reference therein to the breakdown of the marriage there were substituted a reference to the failure to provide, or to make a proper contribution towards, reasonable maintenance for the child of the family to whom the application relates.

...

(5)   Where on an application under this section it appears to the court that the applicant or any child of the family to whom the application relates is in immediate need of financial assistance, but it is not yet possible to determine what order, if any, should be made on the application, the court may make an interim order for maintenance, that is to say, an order requiring the respondent—

(a)   to make to the applicant until the determination of the application such periodical payments as the court thinks reasonable; or

(b)   to pay to the applicant such lump sum or sums as the court thinks reasonable.

(6)   Where on an application under this section the applicant satisfies the court of any ground mentioned in subsection (1) above, the court may make any one or more of the following orders, that is to say—

(a)   an order that the respondent shall make to the applicant such periodical payments, for such term, as may be specified in the order;

(b)   an order that the respondent shall secure to the applicant, to the satisfaction of the court, such periodical payments, for such term, as may be so specified;

(c)   an order that the respondent shall pay to the applicant such lump sum as may be so specified;

(d)   an order that the respondent shall make to such person as may be specified in the order for the benefit of the child to whom the application relates, or to that child, such periodical payments, for such term, as may be so specified;

(e)   an order that the respondent shall secure to such person as may be so specified for the benefit of that child, or to that child, to the satisfaction of the court, such periodical payments, for such term, as may be so specified,

(f)   an order that the respondent shall pay to such person as may be so specified for the benefit of that child, or to that child, such lump sum as may be so specified, subject, however, in the case of an order under paragraph (d), (e) or (f) above, to the restrictions imposed by section 29(1) and (3) ... on the making of financial provision orders in favour of children who have attained the age of eighteen.

(6A)   An application for the variation under section 31 of this Act of a periodical payments order or secured periodical payments order made under this section in favour of a child may, if the child has attained the age of sixteen, be made by the child himself.

(6B)   Where a periodical payments order made in favour of a child under this section ceases to have effect on the date on which the child attains the age of sixteen or at any time after that date but before or on the date on which he attains the age of eighteen, then if, on an application made to the court for an order under this subsection, it appears to the court that—

(a)   the child is, will be or (if an order were made under this subsection) would be receiving instruction at an educational establishment or undergoing training for a trade, profession or vocation, whether or not he also is, will be or would be in gainful employment; or

(b)   there are special circumstances which justify the making of an order under this subsection,

the court shall have power by order to revive the first mentioned order from such date as the court may specify, not being earlier than the date of the making of the application, and to exercise its power under section 31 of this Act in relation to any order so revived.

(7)   Without prejudice to the generality of subsection (6)(c) or (f) above, an order under this section for the payment of a lump sum—

(a)   may be made for the purpose of enabling any liabilities or expenses reasonably incurred in maintaining the applicant or any child of the family to whom the application relates before the making of the application to be met;

(b)   may provide for the payment of that sum by instalments of such amount as may be specified in the order and may require the payment of the instalments to be secured to the satisfaction of the court.

37.—(1)   For the purposes of this section 'financial relief' means relief under any of the provisions of sections 22, 23, 24, 27, 31 (expect subsection (6)) and 35 ..., and any reference in this section to defeating a person's claim for financial relief is a reference to preventing financial relief from being granted to that person, or to that person for the benefit of a child of the family, or reducing the amount of any financial relief which might be so granted, or frustrating or impeding the enforcement of any order which might be or has been made at his instance under any of those provisions.

(2)   Where proceedings for financial relief are brought by one person against another, the court may, on the application of the first-mentioned person—

(a)   if it is satisfied that the other party to the proceedings is, with the intention of defeating the claim for financial relief, about to make any disposition or to transfer out of the jurisdiction or otherwise deal with any property, make such order as it thinks fit for restraining the other party from so doing or otherwise for protecting the claim;

(b)   if it is satisfied that the other party has, with that intention, made a reviewable disposition and that if the disposition were set aside financial relief or different financial relief would be granted to the applicant, make an order setting aside the disposition;

(c)   if it is satisfied, in a case where an order has been obtained under any of the provisions mentioned in subsection (1) above by the applicant against the other party, that the other party has, with that intention, made a reviewable disposition, make an order setting aside the disposition;

and an application for the purposes of paragraph (b) above shall be made in the proceedings for the financial relief in question.

(3)   Where the court makes an order under subsection (2)(b) or (c) above setting aside a disposition it shall give such consequential directions as it thinks fit for giving effect to the order (including directions requiring the making of any payments or the disposal of any property).

(4)   Any disposition made by the other party to the proceedings for financial relief in question (whether before or after the commencement of those proceedings) is a

reviewable disposition for the purposes of subsection (2)(b) and (c) above unless it was made for valuable consideration (other than marriage) to a person who, at the time of the disposition, acted in relation to it in good faith and without notice of any intention on the part of the other party to defeat the applicant's claim for financial relief.

(5)   Where an application is made under this section with respect to a disposition which took place less than three years before the date of the application or with respect to a disposition or other dealing with property which is about to take place and the court is satisfied—

(a)   in a case falling within subsection (2)(a) or (b) above, that the disposition or other dealing would (apart from this section) have the consequence, or

(b)   in a case falling within subsection (2)(c) above, that the disposition has had the consequence,

of defeating the applicant's claim for financial relief, it shall be presumed, unless the contrary is shown, that the person who disposed of or is about to dispose of or deal with the property did so or, as the case may be, is about to do so, with the intention of defeating the applicant's claim for financial relief.

(6)   In this section 'disposition' does not include any provision contained in a will or codicil but, with that exception, includes any conveyance, assurance or gift of property of any description, whether made by an instrument or otherwise.

(7)   This section does not apply to a disposition made before 1 January 1968.

28.—*(1)   Subject in the case of an order made on or after the grant of a decree ofdivorce or nullity of marriage to the provisions of sections 25A(2) ... and 31(7) ..., the term to be specified in a periodical payments or secured periodical payments order in favour of a party to a marriage shall be such term as the court thinks fit, except that the term shall not begin before or extend beyond the following limits, that is to say—*

(a)   in the case of a periodical payments order, the term shall begin not earlier than the date of the making of an application for the order, and shall be so defined as not to extend beyond the death of either of the parties to the marriage or, where the order is made on or after the grant of a decree of divorce or nullity of marriage, the remarriage of the party in whose favour the order is made, and

(b)   in the case of a secured periodical payments order, the term shall begin not earlier than the date of the making of an application for the order, and shall be so defined as not to extend beyond the death or, where the order is made on or after the grant of such a decree, the remarriage of the party in whose favour the order is made.

(1A)   Where a periodical payments or secured periodical payments order in favour of a party to a marriage is made on or after the grant of a decree of divorce or nullity of marriage, the court may direct that that party shall not be entitled to apply under section 31 ... for the extension of the term specified in the order.

(2)   Where a periodical payments or secured periodical payments order in favour of a party to a marriage is made otherwise than on or after the grant of a decree of divorce or nullity of marriage, and the marriage in question is subsequently dissolved or annulled but the order continues in force, the order shall, notwithstanding anything in it, cease to have effect on the remarriage of that party, except in relation to any arrears due under it on the date of the remarriage.

(3)   If after the grant of a decree dissolving or annulling a marriage either party to that marriage remarries whether at any time before or after the commencement of this Act, that party shall not be entitled to apply, by reference to the grant of that decree, for a financial provision order in his or her favour, or for a property adjustment order, against the other party to that marriage.

29.—*(1) Subject to subsection (3) below, no financial provision order and no order for a transfer of property under section 24(1)(a) above shall be made in favour of a child who has attained the age of 18.*

(2)   The term to be specified in a periodical payments or secured periodical payments order in favour of a child may begin with the date of the making of an application for the order in question or any later date but—

(a)   shall not in the first instance extend beyond the date of the birthday of the child next following his attaining the upper limit of the compulsory school age (that is to say, the age that is for the time being that limit by virtue of section 35 of the

Education Act 1944 together with any Order in Council made under that section) unless the court considers that in the circumstances oe case the welfare of the child requires that it should extend to a later date; and

(b)   shall not in any event, subject to subsection (3) below, extend beyond the date of the child's 18th birthday.

(3)   Subsection (1) above, and paragraph (b) of subsection (2), shall not apply in the case of a child, if it appears to the court that—

(a)   the child is, or will be, or if an order were made without complying with either or both of those provisions would be, receiving instruction at an educational establishment or undergoing training for a trade, profession or vocation, whether or not he is also, or will also be, in gainful employment; or

(b)   there are special circumstances which justify the making of an order without complying with either or both of those provisions.

(4)   Any periodical payments order in favour of a child shall, notwithstanding anything in the order, cease to have effect on the death of the person liable to make payments under the order, except in relation to any arrears due under the order on the date of the death.

Domestic Proceedings and Magistrates' Courts Act 1978

1.   *Either party to a marriage may apply to a magistrates' court for an order under section 2 of this Act on the ground that the other party to the marriage—*

(a)   has failed to provide reasonable maintenance for the applicant; or

(b)   has failed to provide or to make a proper contribution towards, reasonable maintenance for any child of the family, or

(c)   has behaved in such a way that the applicant cannot reasonably be expected to live with the respondent; or

(d)   has deserted the applicant.

2.—*(1)   Where on an application for an order under this section the applicant satisfies the court of any ground mentioned in section 1 of this Act, the court may, subject to the provisions of this Part of this Act, make any one or more of the following orders, that is to say—*

(a)   an order that the respondent shall make to the applicant such periodical payments, and for such term, as may be specified in the order;

(b)   an order that the respondent shall pay to the applicant such lump sum as may be so specified;

(c)   an order that the respondent shall make to the applicant for the benefit of a child of the family to whom the application relates, or to such a child, such periodical payments, and for such term, as may be so specified;

(d)   an order that the respondent shall pay to the applicant for the benefit of a child of the family to whom the application relates, or to such a child, such lump sum as may be so specified.

(2)   Without prejudice to the generality of subsection (1)(b) or (d) above, an order under this section for the payment of a lump sum may be made for the purpose of enabling any liability or expenses reasonably incurred in maintaining the applicant, or any child of the family to whom the application relates, before the making of the order to be met.

(3)   The amount of any lump sum required to be paid by such an order under this section shall not exceed £1,000 or such larger amount as the Secretary of State may from time to time by order fix for the purposes of this subsection.

4.—*(1)   The terms to be specified in any order made under section 2(1)(a) of this Act shall be such term as the court thinks fit except that the term shall not begin earlier than the date of the making of the application for the order and shall not extend beyond the death of either of the parties to the marriage.*

(2)   Where an order is made under the said section 2(1)(a) and the marriage of the parties affected by the order is subsequently dissolved or annulled but the order continues in force, the order shall, notwithstanding anything in it, cease to have effect on the remarriage of the party in whose favour it was made, except in relation to any arrears due under the order on the date of the remarriage.

5.—(1) Subject to subsection (3) below, no order shall be made under section 2(1)(c) or (d) of this Act in favour of a child who has attained the age of eighteen.

(2) The term to be specified in an order made under section 2(1)(c) of this Act in favour of a child may begin with the date of the making of an application for the order in question or any later date or a date ascertained in accordance with subsection (5) or (6) ... but—

(a) shall not in the first instance extend beyond the date of the birthday of the child next following his attaining the upper limit of the compulsory school age (construed in accordance with section 8 of the Education Act 1996) unless the court considers that in the circumstances of the case the welfare of the child requires that it should extend to a later date; and

(b) shall not in any event, subject to subsection (3) below, extend beyond the date of the child's eighteenth birthday.

(3) The court—

(a) may make an order under section 2(1)(c) or (d) of this Act in favour of a child who has attained the age of eighteen, and

(b) may include an order made under section 2(1)(c) of this Act in relation to a child who has not attained that age a provision for extending beyond the date when the child will attain that age the term for which by virtue of the order any payments are to be made to or for the benefit of that child,

if it appears to the court—

(i) that the child is, or will be, or if such an order or provision were made would be, receiving instruction at an educational establishment or undergoing training for a trade, profession or vocation, whether or not he is also, or will also be, in gainful employment; or

(ii) that there are special circumstances which justify the making of the order or provision.

(4) Any order made under section 2(1)(c) of this Act in favour of a child shall, notwithstanding anything in the order, cease to have effect on the death of the person liable to make payments under the order.

6.—(1) Either party to a marriage may apply to a magistrates' court for an order under this section on the ground that either the party making the application or the other party to the marriage has agreed to make such financial provision as may be specified in the application and, subject to subsection (3) below, the court on such an application may, if—

(a) it is satisfied that the applicant or the respondent, as the case may be, has agreed to make that provision, and

(b) it has no reason to think that it would be contrary to the interests of justice to exercise its powers hereunder,

order that the applicant or the respondent, as the case may be, shall make the financial provision specified in the application.

(2) In this section 'financial provision' means the provision mentioned in any one or more of the following paragraphs, that is to say—

(a) the making of periodical payments by one party to the other,

(b) the payment of a lump sum by one party to the other,

(c) the making of periodical payments by one party to a child of the family or to the other party for the benefit of such a child,

(d) the payment by one party of a lump sum to a child of the family or to the other party for the benefit of such a child,

and any reference in this section to the financial provision specified in an application made under subsection (1) above or specified by the court under subsection (5) below is a reference to the type of provision specified in the application or by the court, as the case may be, to the amount so specified as the amount of any payment to be made thereunder and, in the case of periodical payments, to the term so specified as the term for which the payments are to be made.

(3) Where the financial provision specified in an application under subsection (1) above includes or consists of provision in respect of a child of the family, the court shall not make an order under that subsection unless it considers that the provision which the applicant or the respondent, as the case may be, has agreed to make in respect of that child provides for, or makes a proper contribution towards, the financial needs of the child.

(4)   A party to a marriage who has applied for an order under section 2 of this Act shall not be precluded at any time before the determination of that application from applying for an order under this section; but if an order is made under this section on the application of either party and either of them has also made an application for an order under section 2 of this Act, the application made for the order under section 2 shall be treated as if it had been withdrawn.

(5)   Where on an application under subsection (1) above the court decides—

(a)   that it would be contrary to the interests of justice to make an order for the making of the financial provision specified in the application, or

(b)   that any financial provision which the applicant or the respondent, as the case may be, has agreed to make in respect of a child of the family does not provide for, or make a proper contribution towards, the financial needs of that child,

but is of the opinion—

(i)   that it would not be contrary to the interests of justice to make an order for the making of some other financial provision specified by the court, and

(ii)   that, insofar as that other financial provision contains any provision for a child of the family, it provides for, or makes a proper contribution towards, the financial needs of that child,

then if both the parties agree, the court may order that the applicant or the respondent, as the case may be, shall make that other financial provision.

(6)   Subject to subsection (8) below, the provisions of section 4 of this Act shall apply in relation to an order under this section which requires periodical payments to be made to a party to a marriage for his own benefit as they apply in relation to an order under section 2(1)(a) of this Act.

(7)   Subject to subsection (8) below, the provisions of section 5 of this Act shall apply in relation to an order under this section for the making of financial provision in respect of a child of the family as they apply in relation to an order under section 2(1)(c) or (d) of this Act.

(8)   Where the court makes an order under this section which contains provision for the making of periodical payments and, by virtue of subsection (4) above, an application for an order under section 2 of this Act is treated as if it had been withdrawn, then the term which may be specified as the term for which the payments are to be made may begin with the date of the making of the application for the order under section 2 or any later date.

(9)   Where the respondent is not present or represented by counsel or solicitor at the hearing of an application for an order under subsection (1) above, the court shall not make an order under this section unless there is produced to the court such evidence as may be prescribed by rules of—

(a)   the consent of the respondent to the making of the order,

(b)   the financial resources of the respondent, and

(c)   in a case where the financial provision specified in the application includes or consists of provision in respect of a child of the family to be made by the applicant to the respondent for the benefit of the child or to the child, the financial resources of the child.

7.—*(1)   Where the parties to a marriage have been living apart for a continuous period exceeding three months, neither party having deserted the other, and one of the parties has been making periodical payments for the benefit of the other party or of a child of the family, that other party may apply to a magistrates' court for an order under this section, and any application made under this subsection shall specify the aggregate amount of the payments so made during the period of three months immediately preceding the date of the making of the application.*

(2)   Where on an application for an order under this section the court is satisfied that the respondent has made the payments specified in the application, the court may, subject to the provisions of this Part of this Act, make one or both of the following orders, that is to say—

(a)   an order that the respondent shall make to the applicant such periodical payments, and for such term, as may be specified in the order;

(b)   an order that the respondent shall make to the applicant for the benefit of a child of the family to whom the application relates, or to such a child, such periodical payments, and for such term, as may be so specified.

(3)   The court in the exercise of its powers under this section—

(a)   shall not require the respondent to make payments which exceed in aggregate during any period of three months the aggregate amount paid by him for the benefit of the applicant or a child of the family during the period of three months immediately preceding the date of the making of the application;

(b)   shall not require the respondent to make payments to or for the benefit of any person which exceed in amount the payments which the court considers that it would have required the respondent to make to or for the benefit of that person on application under section 1 of this Act;

(c)   shall not require payments to be made to or for the benefit of a child of the family who is not a child of the respondent unless the court considers that it would have made an order in favour of that child on an application under section 1 of this Act.

(4)   Where on an application under this section the court considers that the orders which it has the power to make under this section—

(a)   would not provide reasonable maintenance for the applicant, or

(b)   if the application relates to a child of the family, would not provide, or make a proper contribution towards reasonable maintenance for that child,

the court shall refuse to make an order under this section, but the court may treat the application as if it were an application for an order under section 2 of this Act.

(5)   The provisions of section 3 of this Act shall apply in relation to an application for an order under this section as they apply in relation to an application for an order under section 2 of this Act subject to the modification that for the reference in subsection 2(c) of the said section 3 to the occurrence of the conduct which is alleged as the ground of the application there shall be substituted a reference to the living apart of the parties to the marriage.

(6)   The provisions of section 4 of this Act shall apply in relation to an order under this section which requires periodical payments to be made to the applicant for his own benefit as they apply in relation to an order made under section 2(1)(a) of this Act.

(7)   The provisions of section 5 of this Act shall apply in relation to an order under this section for the making of periodical payments in respect of a child of the family as they apply in relation to an order under section 2(1)(c) of this Act.

APPENDIX D

ANCILLARY RELIEF PROCEDURE RULES

D.1 Family Proceedings (Amendment No. 2) Rules 1999

1.—*(1) These rules may be cited as the Family Proceedings (Amendment No. 2) Rules 1999 and shall come into force on 5th June 2000.*

(2) The Family Proceedings Rules 1991, as amended by these rules, shall apply to proceedings commenced by Form A or B on or after 5th June 2000.

(3) Where proceedings have been commenced before 5th June 2000:

(a) the court may, if it considers it just to do so, direct that the Family Proceedings Rules 1991, as amended by these rules, shall apply to those proceedings; otherwise

(b) the Family Proceedings Rules 1991 shall apply to those proceedings as if these rules had not been made.

2. *The Family Proceedings Rules 1991 shall be amended in accordance with the provisions of these rules.*

3. *In the Arrangement of Rules, for the numbers and words from '2.52 Right to be heard on ancillary questions' to '2.68 Application for order under section 37(2)(a) of Act of 1973', there shall be substituted the following;*

'2.51A *Application of ancillary relief rules*
2.51B *The overriding objective*
2.52 *Right to be heard on ancillary questions*
2.53 *Application by petitioner or respondent for ancillary relief*
2.54 *Application by parent, guardian etc. for ancillary relief in respect of children*
2.57 *Children to be separately represented on certain applications*
2.59 *Evidence on application for property adjustment or avoidance of disposition order*
2.60 *Service of statement in answer*
2.61 *Information on application for consent order for financial relief*
2.61A *Application for ancillary relief*
2.61B *Procedure before the first appointment*
2.61C *Expert evidence*
2.61D *The first appointment*
2.61E *The FDR appointment*
2.61F *Costs*
2.62 *Investigation by district judge of application for ancillary relief*
2.64 *Order on application for ancillary relief*
2.65 *Reference of application to judge*
2.66 *Arrangements for hearing of application etc by judge*
2.67 *Request for periodical payments order at same rate as order for maintenance pending suit*
2.68 *Application for order under section 37(2)(a) of Act of 1973*
2.69 *Offers to settle*
2.69A *Interpretation of rules 2.69B to 2.69D*

4.—*(1) In rule 1.2(4), after 'Appendix 1' there shall be inserted 'or 1A'.*
(2) After rule 1.2(5) there shall be inserted:
(5A) In these rules a reference to a Part or rule, if prefixed by the letters 'CPR', is a reference to that Part or rule in the Civil Procedure Rules 1998.

5.—*(1) In rule 2.45(1) for 'Form M12' there shall be substituted 'Form B'.*
(2) Rule 2.45(2) and (3) shall be omitted.
(3) In rule 2.45(5):
(a) the words 'the proper officer shall fix an appointment for the hearing; and' shall be omitted;
(b) for 'rules 2.62(3) to (7)' there shall be substituted 'rules 2.51B to 2.70'; and
(c) after 'application for ancillary relief' there shall be inserted 'and, unless the context otherwise requires, those rules shall be read as if all references to Form A were references to Form B'.

6. *Before rule 2.52, but after the heading 'Ancillary relief,' the following shall be inserted:*

'Application of ancillary relief rules
2.51A.—*(1) The procedures set out in rules 2.51B to 2.70 ('the ancillary relief rules') apply to any ancillary relief application and to any application under section 10(2) of the Act of 1973.*
(2) In the ancillary relief rules, unless the context otherwise requires:
'applicant' means the party applying for ancillary relief;
'respondent' means the respondent to the application for ancillary relief;
'FDR appointment' means a Financial Dispute Resolution appointment in accordance with rule 2.61E.

2.51B.—*(1) The ancillary relief rules are a procedural code with the overriding objective of enabling the court to deal with cases justly.*
(2) Dealing with a case justly includes, so far as is practicable—
(a) ensuring that the parties are on an equal footing;
(b) saving expense;
(c) dealing with the case in ways which are proportionate—
(i) to the amount of money involved;
(ii) to the importance of the case;
(iii) to the complexity of the issues; and
(iv) to the financial position of each party;
(d) ensuring that it is dealt with expeditiously and fairly; and
(e) allotting to it an appropriate share of the court's resources, while taking into account the need to allot resources to other cases.
(3) The court must seek to give effect to the overriding objective when it—
(a) exercises any power given to it by the ancillary relief rules; or
(b) interprets any rule.
(4) The parties are required to help the court to further the overriding objective.
(5) The court must further the overriding objective by actively managing cases.
(6) Active case management includes—
(a) encouraging the parties to co-operate with each other in the conduct of the proceedings;
(b) encouraging the parties to settle their disputes through mediation, where appropriate;
(c) identifying the issues at an early date;
(d) regulating the extent of disclosure of documents and expert evidence so that they are proportionate to the issues in question;

(e) helping the parties to settle the whole or part of the case;

(f) fixing timetables or otherwise controlling the progress of the case;

(g) making use of technology; and

(h) giving directions to ensure that the trial of a case proceeds quickly and efficiently.'.

7. In rule 2.53 and 2.54(1), for 'Form M11', wherever it occurs, there shall be substituted 'Form A'.

8. Rules 2.55, 2.56 and 2.58 shall be omitted.

9.—(1) Rule 2.59(1) shall be omitted.

(2) In rule 2.59(2) for 'Form M11 or M13' there shall be substituted 'Form A'.

(3) In rule 2.59(3) for the words from 'A copy' to 'supporting affidavit' there shall be substituted 'Copies of Form A and of Form E completed by the applicant'.

(4) In rule 2.59(4):

(a) for 'Form M11 or M13 as the case may be' there shall be substituted 'Form A'.

(b) for 'affidavit' there shall be substituted 'Form E'.

(5) In rule 2.59(5):

(a) for 'an affidavit' in sub-paragraph (a) there shall be substituted 'copies of Forms A and E';

(b) for 'an affidavit' in sub-paragraph (b) there shall be substituted 'a copy of Form E'; and

(c) for 'file an affidavit' there shall be substituted 'file a statement'.

(6) At the end of rule 2.59(5), there shall be inserted the following:

(6) A statement filed under paragraph (5) shall be sworn to be true.

10. For rule 2.60 there shall be substituted:

'Service of statement in answer

2.60.—(1) Where a form or other document filed with the court contains an allegation of adultery or of an improper association with a named person ('the named person'), the court may direct that the party who filed the relevant form or document serve a copy of all or part of that form or document on the named person, together with Form F.

(2) If the court makes a direction under paragraph (1), the named person may file a statement in answer to the allegations.

(3) A statement under paragraph (2) shall be sworn to be true.

(4) Rule 2.37(3) shall apply to a person served under paragraph (1) as it applies to a co-respondent.'

11. After rule 2.61 there shall be inserted:

'Application for ancillary relief

2.61A.—(1) A notice of intention to proceed with an application for ancillary relief made in the petition or answer or an application for ancillary relief must be made by notice in Form A.

(2) The notice must be filed:

(a) if the case is pending in a divorce county court, in that court; or

(b) if the case is pending in the High Court, in the registry in which it is proceeding.

(3) Where the applicant requests an order for ancillary relief that includes provision to be made by virtue of section 25B or 25C of the Act of 1973 the terms of the order requested must be specified in the notice in Form A.

(4) Upon the filing of Form A the court must:

(a) fix a first appointment not less than 12 weeks and not more than 16 weeks after the date of the filing of the notice and give notice of that date;

(b) serve a copy on the respondent within 4 days of the date of the filing of the notice.

(5) The date fixed under paragraph (4) for the first appointment, or for any subsequent appointment, must not be cancelled except with the court's permission and, if cancelled, the court must immediately fix a new date.

Procedure before the first appointment

2.61B.—*(1) Both parties must, at the same time, exchange with each other, and each file with the court, a statement in Form E, which—*

    (a) is signed by the party who made the statement;

    (b) is sworn to be true, and

    (c) contains the information and has attached to it the documents required by that Form.

(2) Form E must be exchanged and filed not less than 35 days before the date of the first appointment.

(3) Form E must have attached to it:

    (a) any documents required by Form E; and

    (b) any other documents necessary to explain or clarify any of the information contained in Form E.

(4) Form E must have no documents attached to it other than the documents referred to in paragraph (3).

(5) Where a party was unavoidably prevented from sending any document required by Form E, that party must at the earliest opportunity:

    (a) serve copies of that document on the other party; and

    (b) file a copy of that document with the court, together with a statement explaining the failure to send it with Form E.

(6) No disclosure or inspection of documents may be requested or given between the filing of the application for ancillary relief and the first appointment, except—

    (a) copies sent with Form E, or in accordance with paragraph (5); or

    (b) in accordance with paragraph (7).

(7) At least 14 days before the hearing of the first appointment, each party must file with the court and serve on the other party—

    (a) a concise statement of the issues between the parties;

    (b) a chronology;

    (c) a questionnaire setting out by reference to the concise statement of issues any further information and documents requested from the other party or a statement that no information and documents are required;

    (d) a notice in Form G stating whether that party will be in a position at the first appointment to proceed on that occasion to a FDR appointment.

(8) Where an order for ancillary relief is requested that includes provision to be made under section 25B or 25C of the Act of 1973, the applicant must file with the court and serve on the respondent at least 14 days before the hearing of the first appointment, confirmation that rule 2.70(4) has been complied with.

(9) At least 14 days before the hearing of the first appointment, the applicant must file with the court and serve on the respondent, confirmation of the names of all persons served in accordance with rule 2.59(3) and (4), and that there are no other persons who must be served in accordance with those paragraphs.

Expert evidence

2.61C. *CPR rules 35.1 to 35.14 relating to expert evidence (with appropriate modifications), except CPR rules 35.5(2) and 35.8(4)(b) apply to all ancillary relief proceedings.*

The first appointment

2.61D.—*(1) The first appointment must be conducted with the objective of defining the issues and saving costs.*

(2) At the first appointment the district judge—

    (a) must determine—

      (i) the extent to which any questions seeking information under rule 2.61B must be answered; and

      (ii) what documents requested under rule 2.61B must be produced,

and give directions for the production of such further documents as may be necessary;

    (b) must give directions about—

      (i) the valuation of assets (including, where appropriate, the joint instruction of joint experts);

      (ii) obtaining and exchanging expert evidence, if required; and

    (iii)   *evidence to be adduced by each party and, where appropriate, about further chronologies or schedules to be filed by each party;*

    (c)   *must, unless he decides that a referral is not appropriate in the circumstances, direct that the case be referred to a FDR appointment;*

    (d)   *must, where he decides that a referral to a FDR appointment is not appropriate, direct one of the following:*

    (i)   *that a further directions appointment be fixed;*

    (ii)   *that an appointment be fixed for the making of an interim order;*

    (iii)   *that the case be fixed for final hearing and, where that direction is given, the district judge must determine the judicial level at which the case should be heard; or*

    (iv)   *that the case be adjourned for out-of-court mediation or private negotiation or, in exceptional circumstances, generally;*

    (e)   *must consider whether, having regard to all the circumstances (including the extent to which each party has complied with this Part, and in particular the requirement to send documents with Form E), to make an order about the costs of the hearing; and*

    (f)   *may—*

    (i)   *make an interim order where an application for it has been made in accordance with rule 2.69F returnable at the first appointment;*

    (ii)   *having regard to the contents of Form G filed by the parties, treat the appointment (or part of it) as a FDR appointment to which rule 2.61E applies;*

    (iii)   *in a case where an order for ancillary relief is requested that includes provision to be made under section 25B or 25C of the Act of 1973, require any party to request a valuation under regulation 4 of the Divorce etc. (Pensions) Regulations 1996 from the trustees or managers of any pension scheme under which the party has, or is likely to have, any benefits.*

    (3)   After the first appointment, a party is not entitled to production of any further documents except in accordance with directions given under paragraph (2)(a) above or with the permission of the court.

    (4)   At any stage:

    (a)   *a party may apply for further directions or a FDR appointment;*

    (b)   *the court may give further directions or direct that the parties attend a FDR appointment.*

    (5)   Both parties must personally attend the first appointment unless the court orders otherwise.

The FDR appointment

2.61E.—*(1)   The FDR appointment must be treated as a meeting held for the purposes of discussion and negotiation and paragraphs (2) to (9) apply.*

    (2)   The district judge or judge hearing the FDR appointment must have no further involvement with the application, other than to conduct any further FDR appointment or to make a consent order or a further directions order.

    (3)   Not later than 7 days before the FDR appointment, the applicant must file with the court details of all offers and proposals, and responses to them.

    (4)   Paragraph (3) includes any offers, proposals or responses made wholly or partly without prejudice, but paragraph (3) does not make any material admissible as evidence if, but for that paragraph, it would not be admissible.

    (5)   At the conclusion of the FDR appointment, any documents filed under paragraph (3), and any filed documents referring to them, must, at the request of the party who filed them, be returned to him and not retained on the court file.

    (6)   Parties attending the FDR appointment must use their best endeavours to reach agreement on the matters in issue between them.

    (7)   The FDR appointment may be adjourned from time to time.

    (8)   At the conclusion of the FDR appointment, the court may make an appropriate consent order, but otherwise must give directions for the future course of the proceedings, including, where appropriate, the filing of evidence and fixing a final hearing date.

    (9)   Both parties must personally attend the FDR appointment unless the court orders otherwise.

Costs

2.61F.—*(1) At every court hearing or appointment each party must produce to the court an estimate in Form H of the costs incurred by him up to the date of that hearing or appointment.*

(2) The parties' obligation under paragraph (1) is without prejudice to their obligations under paragraphs 4.1 to 4.11 of the Practice Direction relating to CPR Part 44.'.

12.—*(1) Rule 2.62(1), (3), (5) and (6) shall be omitted.*

(2) In rule 2.62(4):

(a) for 'discovery and production' there shall be substituted 'disclosure and inspection'; and

(b) for 'affidavits' there shall be substituted 'statements'.

(3) After rule 2.62(4), there shall be inserted:

(4A) A statement filed under paragraph (4) shall be sworn to be true.'.

(4) In rule 2.62(7):

(a) for '(a 'production appointment')' there shall be substituted '(an 'inspection appointment')'; and

(b) for the second occurrence of 'production' there shall be substituted 'inspection'.

(5) In rule 2.62(8), for 'a production' there shall be substituted 'an inspection'.

(6) In rule 2.62(9), for 'a production' there shall be substituted 'an inspection'.

13. *Rule 2.63 shall be omitted.*

14. *In rule 2.64(2) after 'final determination of the application,' there shall be substituted 'and subject to rule 2.69F,'.*

15. *In rule 2.66(4) for 'as a district judge has under rule 2.62(5)' there shall be substituted 'to make directions as a district judge has under these rules'.*

16. *In rule 2.67(2) for 'Form M15', wherever it occurs, there shall be substituted 'Form I'.*

17.—*(1) For rule 2.69 there shall be substituted:*

'Offers to settle

2.69.—*(1) Either party to the application may at any time make a written offer to the other party which is expressed to be 'without prejudice except as to costs' and which relates to any issue in the proceedings relating to the application.*

(2) Where an offer is made under paragraph (1), the fact that such an offer has been made shall not be communicated to the court, except in accordance with rule 2.61E(3), until the question of costs falls to be decided.

Interpretation of rules 2.69B to 2.69D

2.69A. *In rules 2.69B to 2.69D, 'base rate' has the same meaning as in the Civil Procedure Rules 1998.*

Judgment or order more advantageous than an offer made by the other party

2.69B.—*(1) This rule applies where the judgment or order in favour of the applicant or respondent is more advantageous to him than an offer made under rule 2.69(1) by the other party.*

(2) The court must, unless it considers it unjust to do so, order that other party to pay any costs incurred after the date beginning 28 days after the offer was made.

Judgment or order more advantageous than offers made by both parties

2.69C.—*(1) This rule applies where*

(a) both the applicant and the respondent have made offers under rule 2.69(1); and

(b) the judgment or order in favour of the applicant or the respondent, as the case may be, is more advantageous to him than both of the offers referred to in paragraph (a).

(2) The court may, where it considers it just, order interest in accordance with paragraph (3) on the whole or part of any sum of money (excluding interest and periodical payments) to be awarded to the applicant or respondent, as the case may be.

(3) Interest under paragraph (2) may be at a rate not exceeding 10 per cent above base rate for some or all of the period beginning 28 days after the offer was made.

(4) The court may also order that the applicant or respondent, as the case may be, is entitled to:

(a) his costs on the indemnity basis beginning 28 days after the offer was made; and

(b) interest on those costs at a rate not exceeding 10 per cent above base rate.

(5) The court's powers under this rule are in addition to its powers under rule 2.69B.

Factors for court's consideration under rules 2.69B and 2.69C

2.69D.—(1) In considering whether it would be unjust, or whether it would be just, to make the orders referred to in rules 2.69B and 2.69C, the court must take into account all the circumstances of the case, including -

(a) the terms of any offers made under rule 2.69(1);

(b) the stage in the proceedings when any offer was made;

(c) the information available to the parties at the time when the offer was made;

(d) the conduct of the parties with regard to the giving or refusing to give information for the purposes of enabling the offer to be made or evaluated; and

(e) the respective means of the parties.

(2) The power of the court to award interest under rule 2.69C(2) and (4)(b) is in addition to any other power it may have to award interest.

Open proposals

2.69E.—(1) Not less than 14 days before the date fixed for the final hearing of an application for ancillary relief, the applicant must (unless the court directs otherwise) file with the court and serve on the respondent an open statement which sets out concise details, including the amounts involved, of the orders which he proposes to ask the court to make.

(2) Not more than 7 days after service of a statement under paragraph (1), the respondent must file with the court and serve on the applicant an open statement which sets out concise details, including the amounts involved, of the orders which he proposes to ask the court to make.

Application for interim orders

2.69F.—(1) A party may apply at any stage of the proceedings for an order for maintenance pending suit, interim periodical payments or an interim variation order.

(2) An application for such an order must be made by notice of application and the date fixed for the hearing of the application must be not less than 14 days after the date the notice of application is issued.

(3) The applicant shall forthwith serve the respondent with a copy of the notice of application.

(4) Where an application is made before a party has filed Form E, that party must file with the application and serve on the other party, a draft of the order requested and a short sworn statement explaining why the order is necessary and giving the necessary information about his means.

(5) Not less than 7 days before the date fixed for the hearing, the respondent must file with the court and serve on the other party, a short sworn statement about his means, unless he has already filed Form E.

(6) A party may apply for any other form of interim order at any stage of the proceedings with or without notice.

(7) Where an application referred to in paragraph (6) is made with notice, the provisions of paragraphs (1) to (5) apply to it.

(8) Where an application referred to in paragraph (6) is made without notice, the provisions of paragraph (1) apply to it.'.

18.—(1) Rule 2.70(1) shall be omitted.

(2)   In rule 2.70(2) for 'discovery' there shall be substituted 'disclosure'.
(3)   In rule 2.70(3):
   (a)   for sub-paragraph (a) there shall be substituted:
      (a)   Form A in accordance with rule 2.61A; or;
   (b)   sub-paragraph (b) shall be omitted.
(4)   In rule 2.70(4) for 'Form M11 or M13 as the case may be' there shall be substituted 'Form A'.

19.   *Rules 2.71 to 2.77 shall be omitted.*

20.   *In Part III references to any of rules 2.52 to 2.70 shall be read as references to those rules as they were before these rules came into force.*

21.   *In rule 3.1(7) for 'intervention by' there shall be substituted 'filing of a statement in answer by'.*

22.   *Forms M11 to M15 shall be omitted from Appendix 1.*

23.   *The following shall be substituted for Appendix 1A:*

'APPENDIX 1A

Notice of [intention to proceed with] an Application for Ancillary Relief

*(*delete as appropriate)*

In the	
	*[County Court]
*[Principal Registry of the Family Division]	
Case No. *Always quote this*	
Applicant's Solicitor's reference	
Respondent's Solicitor's reference	

The marriage of　　　　　**and**

Take Notice that

the Applicant intends **to apply** to the Court or

to proceed with the application in the [petition][answer] for:

- ☐ an order for maintenance pending suit
- ☐ a periodical payments order
- ☐ a secured provision order
- ☐ a lump sum order
- ☐ a property adjustment order

If an application is made for any periodical payments or secured periodical payments for children:

- and there is a written agreement made before 5 April 1993 about maintenance for the benefit of children, **tick this box**　☐

- and there is a written agreement made on or after 5 April 1993 about maintenance for the benefit of children, **tick this box**　☐

- but there is no agreement, tick any of the boxes below to show if you are applying for payment:

- ☐ for a stepchild or stepchildren
- ☐ in addition to child support maintenance already paid under a Child Support Agency assessment
- ☐ to meet expenses arising from a child's disability
- ☐ to meet expenses incurred by a child in being educated or training for work
- ☐ when either the child **or** the person with care of the child **or** the absent parent of the child is not habitually resident in the United Kingdom
- ☐ Other (please state)

Signed:　　　　　　　　　　　　　　　　Dated:
[Applicant/Solicitor for the Applicant]

The court office at

is open between 10 am and 4 pm (4.30pm at the Principal Registry of the Family Division) Monday to Friday. When corresponding with the court, please address forms or letters to the Court Manager and quote the case number. If you do not do so, your correspondence may be returned.

Form A Notice of [Intention to proceed with] an Application for Ancillary Relief

Notice of an application under Rule 2.45

In the	
	*[County Court]
	*[Principal Registry of the Family Division]
Case No. *Always quote this*	
Petitioner's Solicitor's reference	
Respondent's Solicitor's reference	

*(*delete as apprpriate)*

The marriage of   **and**

Take Notice that

The Respondent intends to apply to the Court under section 10(2) of the Martimonial Causes Act 1973 for the Court to consider the financial position of the Respondent after the divorce.

Signed: Dated:

[Respondent/Solicitor for the Respondent]

The court office at

is open between 10 am and 4 pm (4.30pm at the Principal Registry of the Family Division) Monday to Friday. When corresponding with the court, please address forms or letters to the Court Manager and quote the case number. If you do not do so, your correspondence may be returned.

Form B Notice of an Application under Rule 2.45

Notice of a First Appointment

In the	
	*[County Court]
*[Principal Registry of the Family Division]	
Case No. *Always quote this*	
Applicant's Solicitor's reference	
Respondent's Solicitor's reference	

(*delete as appropriate)

The marriage of and

Take Notice that

By [ ] you must file with the Court a statement which gives full details of your property and income. You must sign and swear the statement. At the same time each party must exchange a copy of the statement with the [legal representative of the] other party. You must use the standard form of statement (Form E) which you may obtain from the Court office.

By [ ] you must file with the Court and the [legal representative of the] other party:

- a concise statement of the apparent issues between yourself and the other party;
- a chronology;
- a questionnaire setting out the further information and documents you require from the other party, or a statement that no information or documents are required;
- a Notice in Form G.

The First Appointment will be heard by

(the District Judge in chambers) at

on   20

at   [a.m.][p.m.]

The probable length of the hearing is

You and your legal representative, if you have one, must attend the appointment. At the appointment you must provide the Court with a written estimate (in Form H) of any legal costs which you have incurred. Non-compliance may render you liable to costs penalties.

Dated:

The court office at

is open between 10 am and 4 pm (4.30pm at the Principal Registry of the Family Division) Monday to Friday. When corresponding with the court, please address forms or letters to the Court Manager and quote the case number. If you do not do so, your correspondence may be returned.

Form C Notice of a First Appointment

Notice of a Financial Dispute Resolution Appointment

In the	
	*[County Court]
*[Principal Registry of the Family Division]	
Case No. *Always quote this*	
Applicant's Solicitor's reference	
Respondent's Solicitor's reference	

*(*delete as appropriate)*

The marriage of   **and**

Take Notice that

By [**]** the Applicant must provide the Court with details of all offers, proposals and responses concerning the Application.

An appointment for a Financial Dispute Resolution will take place at

on   20

at   [a.m.][p.m.]

The probable length of the hearing is

At the appointment

- You, and your legal representative, if you have one, must attend this appointment.
- The hearing will define, as far as possible, the issues in this matter and explore the possibility of settlement. If the matter proceeds to a full hearing, the date of the full hearing will be fixed.
- You must provide the Court with a written estimate (in Form H) of any legal costs.

Dated:

The court office at

is open between 10 am and 4 pm (4.30pm at the Principal Registry of the Family Division) Monday to Friday. When corresponding with the court, please address forms or letters to the Court Manager and quote the case number. If you do not do so, your correspondence may be returned.

Form D Notice of a Financial Dispute Resolution Appointment

FINANCIAL STATEMENT

*Applicant/*Respondent
*(delete as appropriate)

In the
*[County Court]
*[Principal Registry of the Family Division]

Case No Always quote this	

Between

Applicant		Respondent
	and	
Solicitor's Ref:		Solicitor's Ref:

Please fill in this form fully and accurately. Where any box is not applicable write "N/A". You have a duty to the court to give a full, frank and clear disclosure of all your financial and other relevant circumstances.

A failure to give full and accurate disclosure may result in any order the court makes being set aside.

If you are found to have been deliberately untruthful, criminal proceedings for perjury may be taken against you.

You must attach documents to the form where they are specifically sought and you may attach other documents where it is necessary to explain or clarify any of the information that you give.

Essential documents, which **must** accompany this Statement, are detailed at questions 2.1, 2.2, 2.3, 2.5, 2.14, 2.18 and 2.20.

If there is not enough room on the form for any particular piece of information, you may continue on an attached sheet of paper.

This statement must be sworn before an Officer of the Court
or a Commissioner for Oaths
before it is filed with the Court
or sent to the other party
(see page 20).

Form E Financial Statement 1

Part 1 General Information

1.1 Full Name

1.2 Date of Birth

Date	Month	Year

1.3 Date of Marriage

Date	Month	Year

1.4 Occupation

1.5 Date of the separation

Date	Month	Year

Tick here ☐ if not applicable

1.6 Date of the:

Petition			Decree Nisi/Decree of Judicial Separation			Decree Absolute		
Date	Month	Year	Date	Month	Year	Date	Month	Year

1.7 If you have remarried, or will remarry, state the date

Date	Month	Year

1.8 Do you live with another person? ☐ Yes ☐ No

1.9 Do you intend to live with someone within the next six months? ☐ Yes ☐ No

1.10 Details of any children of the family

Full names	Date of Birth			With whom does the child live?
	Date	Month	Year	

1.11 Give details of the state of health of yourself and the children

Yourself	Children

2

1.12 Give details of the present and proposed future educational arrangements for the children.

Present arrangements	Future arrangements

1.13 Give details of any Child Support Maintenance Assessments or Child Maintenance Orders made between the parties. If no assessment or agreement has been made, give an estimate of the liability of the non-residential parent under the Child Support Act 1991, in respect of the children of the family.

1.14 If this application is to vary an order, give details of the order that is to be varied and attach a copy of the order. Give the reasons for asking for the order to be varied.

1.15 Give details of any other court cases between you and your husband/wife, whether in relation to money, property, children or anything else.

Case No	Court

1.16 Specify your present residence and the occupants of it and on what terms you occupy it (e.g. tenant, owner-occupier).

Address	Occupants	Terms of occupation

3

Part 2 Financial Details — *Capital: Realisable Assets*

*If you have obtained a valuation within the last six months attach a copy. If not, give your own estimate of the property value. A copy of your most recent mortgage statement is also required.

2.1 Give details of your interest in the matrimonial home.

Property name and address	Land Registry Title No.	Nature and extent of your interest	*Property value

Mortgagee's Name and address	Type of mortgage	Balance outstanding outstanding on any mortgage	Total current value of your beneficial interest
1st			
2nd			
Other:			

NET value of your interest in the matrimonial home (A)	£

2.2 Give details of all other properties, land, and buildings in which you have an interest

Property name(s) and address(es)	Land Registry Title No.	Nature and extent of your interest	Property value
1.			
2.			
3.			

Mortgagee's Name(s) and address(es)	Type of mortgage	Balance outstanding on any mortgage	Total current value of your interest
1.			
2.			
3.			

TOTAL value of the above (not including the matrimonial home)	(B1) £

4

2.3 Give details of all bank, building society, and National Savings accounts, in credit, which you hold or have an interest in. Include PEPs, TESSAs and ISAs. For joint accounts, give your interest and the name of the account holder. If the account is overdrawn, include in Liabilities section at 2.12

You must attach your bank statements covering the last 12 months for each account listed

Name of bank or building society including Branch name	Type of account (e.g. current)	Account number	Name of other account holder *(if applicable)*	Balance at the date of this Statement	Total current value of your interest
1.					
2.					
3.					
4.					
5.					
				TOTAL value of your interest in ALL accounts	(B2) £

2.4 Give details of all stocks, gilts and other quoted securities which you hold or have an interest in. Include PEPs and ISAs. Do not include dividend income as this will be dealt with separately later on.

Name	Type	Size	Current value	Total current value of your interest
			TOTAL value of your interest in ALL holdings	(B3) £

2.5 Give details of all life insurance policies which you hold or in which you have an interest, including those that do not have a surrender value, for each policy.

Policy details including name of company, policy type and number	If policy is charged, state in whose favour and amount of charge	Maturity date			Surrender Value	Total current value of your interest
		Date	Month	Year		
You must attach any surrender value quotations		**TOTAL value of your interest in ALL policies**				(B4) £

5

2.6 Give details of all issues of National Savings Certificates which you hold or have an interest in.

Name of issue	Nominal amount	Current value	Total current value of your interest

TOTAL value of ALL your certificates	(B5) £

2.7 Give details of all of National Savings Bonds (including Premium bonds) and other bonds which you hold or have an interest in.

Type of Bond	Bond holder's number	Current value	Total current value of your interest

TOTAL value of ALL your bonds	(B6) £

2.8 Give details of all monies which are OWED TO YOU. Include sums owed in director's or partnership accounts

Brief description of debt	Balance outstanding	Total current value of your interest

TOTAL value of your interest in ALL debts owed to you	(B7) £

6

2.9 Give details of all of cash savings held in excess of £300. You must state where it is held and the currency it is held in.

Where held	Amount	Currency	Total current value of your interest

TOTAL value of ALL your cash

(B8)
£

2.10 Give details of personal belongings individually worth more than £500.
Include cars (gross value), collections, pictures, jewellery, furniture, and household belongings (this list is not exhaustive).

Item	Sale value	Total estimated current value of your interest

TOTAL value of your interest in ALL chattels

(B9)
£

2.11 Give details of any other realisable assets not yet mentioned, for example, unit trusts, investment trusts, commodities, business expansion schemes and futures (this list is not exhaustive). This is where you must mention any other realisable assets.

Type	Current value	Total current value of your interest

TOTAL value of your interest in ALL other realisable assets

(B10)
£

Now add together all the figures in the previous total boxes (B1 to B10) to give the TOTAL current value of ALL your interest in realisable assets.

(B) £

7

Part 2 Financial Details *Capital: Liabilities*

2.12 **Give details of any liabilities you have. Exclude** mortgages on property dealt with above.
Include money owed on credit cards and store cards, bank loans, hire purchase agreements and any overdrawn bank or building society accounts.

Liability (i.e. total amount owed, current monthly payments and term of loan/debt)	Current amount	Total current value of your share of the liability
TOTAL value of ALL your liabilities		(C1) £

Part 2 Financial Details *Capital: Capital Gains Tax*

2.13 **If any Capital Gains Tax would be payable on the disposal now of any of your realisable assets, give your estimate of the tax.**

Asset	Capital Gains Tax	Total current value of your liability
TOTAL value of ALL your Capital Gains Tax liabilities		(C2) £

Now add together C1 + C2 to give:- TOTAL net value of your liabilities	**(C)**	£

Now take the liabilities total from the realisable assets total (A+B-C), to give:- TOTAL net value of your personal assets	**(D)**	£

8

Part 2 Financial Details   *Capital: Business Assets*

2.14 Give details of all your business interests.   *You must attach a copy of the last 2 years accounts and any other document on which you base your valuation.*

Name and nature of your business	Your ESTIMATE of the current value of your interest	Your ESTIMATE of any possible Capital Gains Tax payable on disposal	Basis of valuation *(No formal valuation is required at this time)*	What is the extent of your interest?	Total net current value of your interest

TOTAL current value of your interest in business assets   **(E)**   £

2.15 List any directorships you hold or held in the last 12 months

Part 2 Financial Details   *Capital: Pensions (including SERPS but excluding Basic State Pensions)*

2.16 Give details of your pension interests.

If you have been provided with a valuation of your pension rights by the trustees or managers of the pension scheme you must attach it. Where the information is not available, give the estimated date when it will be available and attach the letter to the pension company or administrators from whom the information was sought. If you have more than one pension plan or scheme, you must provide the information in respect of each one, continuing, if necessary, on a separate piece of paper. If you have made Additional Voluntary Contributions or any Free Standing Additional Voluntary Contributions to any plan or scheme, you must give the information separately if the benefits referable to such contributions are separately recorded or paid. If you have more than one pension scheme you should reproduce the information for each scheme. Please include any SERPS.

Information about the Scheme(s)

Name and address of scheme, plan or policy	
Number of scheme, plan or policy	
Type of scheme, plan or policy *(e.g. final salary, money purchase or other)*	

CETV - Cash Equivalent Transfer Value

CETV Value	
The lump sum payable on death in service before retirement	
The lump sum payable on death in deferment before retirement	
The lump sum payable on death after retirement	

Retirement Benefits

Earliest date when benefit can be paid	
The estimated lump sum and monthly pension payable on retirement, assuming you take the maximum lump sum.	
The estimated monthly pension without taking any lump sum	

Spouse's Benefit

On death in service	
On death in deferment	
On death in retirement	

Dependant's Benefit

On death in service	
On death in deferment	
On death in retirement	

TOTAL value of your pension assets   (F)   £

10

267

Part 2 Financial Details   *Capital: Other Assets*

2.17 Give details of any other assets not listed above.
Include the following: (this list is not exhaustive)

- **Unrealisable assets.**
- **Share option scheme**, stating the estimated net sale proceeds of the shares if the options were capable of exercise now, and whether Capital Gains Tax or Income Tax would be payable.
- **Trust interests** (including interests under a discretionary trust), stating your estimate of the value of the interest and when it is likely to become realisable. If you say it will never be realisable, or has no value, give your reasons.
- Specify also any asset that is likely to be received in the forseeable future, any assets held on your behalf by a third party and any assets not mentioned elsewhere in this form held outside England and Wales.

Type of Asset	Value	Total net value of your interest

Total value of your other assets	**(G)**	£
Total value of your net assets (excluding pensions) **(D+E+G)**	**(H)**	£
Total value of your net assets (including pension) **(H+F)**	**(I)**	£

11

268

Part 2 Financial Details   *Income*

You must attach your last three payslips and your P60 for the most recently completed financial year

2.18 Earned Income: Give details of your gross and net income in the last financial year, and in the current financial year.

Nature of income (e.g. salary, bonus)	Last financial year		Current financial year *(estimated for the whole year)*	
	Gross	Net	Gross	Net

2.19 Additional Income: benefits etc. Give details and the value of all benefits in kind, perks, or other remuneration not disclosed elsewhere, received in the last financial year and current financial year.

Nature of income	Last financial year	Current financial year *(estimated for the whole year)*

12

Income continued

2.20 Self-employed or partnership income: Give details of annual net profit or loss for the last two accounting years, your share of this figure and tax payable to date of the last accounts and the estimate of income since that date. State the date on which your accounting year begins. Year 2 should be the most recent year, Year 1 the previous year. Please state the "from" and "to" dates for the years concerned.

Nature of income and date your accounting year begins	Details of the last two accounting periods					
	Net profit/loss		Your share of profit/loss		Tax payable by you	
	Year 1	Year 2	Year 1	Year 2	Year 1	Year 2

Nature of income and date your accounting year begins	Net Income	Estimate	
Net income SINCE date of last accounts and estimate for the whole year			*You must attach the accounts for the last two completed accounting years*

2.21 Investment income (e.g. dividends, interest) Give details of net income received in the last financial year, and in the current financial year and state whether it was paid gross or net of income tax. You are not required to calculate any tax payable that may arise.

Nature of income and the asset from which it derived	Paid gross or net (*delete that which is not applicable*)	Last financial year	Current financial year
	Gross / Net		

2.22 State benefits (including state pension) Give details of all state benefits received in the last 52 weeks

Nature of income	Total Income received in the last 52 weeks

13

2.23 Any other income Give details of any other income received in the last 52 weeks

Nature of income	Total Income for the last 52 weeks

Part 2 Financial Details   *Summaries*

2.24 Summary of your income

Your estimate of your current annual net income from all sources (2.18 - 2.23)	Your estimate of your net income from all sources for the next 52 weeks
£	£ **(J)**

2.25 Summary of financial information

	Reference of the section on this statement	Value
Net value of your interest in the matrimonial home	**A**	
Total current value of all your your interest in the other realisable assets	**B**	
Total net value of your liabilities	**C**	
Total net value of your personal assets	**D**	
Total current value of your interest in business assets	**E**	
Total current value of your pension or transfer values	**F**	
Total value of your other assets	**G**	
Total value of your net assets *(excluding pension)*	**H**	
Total value of your net assets *(including pension)*	**I**	
Your estimated net income for the next 52 weeks	**J**	

14

Part 3 Requirements   *Income Needs*

3.1 Give the reasonable future income needs of yourself (e.g. housing, car etc) and of any children living with you, or provided for by you. This may be expressed as annual, monthly or weekly figures (state which), but you should not use a combination of any of these periods.

Item	*Income needs of yourself*	Amount
	sub-total	

Item	*Income needs of child(ren) living with you, or provided for by you.*	Amount
	sub-total	
	Total income needs	£

Part 3 Requirements   *Capital Needs*

3.2   Give the reasonable future capital needs of yourself and of any children living with you, or provided for by you.

Item	*Capital needs of yourself*	Cost
	sub-total	

Item	*Capital needs of child(ren) living with you, or provided for by you.*	Cost
	sub-total	

	Total capital needs	£

Part 4 Other Information

4.1 State whether there has been any significant change in your net assets during the last 12 months, including any assets held outside England and Wales (e.g. closure of any bank or building society accounts).

4.2 Give brief details of the standard of living enjoyed by you and your spouse during the marriage.

4.3 Are there any particular contributions to the family property and assets or outgoings, or to family life, that have been made by you, your partner or anyone else that you think should be taken into account? If so, give a brief description of the contribution, the amount, when it was made, and by whom.

4.4 Bad behaviour or conduct by the other party will only be taken into account in very exceptional circumstances when deciding how the assets should be divided after divorce. If you feel it should be taken into account in your case identify the nature of the behaviour or conduct.

17

274

Part 4 Other Information *continued*

4.5 Give details of any other circumstances which you consider could significantly affect the extent of the financial provision to be made by or for you or for any child of the family e.g. earning capacity, disability, inheritence prospects or redundancy, remarriage and cohabitation plans, any contingent liabilities. (This list is not exhaustive).

4.6 If you have remarried (or intend to) or are living with another person (or intend to), give brief details, so far as they are known to you, of his or her income and assets.

Annual Income		Assets	
Nature of income	Value (state whether gross or net, if known)	Item	Value (if known)
Total:		Total:	

Part 5 Order Sought

5.1 If you are able to at this stage, specify what kind of orders you are asking the court to make, and state whether at this stage you see the case being appropriate for a "clean break". (A "clean break" means a settlement or order which provides, amongst other things, that neither you nor your spouse will have any further claim against the income or capital of the other party. A clean break does not terminate the responsibility of a parent to a child).

5.2 **If you are seeking a transfer or settlement of any property or other asset, you must identify the asset in question.

5.3 **If you are seeking a variation of a pre-nuptial or post-nuptial settlement, you must identify the settlement, by whom it was made, its trustees and beneficiaries, and state why you allege it is a nuptial settlement.

** **Important Note:** Where 5.2, 5.3 (above) or 5.4 (overleaf) apply, you should seek legal advice before completing the sections.

19

Part 5 Order Sought   *continued*

5.4   ****If you are seeking an avoidance of disposition order, you must identify the property to which the disposition relates and the person or body in whose favour the disposition is alleged to have been made.**

Sworn confirmation of the information

I

(the above-named Applicant/Respondent)

of

make oath and confirm that the information given above is a full, frank, clear and accurate disclosure of my financial and other relevant circumstances.

Signed

Dated

Sworn by the above named [Applicant] [Respondent] at

on

before me

A [solicitor] [Commissioner for Oaths] [Officer of a Court, appointed by the Judge to take Affidavits]

Address all communications to the Court Manager of the Court and quote the case number from page 1. If you do not quote this number, your correspondence may be returned.

The court office at

is open from 10 a.m. to 4p.m. (4.30pm at the Principal Registry of the Family Division) on Monday to Friday only.

20

Notice of Allegation in Proceedings for Ancillary Relief

In the	
	*[County Court]
*[Principal Registry of the Family Division]	
Case No. *Always quote this*	
Applicant's Solicitor's reference	
Respondent's Solicitor's reference	

(*delete as appropriate)

The marriage of   **and**

Take Notice that

The following statement has been filed in proceedings for ancillary relief:

Signed: Dated:

[Respondent/Solicitor for the Respondent]

If you wish to be heard on any matter affecting you in these proceedings you may intervene by applying to the Court for directions regarding:

- the filing and service of pleadings
- the conduct of further proceedings

You must apply for directions **within eight days** after you receive this Notice. The period of eight days includes the day you receive it.

The court office at

is open between 10 am and 4 pm (4.30pm at the Principal Registry of the Family Division) Monday to Friday. When corresponding with the court, please address forms or letters to the Court Manager and quote the case number. If you do not do so, your correspondence may be returned.

Form F Notice of allegation in proceedings for ancillary relief

Notice of response to First Appointment

In the	
	*[County Court]
*[Principal Registry of the Family Division]	
Case No. *Always quote this*	
Applicant's Solicitor's reference	
Respondent's Solicitor's reference	

*(*delete as appropriate)*

The marriage of   **and**

Take Notice that

At the First Appointment which will be heard on   20

at   [am][pm]

the [Applicant] [Respondent] [will][will not] be in a position to proceed on that occasion with a Financial Dispute Resolution appointment for the following reasons:-

Dated:

The court office at

is open between 10 am and 4 pm (4.30pm at the Principal Registry of the Family Division) Monday to Friday. When corresponding with the court, please address forms or letters to the Court Manager and quote the case number. If you do not do so, your correspondence may be returned.

Form G Notice of response to First Appointment

Ancillary Relief
Costs Estimate of
*[Applicant]
*[Respondent]

*(*delete as appropriate)*

In the	
	*[County Court]
	*[Principal Registry of the Family Division]
Case No. *Always quote this*	
Applicant's Solicitor's reference	
Respondent's Solicitor's reference	

The marriage of   **and**

PART 1

	Legal Aid Rates £	Indemnity Rate £
1. Ancillary relief solicitor's costs *(including VAT)* including costs of the current hearing, and any previous solicitor's costs.		
2. Disbursements *(include VAT, if appropriate, and any incurred by previous solicitors)*		
3. All Counsel's fees *(including VAT)*		
TOTAL		

PART 2

4. Add any private cases costs previously incurred *(Legal Aid cases only)*		
5. GRAND TOTAL		

PART 3

6. State what has been paid towards the total at 5 above		
7. Amount of any contributions paid by the assisted person towards their legal aid certificate		

NB. If you are Legally Aided and might be seeking an order for costs against the other party complete both rates.

Dated [   ]

The court office at

is open between 10 am and 4 pm (4.30pm at the Principal Registry of the Family Division) Monday to Friday. When corresponding with the court, please address forms or letters to the Court Manager and quote the case number. If you do not do so, your correspondence may be returned.

Form H Costs Estimate

Notice of Request for Periodical Payments Order at same rate as Order for Maintenance Pending Suit

(*delete as appropriate)

In the	
	*[County Court]
	*[Principal Registry of the Family Division]
Case No. *Always quote this*	
Applicant's Solicitor's reference	
Respondent's Solicitor's reference	

The marriage of   **and**

Take Notice that

On   1999 [20   ] the Applicant obtained an Order for you to pay maintenance pending suit at the rate of £   .

The Applicant having applied in his/her petition (answer) for a Periodical Payments Order for himself/ herself has requested the Court to make such an Order at the same rate as above.

Signed (District Judge)   Dated

What to do if you object to this Order being made.

If you object to the making of such a Periodical Payments Order, you must notify the District Judge and the Applicant/Respondent of your objections within 14 days of this notice being served on you. If you do not do so, the District Judge may make an Order without notifying you further.

The court office at

is open between 10 am and 4 pm (4.30pm at the Principal Registry of the Family Division) Monday to Friday. When corresponding with the court, please address forms or letters to the Court Manager and quote the case number. If you do not do so, your correspondence may be returned.

Form I Notice of Request for Periodical Payments Order at same rate as Order for Maintenance Pending Suit

281

New Ancillary Relief Procedure

Note: the overriding objective in Rule 2.51B governs all steps

Phase 1: To end of First Appointment ('FA')

	Step	Party	Timing	FPR
1	Filing of Ancillary Relief Notice (Form A)	Either	Any time after filing Petition	2.61A(1)
2	Fixing of First Appointment **12–16 weeks** ahead (**Form C**)	Court	When Form A is filed	2.61A(4)(a)
	NB: No vacating of date without permission			2.61A(5)
3	Service of copy of Notice in Form A	Court	Within **4 days** after Form A filed	2.61A(4)(b)
4	Filing and **simultaneous exchange** of **Form E**, completed and sworn by each party and containing the information and attaching the documents **required** by the Form and any other documents **necessary** to explain or clarify the information. The **required** documents are • property valuations obtained in last 6 months • most recent mortgage statements • last 12 months' bank statements • surrender value quotes of insurance policies • last 2 years' business accounts • valuation of pension rights • last 3 payslips and most recent p60	Both	At least 35 **days** before FA	2.61B(1), (2)
5	Service of documents required by but unavoidably not attached to Form E (with explanation); but otherwise	Either	At earliest opportunity	2.61B(5)
	NO general discovery before FA	Neither		2.61B(6)
6	Filing and service of • Concise statement of issues; • Chronology; • Questionnaire, **referable to the statement of issues**, seeking further information and documents; and • Notice (**Form G**) stating whether that party will be able to proceed to FDR at the FA and confirmation of service under FPR 2.59(3) & (4), and applicable 2.70(4)	Both Both Both Both Both Applicant	At least **14 days** before FA	2.61(B)(7)
7	Produce first costs estimate (Form H)	Both	Immediately prior to FA	2.61F(1)
	If a party intends to seek a summary assessment of costs, produce a Woolf costs schedule		24 hours prior to FA	2.61F(2)
8	**THE FIRST APPOINTMENT** **Objective**: to define issues and save costs	Both parties to attend personally unless otherwise ordered FPR 2.61D(5)	On date fixed 12–16 weeks after filing of Form A (Step 2)	2.61D(1)
	Directions as to: • answering questions and producing documents; and any further **necessary** documentation; • valuations (joint where appropriate) and experts • evidence to be adduced by each party, further chronologies, schedules			2.61D(2)(a) 2.61D(2)(b) 2.61D(2)(b)
	District Judge *shall* then: **either** direct FDR (this will be the norm)		Date for FDR on Form D	2.61D(2)(c)
	Or (if FDR inappropriate) direct: • hearing for further directions; or • hearing for interim order; or • final hearing; or • adjournment for mediation, negotiation or generally.			2.61D(2)(d)

	Step	Party	Timing	FPR
	The District Judge *may* in addition			2.61D(2)(f)
	• make urgent interim order, provided application duly made in accordance with 2.69F returnable on that occasion;			
	• having regard to forms g (see step 6), treat as FDR			
	• direct pensions valuation			
	Costs			
	• produce written estimate to DJ	Both		2.61F
	• DJ must consider making an order for costs depending on circumstances including compliance with the rules.			2.61D(2)(e)

Phase 2: to end of Financial Dispute Resolution Appointment ('FDR')

	Step	Party	Timing	FPR
9	Comply with all directions made at FA	Both	As per Direction Order and by FDR date	
	Any further discovery only with court permission	Both	By application	2.61D(3)
10	Where FDR has been ordered:			
	Notice to court of all offers, proposals and responses, including all without prejudice and Calderbank offers	Applicant	At least **7 days** before	2.61E(3) 2.69 FDR
	Produce second costs estimate in Form H	Both	Immediately prior to FDR	2.61F
11	**THE FDR APPOINTMENT**			
	Objective: best endeavours to reach agreement	Both parties to attend personally unless otherwise ordered: FPR	On date fixed at FA	2.61E 2.61E(6)
	Ground rules:			2.61E(9)
	• FDR treated as held for discussion and negotiation purposes: see Practice Direction [1997] 3 All ER 768, [1997] 1 WLR 1069			2.61E(1)
	• Conducted by a DJ who will not have anything else to do with the case			2.61E(2)
	• Offer details lodged are not to be kept on Court file after FDR			2.61E(5)
	District Judge may then:			
	• adjourn from time to time;			2.61E(7)
	• make appropriate consent order;			2.61E(8)
	• give further directions; and			
	• fix final hearing			
	Note: Where FDR has failed in a substantial case narrative affidavits of the financial history may be helpful: *W* v *W* (Wilson J, 17 January 2000, unreported)			
12	**Application for interim order**			
	• An application for an interim maintenance or variation order must be made returnable on 14 days notice	Either	at any time	2.69(F)
	• Unless the applicant has filed Form E it must be accompanied by a short sworn statement about his means and why the application is necessary			
	• the other party must file and serve a short sworn statement of means not less than 7 days before the hearing	Either	At any time	2.69(F)
	• A party may at any stage apply (without notice if necessary) for other interim orders			

Phase 3: to final hearing

	Step	Party	Timing	FPR
13	**Directions orders made at FDR to be complied with appropriately**	Both	As per Direction Order	
14	**Statement of Open Proposals** • To be drafted • File with Court and serve on other party	Both Applicant Respondent	After FDR **14 days** before final hearing **7 days after** receipt of Applicant's statement	2.69E(1) 2.69E(2)
15	**Further Directions/adjourned FDRs**	Either party may apply or Court may direct	Any time	2.61D(4)
	A written statement of costs in Form H must be produced at every Court hearing			2.61F
16	**THE FINAL HEARING** NB: Final costs estimate in Form H required		On date fixed at First Appointment (Step 8) or at FDR (Step 11) or otherwise	
17	**Cost after judgment** • Either party may make a *Calderbank* offer • Where a party beats his opponent's *Calderbank* offer, Court **must**, unless it considers it unjust, order the offeror to pay the offeree's costs from 28 days after the offer was made • Where a party beats both his opponents's offer *and* his own offer, the court **may**, if it is just, order that for that period he receive indemnity costs and/or interest thereon of up to 10% over base rate • Factors affecting the justice of making such orders include the terms of *Calderbank* offers; the stage when made; the information then available; conduct of the parties; and their means			2.69(1) 2.69B 2.69C 2.69D

D.2 Pre-application Protocol

1 Introduction

1.1

1.1.1 *Lord Woolf in his final Access to Justice Report of July 1996 recommended the development of pre-application protocols:*
> *'to build on and increase the benefits of early but well informed settlement which genuinely satisfy both parties to dispute'*

1.1.2 *In April 2000 the Lord Chancellor's Ancillary Relief Advisory Committee recommended that there be a Protocol for ancillary relief applications and this recommendation has been accepted by the Lord Chancellor.*

1.2 *The aim of the pre-application protocol is to ensure that:*
   (a) Pre-application disclosure and negotiation takes place in appropriate cases.
   (b) Where there is pre-application disclosure and negotiation, it is dealt with
      (i) Cost effectively;
      (ii) In line with the overriding objectives of the Family Proceedings (Amendments) Rules 1999;
   (c) The parties are in a position to settle the case fairly and early without litigation.

1.3 *The court will be able to treat the standard set in the pre-application protocol as the normal reasonable approach to pre-application conduct. If proceedings are subsequently issued, the court will be entitled to decide whether there has been non-compliance with the protocol and, if so, whether non-compliance merits consequences.*

2 Notes of Guidance

Scope of the Protocol
2.1 *This protocol is intended to apply to all claims for ancillary relief as defined by FPR r. 1(2). It is designed to cover all classes of case, ranging from a simple application for periodical payments to an application for a substantial lump sum and property adjustment order. The protocol is designed to facilitate the operation of what was called the pilot scheme and is from 5 June 2000 the standard procedure for ancillary relief applications*

2.2 *In considering the option of pre-application disclosure and negotiation, solicitors should bear in mind the advantage of having a court timetable and court managed process. There is sometimes an advantage in preparing disclosure before proceedings are commenced. However solicitors should bear in mind the objective of controlling costs and in particular the costs of discovery and that the option of pre-application disclosure and negotiation has risks of excessive and uncontrolled expenditure and delay. This option should only be encouraged where both parties agree to follow this route and disclosure is not likely to be an issue or has been adequately dealt with in mediation or otherwise.*

2.3 *Solicitors should consider at an early stage and keep under review whether it would be appropriate to suggest mediation to the clients as an alternative to solicitor negotiation or court based litigation.*

2.4 *Making an application to the court should not be regarded as a hostile step or a last resort, rather as a way of starting the court timetable, controlling disclosure and endeavouring to avoid the costly final hearing and the preparation for it.*

First Letter
2.5 *The circumstances of parties to an application for ancillary relief are so various that it would be difficult to prepare a specimen first letter. The request for information will be different in every case. However, the tone of the initial letter is important and*

the guidelines in para. 3.7 should be followed. It should be approved in advance by the client. Solicitors writing to an unrepresented party should always recommend that he seeks independent legal advice and enclose a second copy of the letter to be passed to any solicitor instructed. A reasonable time limit for a response may be 14 days.

Negotiation and Settlement

2.6 *In the event of pre-application disclosure and negotiation, as envisaged in para. 2.2 an application should not be issued when a settlement is a reasonable prospect.*

Disclosure

2.7 *The protocol underlines the obligation of parties to make full and frank disclosure of all material facts, documents and other information relevant to the issues. Solicitors owe their clients a duty to tell them in clear terms of this duty and of the possible consequences of breach of the duty. This duty of disclosure is an ongoing obligation and includes the duty to disclose any material changes after initial disclosure has been given. Solicitors are referred to the Good Practice Guide for Disclosure produced by the Solicitors Family Law Association (obtainable from the Administrative Director, 366A Crofton Road, Orpington, Kent BR2 8NN).*

3. The Protocol

General Principles

3.1 *All parties must always bear in mind the overriding objective set out at FPR Rule 2.51B and try to ensure that all claims should be resolved and a just outcome achieved as speedily as possible without costs being unreasonably incurred. The needs of any children should be addressed and safeguarded. The procedures which it is appropriate to follow should be conducted with minimum distress to the parties and in a manner designed to promote as good a continuing relationship between the parties and any children affected as is possible in the circumstances.*

3.2 *The principle of proportionality must be borne in mind at all times. It is unacceptable for the costs of any case to be disproportionate to the financial value of the subject matter of the dispute.*

3.3 *Parties should be informed that where a court exercises a discretion as to whether costs are payable by one party to another, this discretion extends to pre-application offers to settle and conduct of disclosure. (Rule 44.3 Paragraph 1 of the Civil Procedure Rules 1998).*

Identifying the Issues

3.4 *Parties must seek to clarify their claims and identify the issues between them as soon as possible. So that this can be achieved, they must provide full, frank and clear disclosure of facts, information and documents which are material and sufficiently accurate to enable proper negotiations to take place to settle their differences. Openness in all dealings is essential.*

Disclosure

3.5 *If parties carry out voluntary disclosure before the issue of proceedings the parties should exchange schedules of assets, income, liabilities and other material facts, using Form E as a guide to the format of the disclosure. Documents should only be disclosed to the extent that they are required by Form E. Excessive or disproportionate costs should not be incurred.*

Correspondence

3.6 *Any first letter and subsequent correspondence must focus on the clarification of claims and identification of issues and their resolution. Protracted and unnecessary correspondence and 'trial by correspondence ' must be avoided.*

3.7 *The impact of any correspondence upon the reader and in particular the parties must always be considered. Any correspondence which raises irrelevant issues or* *which might cause the other party to adopt an entrenched, polarised or hostile position is to be discouraged.*

Experts

3.8 *Expert valuation evidence is only necessary where the parties cannot agree or do not know the value of some significant asset. The cost of a valuation should be proportionate to the sums in dispute. Wherever possible, valuations of properties, shares etc. should be obtained from a single valuer instructed by both parties. To that end, a party wishing to instruct an expert (the first party) should first give the other party a list of the names of one or more experts in the relevant speciality whom he considers are suitable to instruct. Within 14 days the other party may indicate an objection to one or more of the named experts and, if so, should supply the names of one or more experts whom he considers suitable.*

3.9 *Where the identity of the expert is agreed, the parties should agree the terms of a joint letter of instructions.*

3.10 *Where no agreement is reached as to the identity of the expert, each party should think carefully before instructing his own expert because of the costs implications. Disagreements about disclosure such as the use and identity of an expert may be better managed by the court within the context of an application for ancillary relief.*

3.11 *Whether a joint report is commissioned or the parties have chosen to instruct separate experts, it is important that the expert is prepared to answer reasonable questions raised by either party.*

3.12 *When experts' reports are commissioned pre-application, it should be made clear to the expert that they may in due course be reporting to the court and that they should therefore consider themselves bound by the guidance as to expert witnesses in Part 39 of the Civil Procedure Rules 1998.*

3.13 *Where the parties propose to instruct a joint expert, there is a duty on both parties to disclose whether they have already consulted that expert about the assets in issue.*

3.14 *If the parties agree to instruct separate experts the parties should be encouraged to agree in advance that the reports will be disclosed.*

Summary

3.15 *The aim of all pre-application proceedings steps must be to assist the parties to resolve their differences speedily and fairly or at least narrow the issues and, should that not be possible, to assist the Court to do so.*

INDEX